A catalogue record of this book is available from the British Library.

Printed in Great Britain by besley & copp Ltd., Exeter, Devon.

Published in Great Britain in 2010 by Colin R. Wright, Honiton, Devon.

ISBN: 978-0-9528139-4-1

(Cover image 'The Glen' courtesy of Arthur Dimond, Honiton.)

To Ken & Freddie

HONITON

A Glimpse Back...

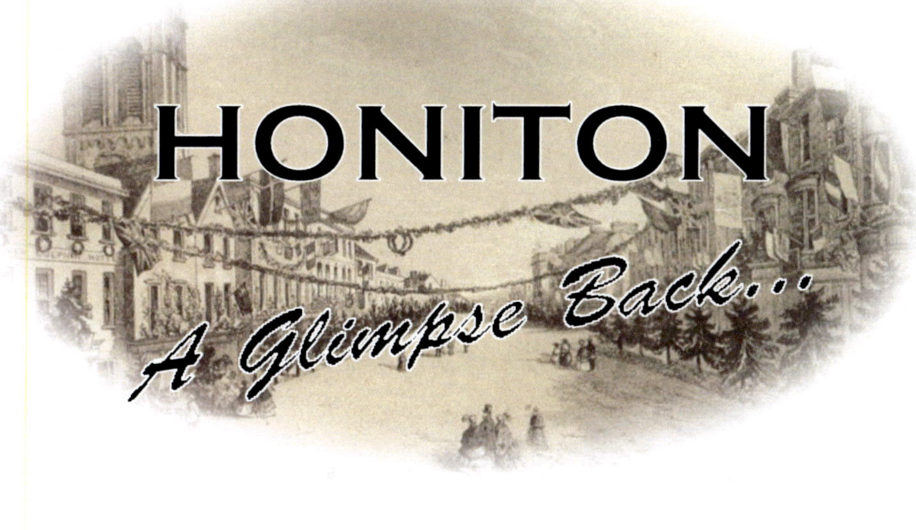

T. Darrant BSc.

Disclaimer and Additional Information

All the information, statistics and details contained within this publication are only as good as the source material. The author has made every effort to ensure that the contents are as accurate and correct as possible at the time of writing and hopes that, you, the reader enjoy the book as much as he has enjoyed researching and writing it.

The majority of the images and photographs contained within this publication have been granted with kind permission of those listed on page 373. In other instances the image(s) are now believed to be in the public domain due to the expiration of their respective copyrights. In all cases, however, the copyright of said images has been researched to the best of the author's ability and no infringement was intended as, in many cases, any relevant copyright holders could not be traced.

Throughout this publication are asterisked numbers which relate to specific locations of particular objects, landmarks, houses etc that either no longer stand or whose location maybe of interest to the reader. The relevant longitudes and latitudes, of each, can be found in *Appendix IV* and one must state that many of these locations are either now on private property or at hazardous locations, i.e. roadsides. This author, therefore, recommends these coordinates be used for reference purpose only with the aid of a map, as visiting such sites may put oneself in unnecessary danger or circumstance of trespass.

CONTENTS

INTRODUCTION

Honiton, a small Devonian market town, has a long and rugged history. It is an ancient town with a history preceding the Domesday Book and the Norman invasion of 1066.

People have been working, living and dying in this settlement for over a millennium and to tell an in-depth story of the town's entire history would be a fantastic notion but almost impossible in reality. The aim of this book is, therefore, to tell the story of this town from the earliest, in-depth, records available. The point in history to which I refer is the mid 19th century when records of peoples' lives first became widely catalogued allowing a picture of their lives to be made, or in this case, written!

This book is heavily weighted on three main sources: the 1851 census showing many personal details of the everyday, undervalued, underpaid and under-represented individual of the time, the tithe map of Honiton printed in 1844 which gives detailed descriptions of the tenants and owners of property and land in the parish and lastly 'The History of Honiton' by R. A. Farquharson, first published in 1868, which is a hugely extensive and brilliant work with many local references to life, establishments and the people residing in Victorian Honiton. These documents give a valuable historical snapshot of the town in these early times and a rare insight into occupations, ages, affluence and many other social factors. It is, therefore, fair to say that this book's focus is that twenty year period (1840-1860) of life and times in Honiton along with a history that both predates and post-dates this era.

Many in-depth histories of the town and its famous residents have been written, and their stories told; this book attempts to tell the story of all the wo/men who resided here at that time and whose lives and experiences have long been forgotten.

As well as the history of the town itself, this book attempts to fit Honiton into the historical jigsaw of the time, incorporating the influences of the period with an in-depth insight into some of the major events that moulded the town into what it was then and what it is now.

This is not the story of Honiton but rather the story of Honiton's people some 53 years before the Orville brothers' first manned flight, 76 years before the first television transmission and 119 years before Neil Armstrong set foot on the moon.

"Much that once was is lost,

For none now live who remember it."

J. R. R. Tolkien

PART 1

Around Honiton

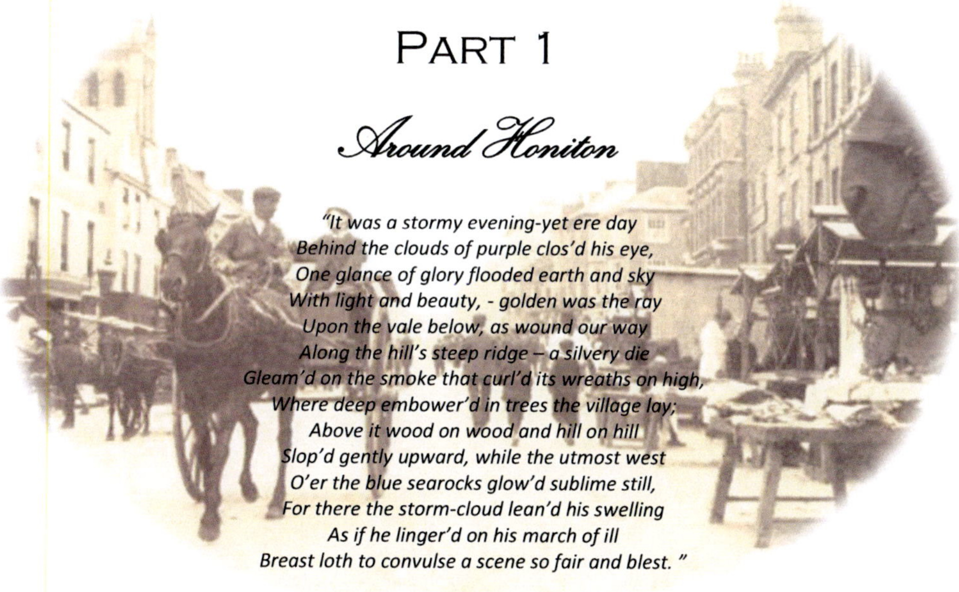

"It was a stormy evening-yet ere day
Behind the clouds of purple clos'd his eye,
One glance of glory flooded earth and sky
With light and beauty, - golden was the ray
Upon the vale below, as wound our way
Along the hill's steep ridge – a silvery die
Gleam'd on the smoke that curl'd its wreaths on high,
Where deep embower'd in trees the village lay;
Above it wood on wood and hill on hill
Slop'd gently upward, while the utmost west
O'er the blue searocks glow'd sublime still,
For there the storm-cloud lean'd his swelling
As if he linger'd on his march of ill
Breast loth to convulse a scene so fair and blest. "

The Approach to the Honiton Vale;
Zarach; Aug 1823

Chapter 1
Location and Setting

"The vicinity, though not so populous as more inland situations, boasts a neighbourhood as replete with friendship, hospitality and politeness."
(Sylvanus Urban 1793)

Honiton is a small market town situated in the rural English county of Devon, seventeen miles from the county capital of Exeter and 157 miles from the country's capital of London. The town is seated in the east of the county and in the 1850s was an isolated country town with a high dependency upon the surrounding countryside for food and income. 'Black Guide to Devonshire' described Honiton as "the prettiest, cleanest and most agreeable of Devonshire towns." In 1851 the population of the town was three and a half thousand and by comparison, Honiton was about the size of the present day Colyton. The town has certainly left its mark on history, not only by giving the world its fine lace but also having been visited by many historical notables, including Horatio Nelson and Charles Dickens. Several members of the Royal Family have also either visited or passed through the town, including King John in 1201, Henry VI in 1452, Catherine of Aragon in 1501, Charles I, who stayed at Marwood house in 1644, Charles II in 1671, George III in 1789, a young Princess Victoria in 1833 and Princess Anne in 2005. The town was also mentioned in Jane Austin's famous novel of 1811, 'Sense and Sensibility'.

This was a time when Devon was a rural and 'wild' county with few, ineffectual means of transportation and poor road networks. As an example, the popular tourist retreat of Dartmoor today was at the time referred to as a "wide barren tract...consisting of naked rushy marshes, and bleak rocky hills, which only [served] for the pasturage of sheep." The land that creates the picturesque Devonian scenery was deemed "waste" unless it could be ploughed or used for livestock and hence the county was a poor, agricultural working community, not the desirable, expensive holiday and retirement retreat of more modern times.

Honiton has two rivers running through and near it; three rivers at the time of this book's setting (1850s). The main river is the Otter which, although "passes the town about half a mile to the north" was, and still is, the main waterway associated with the town, so much so that birth, marriage and burial registers, prior to 1800, referred to the town as "Honiton on Otter"! The Otter obtained its name from the once abundant number of otters that resided in it. It is thought that this river once formed the boundary between the two ancient tribes of the 'Durotrige' and the 'Danmonii'. The stream that actually does flow through the town is called the 'Gissage.' The little brook got its name from a hedge that separated the parish of Honiton from the parish of Gittisham: 'Gittisham Hedge' or 'Gittishedge' which was in time shortened to its present name. One of the earliest references to this stream is in a charter concerning land belonging to 'Geoffrey the Merchant' and 'Nicholas le Cartere' in about 1300 when the stream is referred to as the 'Gissah.'

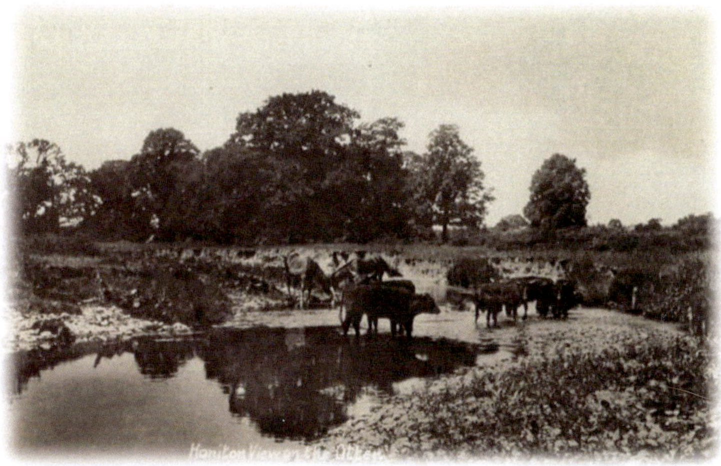

Animals grazing on the banks of the Otter.

The third river that sadly no longer flows through Honiton was described as "a stream of fine clear water...with dipping places before every door." A witness described the stream as "clean water" that added to the "hygiene" of the town. Presumably clean and clear water was not a common sight for travellers of this time! This little river, named 'The Crystal', used to flow from a "cast iron water spout[at the bottom of Kings Road] which discharged water" through an iron trough that is still present in the High Street but today remains dry unless filled with rainwater. This feature of the High Street is a centuries old innovation and written comments of it date back to the 18th century when the "dipping places" were where locals could obtain a supply of water. The 6 foot stone 'source' of the Crystal was blocked up in the 1970s. The iron trough that still runs the length of the High Street was made by local iron founders 'Mickelburghs'.

Honiton parish consisted of 3,046 acres of land, according to White's Directory of 1850 and, as would be expected, the vast majority of this land was farmed, providing employment for the majority of the working population.
The boundaries of the parish were once illustrated by specific markers such as stones and/ or trees. An example of the markers, that existed in 1844, was a boundary stone which used to stand on Northleigh Hill Road, at a junction of what was 'Wadmore Lane' and which is now a footpath that leads through the Honiton Golf Course*1. Another boundary marker was an oak tree that stood a little distance down the 'Farway common road'*2. There is an ancient tale that when a dispute arose concerning where the boundaries of the parishes of Honiton, Farway, Sidbury and Gittisham met Isabella de Fortibus, then the Countess of Devon and Lady of the Manor of Honiton, rode to the approximate spot and, taking a ring from her finger, threw it into a mire and stated that where the ring fell would be the new boundary of the said parishes. This act was said to have taken place somewhere in the vicinity of the present day 'Hare & Hounds'; the road from the said pub to Ottery St. Mary was once known as 'Ring in the Mire Lane'. Isabella is also the lady we have to thank for giving her name to 'Countess Wear' in Exeter.
Another boundary stone, although just outside the Honiton parish, is worth mentioning considering the tale that lies behind it. There was once a boundary stone some 50 yards from the junction of 'Fern Lane', from Offwell, and the A35. Today this crossroads is known as 'Drummerstone Cross' and the name dates back to 1701 when a sailing drummer boy, travelling home from Plymouth with his companion, rested on the stone after navigating the hill out of Wilmington. The boy's greedy and envious companion strangled him where he sat and stole his money. The stone was present until the 1920s when a gardener unwittingly broke it up to make a rockery for his garden.

Honiton stands in the shadow of 'Dumpdon Hill', now National Trust Property. This dominating hill with its curious clump of trees upon its summit was, in the mid 1800s, described as the second largest peak in Devon after Dartmoor and was primarily used for pasture as "cultivated tracts" were "of no great extent" for the soil was not "distinguished by fertility." A Mr. Hoskins visiting "Dumpden Camp" explained that "the mound in the middle was thrown up some years ago by the ordnance surveyors as a point to take angles from." From some of the earliest photos of Dumpdon Hill (1900s) the quaint little clump of beech trees appear quite young; however, Hoskins noted their presence during his visit in 1862.

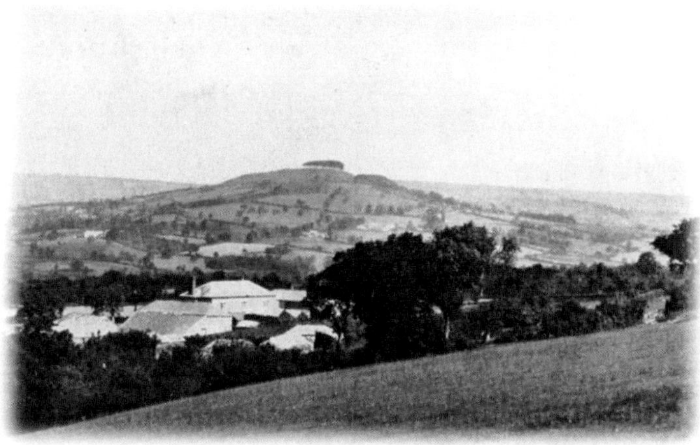

Dumpdon Hill

Chapter 2
General History

"This towne is neere three quarters a myle in length"
William Pole 1790

A Rev. Edmund Butcher who passed through Honiton one summer's morning in 1805 wrote this:

"just before the road descends on the Honiton side of the hill, we gain a view of the town, stretching itself in the vale below, and apparently running away from its church, which in a solitary state, is perched upon a hill, about half a mile from the town. The smoke, which was just rising from many of the chimnies, and which, when illuminated by the morning sun, adds not only a variety, but a beauty to the general picture, was, on another account, a pleasing exhibition to me and my party."

Honiton has a very long and illustrious history but the origins of the town's name are sketchy at best. The spelling alone has changed many times as has been found scattered throughout the centuries of scriptures and documents: *Hanitone; Honetone; Honinton; Hunitone; Hunniton; Honington; Honyton* and *Hunningston* to name but a few! These names have come from many different sources, including The Domesday Book, and even a tombstone within St. Michael's churchyard. The most popular interpretation of this name, quite possibly of Anglo-Saxon origin, is probably the most obvious, "Honey Town", from a once abundant honey trade producing the well known drink of the day, mead. It could have also been from the high demand of bees-wax candles for the pre-reformation monasteries. This argument also backs the theory that Honiton was once situated on the Hill with the old parish church of St. Michael's and that when the villagers retreated to the vale where "thick wood frequented by bees" they started a new trade to go with the new town. It is also thought that anciently the surrounding hills were covered in sweet thyme that attracted a large population of local bees: even Westcote described the surrounding hills as thus.

A certain Gilbert Dyer, writing in 1805, arrived at the theory "that Honiton implies 'The Little Water Land and Town': the parish lies on a small stream" from, once again, the ancient Saxon language. 'An', 'on' or 'un' were all old Gaelic names for 'water'; however, although the 'h' was not originally written it *was* pronounced, i.e. 'Hunitone' would have been written as 'Unitone.' 'I' and 'y' were also Gaelic for 'little' or 'shallow' and as 'ton' is

believed to signify 'habitation' or 'town' we arrive at the present name and its derived meaning: (H) 'on' 'i' 'ton.' One theory was that the town name was connected with ancient local camps called "Honeyditch and "Henabourough". A more less likely theory is that the name was taken from the whetstones, locally named 'hones', which were excavated from a hill near the town (Hone-town).
Another story for the name of Honiton comes from an ancient legend that at one time all the women of the town were barren, unable to conceive, and to remove this curse all the females of the parish retreated to St Margaret's Chapel for a day of fasting and prayer. This leads us to the significance of this legend: the word 'honi' was a Norman word for 'disgrace' or 'shame' and with 'ton' (still meaning town or settlement) Honiton would have been anciently referred to as the 'town of shame/disgrace.' This story of the childless women of Honiton is reflected in the pictoral display on the town seal: a pregnant woman knelling before the Almighty. These arms also show a sprig of Honeysuckle; maybe a once prominent, local plant that gave rise to the name! These are but just a few of the many interpretations of this ancient settlement's name; however, the truth of the matter is that no definitive conclusions have been reached. The generally accepted theory among historians is that the name was simply derived from another Saxon term "Huna's Tun" meaning a farm or settlement belonging to a man named 'Huna'. Huna was a common male Anglo-Saxon name and there is even evidence of a Saxon named Huna who was granted land at Glastonbury by King Eadwig in 957AD, only some 40 miles from the town.

The earliest known residents of the area were, surprisingly, hippopotamus whose remains were found during the Honiton Bypass project of 1966. These animals lived here some 250,000 years ago; however, the earliest evidence of human inhabitants was during the Palaeolithic period. These people made tools from flint gathered from the banks of the Gissage some 25,000 years ago, close to where Dowell Street now runs. There is no recognised human population residing here between then and the Iron Age but it is known that those who lived here in the Bronze Age buried their dead here: some 60 burial mounds have been identified in the surrounding countryside. When a new green was being excavated at the Honiton Golf Club in 1934, a Bronze Age urn containing calcified bones was unearthed! In Roman times Honiton was situated in a strategic position on the Fosse Way being the first point out of Exeter where the countryside became hilly.

Honiton originally stood on the ancient Icknield/Inkfeld Street (once an important trade route stretching to the south-east of England). Prior to the Norman Conquest, the Manor of Honiton was owned by an Anglo Saxon, Drogo, under the Count/Earl of Mortain/Moreton who had inherited it from Elmer. Drogo (born 1003, Île-de-France) married Godgifu, who was the only daughter of Æthelred II (968-1016) and a sister to Edward the Confessor. After William the Conqueror had pronounced himself King of England in 1066 he bestowed the Manor and the title of 'Count of Mortain' (a settlement in France) to his half brother Robert, Earl of Cornwall.

Honiton is described in The Domesday Book of 1086 as having "gelding for five hides, and having lands for eighteen ploughs, with a recorded population of 24 villeins and ten surfs and boarders...a mill ...and 2 saltworkers." A 'hide' (the amount of land deemed to support one peasant) was about 120 acres meaning that Honiton Parish, at the time of Domesday, was approx 600 acres in size; considerably smaller than the period in which this book is set. Three of the five hides were worked by villeins (tenant farmers) meaning that these 11th century yeomen worked 360 acre of land with the remaining two hides consisting mainly of woodland, meadows and pasture. Honiton was also of great importance at this time for it was one of only 8% of the settlements in Devon to have its own mill. This Domesday mill is thought to have been the one that still exists in Littletown.

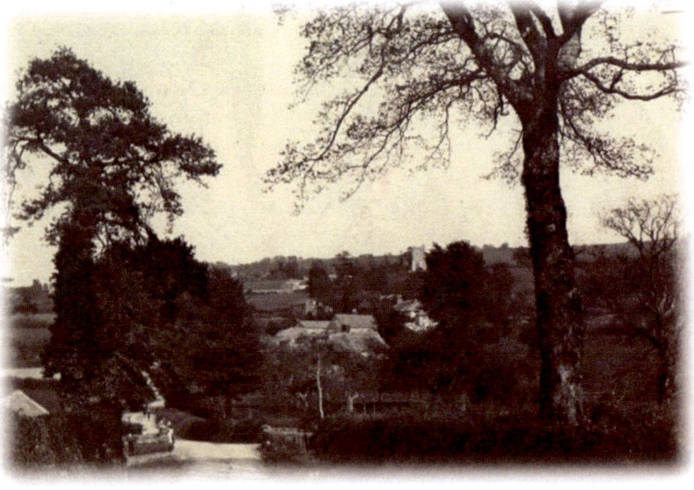

Littletown

The hamlet of Littletown was believed to be the original settlement of the town and even in Victorian times there was a field called 'Littletown Common' which would have once been an equivalent to a village green where the local peasants would have been permitted to communally graze their cattle and sheep.

Robert, Earl of Cornwall and half brother to King William, died leaving the Manor to his only son and successor William. Despite the fact that William had been left some 793 manors in England, he was resentful of the great power wielded by Henry I and demanded from the King the Earldom of Kent which had belonged to his uncle. Henry refused and William fled in an attempt to revolt: he paid dearly for his greed. Henry seized William's lands in England and razed his castles to the ground. When William himself was captured he had his eyes gouged out and was Henry's prisoner for the remainder of his life. After William lost the Manor in the feud, Henry I bestowed the lands to his "faithful and beloved" councillor, Richard de Redvers (of Reviers in Normandy), as well as granting him the 'Earldom of Devon'. Several generations of the Redvers held the Manor of Honiton until the last of the Redvers, Baldwin, died in 1262 after being poisoned. Baldwin had no children so the Manor passed to his sister, Isabella, who had married William de Fortibus. Isabella inherited the Earldom of Devon and gave Honiton its 'Ring in the Mire' and Exeter its 'Countess Wear': explained earlier. Isabella was a strong willed and rich woman and by the time she was widowed, in her mid twenties, she was deemed the richest heiress in England, owning lands in Devon, Hampshire, Yorkshire and Cumberland. She also owned the Isle of Wight which gave her the honorary title of 'Lady of the Isle'. It is not surprising many wished to marry her and even Edward I was known to have been envious of her vast estates. When Isabella died in 1293, aged 56, she had already outlived all her six children and the Manor of Honiton was bought by the envious Edward I who bestowed it upon a man called Gilbert de Knovil. By 1327 the Manor had passed to Isabella's nearest male heir who was Hugh Courtenay. Hugh's ancestor had married the daughter of William de Redvers, or William de Vernon as he was also known, having resided at Vernon Castle. William de Vernon had allegedly been the gentleman who had re-established Honiton from the ancient hill settlement, near St Michael's, to the valley where Honiton stands today and was also the great grandfather of Isabella de Fortibus. Hugh acquired the Manor at the tender age of 16 and it would remain in his family's possession for the next 600 years. The Courtenays had a Manor House in Honiton as early as 1402, which was on the site of the present day 'Montgomery's Hotel'. The

Courtenay home anciently had been 'Powderham Castle' which came into the family in the 1300s.
The Earldom of Devon was also carried on by the Courtenays until the mid 1500s when, in 1538, Henry Courtenay was beheaded for treason and the Earldom was forfeited. Henry Courtenay's only surviving son, Edward, was held prisoner in the Tower of London for 15 years, after which Mary I released him and restored his Earldom. Edward later moved to Italy where he died after being poisoned, unmarried and without children and hence the Earldom died with him.
The last member of the Courtenay family to hold the Manor of Honiton was William 'Kitty' Courtenay. 'Kitty' was born the fourth child to William Courtenay 8th Earl of Devon, the only son out of fourteen children! He sold the Manor, along with other estates, in about 1809 due to his tendancy to live beyond his financial means and later had to flee the country due to persecution for his homosexuality. William Courtenay owned many other Manors and Estates, including many in Ireland. He was famously involved in a scandalous relationship with William Beckford, once the wealthiest man in England. Beckford, aged 19, "fell in love" with William when he was only 10 and the couple's activities became public when "strange goings on" were heard between the two in Courtenay's bedchamber at Powderham. Beckford's association with Courtenay ruined his reputation and people dubbed him 'The Fool of Fonthill' (his ancestral home). In a letter Beckford wrote to Courtenay's aunt he said that his time with young William "were the most delightful hours of [his] existence." Not so surprisingly few looked favourably upon this relationship and even King George III had personally wanted Beckford to be hanged for his involvement with Courtenay. Beckford later married and became a recluse whilst his young lover, Kitty, flamboyantly broadcast his sexuality; more so even than his seducer. Most gentlemen of Exeter avoided him and he even had to abandon plans to build a summer home at Torquay due to local hostility. By 1811 an Essex magistrate had gathered enough evidence on Courtenay to issue a warrant

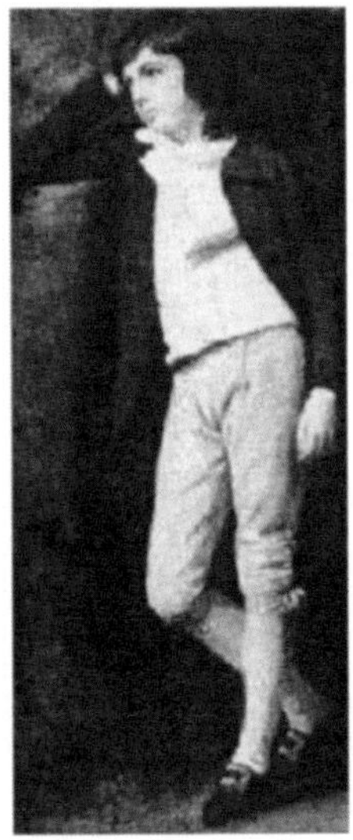

William Courtenay (1768-1835) as a boy .

for his arrest on charges of sodomy. Possibly facing the death penalty, William had no choice but to flee the country and went to France. There were rumours that in 1815 Courtenay returned to England in disguise and engaged some locals of Exeter in conversation as to the perceived reception if he were to permanently return to his native land. Hearing the general opinion was that stoning, tarring and feathering would be the most likely result, he immediately left for Paris, never to return.
William Courtenay later revived the old title of 'Earl of Devon' in 1831, which had been officially extinct for several centuries, and after he died, unmarried and with no children, in 1835, the title was inherited by his third cousin, whose descendants still hold it today. Despite his extravagant lifestyle and many years abroad, William Courtenay remained "dearly loved" by his Devonian tenants and was thus interred in the family vault at Powderham Castle.
The current and 18th Earl of Devon is Hugh Rupert Courtenay (b.1942). Ironically, Hugh Courtenay had his licence to hold civil ceremonies at Powderham Castle revoked by Devon County Council in 2009 due to his refusal to allow a gay marriage to take place there!

Around the time William Courtenay sold the Manor it was said to have been "fourteen hundred acres" in size with an annual value of £2,358.
The Manor of Honiton was sold to 'Messrs Smith, Brook & Townsend' of the East Devon Bank in 1809. The Manor was later held for a time in a frozen state due to financial difficulties of the newly appointed owners and after that was sold several times before being bought in 1847 by Joseph Locke.
Joseph Locke was born into a humble Sheffield family in 1805. He became an apprentice of George Stephenson and in time he became great friends with Stephenson's son Robert: Locke was even a pallbearer at Robert's funeral in 1859. Locke's years with Stephenson sent him on his road to railway engineering where he accomplished many great feats, including his joint engineering project, with Stephenson, of the 'Grand Junction Railway' that linked Birmingham with Manchester and Liverpool, the first commercial passenger railway in the world. On the opening day of the railway it was Locke who was entrusted to drive Stephenson's 'Rocket' which, sadly, resulted in what is claimed to be the first death of the railway when the Rocket collided with an MP named William Huskisson. Undeterred by this event, Locke went on to construct many more railway lines, including many in France, and when he purchased the 'rotten borough' of Honiton, he became its MP until his death.

"Oh! Honiton Town is the place of all places
For honest Electors, and sweet pretty faces,
I would rather live there, when Elections are nigh.
Thank in any Town Corporate under the sky!

Shall I tell what took place on this very day,
When Locke, and when Hogg, had said out their say!
Why they both were elected ;-and as I suppose
For the best of all reasons-There were none to oppose!

Some Tories, 'tis true were most sadly dismayed,
When they found they had lost, full one half of their trade ;
So they'd have a third man, by hook or by crook.
And calling a Cab, their journey they took.

Then they tried Tracey Bridge and Netherton Hall,
But they very soon found it was "no go" at all,
Even Clifton complained,-so to Shute the must jog,
To get a long Pole to stir up the Hogg!

The Baronet bowed, and hinted a doubt,
As to whether their Mothers knew that were out,
So turning long faces towards Honiton Town,
They told eighty two friends, that they were "done brown."

Then Hurrah for the Queen, and long life to Lord John
We must go ahead, now the steam is turned on!
And the time, and the ticket by Honiton clock,
Is freedom forever-We have got JOSPEH LOCKE!
(Written to be sung to the tune 'Derry Down'.)

This song was written by an unknown author to commemorate the election campaigns of Joseph Locke and Sir James Weir Hogg.
Election time was an affair taken very seriously in the town; in one election six men who had pledged their allegiance to Sir James Hogg were publicly named and shamed when they went back on their word. The men's places of business were ridiculed: John Trickey, who ran the Three Tuns Inn at the time, had his establishment renamed "The Twister's Arms" and John Croot, landlord of The Crown & Sceptre, had his tavern referred to as the

"Henpeck'd Weathercock"! Collectively referred to as "the twisters", these men had their names plastered around the town with the warning:

"Honitonians! These Men have disgraced your fair fame!!
BEWARE OF THEM!!!"

Of note, one of the men was called John Major - an interesting name considering his political endeavours!

There was an interesting account of the last election Locke stood for in 1857. The Honiton candidates were Locke, Hogg and another gentleman called Lt. Col. Wortley. Locke had secured his position but by quarter to four in the afternoon of polling day the seat of the remaining MP hung in the balance as Hogg had 117 votes and Wortley 118 and there was still one voter left to cast his vote. The poll closed at four and the Tories were eager to obtain the last voter who was, in fact, holding out for money, before making his final decision. The Tories' agent rushed to the voter and asked "What do you want to go to poll?" The voter replied "£30" and the agent replied "Then you are there" whilst writing a cheque for the agreed sum. The voter dashed to cast his vote for the Tory candidate, Wortley, and on examining the cheque realised he had been conned as there was no signature confirming the amount bequeathed!

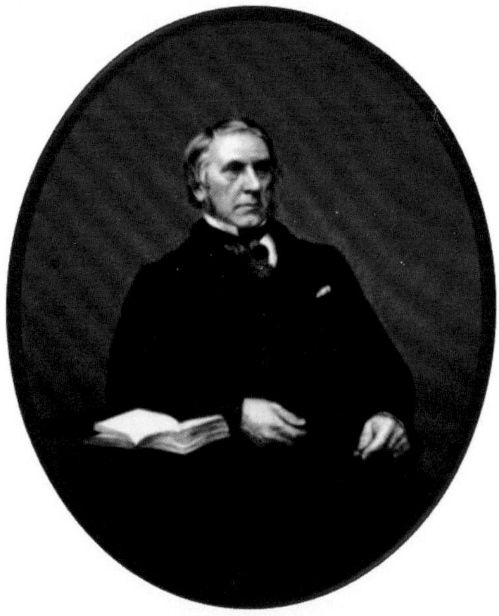

Joseph Locke

In 1838 Joseph Locke married Phoebe McCreary: the couple did not have any children and so later adopted a young Irish child called Minna Maurice, later Minna Locke. Locke himself died on a hunting trip of suspected appendicitis in 1860, aged 55, and his wife dedicated a park in the town of Barnsley to his memory. His obituary in 'The Times' referred to him as "one of the great triumvirate of railway pioneers" putting him "alongside George Stephenson and Brunel."

Joseph's wife only outlived him by 6 years and by that time their daughter was only 18. The following year, in 1867, Minna Locke married James Arcdeckne-Butler and after being widowed only 3 years later, she remarried a solicitor, Charles Lane, whom she spent the rest of her days with.

When Joseph Locke died his widow sold the Manor of Honiton to a London based Jewish banker and bullion broker, Frederick Goldsmid, for which he paid £110,000 in 1863. Mr. Goldsmid died only 3 years after the purchase and by his will it was instructed that the Manor be sold, at which point it was bought back by his son, Sir Julian Goldsmid who was a lawyer and businessman. Like Mr. Locke, the two Goldsmids used the 'rotten' Manor of Honiton as their ticket into Parliament, both standing as the town MPs; however, after the Parliamentary Reform Act of 1867, Honiton was disenfranchised, due to corruption, and the Manor was presumably no longer of any use to the family, for only 2 years later it was sold yet again. This did not halt Julian's ambitions: he later became MP for Rochester and St. Pancreas South and became Deputy Speaker of the House of Commons in 1894.

In 1869 Julian Goldsmith advertised the Manor to be sold as "one lot" which was described as "The Lordship and Manor of Honiton including also the Manors of Battishorne Arundel and Battishorne Paulet." With a total of 33 shops, 20 private houses, 45 cottages and a grand total of 1,838 acres of land the Manor was duly sold. Almost immediately after the sale much of the land was sold off to a number of private purchasers. Eventually, after these 60 years of sales and turmoil, following centuries of stability, the remainder of the Manor and Lordship was purchased by Richard Marker of Combe House, Gittisham. Mr. Marker had previously inherited the vast Combe Estate and was already Lord of the Manor of Stockland, Farway and Gittisham by the time he bought the Honiton Manor in 1873. Combe Estate had been the property of the Putt family since a barrister called Nicholas Putt bought the estate in 1614. A descendant of Nicholas, Thomas Putt (1757-1787), was the gentleman who planted 'Beech Walk' and gave his name to the 'Thomas Putt Apple Tree'. The last Putt to own Combe Estate died, unmarried, in 1844 and the lands passed to his eldest sister Margaretta who had married Henry Marker, the Rector of Aylesbeare. Margaretta died less than two years later and thus Combe Estate was inherited by the Marker family in 1846. The last Putt to reside in Gittisham was one of Thomas Putt's sisters, Amelia, who died a spinster

in 1857 at Pomeroy House, aged 87. With her passing so did the 242 year line of the Putts of Gittisham! One of Margaretta Putt's daughters married Charles Gordon of Wiscombe Park whilst her own two sons, Henry William and Thomas John Marker, both subsequently inherited the Combe Estate. The last 'blood' Marker to hold the estate was Richard Raymond Kitchener Marker who was interestingly a godson of Lord Kitchener, the face of the famous "Wants You" WWI recruitment posters. This Mr. Marker died aged 53, with no immediate family, in 1961. The estate was then inherited by Mr. Marker's first cousin once removed who was, at the time, an 8 year old Canadian boy called Richard Trelawny. The estate was held in trust until Mr. Trelawny came of age and later he adopted his mother's maiden name of Marker and moved to Devon in 1981 to run the estate that now consists of some 4,000 acres, a position still held today.
(for a map ofthe extent of Honiton Manor's lands see Appendix III).

Honiton was first created a borough in 1300 and in the following year the town sent two members to Parliament named Johannes de Swengethrull and Galfridus Toleiner. Johannes was sent to Parliament again in 1311 but after that the town made no more returns until 1641. By the mid-nineteenth century the town had as much political representation as that of Liverpool; both being represented by two MPs. The interesting thing was that Honiton had a population of about 4,000 compared to Liverpool that had a population of over 300,000!
The town was under the jurisdiction of a 'Portreeve' until the election of the first councillors in 1847. A 'Portreeve' or 'port warden' was an early equivalent to a tax collector who ensured the Lord received what he was owed by his people and later the position became similar to that of town or borough Mayor. An ancient charter, granted to the Lord of the Manor of Honiton, permitted the Portreeve to hold "magisterial power to hold monthly courts and to make by-laws for the government of the borough". One of the earliest listed Portreeves of Honiton was Edward Channon in 1689 and other families who have held the title include the Livermores, Blagdons, Gills, Northcotes, Powning and Hakes. After 1847 the town had its own Mayor, of whom the first was Christopher Flood, a local attorney and banker. Prior to 1847 the town had been a corrupt rotten borough where politicians were elected by bribery levying - as Mr. Locke's song states, there were few "to oppose" the standing candidates. In the eighteenth century, exactly half of all the Parliamentary candidates for Honiton were either Younges or Courtenays, two of the most influential and notable local families. The Younge family were long established landowners in the town, dating back to the reign of Henry VII. Some of the

family once resided at Escot House, which was built in 1685, in the 18th century. One member of the Younge family, and the last to represent Honiton as an MP, was George Younge. He spent some £240,000 securing his seat for the town over his political life and by 1802 he was "ruined". This year was his last stand for the Honiton seat and whilst canvassing the streets he was booed and insulted as the voters knew of his financial situation and thus would not be paid anything for their votes. The mother of Christopher Flood, the banker, and wife to 'King Kester' even set light to his wig with a candle in New Street! The 162 year reign of the Younge family had come to an end and Mr. Younge died with no children at Hampton Court in 1812, aged 81. His body was interred at his place of death but was later exhumed and brought to the Younge family crypt at Colyton for a midnight service due to fears that his creditors would seize the body!

In 1201, King John I visited the town and granted a Charter for the weekly market to be changed from the original day of Sunday to Saturday. Many rural settlements obtained rights for annual fairs and weekly markets throughout the middle ages and fortunately Honiton's market, unlike many other towns and villages, survived the Black Death of 1348 after which many other rural settlements were abandoned. It is most likely that John sold the rights of the fair to Honiton, as he did with many other towns and villages, in order to raise money for the numerous wars in which he was involved.

Over the 250 year period between 1670 and 1920, Honiton has had nearly 30 fires that have ravaged part, if not all, of it so much so that, despite its age, it has virtually no remnants left of its medieval past . The first recorded fire occurred in 1672; there were several great fires, the first being on July 19th 1747. It started at 3pm and raged for 13 hrs; it was described as "a great conflagration that burnt half the town." The fire had started in a house opposite the old Allhallows Chapel and destroyed the entire south side of the High Street to the bridge opposite the present day 'Holt' (once Dominoes) along with part of the decaying 'shambles', causing about £43,000 worth of damage (about £7.1 million today). One observer of the aftermath noted that "the place has been eventually benefited; for the houses which are rebuilt are said to be neater in their appearance and more commodious to the inhabitants" and went on to compare the disaster with that of London in 1666: "it rose like a fair and beautiful Phoenix out of its ashes!"

The second of the most devastating fires of the town's history happened on 21st August 1765. The blaze began in a blacksmith's shop behind 'The Blacksmith's Arms,' and once again, the fire started on the south side of the High Street. However, this time the inferno crossed the road due to an inconveniently located thatched property. This fire started at about noon and had obliterated three quarters of the town by the time it was extinguished in the evening. The fire reduced 140 houses to ash and took the life of a certain Mr Darke: it is said that they found his severed arm clinging to the door latch of the old Presbyterian Chapel. The damage from this fire was estimated to be in the region of £10,500, of which less than half was covered by insurance.

A smaller fire on 14th March 1779, thought to have been started intentionally, wiped out a further 14 houses; another fire in 1790 destroyed 39 further houses and again in 1797, 47 homes were engulfed amounting to £10,000 worth of damage. By the early 19th century, the once abundant thatched roofs had been replaced by slate, which were obviously much more fireproof.

Many people may have noticed a solitary thatched Tudor cottage opposite the library. This is, in fact, the only property to survive one of the town's last fires in 1887; its neighbouring slate- roofed houses were built after the fire by local builders. This recently re-thatched cottage is the only Tudor property still standing in Honiton. The last biggest 'small' fire to harm the town, from this period, was the one that devastated the old church of St Michael's in 1911.

Farquharson wrote "that nearly every portion of the High Street has been burnt since 1747!"

(For a full list of fires please see Appendix 1.)

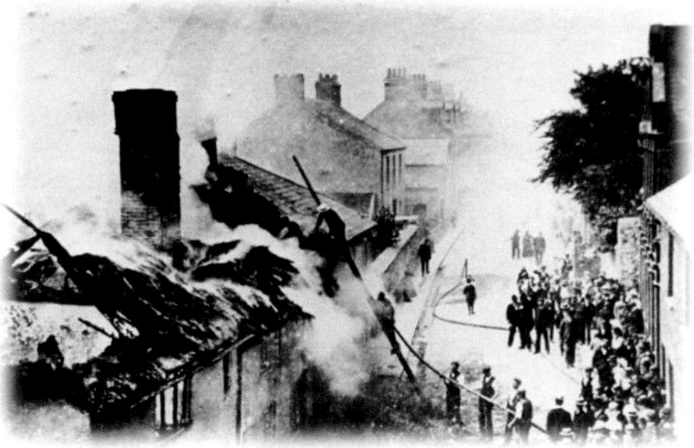

A fire in New Street, believed to be that of 1887.

Chapter 3
Schools & Educational Institutions

"The fate of empires depends upon the education of youth."
Aristotle

Schooling, prior to the Victorian era, was poorly funded and thus poorly attended. In 1858, less than half of children aged between 5 and 10 attended school and of those only 10% were educated to an 'adequate' standard. Education had been a luxury solely for the richer classes; however, by 1844, when the majority of the country was illiterate, the law had changed and stated that all children must attend school for at least 2 days a week. Honiton had had a variety of schools by the 1850s; some institutions for the children of the richer members of Honiton society and some provided to educate the poorer classes.

Allhallows Grammar School: The oldest and most well known of these schools must have been Allhallows Grammar School. Before its relocation, just before WWII, it had stood in the centre of the town for some 400 years. The 'Allhallows Charity', of which the school was a part, was established on 20th July 1524. The earliest documented pupil was one George Humphrey, grandson of the Rector of Honiton, Ozias Upcott, from 1663-1699. This Mr. Humphrey attended the school from 1714-1719. His eldest son, Ozias Humphrey, who also attended Allhallows between 1752 and 1757, went on to become a famous artist. Ozias' road to fame started when King George III purchased one of his miniatures and then commissioned him to paint portraits of his wife, Queen Caroline, along with other members of the Royal family. Other examples of his work include a painting of Elizabeth Lawrence, which can be seen in the Royal Albert Memorial Museum, Exeter and a portrait of the famous horse painter George Stubbs which hangs in the National Gallery, London.
As well as Mr Humphrey, many other famous people started their academic journey at Allhallows:

- George Buckle (1854-1935): attended at some point in the 1860s and went on to be editor of 'The Times' where he worked for 28 years.
- Arthur William A. Beckett (1844-1909) a well known novelist, dramatist, journalist and a man of letters who spent many years on the staff of 'Punch' magazine. He attended Allhallows in the 1850s.

- Thomas Wakley (1795-1862): founded the well known weekly medical journal 'The Lancet.' He was also MP for Finsbury and Coroner of West Middlesex; he would have attended the school in the early 1800s.
- Sir James Bacon (1798–1895): he was Vice Councillor of England from 1870-1886 and would have been a pupil in Honiton in the early 19th century.
- Arthur Francis Pridham (1886-1975): born in Teignmouth, this naval gentleman attended the school in the late 1890s. He commanded various ships including: HMS Concord, HMS Calliope, HMS Curlew, HMS Excellent and HMS Hood. After his retirement in 1941, when he was a Vice Admiral, he became President of the Ordnance Board, a position he held from 1941 to 1945 and was later awarded the Imperial Russian Order of St Stanislas and the Commander Legion of Merit (USA), in 1946.
- Sir Alfred Stephen (1802-1894): born in the West Indies he went on to be a judge and Chief Justice of New South Wales, Australia.
- Sir Arthur 'Bomber' Harris (1892-1984): attended Allhallows in the early 1900s and went on to become 'Marshal of the Royal Air Force'. He was a key figure in the Second World War.
- Lord John Coleridge (1820-1894): he was a great nephew of the famous Samuel Taylor Coleridge and after his attendance at Allhallows in the 1830s he was educated at Eton. He was made the '1st Baron of Coleridge and held the positions of Solicitor General for England and Wales, Attorney General for England and Wales, Chief Justice of the Common Pleas and Lord Chief Justice of England in 1880.
- Sir William Webb Follett (1798-1845): born in Topsham he became an MP and later Attorney-General of England in 1844. A statue of him stands in Westminster Abbey.

From the records there seems to seldom be a student who attended Allhallows who did not go on to do well in life and among the numerous other pupils was a Commissioner of Customs and Excise, an Astronomer Royal, a Quartermaster-General to the Forces and, on a more local note, a Chairman and Managing Director of Heavitree Brewery, Exeter! Former pupils of the school were once known as 'Old Honitonians'.

The schoolroom, standing independently since 1712, served several different functions, later becoming a dining room and later the school chapel, in memory of those who fell in the Boer War, until Allhallows'

relocation. From 1946 to the present it has been The Honiton and Allhallows Museum.
In 1818 the then headmaster Rev. Richard Lewis charged £30/yr for boarders of which, at the time, there were between 50-60 present (in 1866 there were 52 boarders and 16 day boys). The majority of those in attendance were also entitled to a 'Stapleton scholarship' at Exeter College, Oxford. The school was "intended for the sons of gentry and professional men" yet was quite within the reach of sons of "upper tradesmen". The school offered "an excellent classical education, preparatory rather than finishing" and "bore marks of conscientious teaching."
The school has obviously had a number of headmasters over the centuries. However, to give one an idea of how the school was operating in the mid nineteenth century, we may take a look at an extract from an inquiry carried out in 1869 whilst the headmaster was the Reverend J. F. Mackarness, who will also be looked at in greater depth later on.

"The Rev. J. F. Mackarness, the Rector of the parish, is the nominal headmaster; but the work of the school he practically confides to the Rev. T. Izod – the charge for the boarders is exceedingly low, for day boys sufficiently high to deter any but the upper tradesmen from sending their sons...The boarding accommodation was good. The younger boys were taught by a German governess, as I was assured, with good results. The neighbourhood all spoke well of it."

It appears from this report that the level of the teaching was good and that the level of education received was "effectively taught."
As already stated, the majority of the scholars were boarders and these had certain privileges over the day pupils. In 1864 a day pupil was taught at a cost of 35 guineas a year if aged under ten, 38 guineas if aged 10-14 and 45 guineas per annum if aged over 14. However, if any of these boys wished to play with their friends in the playground, that would cost the respective parents another 10 shillings a year and an additional 5 shillings if they wanted access to the library.
The hours of the pupils were virtually as long as the working hours of their parents; school commenced at half past six in the morning and could finish at anytime between half past eight and ten at night. This did, however, include "play time" and the time taken for meals. As a boarder a child could expect four square meals a day, including a "cup of coffee with bread and butter" in the morning and the extra cost incurred by day scholars was included in their annual fee. The average annual school bill in 1864 for a

boarder was £57. The children were also made to attend church twice on Sunday and once on Wednesday and Friday and the scripture was read daily. Examinations were held twice a year and pupils were given between 12 and 14 weeks holiday per annum.

In 1893 the school facilities were enlarged by the erection of a new school room; over the entrance was placed an attractive stained glass window in memory of Rev. J. F. Mackarness who was headmaster for many years. This building today is now known locally as Mackarness Hall and serves many purposes, from a polling station to the venue of many local events. During WWII it served as a dining room for the first of the evacuees to reach Honiton on September 1st 1939.

It was apparently the ambition of all the schoolboy batsmen to hit a six which would smash one of the windows in Pulman's cottages (owned by the father of the once well known Edgar William Pulman) which were once located opposite the cricket field. This feat was once said to have been achieved and the lady resident angrily brandished a shattered chamber pot out of the broken window!

In 1933 the school had 100 boarders and 20 day pupils all governed by some 9 masters, not including the headmaster, matrons and the school doctor. The school also had sporting facilities for rugby, football, cricket and hockey.

The school also employed local artist Alfred Leyman (1856-1933) as a teacher of art. Alfred Leyman captured many rural scenes of the Devonian countryside and coastline which today sell for hundreds of pounds.

The Grammar School itself was extended bit by bit over the years, including the acquisition of the playing field of 'Allhallows' as a cricket ground, a new dining room in 1906, which is now part of Allhallows Museum, a new library and rebuilt gymnasium in 1909, a science laboratory was added in 1921 and an open air swimming pool at the top of School Lane. For use of the swimming pool scholars were charged an additional five shillings for use during the summer months. In the early 20th century, fees were cheaper for the sons of the clergy and on arrival all students were given "two pairs of sheets, two pillow cases, six towels and a spoon and fork." By this time the fees for day boys had also fallen dramatically to only 10 guineas a year.

It was becoming apparent that the school's confined town centre location was restricting expansion and inhibiting the teaching and lodging of the 175 students. By summer 1938 the school had out-grown its situation and the whole establishment was relocated to a large Victorian mansion, built in about 1878 by the Peek family, in Rousdon, some 15 miles away. The cricket field was retained by the town and the separate parts of it were

broken up: the present day Honiton Working Man's Club' was once a part of the school.
After its move, Allhallows Grammar later became known as 'Allhallows College' but in 1998, with falling attendances and financial difficulties, the school sadly closed permanently.

The Charity School: a Charity School was established in Dowell Street in 1713 by a Mr. Shepard, MP for the borough at the time. It was written that as Mr. Shepard had had "great satisfaction" witnessing "the Charity Children on the Thanksgiving Day in the Strand" he decided to set up A Charity School in Honiton of whom the master should be "capable of playing on a organ" and that he should be paid between £30 and £40 per year. This School was free to all the poor children of the parish and cost £300 to establish which was raised from voluntary contributions. In 1717, some 4 years after the school's foundation, there were 30 boys in attendance and was one of only 32 Charity Schools in the whole of Devon. The school once stood where Honiton Scout Headquarters is now located.

The National School: The aforementioned Charity School went on to become the National School that was founded in 1829 with room for 140 boys and 90 girls. This new school was set up by the Rev. V. H. P. Somerset with the aid of a London grant of £150 towards the building. The master of the new school was on a salary of £50 a year. The school went on until 1860 when it moved to a bigger site in King Street. The new site was constructed on land donated by Charles Tucker in 1820 to the Church of St Michael's. Construction was finished in 1861 and the new school could hold 400 pupils; it was later extended to take a further 92 and by 1906 had room for 600 students. When the school opened, one of its first teachers was Richard Drewe who was only 15 years old, not much older than the pupils! At the time of its closure in 1940, the school had both a primary and senior faculty which had long outgrown its old site and pupils were therefore transferred to the newly constructed Honiton Community College and Honiton Primary School which, of interest, were referred to in the 1950s as "St Paul's Senior School" and "St Paul's Junior School". The closure of such small, rural country schools was common around this time. In the thirty years after WWII there was a need for 5 million additional school places. This was due to a population explosion - the baby boom years - and an increased school leaving age. The ideals of these new schools were to be completely different from the former 'dark, heavy [and] imposing' establishments of the previous century and instead were to be

environments that were 'bright and airy' so as to not intimidate scholars and Honiton was no exception to these post war trends.
The National School's original site in Dowell Street later became a motor cycle repair shop of a Mr. Cowell and later the premises of Honiton 1st Scout Group in 1936, when Mr F. Cottrell of Marwood House donated the property to them. The 'new' site in King Street, after the school's closure, became the offices of 'Hansford & Co.', a local building company and later, in 1987, flats for the elderly (Homelace House).

The British School: The British School was established in 1834, constructed right next to the Independent Chapel. The cost of this building was £320 with a £150 grant from Parliament. It was founded to educate "the children of the poor in Honiton according to the principles of the British and Foreign School Society." The schoolroom was also used on the Sabbath for Sunday school.
A report filed by the Committee of Council on Education in 1850, at which point a combined total of 60 girls and boys were in attendance, had the following to say about the school:

"This school has not improved since the date of my last visit, nearly two years ago, but rather the reverse. The defect in this case does not appear obviously to be of instruction, capacity, proper demeanour, or desire to do the best but of the tact and energy to employ every available power to the training and instruction of the children. In fact, the school exhibits less of either discipline or instruction than it is possible to conceive in the presence of so respectable a master. The methods are defective in every exercise there is a want of purpose either to teach or learn among the monitors and children: and the progress, therefore, is slow and blundering. Five boys at the top of the school , including one chiefly taught elsewhere, have superior ability to reading, writing, spelling, and arithmetic: but in grammar and geography all are equally deficient...All this might be excused in so poor a town as Honiton, if the mass of the children were being well and industriously educated in the simplest elements, with habits of order, industry, and cheerful obedience; but such is not the case; and the poor and backward state of the town generally therefore, does but awaken the more regret that this school is not one of a vigour proportioned to the want of it."

The report also went on to say that the building's "erection and continued existence" was all the work of the Independent Chapel's minister, Rev. W. Wright. The building still exists today and is Grade II listed.

Woodgates Academy: another academic establishment was the 'Honiton Classical & Mathematical Academy' otherwise known as 'Woodgates Academy'. This school was a private boarding school for boys up to the age of 16 and was located in New Street. Its headmaster was one William Woodgates who was proprietor for over 30 years. The school had been founded by a Mr. Trenow in the early 19th century and had previously been located in the High Street. The original school was described as a "large middle class school for boarders and day boys". When Mr. Woodgates took over the school in about 1825 he relocated it to the large house in New Street, called 'The Laurels', and for the following 30 years "conducted a flourishing academy". In 1851 the school had 31 boys in attendance, although there were "generally from 100 to 150 boarders. Aside from the "spacious school-room" there was also "a beautiful playground, for the accommodation of the boys". One description of the school said that it "offered a commercial, nautical, mathematical and classical education', named history and geography [were] among the subjects taught, but not English; only Reading, Writing...English Grammar...and English Composition".

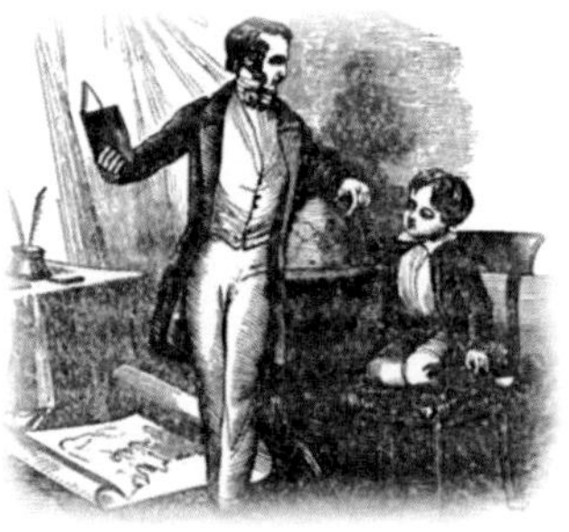

At one point the Woodgates family had quite a hold on the town when it came to academia which will be explained later (*See Residents and Residence Section*).

Summerland College: this school for girls was founded in the 1870s by two sisters, Jessie and Elizabeth Eastman, the daughters of an Independent Minister. The school, like Allhallows and Woodgates, was a boarding and day school for girls aged up to 16 years old. In about 1890 Jessie left for another school in Wales, leaving Summerland in the hands of her sister. In 1894 Elizabeth died at the age of 39 and another two sisters named Fanny and Gertrude Grimbley took over the school.

"The Misses Grimbly, whilst careful of the intellectual training of the pupils under their charge, by no means neglect their physical culture. Real home life is associated with all kinds of healthy exercise- croquet, tennis, and such-like, and both day pupils and boarders are encouraged to develop 'mens sana in corpora sano'. Children attend this school from the earliest age, and the kindergarten department has proved most successful."

These two sisters ran the establishment until their retirement in the early 1920s when the Misses Harrison took the reins. The Harrisons retired in the early 1930s and the school became unisex. A Miss Barralet was principal for a few years when the school boasted having "qualified staff"! The school was later taken over by one of its teacher, Miss Edith Tucker. When Miss Tucker retired, just after WWII, the school closed and is now a private house called 'Claywell'. Edith Tucker died in Honiton in 1985 aged 79. In 1881 the school had two headmistresses, two English teachers, one French teacher, a cook, a maid and eleven pupils from as far away as Pembrokeshire.

Some twenty years prior to the establishment of this facility there was another boarding school known as 'Summerland' run by another two sisters called Sarah and Betsy Dyer in the building now occupied by 'Bay Associates Ltd' (62 high Street). This school disappeared in the mid 1840s and became a grocers shop.

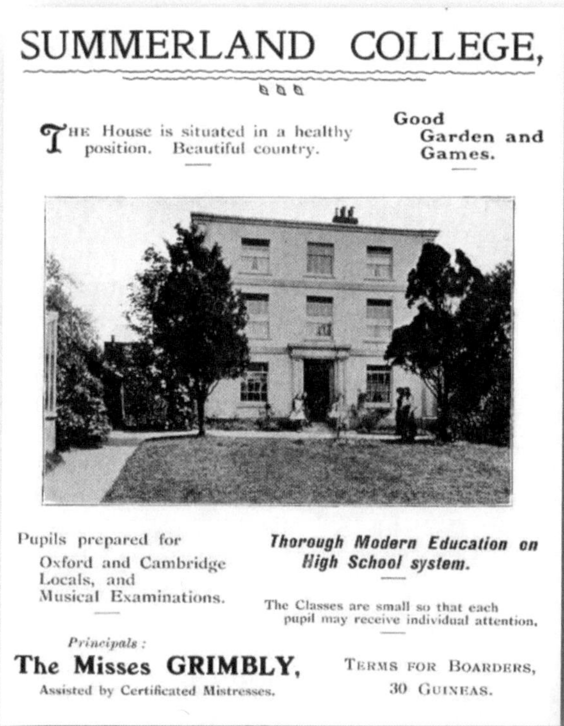

Chapter 4
Churches & Places of Worship

"This hill is a favourite walk with Honiton folk for it leads to the spot where their dearest associations lie and where are peacefully slumbering the forefathers of the town."

Description of the Church of St Michael's: R. A. Farquharson, 1891

There was known to have been a "church" in Honiton as early as 1263 and although no name is given in the document stating this fact, this is believed to be one of, if not the earliest reference to, any place of worship in the town.
The parish church of Honiton today is St. Paul's, situated very majestically in the centre of town and dominating many neighbouring properties with its ever present shadow. The original parish church of Honiton, however, seems to have changed several times; not only its location but also its name. By the 1850s the town also had some long established non-conformist places of worship.

St. Margaret's Chapel

St. Margaret's Hospital, with a chapel also present, was established as a hospital for four leprous people with originally two residential cottages for those afflicted by the illness. References date back to the 12th century but the earliest reputable record for this building is 1374. Mr. Aberdein, a local historian during the Victorian period, believed this small chapel to be the original parish church. However, although it is highly likely that this was at one time the case, other evidence suggests an even earlier church. Falco de Breaute held a palfrey in 1221 for 'a yearly fair at the Manor of Huneton on eve day and morrow of All Hallows' and it was always customary to hold the annual fair on the day of the parish's patron saint which the local church would have also been named after. This suggests that the old chapel of Allhallows was the earliest church of the parish. Then 26 years later in 1247, a licence was granted for the fair day to be changed to the feast of St Margaret (July 25th). St Margaret is also Patron Saint of Pregnant Women/Unborn Children which gives credence to the old Honitonian legend when all the women were barren. The actual date of the original construction is not known but it was built on land originally owned by the smaller Honiton Manor of 'Batishorne.'
The Chapel was thought to have been founded by a Knight named William de Tracy in the late 12th century. William de Tracy was one of, and allegedly the principal of, the four knights who murdered Thomas a Becket

in December 1170. After the incident, England was in a state of shock; Becket had been England's foremost religious man and on his murder 100,000 pilgrims flocked to the sight of his death. Tracy and the other 3 knights accused of his murder were called to Rome to be judged by the Pope himself. Despite their penitence, he declared that they should be exiled and fight for a number of years "in knightly arms in The Temple for 14 years" in Jerusalem. It is said that whilst on this crusade Tracy fell ill with leprosy yet miraculously recovered. On his return, and in thanks for his recovery, he founded the chapel and hospital of St Margaret's. He also founded a building for four further leprous people called 'Coismas' in France. Tracy performed a number of further commendable feats in an attempt to recompense for his crime, including founding and extending at least three further churches in both France and England. However, it appears Tracy was never truly forgiven. The place and time of William de Tracy's death is unknown. One of William de Tracy's daughters married a member of the Courtenay family. Interestingly, 'Saint Margaret of England,' (another St. Margaret) who died in 1192, was a close relation of Thomas a Becket!

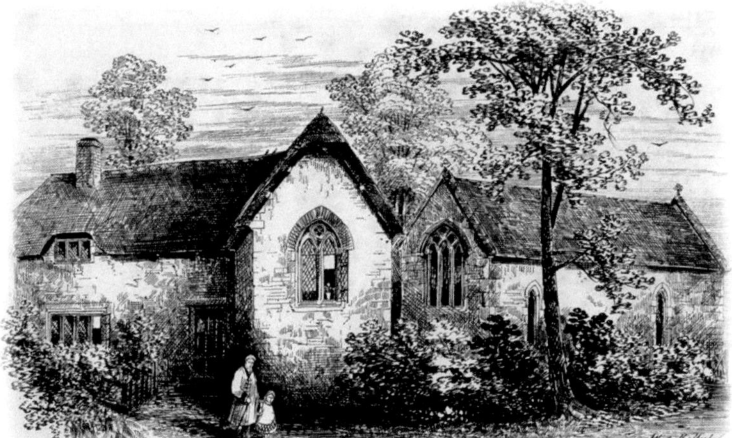

✠ Saint : Margaret's : Hospital : and : Chapel : Honiton : Devon.

Leprosy was the most feared disease of medieval England and sufferers were social outcasts, forced to wear a cloak and a bell to warn others of their approach. It was deemed to be an affliction brought about by "divine judgement" as punishment for a sinful life. It was a horrific disease which was known as the 'living death'. Once one had contracted the illness the sufferer could expect to have their fingers and toes melt away, the collapse and disintegration of the nose, leaving a gaping wound through which a pungent liquid would flow, as well as a coarse and croaky voice from an ulcerated larynx and wholly one would be a 'deformed, stinking, blind and repulsive individual'. It was for these reasons people were utterly terrified of it and why the Honiton Hospital was established some miles from the town itself. There was most probably a lot of local controversy when St. Margaret's was established, having a community of sinful and contagious residents so near to the town!

William de Tracy took his family name from his ancestors who had originated from a village called 'Tracy' in Normandy and had come over to England during the Norman Conquest. This name has had much influence both locally to Honiton and locally to Devon: Bovey Tracey takes its name from this ancient family and 'Tracey House', now destroyed, of Awliscombe; some surrounding landmarks also owe their name to this family.

One of William de Tracy's descendants, Thomas Chard (last Abbott of Forde, Dorset), re-founded the then 400 year old, decaying chapel in the 16th century; the rebuilding was completed in 1530. In 1642 a new regulation was made which extended the Chapel/Hospital's aid to those of Honiton parish who were poor as well as leprous.

The Chapel, at one point, had a small graveyard and it is said that those convicted and executed under the notorious 17th century Judge Jefferies' Assizes were buried here. 17 criminals convicted and executed at the County Lent Assizes of 1590 were also interred here, the Assizes being held in Honiton due to a plague epidemic in Exeter.

St Margaret's Chapel is now a private residence located at the west end of the town, originally "about half a mile from the town" now opposite the Honiton Motel. The chapel was still in use well into the twentieth century when "occasional services" were held and up until the 1930s Holy Communion was administered there by the Rector of Honiton on St Margaret's day.

The small bell that hung in the chapel was inscribed "God preserve the House."

(More information on the hospital and charity of St Margaret's can be found in the Chapter 'Poor of the Parish.')

Church of St Michael's

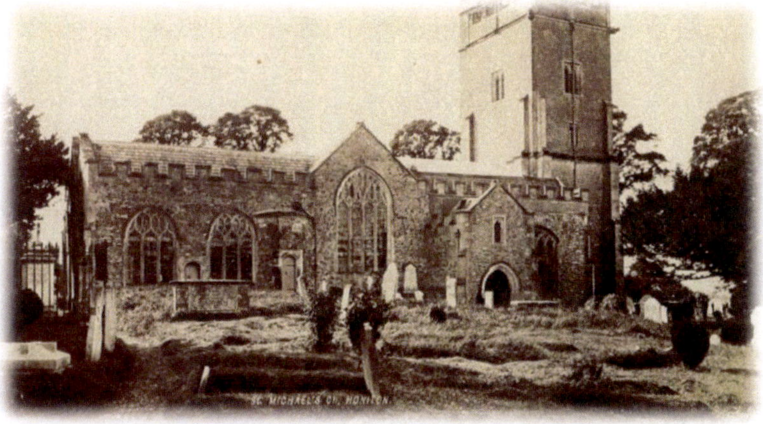

The long established Church of St. Michael's was the parish church of Honiton for many hundreds of years. 'Mate's Illustrated Honiton' suggested the following:

"Go to St Michael's churchyard on a fine day, and amidst the quiet of God's acre, look around on the panorama unfolded by nature. No pen can describe it, no painter's brush can adequately depict a scene so charming."

It is believed to have originally been built by Mendicant Friars as a roadside Chapel for travellers: the road on which it is situated was originally the 'Great Western Road', which centuries later was relocated into the valley. Early 20th century excavations even suggest evidence of an earlier Saxon place of worship. One theory for the church's isolated location was that this was the original site of early Honiton, for although today the church is within the town's urban boundaries, back in the 1800s it was "half a mile south of the town." It has also been suggested that the once little hamlet of 'Littletown' was the remains of medieval Honiton for, like the church, this small collection of houses was also located on the Great Western Road. Another more far-fetched myth was that the Church owed its situation to the Devil, who forced the builders to relocate the preferred site of the once Union Workhouse (now Honiton Hospital) to its present situation on the hill. The Devil would carry the stones up to the hill's summit at night whilst the builders attempted to bring them back down the hill in the daytime but after many days of this occurrence the townspeople gave up their feud. However, in order to provoke any further involvement with Beelzebub, the people devoted the completed church to St Michael, conqueror of the Devil. However, as many churches located in hilly positions were dedicated to St. Michael, this folk tale is probably more far-fetched than most!

Farquharson (author of the well-known 'The History of Honiton') stated that the Church's history went back to 1326 but also stated that the first authentic record of this ancient building was some 80 years later in 1406 when it was mentioned in the Will of a John Chepman. This document, however, only referred to the church as a 'small chapel.' Mr. Chepman's Will also gives credence to the theory that St. Michael's was not the original parish church, for in his Will he left bequests to both Allhallows and St Michael's. However, the sum left to the former was far more substantial than that of the latter, suggesting Allhallows was of more importance! One of the next reputable recordings of this church was in another gentlemen's Will which was proved in 1506. This man was a Mr. John Takell and he kindly gave 12d to the thirty nearest parishes of Honiton to "pray for his soul." Both Mr. Chepman and Mr. Takell were interred within the church itself.
St. Michael's was largely extended and this was initiated by Richard Courtenay, the then Lord of Honiton Manor, who was also a nephew of William Courtenay, Archbishop of Canterbury. Progress, however, in the restoration was slow and by his death in 1415 work had ceased. The job was not taken up again until some 70 years later by Richard's grandnephew who completed the construction of a tower and the nave in about 1480. Peter de Courtenay, Richard's grandnephew, who later became both Bishop of Exeter and Winchester respectively, also donated an "elaborately carved screen" of oak in 1483 which, by the late 1850s, had been "disfigured by the hand of vandalism." By 1864 this "oaken screen" was said to have been "unhappily disfigured with paint" possibly an attempt to cover the formerly mentioned "vandalism."

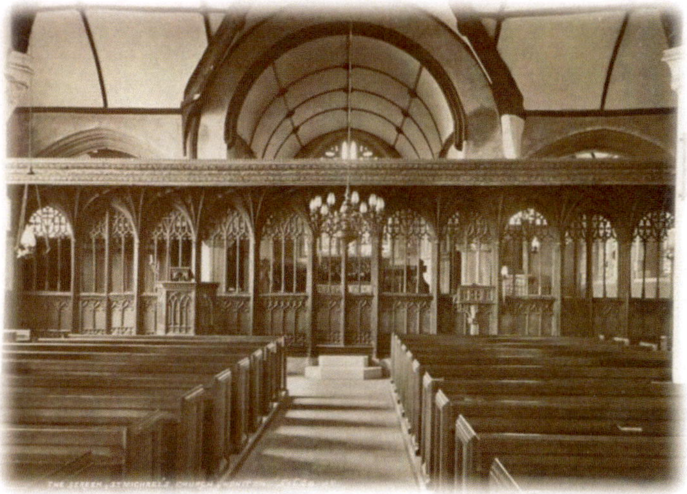

The beautifully carved oak screen that was lost in the fire of 1911.

The church's aforementioned generous benefactor (Peter de Courtenay) died on 22nd September 1492 and further improvements were contributed by other wealthy local parishioners, including the already mentioned John Takell and his wife Joan. Joan Takell left many bequests in her Will, including monies to the daughters of John of Gaunt, giving one some idea of this lady's former notability. It is thought that the ongoing rebuilding and restoration of the church from benefactors was actually a complete conversion from the earlier "small chapel" to a parish church. Whether this was done due to population increase, a generous gift or the relegation of an earlier parish church is not known.

This "fine old building" was the parish church for over 500 years and up until 1868, when the sexton's house was built, even had stables for the horses of its parishioners.

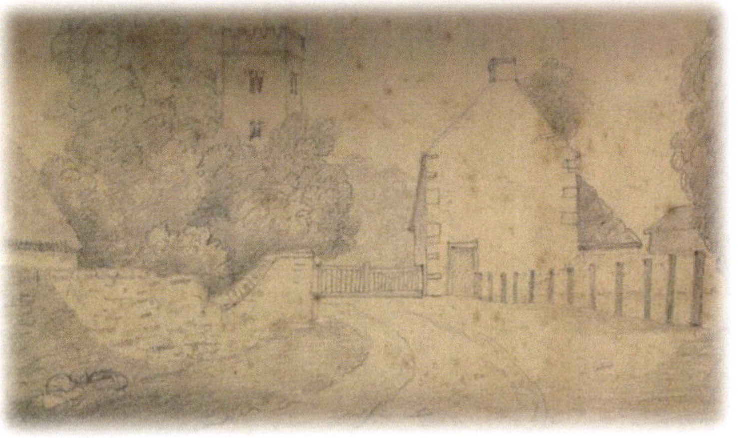

Drawing by Richard Farquharson of St. Michael's before the extension of the graveyard. The property on the right is the sexton's house.

Two observers writing in 1793 and 1805 both noted the churchyard to be "rather small" as well as the fact that "it [had] few, but some old tombs". So few, in fact, that one of these gentlemen listed them all! In 1818, however, a certain Mr. John Evan wrote that "the church-yard was crowded with graves!" Among the souls laid to rest in the churchyard are a few people who are worth mentioning. Firstly, Thomas Marwood: the physician to Her Majesty Queen Elizabeth I whose tomb was constructed of black marble. He died a Catholic, in Honiton, on September 18th 1617 at the grand old age of 105. He had travelled to settle in Devon, from London, at the age of eighty and married his second and third wives at the respective ages of 87 and 94! This tomb seems to have been so important to the church that the Lord of the Manor of Widworthy actually funded its restoration in the late 1830s. James Rodge was another gentleman laid to rest in the graveyard in 1617 and by the inscription on his tomb he has been found to be the oldest recorded lace dealer in England. This may not be so surprising considering the famous centuries old Honiton lace trade. No tombs dating prior to that of James Rodge's grave are mentioned by past visitors, which is not so surprising as prior to the 17th century, graves were simply marked with a wooden cross, which in time would obviously simply rot away.

The grave of Thomas Baker can also be found here: a butterman who was robbed and murdered at the 'Hand and Pen Inn' on the Exeter Road some

9 miles from Honiton on April 17th 1724. The event seems to have been so shocking to the local community that a memorial to mark the place of his death, known as 'Baker's Monument', was erected although this has long since disappeared.

In 1844 St. Michael's churchyard was approximately a quarter of what it is today. The observation of a "small" graveyard, made in 1818, must have been correct for only 20 years later a large proportion of a field, ironically called 'Churchyard Field', was acquired from the Honiton Manor to extend the burial grounds. The entrance to the churchyard was also extended nearer to the road. When entering the churchyard today it is worth noting the dates on the graves to your immediate right, for the majority of them are from the second half of the Victorian period compared to the earlier internments nearer to the church. By the time Farquaharson wrote his local book 'The History of Honiton' in 1868, he had stated that the "new burying grounds" were "nearly full." As more practical methods of disposing of the dead, such as cremation, were not to be made legal for another 20 years and the fact that under common law "all citizens had a right to be buried in the churchyard of their home parish", space for the deceased was always in demand. A certain Moses Read, who was gravedigger in Honiton from 1843-1868, apparently interred 2,050 people over his 25 year employment period. This "new burying ground" today is an old, overgrown, fenced off portion of the cemetery where sheep may often be seen feeding and where even the most preserved headstones are often illegible. In later years a massive proportion of a field to the east of the church called 'Downton's Field' was obtained for burials; the other half of this field today is a private residence. A further one acre plot was bought from the Lord of the Manor, Richard Marker, in 1890 for the sum of £139.16s and yet another acre was purchased in 1929.

In 1770 an attorney by the name of William Baker planted a yew tree on the grave of Ann, his daughter, and by 1793 one observer noted that the churchyard was "adorned with eight fine spiral yews" which were planted by a man called Sergeant Sheppard. All the yews were planted from the respective planters' gardens. These fine trees are still present today and give the path to the church entrance a dark, foreboding appearance.

It was customary in earlier times to use broken headstones for any needed purposes: there was once "upping stocks" which stood near the church gates that were used for the convenience of tying or mounting riders' horses; these were made up of fragments of ancient graves.

By 1870, some 30 years after the new church of St. Pauls had been built, services were held here once a month. In 1896 the church underwent a restoration at a cost of £800, the equivalent of nearly £80,000 today, when the galleries were taken away and the inside was completely re-seated to accommodate 200 people. The organ that had also been present in this ancient building since 1700 had also been removed some 15 years earlier in 1881 due to its "decayed" condition.

Unfortunately, all of this restoration was in vain for a great fire completely gutted the church on March 26th 1911. The fire was thought to have been caused by sparks from the heating apparatus' furnace igniting the woodwork of the roof. The church was, however, restored at a cost of £2,900 and re-dedicated in August 1912.

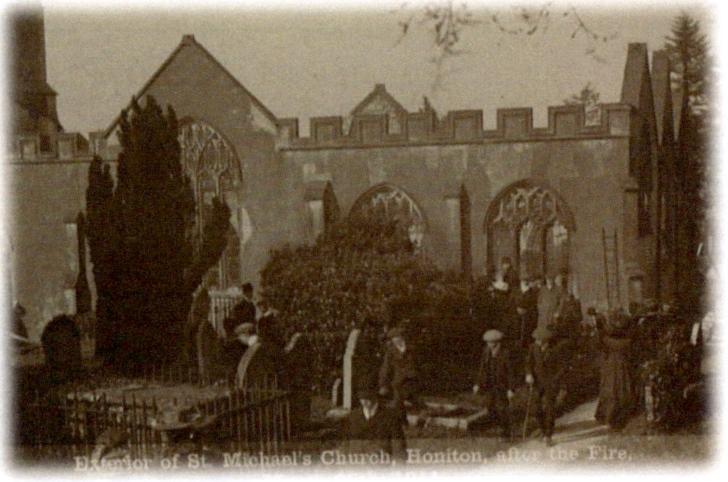

Still standing today, the church is still used for weddings, christenings and, mainly due to no space at the new church, burials of the departed. In the 1930s, services continued to be held twice monthly and the church was open "daily" for visitor and worshippers. Even up until the 1950s, monthly services were still held at the old Church.

The first recordings of the parish after the Reformation, of a birth, marriage and burial, were made in this church's register on 26th March, 29th May and 3rd April 1598 respectively.

This fine church has always had a place in the town's heart and now is a place where concerts and other local events take place. Today this 'Chapel-of-Ease' is a Grade II* listed building.

We now leave St Michael's with a quote to the Church from a Victorian visitor named Wilson:

"Such is the Scene around me now
a little churchyard on the brow
of a green pastoral hill.
A place where all things mournful meet
and yet the sweetest of sweet
The stillest of still."

The Rectors of Honiton

Although a full list of the Rectors of Honiton can be found in *Appendix II* of this book, here is some additional information on some of the prestigious men and women who served this community's religious and personal needs throughout the centuries.

- Walter: the first known Rector of Honiton in 1224 whose sister, Alice de Bristol, donated lands at Butterleigh and Slade to a convent there and he himself donated lands to St Nicolas' Priory, Exeter.
- Edward Fishacre: was rector of Honiton during the reign of Henry IV. He died in 1416 as the Vicar of Cullompton.
- Robert Fynor: rector from 1408; he was a nephew of Sir Philip Courtenay and was at one point a clerk for the Bishop of Norwich. When he died the chancel of St Michael's was said to be "in a dilapidated state": maybe not the most proactive of the town's rectors!
- Richard Denys: was 'cessioned 'from his post in Honiton but was thought to have latterly been appointed to Powderham where he died in 1533.
- Philip Bale: came to the parish in 1539 during the reign of Henry VIII. One of his wives was at one point the 2nd wife of Sir William Courtenay.
- John Eedes: born 1583 and before the calling of Honiton he had been Vicar of the smaller parish of Clyst St Lawrence. Being a supporter of Charles I, he was ejected from his post. He was described as "a severe sufferer for the cause of Royalty" and was a "very worthy person and much of a gentleman...that died before the Restoration of the Monarchy".
- Francis Sourton: was ejected from his position due to nonconformity and was imprisoned for a short while in Exeter Jail; however, due to the fact he had married an aunt of Sir

William Courtenay (who was High Sheriff) he was released soon afterwards. He was described in one text as "a man of great energy in his parish". He was educated at a 'free-school' in Plymouth later 'Exeter College' and was said to have been "a man of great learning...an excellent preacher...and surprisingly humble" whose sermons were "kept as a treasure". There was once a piece of land on Marlpits Hill named after him.

- Ezra Cleveland: born 1661 he became the rector of Honiton in 1699 after having been the Rector of Powderham from 1697. He was a prolific author and wrote a book about the Courtenay's family history. He was also Fellow of Exeter College, Oxford where the young Sir William Courtenay had been his pupil. He died in 1740, having served the community for 40 years, outliving both his wife and son who had fallen victim to smallpox. Interestingly, two cousins of this gentleman were thought to have been involved in the Monmouth Rebellion and on being dragged before Judge Jeffries were sentenced to 10 years exile in America where they were sold as slaves.
- Hon Charles Bertie: a Professor of Natural Philosophy at Oxford, he was the youngest son of James Earl of Abingdon and a brother to one of the Lady Courtenays. He died in 1746 aged 69 and was buried at Kenn, near Exeter.
- Charles Bertie: born in 1704 and son of the above; this gentleman was rector from 1761 and in 1784 married, for what was thought to be the first time, to a 64 year old spinster, himself being 82!
- Edward Honywood: was previously Chaplain to the Prince of Wales "this gentleman used to walk to church in a cassock, bands and well powdered wig, and his great delight was to make his clerk, an illiterate man, read the lesson when it contained a lengthy list of Hebrew name"! He was also supposed to have once ridden into town whilst a riot was ensuing and dispersed the crowd with a hunting whip. He also had a brother, Sir John Honywood, who was MP for the town from 1802-1806 who gained support from the Courtenay family after marrying the eldest daughter of the 2nd Viscount.
- Villiers Henry Plantagenet Somerset: born in 1803 he was directly descended from John of Gaunt being the third son of General Lord Charles Henry Somerset and Elizabeth Courtenay. An Oxford educated man he came to Honiton at the age of 24 and in

1843 was presented with 'a service of plate' from his grateful parishioners. His premature death in 1855 came as a sad shock to the town.

- John Fielder Mackarness: he was born in 1820 and was educated at Eton. Before coming to Honiton he was the Vicar of Tardebigge, Worchesershire, and an honorary Canon at Worchester Cathedral. He came to Honiton in 1855 and married a daughter of Sir John Coleridge, a great niece of the famous poet Samuel Coleridge Taylor, and allegedly moved to the East Devon parish so his wife could be near her parents in their retirement. He was described as "a true pastor" holding "Sunday afternoon services, in a shed, for navvies living in huts near the site of the railway tunnel being built between Honiton and Axminster". He also changed the location of the Rectory from the present 'Old Rectory Farm' to the old Rookwood Rectory, now destroyed. In 1870 he was invested with the prestigious title of Chancellor of the Order of the Garter. Many of the Devonian clergy apparently mistrusted him due to his views on the disestablishment of the Church of Ireland. However, this did not stop him becoming the Bishop of Oxford in 1869. He died 20 years later still holding this respectable post.

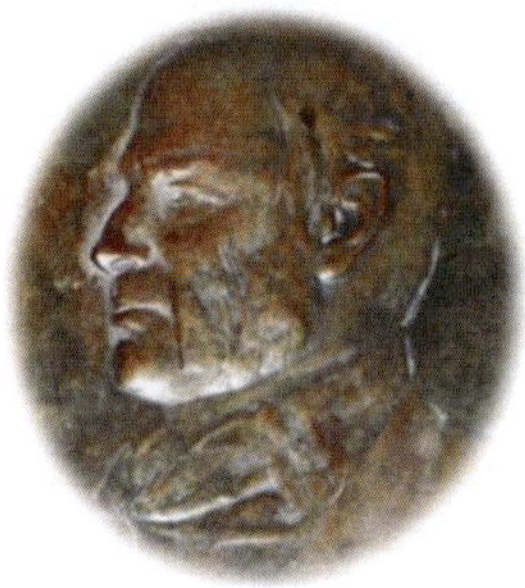

- Michael Ferrebee Saddler: born in Yorkshire he started as Curate of Pidely cum Fenton, Huntingdonshire; then went onto be Vicar of Bridgewater and rector of St Paul's, Bedford before coming to Honiton in 1869.
- Hugh John Fortescue: born in Poltimore, Devon in 1844, his father was a Canon of Worchester Cathedral and he and his family once lived in the Cathedral's west end. Hugh's grandfather was the 1st Earl of Fortescue and

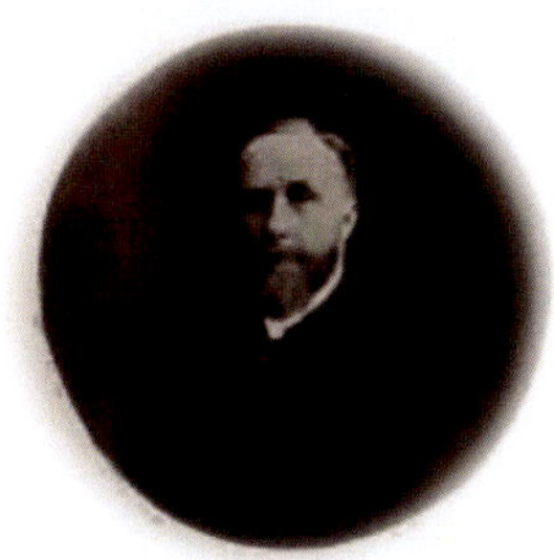

held the positions of Vice Admiral and Lord Lieutenant of Devon for some 50 years. The family lived at Castle Hill in Devon and had its roots in Devon stretching back to the 14th century. Hugh, himself, was Curate of St Mary's Riddle, Worcestershire before being posted to Honiton. Mr. Fortescue never married and lived with his sister, Eleanor, all his life. He left Honiton in 1895 and died in Margate in 1907. His three surviving sisters, in 1909, erected the Lynch Gate at the Church of St. Michael's to his memory.

- Frederick Leslie Courtenay: this gentleman succeeded the Rev. Fortescue and was born at Powderham Castle in 1875. After his father's death he became the 16th Earl of Devon and was Mayor of Honiton from 1929 to 1933. His grandson Hugh Rupert Courtenay is the current Earl of Devon.
- Andrew Augustine Fane de Salis: born 1901 the son of Cecil Fane de Salis a barrister of Dawley Court, Uxbridge. His Uncle was the Bishop of Taunton and he was descended from Italian nobility. He was educated at Exeter College, Oxford, spent five years in the Indian Church Establishment and before coming to Honiton was the Curate of Heavitree from 1934. He died in February, 1962.
- Richard Andrew Babington: born in 1927, his father was Archdeacon of Exeter. He left Honiton in 1972 for Blandford, Dorset where he died in 1993.
- Robin Mark George Morrell: was rector of Honiton from 1972-78, a position he left to become Lay Diocese Training Officer of Southwark. He later became the Assistant Chaplain of HM Prison Brixton. He died in 2010 aged 80.
- Jane Barbara Hedges: born 1955, she was educated at Durham University and held her first post as Curate of The Church of St. Columba, Farham, Hampshire. She later became Rector of Honiton in 2001, a position she held for 5 years after leaving to become a Canon of Westminster Abbey. She was also the first female Rector of the town.

As can be seen, there are a lot of connections between Honiton Rectors and the Courtenay family. This may not be surprising as they were Lords of the Manor and Patrons of the rectory. It is also evident that Honiton has had many a rector from much more than a humble background!

Chapel of St. Thomas

Another very early Chapel recorded in the town was that of St Thomas, dedicated to the once again referred to Thomas a Becket. This chapel "Capella beati Thome de Honetone" was licensed for holy worship as of 27th February 1332 by Bishop John Grandisson of Exeter. It can also, from bequests, be established that it was still in use in 1406 and was still standing up until 1528 but where this place of worship was, or when it was destroyed, is not known.

Allhallows Chapel

Prior to the construction of the parish church of St Paul's, there was a medieval chapel called Allhallows or All Saints, of which the earliest recording was in 1327 which was reputed to have been constructed of "flint".

Throughout this chapel's long history, it seems for most of its life to have been in a state of disrepair rather than a fully functional place of religious worship. An early account of this was when a John Chepman, mentioned earlier, left a sum of £10 in his Will dated 1406, to aid the repair of the roof. By 1418, some ten years later, the chapel was in a similar state with a period "of forty days" being granted "to all who contributed towards its support."

In 1426 an enquiry was held when one member of the parish was supposed to have assaulted the chaplain and spilt blood on sacred ground. In 1429 a petition was sent to the Pope by the people of Honiton asking for "mass celebrated daily at dawn by a fit priest" at the chapel as the climb to the parish church of St Michael's proved almost impossible in bad weather. By 1710 the chapel was virtually derelict and only 2 years later the nave and tower were pulled down and the site remained vacant with the chapel being used as no more than a place to house ladders and a general town storage depot. At this time, a travelling observer described the chapel as having "a low obtuse spire with three small bells." Thirty years following this, in 1743, a complete reconstruction was initiated: unfortunately, by the mid 1760s, reconstruction had been so slow that little more than a tower, cupola and six bells had been completed. Later that year the entire building was engulfed by the great fire of 1765. The fire did not end the life of this ancient chapel and it was reopened for worship on July 6th 1769. This new building was described in one chronicle of the time as "a square embattled tower of flint, with six bells, a clock and chimes." In 1790 the building was extended and weekly services were held on Wednesday and Friday by the then Master of the Grammar School. "The dead time of the year" being the six weeks before and after Christmas, was when Allhallows

was used for all the Sunday services instead of St Michael's, the then parish church!
The last service ever held was in August 1835 when the following morning the entire site was cleared to make way for the new parish church of St Paul's.

Church of St. Paul's

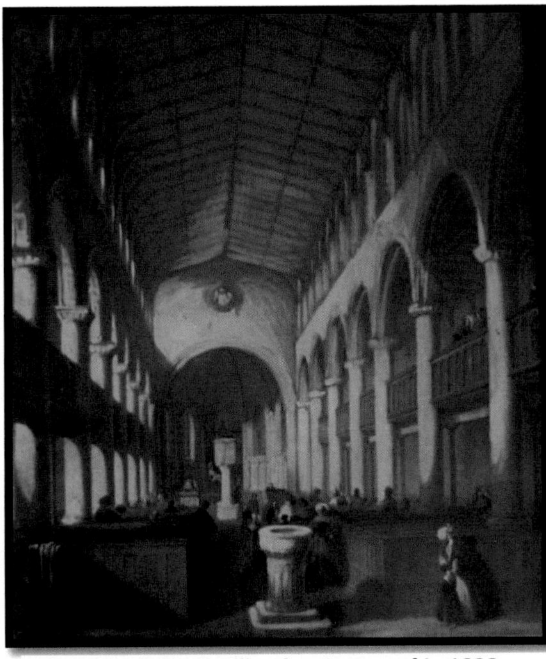

The interior of St. Paul's when it opened in 1838.

Due to the continuing struggle by locals to climb Church Hill every Sunday for Holy Communion, permission for the construction of a new parish church of St Paul's was granted by an Act of Parliament in 1835. It was designed by the famous architect of the time Charles Fowler, born in Cullompton. He had had an illustrious career before his Honiton enterprise, having designed the markets of Covent Garden and Hungerford, London and a bridge across the River Dart at Totnes. After his Honiton project he went on to design the 'Devon Lunatic Asylum' in Exeter in 1845, as well as becoming Vice President of the 'Institute of British Architects.' Fowler was also commissioned by William Courtenay 10th Earl of Devon to make Powderham Castle, home of the old Honiton Lords, "of a character consistent with an ancient castle" in 1835.

The new church was built in the centre of town and construction began in early spring, 1837. Prior to this, the medieval Allhallows chapel and some houses in its immediate vicinity were removed. There had been early proposals to build the new church in King Street where the National School stood as this was the original reason for Mr Tucker donating the land. The foundation stone was laid on the 25th October 1835 by local businessman and attorney, Christopher Flood (Lord of the Manor of Monkton). Fowler's designs for the new church were carried out by the highly respected local builder Mr. William Lee. The church was built in the "Norman style" and was made largely out of stone from Beer. Churches were usually constructed so that their altar resided in the east, as this is the compass point believed to be from where the second coming of Jesus will occur. Yet due to special limitations the building thus runs north/south with a tower 104 feet high. The original estimate for this building was £6,600 but with the sum of £2,200 being spent on the purchase of the needed surrounding land and additional exterior work, the sum was almost doubled to £11,000, about £920,000 in today's money. All of this money was raised by voluntary subscriptions, except for a small grant given by 'The Society for the Enlargement of Churches and Chapels.' I now quote from one chronicle printed in 1838:

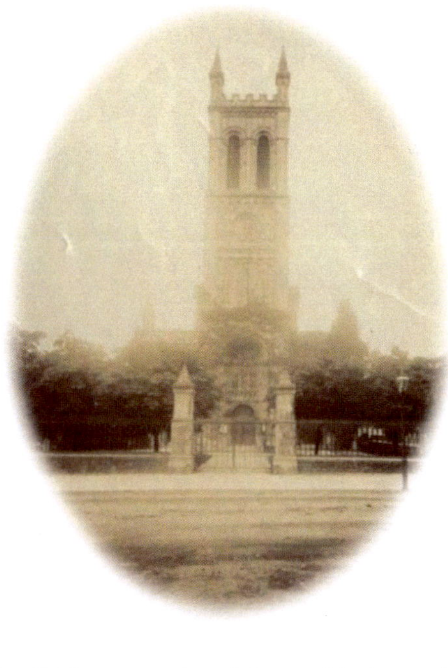

"This is indeed, a noble and splendid demonstration of the good feeling and zeal which prevail among the respectable classes in Honiton, in favour of their national church; not the result of the munificence of one wealthy individual, but the combined and popular expression and effort of many hundreds, who now look with becoming and highly-commendable pride and satisfaction on the beautiful temple which they have reared for the honour of God, and illustration of his laws."

The building was officially opened by the Bishop of Exeter on 24th April 1838 and the parishioners of Honiton stood in awe at this fantastic 100 foot long building with seating for 1,550 people.
The interior of the new church was so described in the year of completion: "The aisles, on each side are lighted by seven handsome windows; and above the roof of each aisle, is a chaste range of fourteen Norman windows, opening in upon the nave. The lower division of the circular wall of the chancel, is thrown into niches or panels, which are separated by columns, and crowned by circular arches; and over them five beautiful windows throw in their light full on the altar."

In a time when religious commitments were much more important than more modern times good seating within the parish church was a high priority for those who could afford it. In 1878 one Mr. Ackland, a local coal merchant, paid one pound and ten shillings for the rights to a centrally located pew within St. Pauls and ensured, through legal documentation that this seat be reserved for himself and "his heirs"!

Only eleven years later in 1849 it became obvious that serious structural damage had arisen in the new church and a massive reconstruction project was initiated. The whole roof was replaced, at a cost of £1,000, as well as the organ which had become damp through the inefficiency of the ceiling. The church had had "one great fault" having had the roof made of "experimental iron... which by expansion broke the covering of tiles and Roman cement." The architect, Mr. Fowler, had a law suit taken out against him and was ordered to pay "heavy damages" for his incompetence.
During this time of repair the clock and chimes taken from the old Allhallows Chapel were installed in the church; their restoration was carried out by a local clock maker Matthew Murch in 1851.

The church tower contains eight bells, of which 6 were cast in about 1780 after the terrible fire of 1765 obliterated the original bells of Allhallows Chapel and the remaining two were added in 1949 when the original six were re-cast. These bells measure from between 29 inches to 40 inches in diameter.
The church was greatly changed during the incumbency of Rev. Mackarness who was rector of Honiton from 1855-1869.
The Church was said to have "a good copy of Raffaelle's "Transfiguration" for it's alter piece" in 1864. The Church was once fronted by iron gates

and railings that disappeared with the arrival of the War Memorial which was erected and unveiled by Juanita Maxwell Philips in 1920.
The church underwent massive restorations in the mid 1980s. A total of £250,000 was estimated for the work and amongst the fears of finding the cash there were serious discussions about re-establishing Holy Communion at the old parish church of St. Michael's and selling the one in town! Less than a decade later another £100,000 was needed for the replacement of the Church organ which, like its predecessor that had been installed in 1872, had fallen victim to water and heat penetration.

The Independent Chapel

The Independent Chapel, located at the eastern end of the High Street, is a long established place of worship with an interesting history.
Up until 1970 its parishioners believed the building was some 70 years older than it actually was. The assumed year of construction, 1695, was incorrect and it was found that it was actually consecrated in November 1771! However, the roots of this congregation in Honiton go back far earlier than that date. The earliest mention of Honiton non-conformists was in 1655 when they were referred to as "Particular Baptists" and the actual formation was around the time of the Act of Uniformity in 1662 when all in Christendom were required to use the same prayer book. It was shortly after this that 5 non-conformists were executed in Honiton under the orders of Judge Jefferies with their bodies being exhibited on the Shambles. A small chapel was founded for this breakaway congregation in 1696, next to the site of the present day chapel: the original chapel was later destroyed in the fire of 1765. The present day chapel stands on the same site and the original lease was granted for 500 years at an annual rent of 3s. 4d. Despite the chapel's long history it was unfortunate for its parisoners that marriage in such a non-conformist establishment was

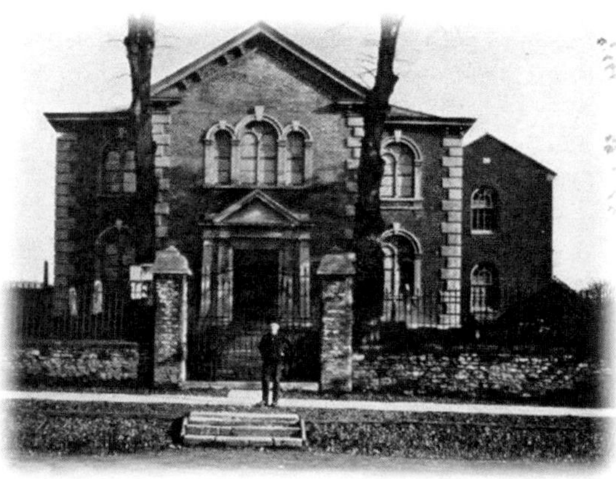

illegal until 1838, and in 1837 Honiton's Independant Chapel was one of only 63 in the entire county!
The land on which the church was built was finally bought when the estate of the late owner passed to his nephew who sold it to the chapel for only £5 in 1844, even though it had been sold to his uncle for £42 some 55 years before!
Between 1852 (on the death of Mr. Wright, the then rector) to the start of WWI, the church had 10 different ministers, a large number for a town where many other churches had ministers for a number of decades.
One minister worth mentioning was a Mr. George Thomas who was installed in 1876. After only 15 months of his installation, 40 out of the 56 members asked him to resign, which he refused to do, until 1879 when he left without warning.
The aforementioned Rev. William Wright came to be "Lay Pastor" of the independent Chapel in 1819 and stayed for 3 years before taking up another position in Essex; however, several years later in 1829 the parishioners invited him back and he accepted the invitation. He died in 1852 and after having invested so many years in the British School, which then stood next to the chapel, he was buried by the schoolroom door so the children could pass his grave each day. Ironically, one of the children he had baptised at the chapel became the Rector of Widworthy in the same year that he died. Prior to his death, Mr. Wright lived in the property next to Edmund Stamp's premises in the High Street.
In 1834 the Rev William Wright, who was minister at this chapel for a total of 24 years, planted "4 chestnut trees in the graveyard" of which one still remains today. This remaining tree is probably the oldest 'living' resident of the High Street today!
In 1869 the chapel arranged to purchase a "Parsonage House" and picked a suitable property, located opposite the church and called "The Old Manse", for the sum of £375. Still known as 'The Old Manse' this house was built in the early 19th century and it is currently home to 'Shades' hairdressers.
In 1902 there was a petition to lay some matting in the chapel to "lessen the clatter of hob-nail boots" worn by so many of the parishioners!
The Chapel today is still a place of divine worship and apart from the loss of its fine looking wrought iron fencing, which was lost in WWII, it has changed very little since its earlier days. The chapel is now known as 'Honiton Evangelical Congregational Church'.

The Baptist Congregation (Honiton Baptist Church)

The Baptist congregation takes it roots back to 1817 when a few members of the new Independent Chapel left due to poor relations with the minister. They met in a schoolroom located on the site of the present day chapel for several years before moving to a single room near Clapper Lane. After this they moved to an old Military Store in King Street, finally purchasing their own chapel in Silver Street which they had bought from the Wesleyans for the sum of £350 in 1831. On July 28th 1852 the foundation stone for the present day Baptist Church was laid and completion was in 1853.

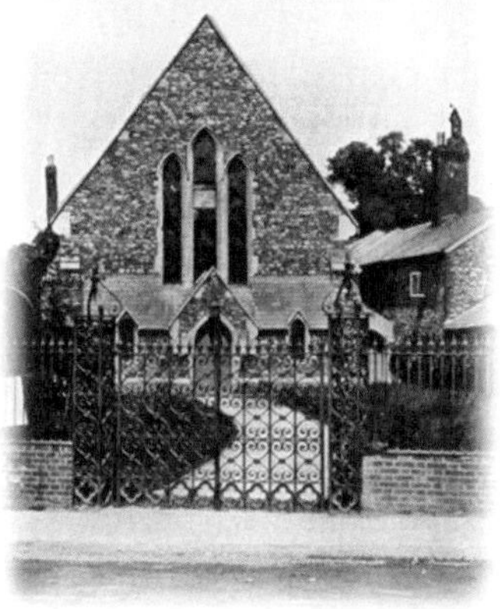

This site was bought from the Lord of the Manor of Honiton for the sum of £250 and the total cost of construction was £1,400, about £132,000 in today's money. In 1867 the church opened new schools: the money needed was raised by the congregation along with the sum of £72 paid for the old Silver Street Chapel that was converted into a private residence. The Chapel originally had wrought iron gates present in front of the building. The first set disappeared in a WWII salvage drive and some later ones were erected in 1949. These second gates were also later removed in 1981 to improve access.

The Wesleyan Congregation

The Wesleyan Congregation, also originating from a small group of breakaways from the Independent Chapel, came to be in the early 19th Century. Their first place of worship was a malt house just behind the High Street, opposite the old Kings Arms Inn. Several further moves followed, including a cottage in Silver Street and a blacksmiths shop in the same road which was converted to a chapel. This chapel was the one sold to the Baptist

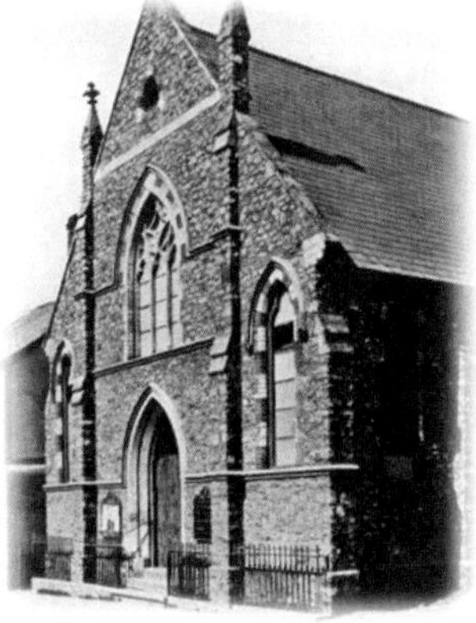

Church in 1831. They then moved to a powder store in Queen Street which came to be known as "Queen Street Chapel" and was once situated in the eighth property, from New Street, on the North side of the road. In 1875, the congregation moved to a newly constructed chapel in New Street which had once been two cottages. This chapel is now the Town Council offices and the Wesleyans or Methodists meet in a small building behind the old church now known as 'Honiton Methodist Church'.

The Royal Catholic Church

Catholicism was abandoned in Honiton during the reformation with the last Catholic Rector being Philip Bale who left his post in 1559. Catholic worship did not cease to be in Honiton though: Thomas Marwood, Elizabeth I's physician, defiantly had etched on his tomb 'departed in the Catholic Faith' in 1617.

A place of worship for Catholics did not return to the town for some 320 years when Hon. Colin Lindsay, youngest son of the Earl of Crawford, and his wife Frances gained permission from the Pope to set up a family Chaplain at their home at Deer Park House in 1877. Although this grand country home is in the parish of Buckerell, local Catholics held mass there which was the first the area had seen in over three centuries. This was all for good reason for only 40 years earlier, in 1837, there were only eight Catholic churches in the entire of Devon. This rebirth of Catholic worship in Honiton was initially only performed during the summer months as the Lindsay family returned to their London home during the winter. The Lindsay family had a very active role in the Roman Catholic Church and all but the eldest of Colin Lindsay's children converted to Catholicism. His daughter Mary became a nun in Bristol and two of Mr. Lindsay's sons went on to be Chamberlains for, between them, Popes Leo XIII, Pius X, Benedict XV and Pius XI. After Colin and his wife Frances died in 1892 and 1897 respectively, their fourth son, Leonard Cecil Colin Lindsay, accepted the responsibility of his parents' mission. However, the Deer Park passed to the Lindsay's oldest son William who was not a Catholic. William Lindsay agreed that mass could be held at the Deer Park until Christmas 1897. A new site for worship was, therefore, required and two of Leonard's cousins donated an Iron Church, originally built in East Sussex, which was dismantled and re-erected on a plot of land on Church Hill. It was also Leonard Lindsay who bought the property once known as Broomhills in 1915, now known as St Rita's. The Lindsays lived at Broomhills until 1931 when they donated the property to the diocese on the condition that when the site of the old Iron Church was no longer needed by the mission, it would revert back to them. This happened only 4 years later when the old church of corrugated iron sheeting that had served its purpose non-stop for some thirty years, not only became too small for the congregation but was also in a great state of disrepair and was later demolished. The site is currently home to the private residents of number 41 Church Hill. In 1927 a house in the High Street was purchased for the residence of the then Catholic Priest Rev. William Fox. Ironically, it was a house called 'The Old Manse', the house that was once home to the Reverend of the Independent Chapel! (The house still exists today and is located at 57 High Street)

The present Catholic Church was founded in 1937 on a plot of land just in front of the present St Rita's Centre. Leonard Lindsay died in London at the ripe old age of 84 in 1941 and with the death of his wife Claire nine years later "the last direct link with the Lindsay family was extinguished." The old chapel at the Deer Park still exists and is currently used as a snooker room. Although divine worship is no longer performed here, the font and bell from the chapel can still be found in the grounds.

Chapter 5
Other Local Facilities & Amenities

"The farther you are from the city, the less amenities they have."
Dave Lardinois

Police Station

The original police station was located in Dowell Street and can today be found with a blue plaque commemorating its former location. It was not much more than a small cottage with a side door to the cells, for prior to 1856 Honiton only had one officer patrolling the town.

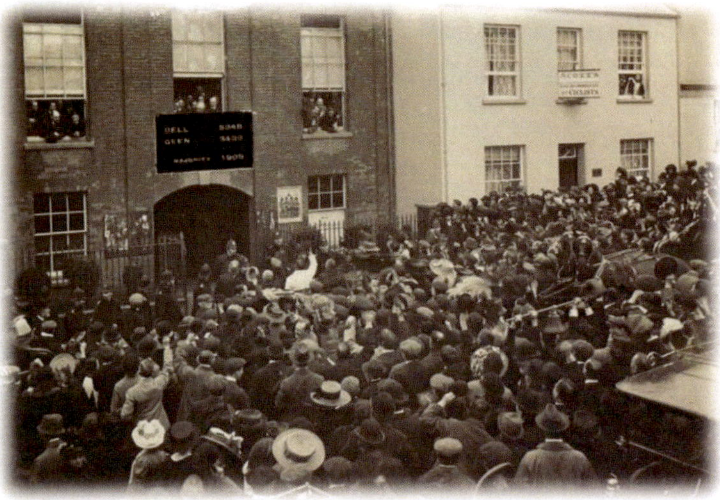

The General Election of 1910 giving one a glance at the old Victorian Police Station.

In 1856, the Borough Police Act came into effect which saw a massive reorganisation of the police force. From the local Quarter Session notes of the time it was proposed to have 1 constable for every 1300 people or every 6005 acres of land and this was adopted the following year. Gerald de Courcy Hamilton became Devon's 1st Chief Constable in 1856, a position he would hold until 1891. There was to be a new class system of the constables to patrol the county. These constables were split into three categories: 1st, 2nd, and 3rd class with 60 1st class officers to be paid 20 shillings a week, 130 2nd class constables at a pay of 18 shillings a week and

73 3rd class constables earning 16 shillings per week. £5,000 was borrowed to provide housing for the new recruits in their respective parishes: Honiton was given 1 sergeant and 3 constables along with new living quarters and the construction of 3 prison cells for evil doers.
By the early 1860s, a new police station had been built, on the same site as the present day premises. The site in question was owned by local attorney, Edmund Stamp, and consisted of a small collection of thatched, three roomed, workers cottages of which £175 was paid by the authorities. One interesting example found of the residents of the police station was in 1881. The superintendant was a John Nicholls living with his wife and children. However, there was one other resident called Mary Ann Middleton, presumed to be about 45 and her occupation was listed as 'lunatic found wandering'. An officer had obviously found this woman wandering the streets and locked her up in one of the cells: an interesting example of Victorian attitudes towards the sick and needy!
The Victorian Police Station was knocked down in the 1970s along with three adjacent thatched cottages and a shop to make way for new, more 'modern' premises. No cells are present at Honiton today and all arrestees are taken to Exeter.

Town Hall

The exact locality of the early town hall is somewhat of a mystery - one of the earliest entries this author could find was in a publication of 'The Gentleman's Magazine' of 1793 which stated that "The usual routine of officers were chosen, and met in the *town-hall."* It has been noted that polling for the local elections once took place in 'The Shambles' and after they were demolished in 1823 elections were held in the newly built 'Market House'. From a newspaper article of the time it has been established that the Market House became the "Townhall" from at least 1824. It is, therefore, quite probable, from dates and other facts, that the old shambles, later removed and replaced by the 'Market House', could have been the earlier location of the Town Hall.
Another Town Hall was later built in 1859 on part of the site once occupied by the old 'Carpenters Arms' which burnt in 1850.

The Gas Works

Gas was a pioneering innovation of the early 19th century which, for the first time in history, allowed a form of adequate lighting after the sun went down.

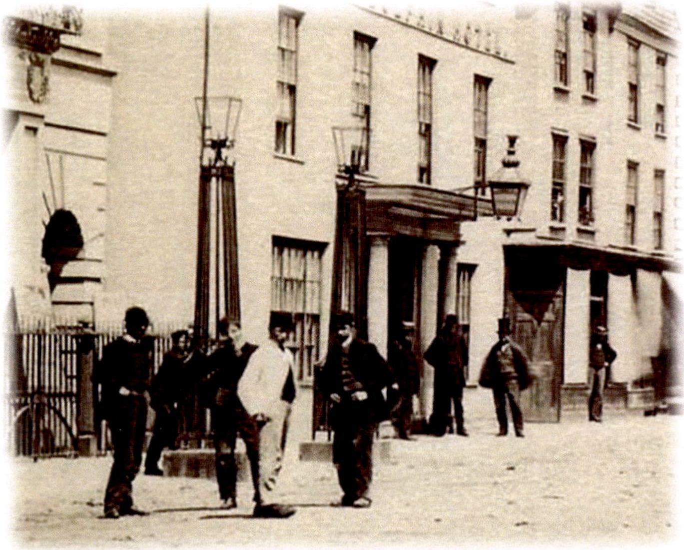

An example of the gas lighting outside the Dolphin Hotel c.1882

Devon, despites its rural isolation and distance from the capital, was well ahead of its time when it came to such feats of science. Gas lighting first lit the streets of Exeter in 1817, only 5 years after London and 3 years before Paris! Electric street lighting came to Exeter in 1889, a mere decade after the first street in Newcastle was illuminated by the new incandescent bulb. Gas arrived at Honiton in 1835 when the Gas Works was constructed in King Street at a cost of £2,700, and the town was first lit on Friday, 23rd May of the same year. In 1850 gas was supplied to customers at a cost of nine shillings per 1,000 cubic feet of the product yet only 3 years later the Board of Directors capped the cost at seven shillings for the same amount. In the twentieth century all customers' homes were fitted with either a penny or shilling slot meter which was collected every quarter. The works later became known as 'The Honiton Gas and Coke Co. Ltd' and in 1903 was responsible for the lighting of the town's 63 street lamps. In 1851 the Gas Works had a live-in 'lessee' who employed two men and a boy and by 1861 the works had a 'manager' employing a stoker and, interestingly, a 12 year old boy! In 1853, The Honiton Gas and Coke Company was run by a Board of Directors, namely Thomas Avery, William Woodgates, John Murch and Richard Tucker and was governed by a Board of Trustees. The lease was sold on a ten year term, of which the lessee was bound to pay £100 annually. The works, up until its closure, also provided accommodation for the gas work's manager and his family in a house and garden that was situated on the site.

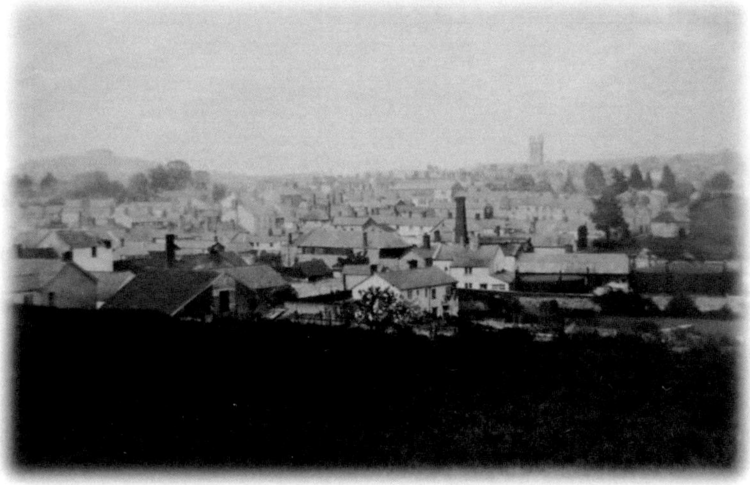

A view of Honiton from what is now part of Millers Way. The protruding chimney and gas tanks (right) is where the old gas works used to stand.

The gas works remained in operation independently until 'The Gas Act' of 1948 which nationalized all of the country's 1,062 privately owned and municipal gas companies. All of these companies were merged into twelve Area Gas Boards, each with its own management structure. Honiton became a part of the 'South Western Gas Board' and the old Gas Works was thence operated under the new system. In 1995 British Gas inaugurated an emergency excavation of the site's old soil after contaminants from an 18 ft tar well, originally used for storing by-products of the gas making process, had been found seeping into the Gissage. The site of the Honiton Gas Works still remains, unused, just to the east of the bridge in King Street, though the buildings have long since vanished. Before the loss of the Gas Works, the town acquired an electrical supply from the 'East Devon Electricity Co. Ltd' in 1930. In a town that was still set in its Victorian ways, an "attractive showroom" was setup in the High Street to "demonstrate the advantages and economies" of the new "electrical methods." New methods of preparing meals were given by a cookery expert every Thursday afternoon to promote and sell the new source of power and to introduce local people to the new electrical appliances which could be hired "under schemes of hire or hire-purchase."

Chapter 6
Local Weather & Climate

"When two Englishmen meet, their first talk is of the weather"
Dr. Samuel Johnson

The winters of the Southwest were always considered "milder" than those of other English counties: in 1830 Devon was described as being "from three to four degrees higher than that of London." Devon's air was described as "generally dry and warm, and the harvest earlier than" other South western counties. For this reason it was "proverbially favourable to the cure of pulmonary complaints." This mild, warmer climate was "beneficial in cases where the organs of breathing [were] long affected" and people with a "dry cough" were advised to visit this location. On the other hand if "patients" were "languish and weak, and [were] affected with a cough of a different description to the other- that is to say, where the expectoration [was] copious, showing the sources of this expectoration to be in a very relaxed state" then the climate was said to be "injurious" to the individual! Obviously, nineteenth century medicine left much to be desired but the point is many sick people of the time used Devon, especially towns such as "Sidmouth," as a retreat to rest and recuperate from such respiratory complaints.

In 1837 the annual rainfall of England was said to be 23.06 inches, nearly half of what it is today (40.16 inches over the 2002-2007 period). This was obviously a much drier time, which I am sure many of us would appreciate in these wetter, modern times!

The mean temperature for the Southeast for the 1850s was 2.8'C for winter, 8.9'C for spring, 15.7'C for summer and 9.6'C for autumn: 9.1'C on average, annually, compared to the Southwest averages which were 6.9'C for winter; 9.8'C for spring, 15.8'C for summer and 12.1'C for autumn: 11.4'C on average, annually. Although the summer averages are virtually the same, it is still obvious that the Southwest was overall a much warmer part of the country and could be compared with winters similar to those of "Madeira." The regional average temperature for 2008 for SW England was 9.9'C; this is a drop from the mid nineteenth century readings but if assessed over a period of time, the temperature has probably not changed that much.

Another report published in 1859 tells of how rainfall of the late 1850s affected country communities. The "tow years" preceding 1859 had seen below average rainfall, "especially in the winter months" which had caused "wells, streams and other sources" of water supply " to be unusually low" with many of them becoming "dry." In the summer of 1859, Devon and Cornwall experienced an extreme "drought" which was not the status quo for this "moist" region. The whole winter of 1857-1858 was also described as an "extreme dry winter." Once again, the annual rainfall for 1856, 1857 and 1858 were given which were 27.8, 24.3 and 16.3 inches respectively. The 1850s in England seemed to be extremely dry, which would have undoubtedly caused many problems for residents and farmers, naturally including those in Devon.

Freak weather and climate change are hot topics today, with homes flooded and nearly every recorded meteorological record being broken on a monthly basis. It is, however, probably not so well known that Honiton also had more than its fair share of extreme weather.

- The poor weather of 1765 led to high prices of flour and provisions generally in Devon. At Honiton on July 30th of that year, weeks before the great fire, locals "seized the bags of corn lodged by farmers in the public-houses, brought them into the market, and sold the corn" to the poor "at their own price" of "5s 6d per bushel" and then returned "the bags to the owners." They then proceeded to burn several of the local flour mills. These protests were not confined to Honiton but were more county- wide riots.
- On January 31st 1809, the mail en route from London to Plymouth was delayed due to "the breaking down of several bridges, and flooding on roads." Honiton itself had a whole bridge "entirely washed away" which had cost thousands of pounds to erect only a few months before. The total cost of this flash flooding was thought to be £30,000. This incident followed only two years after a bad storm in 1807 which had carried weiring down from Littletown and destroyed the originally wooden footbridge over the Gissage.
- A large thunderstorm in 1854 lead to "a flock of thirty-one sheep which had sought shelter under an Oak tree near Honiton" being killed by a bolt of lightning.

- The 'Honiton and East Devon Poultry Show' that was held on 28th and 29th December 1853 had visitors deterred by a "heavy snow-storm" - hard to believe in these modern, almost- snow -free times.

Chapter 7
Town Statistics

"There are two kinds of statistics: the kind you look up and the kind you make up"
Rex Stout

Age and Population

In 1851, Honiton had a population of 3427 people: 702 families living in 692 houses, giving an average household size of 4.9 people, compared with 2.4 people in 2004. This may seem a much smaller amount than one might think for this era. The average number of children under the age of 16 living in each household was only 1.9: much smaller than the national average today of '2.4 children' yet surprisingly unchanged when compared with the 2004 statistic for Honiton of 2.0!
By the end of the nineteenth century the population had not increased. In fact, it had actually fallen to 3271 in 1901 and the number of houses had also hardly increased; by 1891 the number of houses had risen by only 3 since 1851. This may not seem so strange considering the fairly neutral population rise. However, from 1831 to 1891 there was a recording of 32 houses allegedly being built at each of the ten year intervals, so whether these houses were never finished or old properties were pulled down in place of the new, it does not appear than Honiton spread beyond its ancient boundaries for the entire Victorian period!

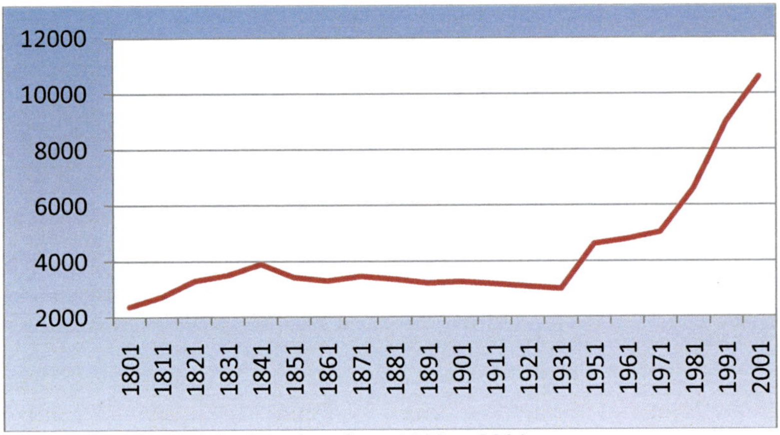

The population growth of Honiton from 1801 to 2001.

As can be seen from Figure 1, the population growth shows a steady rise in the earlier part of the nineteenth century up until about 1840, which was a time of successful trade. The trading era took a drop about this time and the growth remained stagnant for the next 80 years, even despite the arrival of the railway in 1860. The population in 1831 was 3,509 compared to that of 1931 when the population had actually fallen to 3,008! The first real growth is seen after the Second World War with the majority of growth taking place in only the last 30 years! Data is not present in this figure for 1941 as no census was taken during the war.

This rather neutral increase in population growth can be rather deceptive, for the actual number of people who were born in Honiton between 1851 and 1901 does show a steady increase.

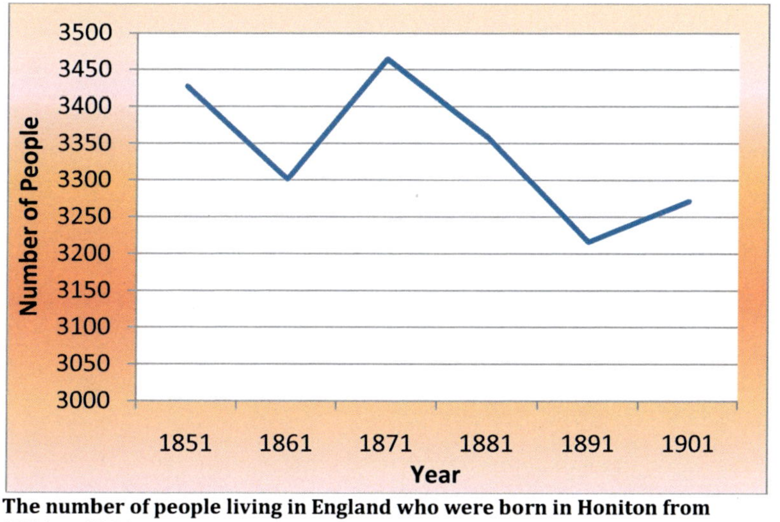

The number of people living in England who were born in Honiton from 1851 to 1901.

The actual population of Honiton was, in fact, increasing. However, probably due to the hard times in country areas, many of these people who *were* born locally moved to the cities for employment.

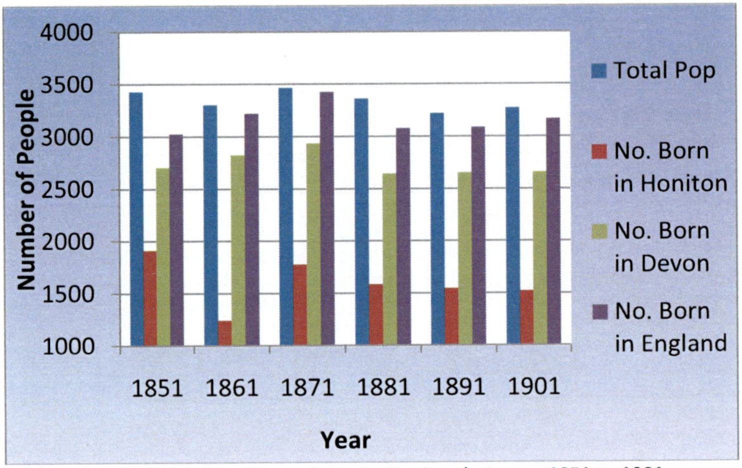

The location of the births of those living in Honiton between 1851 to 1901.

Overall the number of people living in Honiton from 1851 to 1901 may not have varied exceptionally but once again it does show a definite decrease in the number of people who stay in Honiton from birth. There were a small number of people living in Honiton who were not born in England which may be surprising considering the town's once rural location. In 1851, not including those born in Honiton itself, only 190 people living in the parish were born within a 5 mile radius of the town. However, between 1851 and 1901 there was an average of only 33 people living in the area who were born elsewhere in the UK (Scotland, Ireland and Wales). These two facts may seem contradictory but it tells us that although people moved a lot within the local vicinity, long distance re-location to the Honiton area was a rarity.

In 1851, Honiton had a relatively young population with the average age of its residents being only 28 years.

The town did, however, have more than its fair share of brushes with disease and death. In 1348 the Black Death "severely visited the neighbourhood." 1724 saw a smallpox outbreak where 29 people died of the disease in a space of only one month. Smallpox struck the town again some 30 years later in 1754 when the death toll rose to fifty. 1780 saw, probably, the worst outbreak of the disease when the annual death toll rose to double that of the average. Cholera was also an unwelcome guest that visited the town in 1847, 1866 and 1867. The latter two years saw the death of 81 and 117 people respectively.

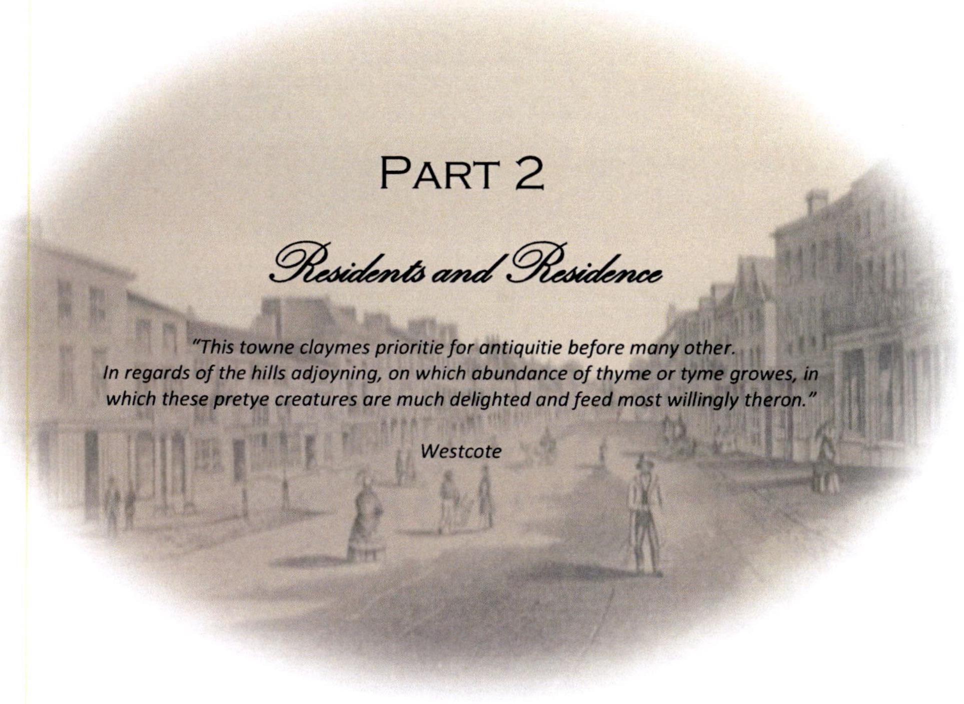

Part 2

Residents and Residence

"This towne claymes prioritie for antiquitie before many other. In regards of the hills adjoyning, on which abundance of thyme or tyme growes, in which these pretye creatures are much delighted and feed most willingly theron."

Westcote

Chapter 1
High Street

"The town is well-built, and consists chiefly of one broad steet, nearly a mile in length"
White's 1850

In the 1850s, Honiton town consisted of a total of just over 30 roads, lanes, passages and drangs compared to the 280 odd of today. There were only several main roads with most of the remaining being small passages and terraced cottage hideaways.

West End
This was the beating heart of the entire town with a large range of interesting shops and businesses. Located in this street were a large number of drapers, hairdressers, solicitors, surgeons and particularly inns - 21 to be more precise! Many of these inns were the remnants of the booming coaching era of the previous century which had already been witness to the closure of some 19 inns. Many of the wealthier members of the community resided in this section of road from Exeter to London and compared with today, it would be hard to recognise. The 'High Street' today is known throughout its length by this name but up until the early 19th century the more central section was known as 'Fore Street' with only the upper section being known as the 'High Street.'

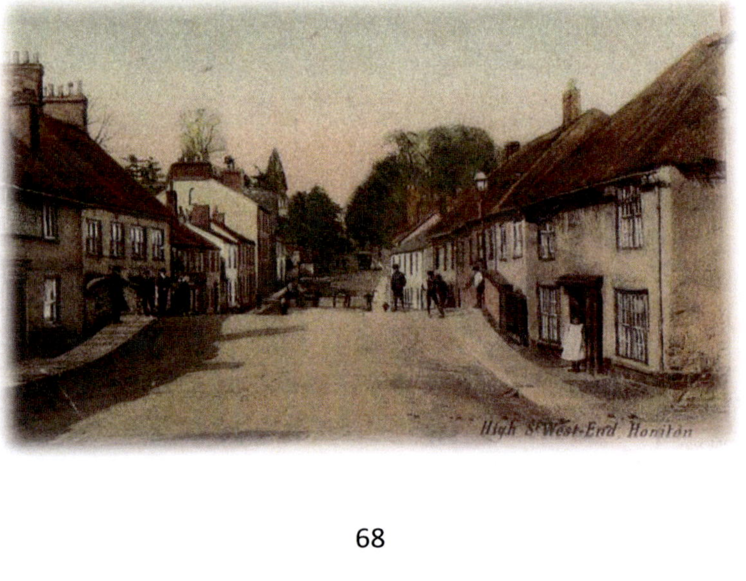

This was a simple name arrangement with each section of street simply indicating its location in the town. This was reflected in others of the town's roads. For example, 'King Street' was, as early as 1750, known as 'Hind' or 'Back Lane'(and only later referred to as 'Street') once again because of its rear location to the main street.

The West End of town, at this time, was a smaller reflection of those who lived in the centre of town or the more westerly Bramble Hill: not as affluent yet not the worst place to live! This area consisted of a mixture of lower paid residents living alongside a select few of more prominent entrepreneurs.
Just before Bramble Hill on the north side of the High Street lived a widow named Emma Danby with her widowed daughter, Julia Danby, and her 4 grandchildren, Emma, Edward, Susan and Chester Webb. Emma was a wealthy woman; probably due to the fact her late husband, John Harvey Danby, had had links with the indigo trade in Bengal. Her grandchildren were born at Fort William, Calcutta to her daughter Emma Jane Webb and her son-in-law Allan Webb. Emma Webb's husband was an Assistant Garrison Surgeon and their children were presumably in their grandmother's care due to their parent's absence. Edward Webb went into the army, like his father, in 1858 at the age of 16. The couple's oldest child, Allan Becher Webb, worked in South Africa for 28 years and became Bishop of Graham's Town: in 1898 he returned to England and became Dean of Salisbury until his death in 1907. Allan B. Webb was, interestingly, born on the 'Jumna Steamer' in Bengal.
This section of High Street was also home to the town's only listed farrier, Thomas Woodland, who had formerly been landlord of the 'Smith's Arms' and was also one of the town's many blacksmiths, probably from where the pub got its name.

A short distance from 'Diggories Lane' lived an elderly couple by the names of William Vincent, a tailor, and his wife Mary who was an 'artificial fly maker' (fishing tackle). Living with them was Mary's Mother, Hannah Holland: Honiton's oldest resident of the time aged 91 and one of only 2 people over the age of 90.

Further up the north side of the High Street was a certain Thomas Bedwarden with the unusual occupation of 'marine store dealer' which, as unusual and interesting as it sounds, was actually a scrap metal dealer!

Albion Davey and his wife Amy lived in the property now occupied by 'Ford Simey Solicitors'. Albion was one of the town's foremost maltsters and his wife Amy had been, before her marriage, Amy Lathy who had been granted a Royal Warrant for lace making in 1830 (*for more information on Amy Lathy see Part 3*). Albion's mother ran a grocery store next to the Dolphin, now 'Bath Travel' (113 High Street). Albion and Amy married quite late in life and their only son, another Albion, died young. Albion later retired and died in 1871, whereas Amy continued to work in the lace trade until her death in 1875 aged 78. Both were buried at St Michael's.

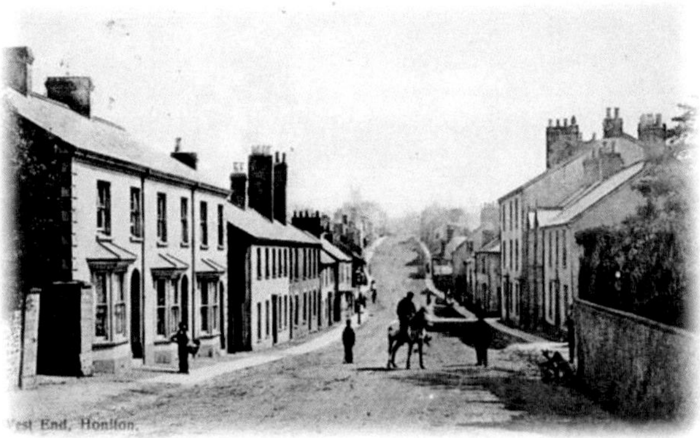

On the corner of Lees Buildings was the home of Anna Maria Churchill, a widow of 86 and the former mistress of the workhouse, along with her daughter's family. Mrs. Churchill is thought to have been the former governess of the old Honiton Workhouse that once stood where 'Summerland Place' now is. Her son- in- law, whom she lived with, was Joseph Manley, Registrar of Births, Marriages and Death and High Bailiff of the County Court. A total of eight people resided in this house, presently to the right of 'Ying Wah,' along with a house servant of 16. The rest of Mrs Churchill's family lived close by. A few houses down from present day Crown Court lived a Mrs Emma Roach, a widow of 43, her daughter Dorothy aged 12 and her brother James Churchill. It seems quite ironic and unfair that the overseeing of the poor had obviously left this family in a rather affluent state. Anna's former husband, for example, owned the old 'Crown and Sceptre Inn' and the entire row of workers' cottages behind it! Whether their connection with the workhouse made them unpopular with the local residents is unknown but both had respectable occupations: Emma was a school teacher and her brother a bailiff.

A close neighbour of the Churchill offspring was a certain William Lee with his wife Jane and their 6 children. Jane's brother Richard Minifie, who was a baker, lived only a few doors down from them and his business had done well enough to enable two of his daughters to become a schoolmistress and a governess and his son a clerk, a profession that could have earned him as much as £110 per year. William Lee (1800-1853) was a well known and respected builder around the town at the time. He had been responsible for the construction of St. Pauls, the new parish church, not the cathedral in London! Earlier in life he had been in partnership with his half brother John (1793-1834) who was described as an "architect and surveyor." John had designed Combe Royal Rectory in 1827 and in 1826-27 both he and his brother repaired and refitted Upottery Church. Both William and his brother had come from a well established family of carpenters and joiners in Honiton. William had a stonemason's yard, sheds and 'tillage plot' roughly where 'Hansford Court' is today in King Street. After William's premature death in 1853 his eldest son, another William Lee, continued his father's business. His son did not practise as an architect, like his father, but was one of only 15 contracted county bridge repairers, on an annual income of £47. It was he, who in the summer of 1855, was called upon to repair Langford Bridge which had been damaged by flooding. The damage amounted to £39 - quite a sum for the time.

The west end of town was also home to the probably not so popular gentlemen Henry Glanvile Chubb who was the district Inland Revenue Officer who resided in the property now occupied by 'Ying Wah' Chinese takeaway (152 High Street).

Daniel Harwood, a Chelsea Pensioner of 64, lived a little further down the High Street. He had served with the 45th regiment from 1809 to 1829 when he was discharged. In 1851 he was the Unitarian Minister of the Bridge Chapel.

On the corner of Dowell Street was once a butcher's shop. It was run by a John Hook from the mid 19th century until his death in about 1886. After John's death his son, William Tucker Hook, took over the business and later ran it with his son, Seabourne Hook, when it became known as 'W. T. Hook and Sons'. When William died in the 1890s, Seabourne became the sole proprietor but he retained the name of 'W. T Hook and Sons': he was also Mayor of Honiton 3 times. Seabourne Hook obtained his strange Christian name from his mother's family. His mother's mother was Susanna Seabourne, wife of Robert White the local iron founder. The butchers remained in the Hook family until the early 1920s when it was taken over by Reginald Dommett. Seabourne, at one point, established another shop further up the High Street and when he retired it became the premises of Mr. Moor who turned it into a garage, which today is 'Honiton Photographic'. John Hook's other son, Henry, started his own butcher's shop a little further down the High Street in about 1860 (181 High Street). Henry's son, William Burrough Hook, took over the shop when his father died. These premises were in business as 'Hook's the Butchers' until only a few years ago. One could expect to pay the following prices if shopping at 'W. T. Hook and Sons' in 1892: beef shoulder 4 ½d per lb; pork, bacon and mutton were priced at 5d per lb; mutton cost 6d per lb and beef suet was a reasonable 3d per lb! Seabourne Hook died in Exeter in 1942 aged 78.

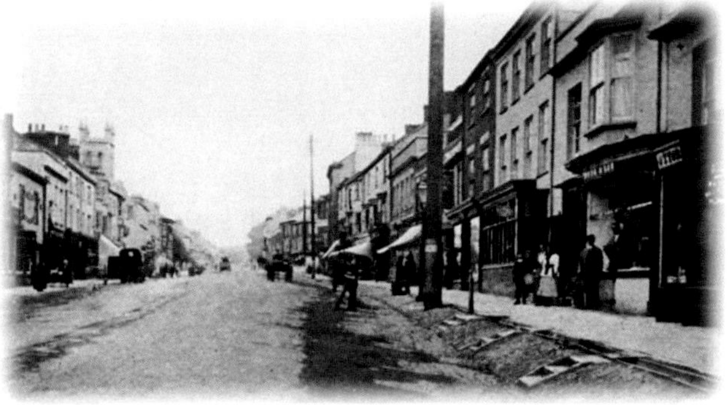

Hook's Butchers (on the right) that later became Moor's Garage.

Next to the Hooks, now on the corner of Dowell Street (159 High Street) lived three spinster sisters by the name of Peggy, Betty and Mary Marsh. Their father had been a maltster and had also been a local electorate known as 'Wheezing Marsh' due to his asthmatic condition. The Marsh family had lived in the town for well over a hundred years. All three of the sisters were annuitants, presumably from their father's prosperous career. Peggy had also been one of the 350 "young ladies" dressed with "white ribbons" who had welcomed George III into town in 1789. Peggy Marsh was good friends with Richard Farquharson, the author of 'The History of Honiton', so much so that he devoted his 1868 publication to his "dear old friend" then, allegedly, the oldest resident in town! Although Peggy was the oldest, both Mary and Betty passed away in their 70s in 1852 and 1854 respectively. After the death of her sisters Miss Marsh employed a live- in servant called Mary Croydon to whom she left a weekly allowance of 2 shillings in her Will. Mrs Croydon did not have much time to enjoy this money as she herself unfortunately died a few months later, already being 75 when her mistress of 97 passed away. Miss Peggy left the majority of her estate to a distant relative named Thomas Marsh of Dulverton along with many other bequests to friends in town. She was buried in 1871 in St. Michael's graveyard, at her request, with her parents and sisters.

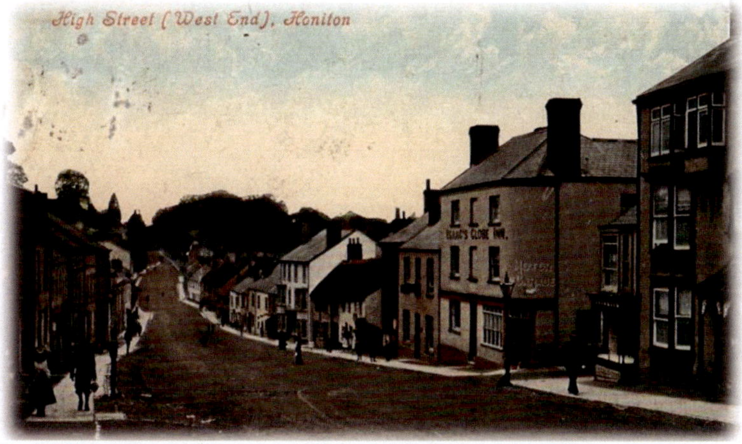

Hook's Butchers on the corner of Dowell Street and the Misses Marsh reisdence adjacent.

The house in which Miss Marsh lived was built in 1805 by Mr Lee's family. A close neighbour of the Marshes was Honiton's very own Hussey's auctioneer. James Hussey lived with his wife and family two doors up the High Street and was the town's main auctioneer. The family property was built by William Lee in 1839 and his family are known to have auctioned livestock at Honiton Show from the early 1900s until quite recently. James Hussey was born in Gittisham in about 1812 and was married twice: first to Ann Lee who died in the 1840s and then to Dionisia Davey in 1847 and between his two marriages produced 10 children. He died in Honiton in 1896.

The family offices were once situated at 66 High Street but in 1995 were taken over by Stags Estate Agents.

Town Centre

The central section of the High Street was indeed the real commercial centre of the town's affluence and business. This was where the wealthier shop owners resided and successful businessmen kept their places of work.

This area consisted of drapers, tailors, hairdressers, chemists, merchants, fine craftsmen and a large proportion of the town's elite.

A few doors up from the Marshes was a boarding school for girls run by Marianne Luckham. Miss Luckham ran the school, which was situated in the old, old! Honiton lace shop (145 High Street: today Pilgrim Antiques), and previously a building, now demolished, presently occupied by the site of the Post Office. Miss Luckham ran the school with her niece for some 15 years and in 1851 she had 7 pupils in attendance. The shop later became the premises of Mr. Fred Lemon who ran a radio and television store from the mid 1920s. Mr. Lemon was a qualified blacksmith, a profession taught to him by his father William Lemon. William ran a successful business near the railway station where he was responsible for fitting shoes to all the horses owned by 'George Blays' and 'Miller & Lilley'.

Situated in the present day 'The Honiton Antique Centre' (136 High Street) lived a certain Mr. Benjamin Ward, his wife Elizabeth and their 7 children. Mr. Ward owned a large coach building company and in 1851 he employed 15 men. He later converted his property into a tavern known as the 'Clarence Hotel'. The couple's oldest son was Joseph Ward who started his working life in his father's coach building business; he later spent some time in the colonial services in India where 2 of his 3 children were born. He later moved to London where his wife was born and gained employment as a railway official. Another of Benjamin Ward's seven children was a young girl named Ann, who later went on to become the well known and respected Mrs Fowler, the lace manufacturer. Miss Ward married William Fowler, a Somerset farmer's son, in 1876 who, at the time of their marriage, was a lace manufacturer. It was Ann, however, who developed and extended the

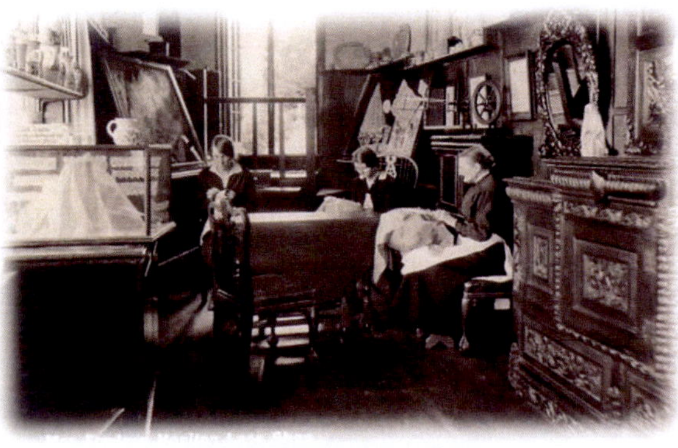

Mrs. Fowler's Lace Shop.

business into the successful, international one of the late Victorian era. Ann Fowler won numerous awards for her designs, including a bronze medal in 1886 at Edinburgh, a silver medal in Paris in 1900, a gold medal at Chicago 1893, another gold medal at St Louis in 1904 and the grand prize at the Franco-British Exhibition of 1908. In her later life, Mrs Fowler worked with her niece, Bessie Dalton Ward, daughter of her brother William. Her first shop was at 145 High Street and she later moved to the east end of town. Her husband, William, changed trades from lace manufacturing to drapery and died in 1908. Mrs. Fowler lived until 1929 and died at the grand old age of 90. Ann's brother, William, remained in Honiton and went on to become a manager for a local manure merchant! The premises where Mr. Ward ran his successive businesses were, in more recent times, 'Honiton Woodcraft'.

Next to Mr. Ward, in the property now occupied partly by 134 High Street, lived the Spurway family who ran a printers and stationers business. The business was thought to have been started by James Spurway of Colyton, a former postmaster of Honiton. The business was later run by his widow, Grace (a cousin of Christopher Flood, the banker), and then by his unmarried daughter, Mary. The business ceased in the 1870s when Mary died.

Situated in what is now 'Honiton Job Centre' (128 High Street) were the offices of a certain Edmund Stamp who was mayor of Honiton on no less than four occasions and was a town alderman from 1857 to 1876. Edmund was born in Honiton to the son of a local baker. He attended Honiton Grammar School and practised as a local solicitor and Attorney at Law for a "large" and "highly respected" business. Edmund was also quite a prolific land and property owner; he is known to have owned 14 cottages/houses, several yards and gardens, a field in King Street now partly occupied by Fairfield Gardens and a malthouse! Mr. Stamp was twice married; his first wife was the sister of the manager of the Honiton branch of the National Provincial Bank and after her death he married a French lady. He had a total of 7 children; his only child with his second wife died young and his oldest child, Edmund Archibald Stamp, later joined his father's firm. There were seldom less that 4 servants working for Mr. Stamp which is not surprising considering he would have been earning around £700 a year at a time when a good weekly wage was £1 per week!
He must have also been interested in the local agricultural trade for he won second prize at The Honiton and East Devon Poultry Exhibition in 1854.

Mr. Stamp died in 1888 at his home in the High Street which his father had built in about 1810.
The property in which Mr. Stamp lived later became the home of one of Mrs. Pankhurst's suffragettes: Mrs Juanita Maxwell Phillips. Juanita was born in Chile, a twin, and the youngest of thirteen children to Thomas Comber, a South American merchant. Mrs. Philips moved to Honiton in 1906 after her marriage to Thomas Phillips who was also a solicitor and later a partner of the local firm 'Every & Philips'. She had a successful career in Honiton becoming a councillor, Justice of the Peace and the first female Mayor of a West Country town, an achievement for which she won a 'silver salver'. Her first public duty was the unveiling of the War Memorial outside St Paul's in 1920. She was also a County Councillor and played a key role in preserving Allhallows Playing field for use by the town after Allhallows School left in 1938. Having no children of her own may have been why she devoted so much of her time and money to the welfare of the town's offspring and was for a time President of the Honiton Infant Welfare Centre. Mrs. Phillips was awarded Freedom of the Borough of Honiton in 1938 and died peacefully in Torquay in 1966 at the age of 86. Her ashes were interred, with her husband's, at Awliscombe churchyard. The house was once known as 'Sudbury Lawn' which was jointly named after Juanita's and Thomas's repective family homes of 'Sudbury' Lodge in Wembley and South 'Lawn' in Worcestershire. In the 1950s the property was used for the town Council Offices where the local Council met on the fourth Wednesday of each month at 6pm. At the back of the property were once garages that Mr. and Mrs. Philips had converted into their own private theatre known as 'Little Theatre' which the couple gave up in WWII so that it could be used as a food office. This building still exists and has been 'Meadow View Chapel' since 1960.

Next door to this property lived a brush maker by the name of John Godolphin. Mr. Godolphin had quite a successful business in the property which is now 'Everys Solicitors,' (formerly Dunnings; 130 High Street); well enough to allow his children to gain their own respectable trades, including a saddler, a chemist and his son, Edwin, a watch and clock maker.

In the property that is currently 'Barclays Bank' (106 High Street) and known as 'Fruidge House', once lived William Woodward who was Mayor of Honiton in 1850 and town alderman for 11 years. His profession was a surgeon which he practised in the town for some 30 years before leaving in 1859; he was also a member of the Royal College of Surgeons, London as well as being a General Practitioner. As a surgeon Mr. Woodward would

have expected around 5 shillings per patient, making medical care difficult for many. Surgeons of the town were also known to have restricted their visits to within 2 miles of their home.
Dental care was also out of reach for the poorer classes. If one had eaten too many sweets a dentist would charge 10s.6d. for two fillings and if one had tormented their teeth for a number of years, one could expect to pay as much as £21 for a full set of false teeth!
An interesting case was found which documented Mr Woodward's early work. In 1816, Mr Woodward was called to a woman who had suffered severe abdominal pains shortly after the birth of a child. The woman's symptoms were a fever and a rapid pulse of 106. The doctor's first task was to remove from "a large orifice in the arm sixteen ounces of blood after which she became slightly faint"! Later the same day her symptoms had returned and another "sixteen ounces... of blood were taken from the same orifice." At half past nine of the same day her pulse had risen to 120 so the doctor removed a further "nine ounces" from "a vein in the other arm." Further treatment administered to this poor patient involved: "a large blister" and "leeches" being applied to the abdomen and her belly was "fomented with a warm decoction of poppy heads"! The woman did, surprisingly, recover: as the existence of germs, etc. was not known about until the end of the 19th century, these methods, which had been in practise since mediaeval times, were obviously still the pinnacle of medical foresight!
William Woodward was born in Dublin but settled in Honiton where he met and married his wife Elizabeth Basleigh in 1821. The couple did not have any children but remained married for some 40 years. Mr. and Mrs. Woodward relocated to Carshalton in Surrey where they lived in a property called 'Honiton Villa'.

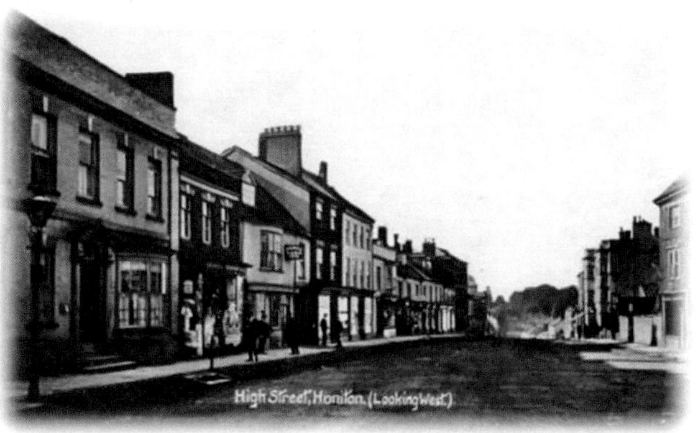

Fruidge House, left, prior to its reconstruction.

The property in which Mr. Woodward lived underwent an attempted restoration in 1961 which, unfortunately, failed leaving the entire building needing to be rebuilt. However, it kept its former appearance and original bay windows, although the building was originally much darker in colour. Despite its reconstruction, the property is still Grade II listed today. The property is thought to have been a surgery from the early Victorian period straight through to the late twentieth century. The last physician to have resided there was Dr. Duncombe S. Steele-Perkins. Dr Steele-Perkins came from a prosperous Exeter family and settled in Honiton with his wife Sybil in the early 20th century. He was 'a highly respected man' and was an active member of the Honiton Golf Club where he was made an honorary life member. His son, Sir Derek Steele-Perkins, later became Surgeon Vice Admiral and Medical Officer to Queen Elizabeth II, attending her during her voyages on the Britannia. Dr. Duncombe, himself, died in Honiton in 1958. 'Fruidge House' was so named by the Steele-Perkins family being the ancient home of the Skinners, a female branch of the family.

Across the road at the old 'Golden Lion Inn' resided Richard Tucker and his wife Elizabeth, at what was then the town Post Office. Mr. Tucker was known to have been Honiton's postmaster since at least 1837 and an earlier predecessor is known to have been a certain James Spurway in the early 1820s. Richard was born in Tilshead, the youngest child of a schoolmaster, and moved to Honiton at an early age where he took a teaching position at Woodgates Academy and later became area postmaster. In 1841, the Post Office was situated in the property now occupied by 'Boots' (123 High Street); by 1844 it had moved again before finally settling at the old Golden Lion Inn. Richard Tucker remained

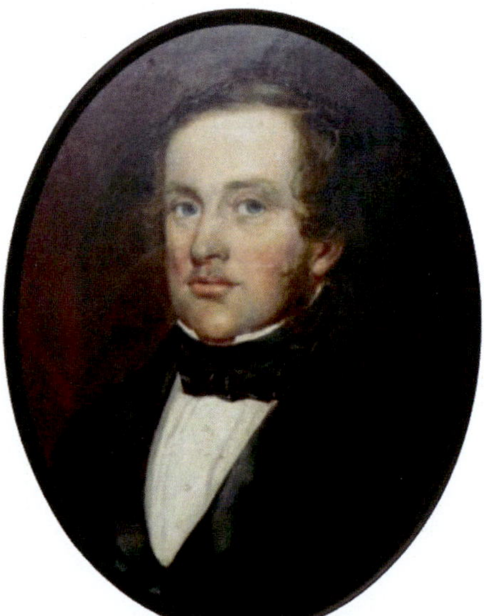

Honiton Postmaster Richard Tucker

the postmaster throughout all these moves. Mr. Tucker married the sister of local watch and clock maker Matthew Murch and with her had no less than 9 children! Before the Golden Lion, Mr. Tucker was postmaster in the old Post Office which was located two doors down from The Golden Lion, now 'Wing Hong' Chinese Takeaway (147 High Street) and with the closure of the inn in 1851, Mr. Tucker moved to the new and much larger premises. Richard Tucker was postmaster for over 30 years until he resigned in 1867 for unknown reasons. He died in Bailbrook House, Bath in 1883 of "Erysipelas of the head and throat" which was a nasty skin infection.

It appears that most of Mr. Tucker's children did well for themselves. However, one is worth mentioning for his versatility. Richard Woodgates Tucker, his eldest child, was listed, in 1878, as a watchmaker, jeweller, silversmith, optician, piano forte dealer and agent for Wilcox sewing machines! Another of Richard's sons, John Murch Tucker, had a series of unfortunate events befall him in the late 1850s. John Tucker had been courting the daughter, Jane, of local iron founder Robert White since he was in his early teens. They were thought to have met through John's mother, for whom young Jane once worked as a milliner, and the couple were engaged to be married in 1859. Jane, however, fell pregnant by another man called Thomas Kerslake, a coal merchant of Cullompton, some twenty years her senior, only months before their wedding. Apparently, Miss. White had been led astray by the married man and from a court hearing that followed it was stated that Mr. Kerslake had driven Jane in a cart to Hembury Fort where he had thrown her over the "seat of the cart and took liberties." Miss White was said to have "resisted" but Mr. Kerslake later had made "connection" with her several more times and after finding she was with child Miss White ran away with Mr. Kerslake. She wrote a letter to John stating that "he would never see her again" and that "he was to try and forgive and forget her" as she was soon to be married to Mr. Kerslake. There was "no doubt" that John Tucker "loved her" and never did marry his young bride which must have affected him for the rest of his days. Prior to this incident he had started an apprenticeship as a silversmith, thought to be with his uncle Matthew Murch. He did not complete his term with Mr. Murch and for a while, after the loss of his betrothed, worked as a clerk in his father's post office. He later enrolled on a career in the church and from 1887 to his death, aged 64, in 1907, was Vicar of Syston, Leicestershire. Mr. Tucker remained a bachelor until aged nearly 50. Jane herself fled to Teignmouth where she had her child but later returned to Honiton as she grew tired of Mr. Kerslake "having continual intercourse with her"! She did, however, eventually marry her sugar daddy some 4 years later in London, where her father had sent her to work as a draper's apprentice. Her father, Robert White, appears to have also been devastated by the series of events for he said that "he had lost the comfort and solace of a virtuous daughter's society" and that her conduct, leading to a "ruined character" and "illegitimite child", showed that she had "the wisdom of the serpent" rather than the "innocence of the dove" - how he had once looked upon her. She had even made her partner, John Tucker, drive her to Exeter where she had arranged to meet and escape with Mr. Kerslake, telling John that she had wished to go shopping!

The son of local auctioneer James Hussey, John, became the town postmaster shortly after Mr. Tucker's departure, a position he held for the next twenty years.

The old Golden Lion, or 'Manor House' as it is now known, later had 20 properties built behind it. These were known as Manor Place and even into the mid- twentieth century had poor sanitation facilities with a pit where rubbish was left for infrequent collections. By the 1970s this small collection of houses had fallen almost derelict and they were demolished, to the distress of many local people.

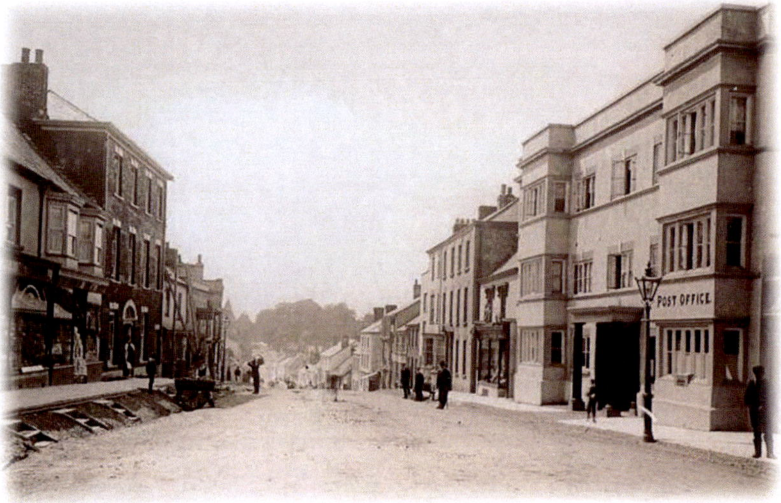

Honiton's old Post Office

To the left of the Post Office once resided Henry Knott Vern, who was the Curate of Monkton and next to him lived Joseph Flood and his family.

Joseph Flood was a professor of music, was the organist at St. Michael's and later went on to become the organist at St. Pauls. Joseph was, undoubtedly, a great lover of music; he even named one of his children – William Haydn Flood - after the composer, Joseph Haydn. Another of his son's, Edwin Flood, was apparently quite a gifted musician and composer who wrote many musical pieces including 'The Sabbath Bells' as well as many other works which can still be purchased on some internet book sites! Edwin had, prior to his father, also been organist at St Paul's before his premature death in 1848 at the age of 24.

Living next to the Three Tuns was Captain James Basleigh who, as well as living next door to an inn, owned the White Hart situated further down the High Street. James Basleigh was born in Mid Street, the son of a barber, and was quite a well known figure who "took a leading part in local matters." He became a Captain in 1808 and served under the command of both Col. Sir G Younge K.B. and Sir John Kennaway. He was Mayor of Honiton twice and was an alderman from 1846 to his death in 1873. Mr. Basleigh was a sly individual and lived 'in sin' with a "succession of mistresses" and had several illegitimate children. He eventually chose one of these women to be his first and only wife at the age of 69, in 1855; maybe because she had already borne him three children! The lady in question was an Elizabeth Bagwell who was some 30 years his junior. His oldest child by her, James Harry Bagwell, was a student at Woodgates Academy. In a skit published in 1840, the following verse was written about him...

"To the Captain a card must be sent
Sure no one has greater pretention
To attend at a fair lady's rout
As a guardian or what we wont mention."

Farquharson described him as "almost dwarfish in person" and that he "considered himself of great consequence." Capt. Basleigh funded a new doorway at St. Michael's Church and used the additional space inside to enlarge his own pew! He was also a grocer and wine merchant in partnership with Thomas Avery, who lived next door to him until his death. He was a Trustee of Allhallows Grammar School and, with his partner Mr. Avery, ran a 'Fire & Life Office' named 'The Phoenix & Pelican'. Thomas Avery must have got on well with his business partner for he named one of his children after him who later also went on to become mayor in 1892! Mr. Avery's daughter, Mary Ann, married local draper Charles Read who

later lived at Ridgeway House and another child, Thomas, also established a grocery business in the town and retired to St. Leonards, Bramble Hill.
In the shop that is now 'Herbs & Acupuncture' (104 High Street), Henry Tovey ran his watch and clock making business which he established in town in 1849/1850: prior to this it was the shop of a silversmith called George Turner.
Mr. Tovey's business was in Honiton for nearly a century with his children and grandchildren succeeding him. To compete with the other numerous clockmakers in the town he had two clocks situated in his shop window: one showing 'Greenwich Mean Time' and the other showing 'Honiton time!' This ploy obviously worked for after only ten years of its establishment, business was booming: Henry had a journeyman and 2 others working for him, as well as extending his professional skills to become a jeweller. Henry was born in Bedminster in 1823 and it was his youngest son, William Alfred Tovey, who continued the business after his father's death in 1902. William's son, Stanley, who married a sister of Harry Roy Read - the founder of Reads Garage - continued the business after his father's retirement, at which time they offered an additional optician service to their customers. The business finally ceased just before WWII when Stanley sold it to a Mr. Real. Both Henry Tovey and his son William were members of the Independent Chapel and led active roles in the church, both becoming the church secretary at different times.

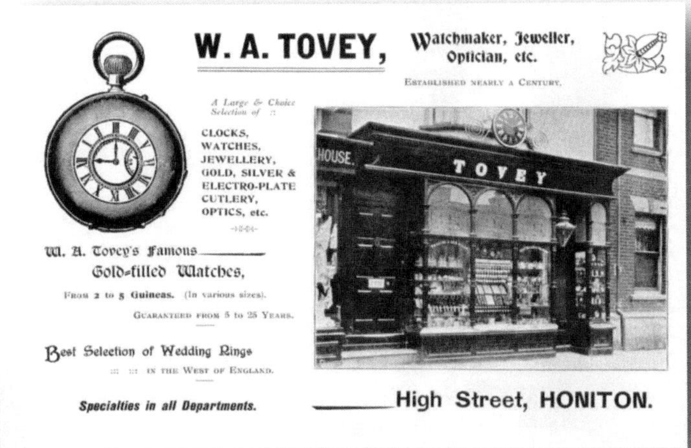

Henry Tovey was an active member of the church for 54 years and teacher of the Sunday school for 33 years. He and his wife Sarah are buried in the chapel's grounds "just by the church steps."
Among the many businesses located within the centre of town was a sweet shop run by Mr. Rippon, a chemists run by a Mr. Creak (now HSBC), a saddler and harness maker who worked out of which is now 'Livingston's Jewellers', a butchers run by John Crees, which today is 'Just Cards', a tea dealership, which is now 'Humbert's Estate Agents' and another lace dealership run by an Elizabeth Baker.

William Rogers was a town alderman for only 3 years from 1849 to his death in 1852. By trade he was a successful hop merchant and with his wife Elizabeth had 5 children. He was also a local property owner and had some 20 cottages under the manor as well as a plot of land at Littletown. His son, John Robinson Rogers, had an interesting education: he was a Doctor of Philosophy and an analytical chemist with a degree from the University of Giessen, Germany. This University's heyday was the mid-nineteenth century and Mr. Rogers was a student of Justus Von Liebig, a famous individual who founded the chemistry department and was "the founder of modern agricultural chemistry and inventor of artificial fertilizer." Such a prominent education was rare in Victorian Honiton and he went on to be a local chemist. Unfortunately he died in his early 40s leaving a wife and young daughter who, after his death, moved to his wife's home county of Shropshire. Elizabeth, William's widow, sadly had to bury another son, William Guppy Rogers, in1861 as well as outliving her other son John and her husband. One touching note found in William Rogers' Will was that he left his 'mourning ring', bought in memory of his own father, to his son John. After her husband's death, Elizabeth moved with her three daughters to the property now called 'Bramble Hill House' until her death in 1873. Her three daughters never married and after their mother's death moved to Hampshire and lived off their inheritance until their respective deaths. William and Elizabeth's oldest daughter, another Elizabeth (Stokes Rogers), married local banker Herman James Lott and was the only one of all their children to carry on the family line with their other only remaining grandchild, Annie, dying a spinster. Elizabeth Lott was widowed early in life and lived at Summerland Place.

On the site now partly occupied by 'Budgens', standing side by side were the businesses of brothers, John and Matthew Murch. Budgens, today, stands on what were originally two, three storey Georgian properties. These two premises later merged to became the 'Honiton Garage' owned

by the Harris family and when the owners relocated to the west end of town in the 1960s and the regal old buildings were later demolished and redeveloped. Over the years the premises have been a variety of supermarkets including 'Price Right', 'International Stores', 'Gateways', Somerfield and Budgens, as it is today.
The Murches came from an old Honiton family and were from a long line of jewellers. The family was thought to have originated from refugees from Flanders in the reign of Elizabeth I. The oldest recorded member of the family to deal in jewellery was a John Murch of Plymouth who died in 1723; however, the Murches had been recorded as goldsmiths as far back as 1684. This John Murch of Plymouth had three sons, one of whom settled in Honiton in 1739; it was John's great grandson, William, who was the father of Matthew and John. William Murch was married twice and in total had twelve children, one of whom was a Jerom Murch. Jerom, a brother of Matthew and John, was born in 1807 and went on to become Mayor of Bath 7 times and was knighted by Queen Victoria. William's daughter married the postmaster Richard Tucker.

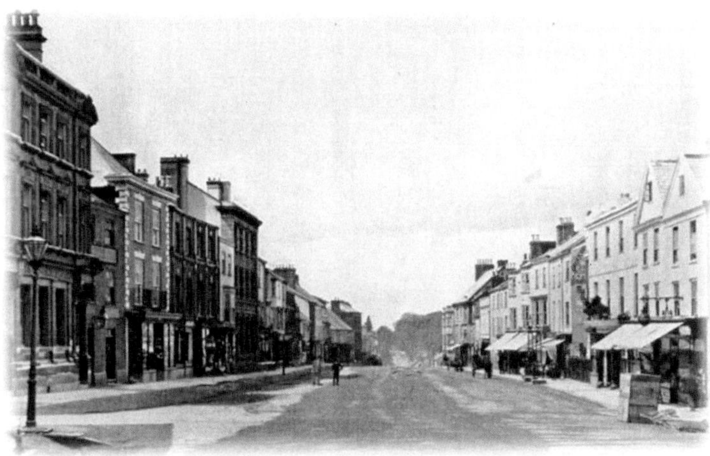

High Street looking west.

By trade, and following in his paternal grandfather's footsteps, Matthew Murch was a watch and clock maker. Matthew Murch's business was located in the shop now occupied by 'Julian Graves' (92 High Street). Matthew built the clock face of St Paul's church in 1846 and, in more modern times, his watches have been known to sell at Christies. Another example of Matthew's work was an 'oak cased 30 hour long case clock' which sold at Bonham's in Honiton for £648 in 2007. Matthew was Mayor of Honiton only once and died in office; he worked in Honiton from 1823 until his death in 1865 and, as well as being a watchmaker was, at various times, a jeweller, silversmith, stamp distributor and an agent for Sun Life & Fire Office. He was also the owner of 8 cottages, stables and gardens in the town, including his own premises. Matthew Murch's son, John, also went on to be Mayor in 1882.

John Murch, Matthew's half brother, had his ironmongery business next door and he, also, was a Mayor of Honiton in 1866 as well as being a town alderman, like his brother. John was also responsible for the construction, in August 1866, of an iron bench near the summit of Church Hill where it amazingly still stands today. Under the bench is a large stone said to be one of the stones that the devil dropped whilst relocating the construction site of St Michael's! Satan was also said to have rested on this stone during his many trips up the hill. There are other examples of such benches scattered around the town. One still standing in Kings Road was dedicated to former Mayor and local doctor, Samuel Devenish, in 1856. Another three, that stand at the bottom of Marlpits Hill just outside Lower Marlpits Farm, at the top of Beggars Lane and lastly one on the A35/Springfield Road junction, were built to commemorate the Coronation of King Edward VII in 1902, and lastly two that sit at the bottom of Northcote Hill and at the Weatherill Road/Lower Brand Lane junction to commemorate the abolition of the road tolls in 1910. All of these 'ancient' benches, when built, were situated out of the 'urban' boundaries and would have served as resting points for people from a time when walking was not just a leisure activity!

Matthew Murch's mother-in-law, Sarah Trump, who was living with the family in 1851, was, at the time, the oldest resident in Honiton at the age of 96.

Another member of the family, John Murch, was responsible for the construction of the clock face of Sidbury Church in 1817.

Whilst most of Matthew Murch's family did well for themselves, his son Edward fell into disgrace. Edward started as a chemist in Torquay and married a schoolmistress. However, by 1881 he was living at Her Majesty's expense in Sussex! Mary Murch, the youngest child of Matthew Murch, married her 1st cousin, Richard Woodgates Tucker. Another son of Matthew's, John (1831-1919), married the daughter of the former landlord and landlady of the Angel Inn (William and Elizabeth Lee) and their son, another John Murch (1871-1959), was a very well known local figure who played a vital part in the foundation of Allhallows Museum, to which he

gave his own personal collection of Honiton history and, rightly so, had a gallery in the museum named after him.
In 1854, the family lost their beloved father, William Murch, aged 86 and his obituary read thus:

"by unbending rectitude, by uniform cheerfulness and by manly piety...he founded the little chapel in which the Unitarian congregation of that town now assemble, and, according to his means, steadily and zealously supported its interests through a large part of a century... Afflicted with paralysis during the last thirty-two years, he was withdrawn from the more active scenes of life. The blessing, however, to him beyond all price, of being able to study the Scriptures and attend public worship, was still spared to him... his family and friends to cherish his memory."

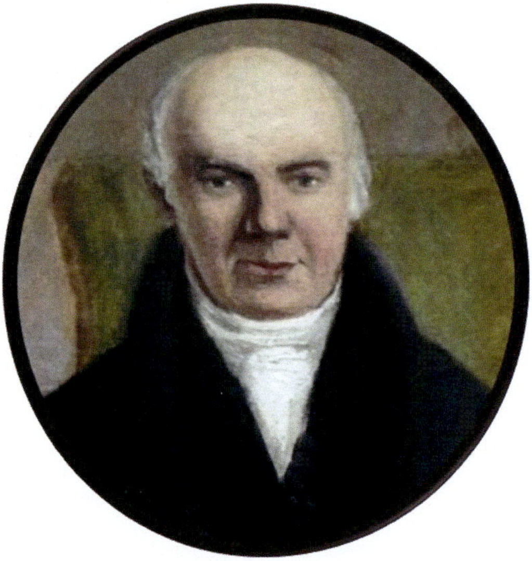

William Murch.

The Murch family suffered further loss on November 9th 1856 with the death of the beloved matriarch of the family, Ann Murch, aged 81, William's widow. Matthew Murch suffered more than the rest for on the same day his wife Sarah died aged 57. His mother was a much loved local figure and her obituary read:

"The obituary notice which merely tends to gratify private affection is scarcely justifiable... Mrs Murch belonged originally to the family of Burnards at Colyton in Devonshire some of those good old middle class religious Nonconformists who from the time of the Ejected Ministers formed the strength of the English Presbyterian Church. The ministry of the Rev Joseph Cornish who through more than fifty years was the faithful shepherd of the little flock at Colyton fostered the principles so dear to the

heroes and martyrs of 1692. And rarely has the great practical result of those principles strength of character been more strikingly exemplified than in the late Mrs Murch. Placed soon after her marriage and settlement at Honiton in circumstances of difficulty - called upon to guide, instruct and care for two families - she was yet never deficient in the requisite vigour and energy. It was probably in after life, when longer trials had had their chastening influence, that the sweeter qualities of the Christian character were most plainly seen. And beautiful was it as, advancing into extreme old age, whether joy or sorrow prevailed in her circle, to see her mind as vigorous and her sympathies as fresh as they could possibly have been in early life. Well may it be said of this venerable and excellent woman, that her children and children's children rose up and called her "Blessed." Even absence and distance had no effect in lessening her interest in all that concerned them; and they, on their part, felt that the longer she was spared to them, the more precious were her example, her counsel and her love. Nor let it be forgotten that amidst family and business cares, through long years when the world had heavy claims upon her, she failed not to cultivate refined and elevating tastes. Happily, the severe illnesses by which she had been occasionally tried for some years, were succeeded before the great change by comparative ease and comfort. Almost to the very last she was allowed much of the social intercourse she loved; so that when the blow came those around her felt how mercifully it had been dealt. In the beautiful cemetery of the old church at Honiton just as the sun was sinking beneath the distant hills, her sons placed her remains in the grave where, three years before, in sight of the same golden clouds, they had left those of their beloved father."

William Murch, in life, had been an ironmonger and is, interestingly, the only inhabitant of St Michael's churchyard to be buried in an iron tomb! Most of the Murchs were attendants at the Independent Chapel and it is here where Matthew Murch was interred in 1865.

Situated on the site now occupied by Lloyds TSB were originally two, three storey, terraced houses that were home to a draper and tailor respectively. There is evidence to suggest that these two buildings housed these types of businesses as far back as 1750. It was only later, at the turn of the 20th century, that these two houses were demolished and the grand building that 'Lloyds TSB' bank occupies today, was built.

Two doors up from the old White Hart Inn, now believed to be the left side of Honiton Toy Shop (87 High St) and which not so long ago was 'East

Devon Electronics' which, after its closure in 2001 became an extension of the toy shop, lived a retired serge manufacturer by the name of Abraham Ash. Although Mr. Ash was born in Honiton in 1803, he was not actually christened until 1822, two years before he married his wife, Sarah. His skills were no longer in demand in the town by the 1850s, which is probably why he retired at some time in the 1840s, but his former business must have done well for him to retire from work at 48! Mr. Ash's son, James, lived 4 houses up and was a draper.

An interesting point worth mentioning relates to the household of Richard and Grace Frost, two doors up from Mr Ash. In the census of 1851, it is Grace, and not her husband, who was listed as 'Head' of the household, even though he was the bread winner. This was exceptionally rare in the 19th century and when, in the same year, a woman of Portsmouth likewise appointed herself 'Head', the story made the newspapers! This woman, apparently, gave her occupation as 'mangle worker' and listed her husband's as 'turns my mangle'!

In 1851, on the east corner of New Street, was a grocer's shop and for much of the 20th century it was a clothes shop called 'Hoskins.'

Part of the old 'A. Dimond & Co.' shop (originally 74 High St) was, at this time, a printers and stationers, owned and run by John Knight, which later went on to the actual premises of A. Diamond & Co Stationers, after Mr. Knight's death. Mr. Knight was the son of a Honiton baker and he died in the town in 1888 having been in business for 50 years. He was also the official printer of the Liberal Party's material and was a town alderman. Both Mr. Knight and his wife Phoebe are interred at St. Michael's where their resting place can still easily be found.

'Shauls Bakery' (76 High Street) was once a wine and spirit shop that belonged to Walter Willey Harris who took it over from his uncle Joseph. Mr. Harris had a store in Northcote Lane which later became a repairs shop for 'Honiton Garage' and more recently 'The Pit Club'. Walter ran the business from the late Victorian era until his retirement in the mid 1920s when Mr. & Mrs. Foale took over the premises. After the Foales' departure, the shop was split into two premises; on the left side, a butchers shop and on the right, the once well known and liked Honiton man, Mr. T. A. Bambury, continued the Foales' grocery business until his retirement in 1967. Mr. Bambury died in 1989. The shop today is Grade II listed and is believed to be an 18th century building.

Living in part of the former premises of 'A. Diamond & Co' was an unmarried sister of Matthew and John Murch who was a school mistress.

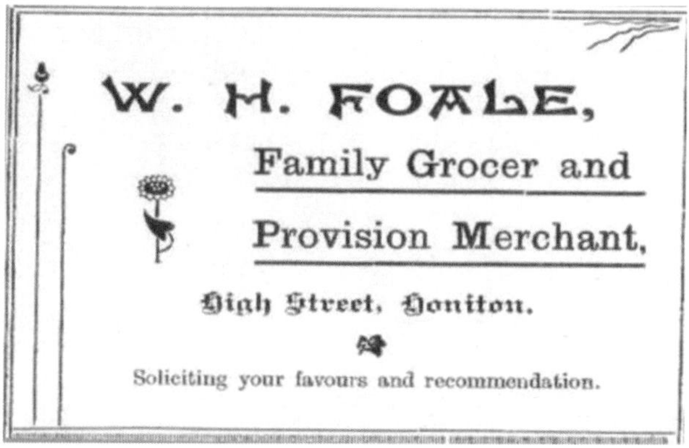

The 'Crusty Cob' bakery and 'Boots' chemist (70 High St) are currently two separate shops located in what was once a building housing only one business, ironically a large bakery run by a Mr Charles White. The chemist Boots currently has two entrances, one of which was originally an alley way that ran between the old bakery and the building next door to a small cottage located at the rear. This 18th century building was once known as 'Old House' and in the early twentieth century was the town 'Working Man's Club'.

Dr. Edward Christopher Holland practised as a surgeon in the grand three storey house now occupied by Stags Estate Agents (66 High St). Previously this house was owned by Husseys Auctioneers and in the 1930s was the home of the headmaster of the Allhallows Grammar School.
Dr. Holland, born in Lambeth, settled in Honiton in about 1835 after marrying his wife Henrietta (from Kingsbridge) in Farway in 1834 and by whom he had one daughter. He was one of the District Surgeons of Honiton Union and a general practitioner. What is interesting about Dr Holland was that he was a practitioner of Homeopathy: definitely a pioneer, especially in a small Devonian town in the mid-nineteenth century and particularly so when many experts still question its effectiveness today! E C Holland was also the union- appointed doctor of the inmates of the workhouse and because of his practise of homoeopathy he got into trouble with the Poor Law Commissioners in 1850. It was stated that this method of treatment "was not recognised by the constituted medical authorities of the country" and they insisted that he refrain from such practises. Another practitioner of the time even went so far as to describe the practise as "evil" and "utterly opposed to science and common sense"!

Dr Holland, however, stood his ground and was quoted that treating the inmates with the proposed conventional methods "in many cases ...was wholly inefficacious, and in others worse than injurious in its consequences". Judging from the example of Dr. Woodward's treatment methods, mentioned earlier, he may have had a point! However, despite his defence, he was removed from office.

A documented case of Dr Holland's in 1846 gives an interesting insight into his methods of treatment. In the January of that year Dr. Holland was called upon to treat a patient in Luppit who had been suffering from an ongoing disorder of severe vomiting which had lead to weight loss and apparently impending death. After a failed prescription, he decided to administer a dosage of "Arsenic" with the homeopathic argument in mind that "like cures like"! Amazingly this treatment appeared to work and the lady recovered and claimed that he had "saved her life". The affliction returned, however, several months later, shortly after her wedding and even after Dr. Woodward was called upon to assist, she died of what was put down to ulceration of the stomach. In a letter that Dr. Holland wrote in 1849 concerning an outbreak of cholera in the town, one would think the local authorities may have given his methods a trial for it was found that of the 15 patients, a total of 5 had died, the first four having been treated by a conventional physician whereas the remaining 11 were treated by Mr. Holland, 10 of whom completely recovered!

After his dismissal, Dr. Holland practised in Norfolk, and after his wife's death in 1867 he remarried in the following year and later relocated to Bath, where he died in 1886.

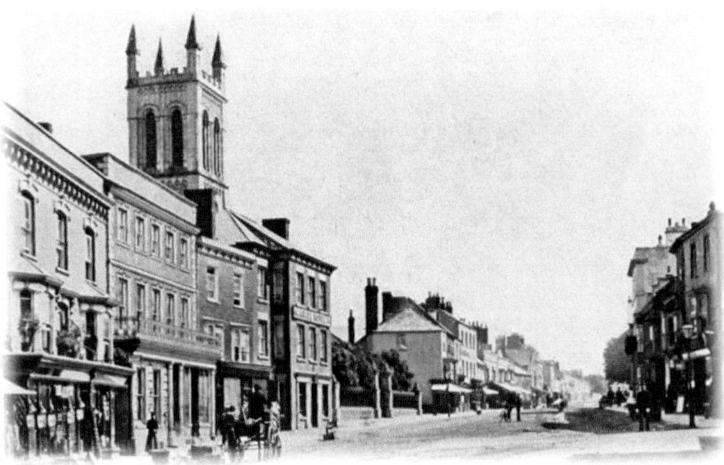

High Street looking east.

Next to the doctor lived a retired grocer by the name of Daniel Pidgeon who lived in one of two fine old terraced houses destroyed in 1967. The houses were once owned by Allhallows School and were at one point housing for the boarder students. Collectively these two houses were known as 'Baker House' during the properties' use by the school and the two front doors were never used at this time, as students entered from the rear. The second floor was where one of the dormitories was situated and the room apparently became so cold in the winter months that jugs of water, used for washing in the morning, often had turned to ice during the nights.

Mr. Pidgeon had previously owned a grocers shop on the corner of New Street in the property now rented by 'First Choice' and by the 1850s he was living off income from rented properties. His brother John had had a wine merchant business in the property next door and he had married the sister of Marianne Luckham, the school mistress. Both John and Daniel came from a long line of merchants and grocers who had been established in Honiton since the late 18th century. One of John's sons - surprisingly a naval pilot! - died in Calcutta. Several members of this family have made their mark on history: another Daniel Pidgeon was a member of the London Geological Society, to whom he left £1,000 in his Will and which was used to set up the 'Daniel Pidgeon Fund' for Young Geologists; Daniel's son, Winter Randell Pidgeon, was a co-author of a US Patent in 1903 for a new type of clutch. A cross-country runner and 2012 Olympics prospect is also descended from this family.

In the ornate, three storey property called 'The Gables', which used to stand where the Post Office now is, lived the Cox family.

Mr. Isaac Cox, a solicitor, married yet another member of the Murch family, Elizabeth Murch, in 1811 at St. Michael's. Mr. Cox was a committed Presbyterian and his religious and political views were noted as being at times "exceedingly unpopular"! He was a very active member of Honiton society and was a County Coroner. Mr. Cox died of heart disease in 1831 and was described in his obituary as "a good man deprived of existence". His son, Isaac John Cox, married the widow of the late John Melhuish and became an attorney and town clerk, like his father, and steward to the Lord of the Manor and in 1851 lived in the property to the right of the Red Cow. 'The Gables' was pulled down after the last doctor to reside there, Dr Finlay, retired in the 1960s due to its poor state of repair. "Attorneys always flourished in Honiton" and in 1847 there were twelve practising solicitors in a town with a population of just under 4,000!

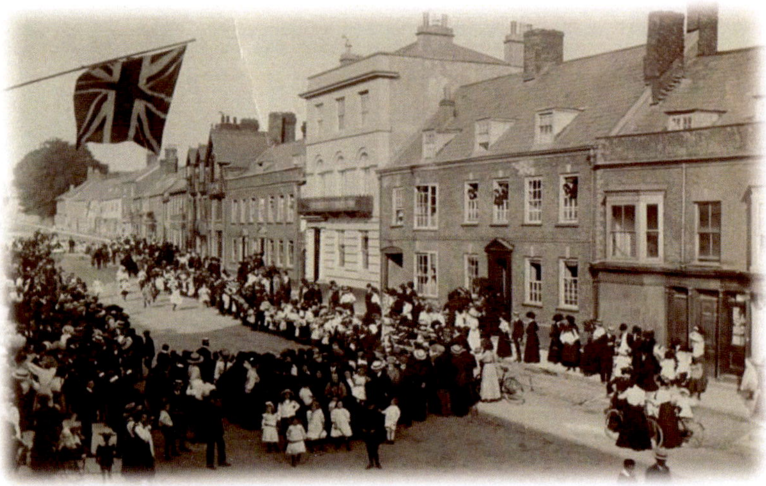

The toll abolition celebrations of 1910 showing the old setup of properties on the south side of the High Street. 'The Gables' is the property two up from the three storey pale building (was home of Dr. Holland).

<u>East End</u>

The East End of town pretty much resembled that of the west; however, rather than the mixed social classes of the west, prosperity dwindled the further from the centre of town one went.

Dr. John Clapcott Jerrard ran his surgery in an eighteenth century property now known as Carlton House (next to the Post Office). Dr. Jerrard, a Dorset man by birth, ran his surgery "for many years and had a high reputation for skill". His eldest son, John Hutchings Jerrard, also became a doctor and for some time practised from his father's surgery. If it has not become apparent, many parents of the time gave the mother's maiden name to their children as a middle name, as in the case of John Clapcott and John Hutchings. J. C. Jerrard was a councillor, became borough mayor 4 times, and was an alderman from 1846 to 1864. He was awarded a silver medal from the 'Society of Arts' in the 'Class of Mechanics' for a bed he designed for invalids in 1831. I will now quote another medical case which gives a further example of the medical procedures of Victorian practitioners, in which Dr. J. C. Jerrard was called to attendance. In 1843 a girl of eleven had fallen while at play and a scythe had penetrated her abdomen causing a proportion of her intestines to protrude. After dressing the wound, Dr. Jerrard gave "dose of castor oil...which operated well in the night". The next morning, you guessed it: she was bled of 16 ounces of blood and a further 16 in the evening! Her treatment was well received and she recovered. Bleeding was the main way of treating sick people in an attempt to rebalance the body's fluids. In the 18th century one girl, who was suffering from a "suppressed" menstrual cycle, was bled no less than 1,020 times from the age of 16 to 19! Her symptoms of "vomiting" and "epileptic attacks" were apparently cured after partaking of "a journey in a rough vehicle"!

Dr. Jerrard's son married the daughter of a Mr. Golesworthy and latterly resided in a property in New Street now known as 'Fairfield House' which is now the Social Services Offices. John Clapcott Jerrard sadly outlived both his wife and his son until he himself died, at Honiton, in 1877 at the age of 83.

John Hutchings Jerrard was a town alderman for a short time and also a lieutenant in the 13th Devon Rifle Volunteers. John Hutchings had 5 daughters and a son, John Henry Jerrard, who was his youngest. John Henry attended Allhallows School in 1886 and went on to become a doctor like his father and grandfather, and operated from his father's practice for a number of years. This Dr. Jerrard donated a field to Honiton after his passing in 1942. It was originally donated for the purpose of being a new site for a "cottage hospital" but as the NHS was established only 5 years after his death there was no longer any need for it. The land was therefore sold to developers, of which the proceeds went to the construction of the 'Jerrard Wing' of Honiton Hospital, which was completed in 1957, and the housing development was aptly named after its kind benefactor. The garden adjoining his house was once concealed from passersby by an 8ft wall that ran the length of New Street car park to the thatched cottages further up. In these gardens, Mr. Jerrard kept his greenhouses where, among other things, he grew grapes.

His house, during the war years, was used as a 'home girls' hostel much to the liking of the American soldiers stationed in the town: it was said that barbed wire had to be put in front of the windows to keep the soldiers out and the girls in! The premises also housed the town library for a few years in the 1960s before the construction of the present day facility in 1974.

Living in the listed, 18th century building now occupied by 'The Boston Tea Party' lived an elderly widow called Ruth Tooze. Mrs. Tooze was yet another member of the Murch family, the sister of Matthew the watchmaker. She was also a rich woman who owned a couple of cottages with some land which were located directly opposite the bottom of Mill

Street. She also owned several other plots of land around the town. She lived with her sister, another elderly widow called Eliza Rigby, her daughter and her son-in –law, who was interestingly the Curate of East Teignmouth - quite a commute in those days! This property (53 High Street) has had a variety of interesting owners and uses over the years. For the latter part of the Victorian period, after Mrs. Tooze died, it was occupied by the Vicar of Monkton, Henry Knott Venn, from whom it is believed the house gets its name 'Monkton House.' Rev Venn's brother lived for a short time further down the High Street and he was the curate of Buckerell. In the early part of the 20th century it was an antique shop owned by a German gentleman, Mr. Schofield, who was thought by many local people of the time to have been a prisoner of war during WWI. The building later became 'The Highland Fling' cafe. It later reverted back to an antique shop run by a Mr. Woodhead and then back to a cafe again!

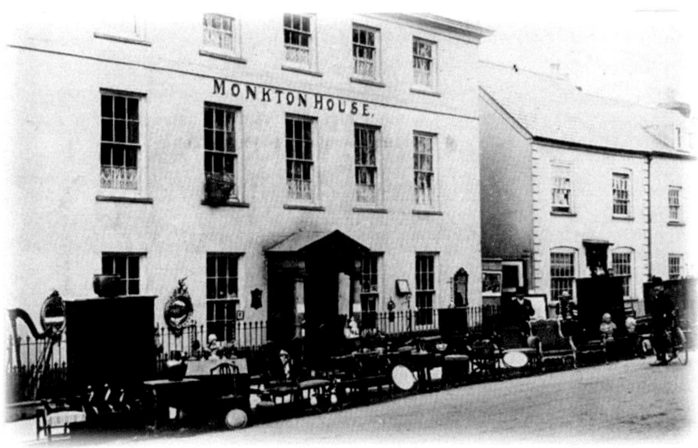

Monkton House, when it was an antique shop in the early 20th century.

Ruth Tooze's neighbour, William Eames, lived in the shop which is currently called 'Hybrid' (51 High Street) and was a prosperous 'plumber and glazier' yet sadly was not as fortunate with his children as with his business. William had six children in total and three of them were born deaf and dumb. After the death of his son, Richard Salter Eames aged 4 in 1850, he lost both his daughters the following year: Harriet Jane at the age of 10 and Eliza aged 6. Son, Frederick William, started his working life as a painter but sadly he also died at the age of 22 in 1872. With only two children remaining it must have been awful for William to witness his son George Miles's committal to the Devon County Lunatic Asylum in the 1870s. George Miles Eames spent well over 20 years in this institution where he is thought to have died. William Eames died in 1881 aged 64 after which his wife Elizabeth went to live in Staffordshire with her youngest son and his wife, Richard and Sarah, along with Sarah's family. Richard worked as a grocer and corn dealer. Incidentally, Richard's wife Sarah was a daughter of the well known Honiton watchmaker Henry Tovey. The property in which they lived was built in 1710 and later became the 'Queen Anne Restaurant.'

The jewellery shop right next to the Red Cow was formerly the home of a Mr. Henry Anning. Mr. Anning was an ornithologist and naturalist and both he and his wife Elizabeth were Honiton born and bred. He had 4 children, of which one of his sons, Henry Christopher, was probably one of the only male lace-makers in town! Henry remarried after his first wife died and he himself died in 1884. His widow, however, carried on his work and was listed in 1902 as an "animal & bird preserver" only 13 years after the establishment of the RSPB. Mrs. Anning at the time of this listing was nearly 90 years old!

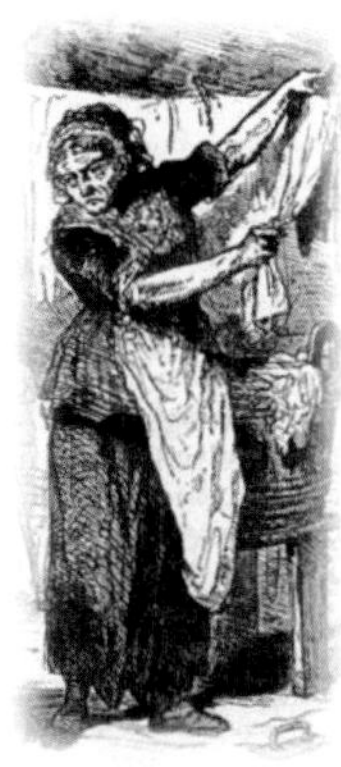

Next to the Annings, in the old Bull Inn, resided a 67 year old washerwoman and her unmarried daughter. I mention this woman, who was called Mary Crabb, as she was stated as being 'Parted from Husband'; where her husband was and why they were parted is unfortunately unknown. The Bull had closed some years before and later, in the 20th century, the cottage merged with the Red Cow.

Three homes up from Clapper Lane live Edward Ford, a tea dealer, his wife Maria and their 10 children; they would go on to have 4 more! Edward was born in Honiton; his wife, however, was born in Sicily where her father Major General John Slessor, who fought at the battle of Waterloo, was posted for a short time. Among the various famous individuals in his pedigree, Mr. Ford also had a great military ancestor: he was a nephew of Captain George Blagdon Westcott, one of Honiton's most famous children. Capt. Westcott, the son of a Honiton baker, sailed on the HMS Victory and HMS Majestic and had a prestigious naval career spanning more than three decades. He was also one of Horatio Nelson's Band of Brothers at the Battle of the Nile where he was killed by a musket ball shot to the throat in 1798. It was Westcott's mother (Susanna Westcott), Edward Ford's aunt, who was fortunate enough to be presented with one of Horatio Nelson's own gold medals in 1801, when Nelson learned that Captain's Westcott had not received his own. Whilst awarding Susanna with her late son's award, he said "You will not value it less because Nelson has worn it." Mrs Westcott, at this time, was living in the property formerly known as 'The Gables' and was bed-ridden with illness and had to be dressed and brought downstairs to meet the Admiral. Whilst in the town Nelson made a visit to a linen draper called Richard Smark (a maternal great uncle of Richard Farquharson, author of 'The History of Honiton') ""to buy some gloves"" and holding out his hands said "you see I only want one""! Nelson was quoted, from a letter addressed to Lady Hamilton:

"At Honiton I visited Captain Westcott's mother — poor thing, except from the bounty of government and Lloyd's, in very low circumstances. The brother is a tailor, but had they been chimney-sweepers it was my duty to show them respect."

Captain Westcott's legacy lives on in the town in the form of a road that was named after him called 'Westcott Way'.
Edward Ford was also descended from Thomas Marwood, the famous local physician who died in 1617, and even more coincidently he lived just across the road from a distant cousin, the Rev Marwood Tucker, who once resided at Marwood House. It is not thought that these two gentlemen knew of the link between them. He had another distant cousin, Ezra Cleveland (once Rector of Honiton), and Edward's father, Humphrey Ford, had been a well known local politician. His family had also, at one time, owned and worked at the Honiton Pottery.
Despite the fact the Fords were well settled in Honiton, the entire family emigrated to Australia at some point between 1851-1853, a journey that could have taken up to four months. With the departure of the Edwards family from Honiton, the Ford family line in the town died out. Edward died at the age of 70 in 1870 and his wife Maria at the age of 99!

Not far from Mr. Ford lived the widow of another of his relatives. Edmund Westcott was one of Edward Ford's cousins: likewise a relation of Capt. Westcott. However, he sadly died of diabetes at the age of 39 in 1850, leaving a wife and 8 children. Fortunately for his wife she managed to climb from being a poorly paid lace- maker to a lace dealer and many of her children went on to gain respectable employment. Ellen, Elizabeth's youngest, never married and by 1881 was in the Union Workhouse: employed as a schoolmistress that is! The family lived in the property to the left of the present day 'Merchant House Antiques'.

A bit of a sadder tale now with relation to one of the Westcott's neighbours who was Edward Bishop. His father was a 'common labourer' although Edward himself had started as an apprentice tailor before which time he worked in the same profession as his father. However, he never qualified and remained a labourer, even after he became crippled at some point in the 1860s. Whether working in this weakened condition was too much for him, he died in 1876 in his mid 50s.

Not far from Mr Bishop lived Mr Jasper Salter, who Farquaharson described as "the wag of the town". Mr. Salter was a butcher and farmer by trade and was said to be "always playing practical jokes" on the good folk of Honiton. One time, for example, he had had an argument with his wife Sally and she refused to speak to him. Jasper, therefore, sent for Dr. Holland stating that his wife had been "taken speechless". When the doctor arrived he found Mr. Salter in his chair smoking a pipe and his wife going about her daily business. Confused, Dr Holland questioned Sally as to why he had been summoned so urgently at which she replied "That's, that old fool" pointing to her husband. Jasper, never missing a trick, suddenly exclaimed "Lord Doctor...what a man you be you've cured her at once". For the next hour Mrs. Salter apparently "proved she had the use of her tongue"! Another example of his poor wife's endurance came when they attended a gathering in Payhembury. Jasper and his wife travelled by horse to the club, with his wife riding pillion behind him, as was the custom of the time. As the night progressed Sally wished to return home but Jasper, having a good time, was reluctant to leave so she started back on foot. Several minutes later Jasper mounted his horse and overtook her: "Jasper...let me get up" yelled his wife "who be you my dear" was his reply "what would my wife Sally say if she heard I took up a strange woman"! Continuing the pretence of not knowing her he made the poor woman walk the whole 6 miles back. Despite their differences they had three children and were married for 50 years. Jasper Salter suffered with blindness later in life and died in 1854, 75 years of age and his wife Sarah (nicknamed Sally) a few years later. His son, Daniel, continued his father's business where he lived with his unmarried sister.

The remainder of the north side of High Street consisted of a mixture of wealthy landowners, retired merchants and some poorer members of Honiton.
Returning to the south side of the street we come upon, amongst others, an umbrella maker and one of, if not the only, town chimney sweeps. Only a few doors from the old Kings Arms Inn, Richard Swaine lived with his wife Mary and their children who had several interesting names, including Mahala and Adolphus! Most of his children seem to have relocated to London, possibly due to lack of employment, so common at this period.

Peter Darke and his wife Susan lived in one of the old properties near the 'Honiton Antique Toy shop'. Peter was a dyer and the 'Darke' family name had long established connections with the town. The now 'Grove Antique Centre', where Dr. Terry and Catherine Glanville lived for many years, was reconstructed, after one of the many fires, by a George Darke and his wife. Peter had two known brothers, one, James, who was a boot and shoe maker and John who was once landlord of the White Horse Inn. Their father, another John, had also been the clerk of the Honiton New Meeting House. Peter's son, John Flood Darke, moved to Somerset where he was a tailor and sadly died in the workhouse at the age of 75.

Living in the property now occupied by the Carlton Inn lived Sarah Fildew, a widowed schoolmistress and her family. Sadly, residing with her was her young daughter Caroline Paine who had also been widowed some 5 years prior. Caroline had a young daughter by the same name and, although bereaved of her spouse at the tender age of 25, she lived to her late 60s and never remarried. Her daughter went on to marry a Mr. Bennett (31 years her senior) who was a commission agent; whether she married for love or money will unfortunately never be known!
Another interesting couple were Mr. and Mrs. McLeary. Like the Frosts not far away, John McLeary's occupation was listed as being an assistant to his wife who was a laundress: not exactly a very common type of employment for a Victorian man. However, unlike the Frosts, he was officially the 'Head' of the household. Mrs. Mcleary could have expected to earn about 1 shilling a day for her endless labours and would usually work 6 days a week from 9am to 8pm or, in many cases, even later...

"She mustn't think, but must work on, washing the bedclothes until she could wash no longer. Wash Wash, all the week long; it was only by working till one o'clock in the morning that she sometimes managed to get the Sabbath free of washing....a strange weakness came over her. She

thought of the endless work that awaited her in the cellar, the great copper on the fire, the heap of soiled linen in the corner, the steam rising from the wash-tub, and she felt she had not enough strength to get through another week of such work."

(George Moore writing about a laundress in 1894)

Even if not a laundress, housewives of the time still had the weekly wash to deal with, which was often undertaken on Mondays. One text of the time advised the respective wives to rise at 2am on laundry day!

Now, concluding this long journey down the High Street, we end with a woman known as Elizabeth Thorn who was a 35 year old seamstress. She had three children although she was not, and had never been, married! Her children were called Sarah Ann, James 'Hopping' and John 'Hopping' Thorn and, interestingly, next door to her lived an unmarried 34 year old gentleman by the name of Thomas Hopping: much more went on behind those closed doors than the authorities cared to know about! Whether Thomas' elderly mother did not approve of her son marrying this woman is unknown but three children out of wedlock was no joke in Victorian England. Elizabeth was one of only 3% of women in the country who were unmarried with children. The local Poor Law Commission did not look too well on this matter either and due to individual parishes not wanting the burden of such individuals, Miss Thorn and "her bastards" were removed to her home parish of Awliscombe in 1853. The family are believed to have lived in the property now occupied by the antique shop 'Upstairs, Downstairs.'

Chapter 2
New Street & Brookhill

"A street to connect the old town with new
It thus became town road number two"
The Author

New Street

New Street, at this time, was a narrow lane with a large number of terraced cottages compacted into its little space. It was the main route out of the town to London for a long time, with coaches travelling up New Street into Queen Street and then joining the now A35 at the Copper Castle Tollhouse. Sadly, this little road has lost much of its former character with the destruction of many of its former properties through either fires or demolition. It was inhabited by a collection of lower income families and numerous shopkeepers.

Brookhill (Brook Hill) was formerly the name of the lower part of what is now Church Hill. However, apart from St. Michael's, the town ended at the Union Workhouse, now the site of Honiton Hospital. It was named after a small 'brook' that ran from the Glen and under New Street. The stream then ran parallel to King Street before joining the Gissage. Despite its pleasant sounding name, one could be forgiven for thinking Brook Hill was a more affluent area but this was not the case: it comprised a collection of some 25 cottages, long since demolished, just a stones throw from Summerland Place whose inhabitants included labourers, laundresses and lacemakers.

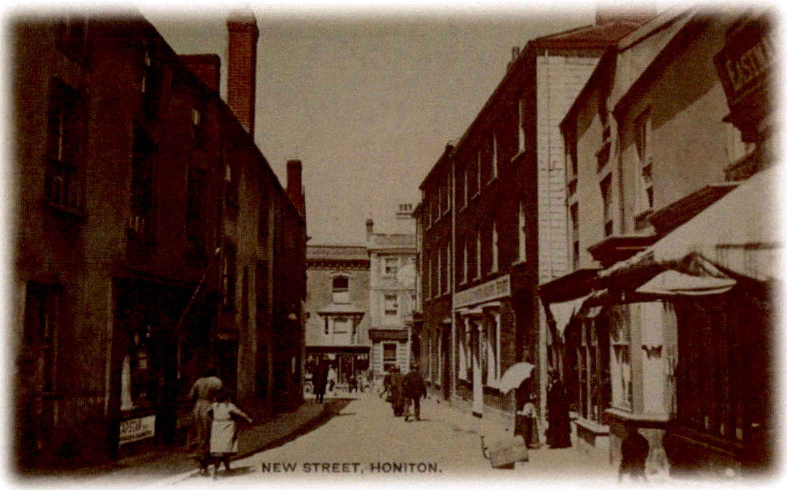

New Street looking north; much narrower in this photo from the early 20th century, prior to the widening of the 1960s.

Located in the shop now occupied by 'Philip & Jenny Family Butchers' lived another of the town's solicitors, Alfred Guppy, along with his younger sister, Sarah Ann.

A little further up lived William Porter, a 73 year old saddler and his schoolmistress wife, Frances. William had somehow become blinded in 1846 and due to his disability he was receiving parish relief and was thus deemed a 'pauper'.

Prior to the widening of New Street in the 1960s, there was a small collection of houses and shops directly behind the old Black Lion Inn. Within these long gone houses resided a saddler, a cordwainer and hairdresser, a wheelwright and a tailor.

Living not far from the Guppys was the Flood family. The household consisted of Betty Flood and her spinster and widowed sisters, Sarah Flood and Margaret Croft and Margaret's 3 children. The sisters were the daughters of William Flood, a shoemaker who was a cousin of Christopher Flood, a local banker. Betty Flood had the most prominent occupation as a school mistress and after her death, Margaret and Sarah moved in with their other unmarried sister, Elizabeth, where they all lived as poorly paid dressmakers. By the 1870s, death had claimed Elizabeth and Margaret was working as a newsagent to support her one remaining sister, Sarah, who had developed dementia. In 1875 the cottage in which they lived was demolished to make way for the new Wesleyan Chapel, now the Town Council Offices. The family moved to Queen Street and Sarah died in 1878 aged 74. Margaret Croft worked as a washer woman until about the age of 80 when she moved in with her son-in-law. Margaret died, poor, in 1891 aged 89. Margaret's father's cousin, Christopher Flood, died the equivalent of a millionaire whilst his extended family lived, worked and died in relative poverty! Another relative of the Floods was George Lott Flood who lived the other side of New Street and was a 'hatter'.

William Woodgates ran 'Woodgates' Academy' formerly located in what is now, and then known as, 'Laurel House'. William owned the Academy as well as a couple of cottages, long since demolished, that backed onto the Academy's land and which were located in Queen Street. He was described by Farquaharson to have been "one of the most hospitable, kindly hearted creatures, that ever breathed and treated his pupils as though they were his own children". He was nicknamed 'The Bacon' from his "portly persona" as well as "The Warbling Pedagogue". He married the sister of the postmaster, Sarah Tucker, and with her had 9 children: his brother, Matthew, married another sister of the postmaster, Matilda Tucker! Two of his daughters, Annabelle and Catherine, married two brothers by the name of Browne whom they met whilst working at their father's school as assistant masters. Another daughter, Emily, established a school for girls almost opposite in New Street near the Star Inn where she was assisted by her sister, Annabelle, and at one time her younger sister Matilda was a student there.

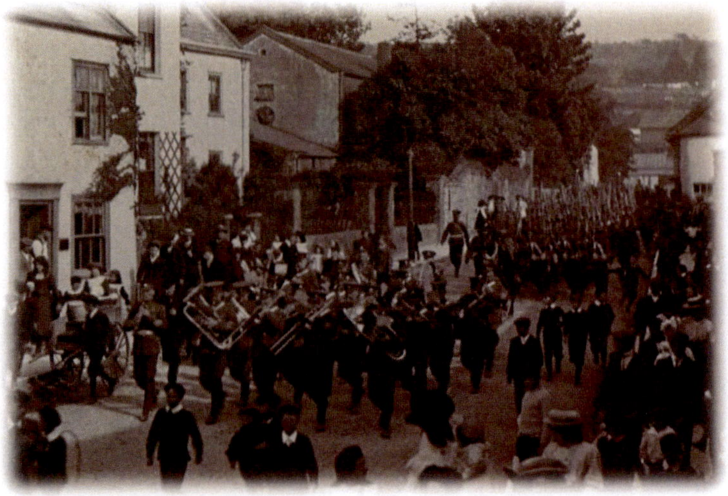

A procession in New Street located roughly where the Woodgates family once resided. The site to the left is where Honiton library now stands.

William Woodgates' eldest son, William, was an officer in the Oriental Colonial Service and another son, James Richard Woodgates, became master of Allhallows Grammar school on February 12th 1851. However, for unknown reasons, he resigned 4 years later on April 25th 1855. James' daughter, Emily, went on to marry a well known poet, Percy E. Pinkerton, in 1909 who, among other works, wrote lyrics for Edward Elgar. William himself died in 1854 aged 50 and his passing was seen as a great loss to the town. His wife died 14 years later, sadly having outlived several of her children, and was buried with her husband in St Michael's. Their ornate, moss covered grave can still easily be found not far from the church, along with many other members of the Woodgates family.

Robert Henry Aberdein was an attorney who was a neighbour of Mr. Woodgates and in 1851 was also County Coroner and Clerk of Honiton. Mr. Aberdein had been born in Honiton in 1793 in the property opposite the Baptist Chapel, the only son of a Scotsman, another Robert Aberdein, who had settled in the town as a draper. His father had first married a Mrs. Lydia Maynard, a lady who, at the time, was head of the lace trade and whose first husband was a member of the Maynard family who were formerly very prominent in the wool/lace trade of Honiton. After Lydia died, leaving him no children, he married a housekeeper, Elizabeth Youatt, who was described as one of "high intellect" and was known locally as "Eliza the mad, nurse of the mob". From this marriage he had 3 children, two of whom were daughters who were said to have "inherited their mother's abilities"! Robert's father also played a key role in assisting the failing lace industry when in 1817 he, along with other local manufacturers, managed to "deliver Honiton lace at the wholesale price to subscribers". This gave the estimated 100 out of work lacemakers a guaranteed income of 3s a week.

Robert himself was educated in a private school in Kentisbeare and was called to the bar in 1815. He first practised at Andover where he married a Mary Wakeford, a daughter of one of the partners of the Andover Bank. He then moved back to Honiton where he went into partnership with a local man, Issac Cox. After the death of Mr. Cox in 1831 he became one of the County Coroners and with the establishment of the County Court he became the first clerk of the Honiton Division. In 1857 he was 'Under Sheriff for Devon' and also stood as Steward of the Manors of Widworthy and Dulverton, as well as sitting as Mayor of Honiton three times.

Mr. Aberdein was a keen local political figure, remaining throughout his life a "consistent whig". He attended the Independent Chapel and was the Church Secretary for nearly 20 years; one of the Chapel's pastors, William Wright, married his sister Georgina Caroline Aberdein.

Robert Aberdein was referred to locally as "James" as he was said to have "looked both ways" when it came to political questions. He was described as "a very handsome man", "of good attainments and pleasing manners" as well as a man "of science" who "possessed a large fund of information" especially on local history on which he gave several local lectures: I would personally liked to have met him for the sake of this book! There was also some speculation as to whether Richard Farquharson, author of 'The History of Honiton', had actually stolen information from these lectures in order to complete his own book; maybe that is why Mr. Farquharson referred to him in the preface!

One of Aberdein's sons went on to work for the Royal Mint and his daughter married a Lt Colonel; Robert died in 1860 aged 65. Both his sons died young without children leaving the family line from his father extinct. After the death of Mr. Aberdein, Mr George Tweed of London moved to Honiton and took over his offices. Mr. Tweed practised as a solicitor in the town over the following 30 years; however, his son Cyril Neville Tweed had much more involvement in town life.

Cyril Tweed was born in Queens House, New Street in 1875 and during his life provided services to the town which one might say were invaluable. He became Deputy Town Clerk in 1901 (a position he held until 1905), was a council member from 1908-1928, an alderman of the borough from 1922-1928, Town Clerk from 1926-1932 and was Mayor 5 times in 1908, 1909, 1916, 1917 and 1935. He was also Deputy Mayor eleven times, a governor of Allhallows School and was Coroner for East Devon after his brother's death in 1921. In recognition of his life's work for the town he was made the first Honorary Freeman of Honiton on 20th February 1936. Mr. Tweed's place of business was described as a "scrooge type of office with high desks and stools". When he retired his offices were closed. Cyril Tweed died in Honiton in 1957.

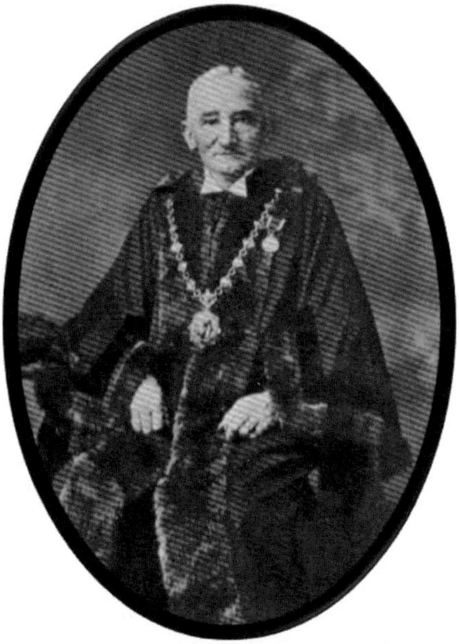

Cyril Tweed

On the site now occupied by the local Social Services offices Dr. Samuel Devenish ran his surgery. This surgery would later be taken over by the Jerrard family. After Dr. Devenish died, a bronze fountain was erected by the town to his memory in 1863; he was buried in the yard of the Independent Chapel. It once stood in New Street, near the entrance to the present day New Street Car Park; it was later relocated to the High Street before it was permanently removed.

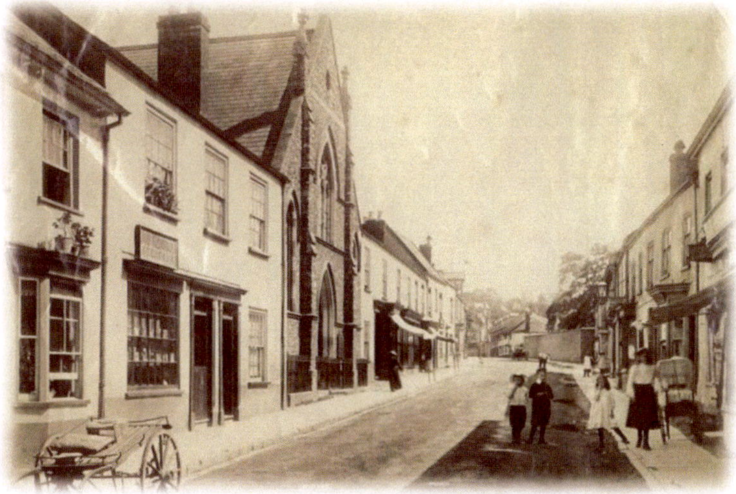

New Street c.1900. The wall on the right in the background was at this time Dr. Jerrard's garden and is today New Street car park.

Believed to have resided in one of the old Tudor cottages that once stood in New Street (opposite the present day Library) lived William Holcombe Russell who had an interesting profession as a 'wood and ivory turner', the only person in town at the time to work with such materials. A skilled artisan, this gentleman would have worked wood and ivory into items such as snooker balls, chess pieces and piano keys. Mr. Russell must have been a well known and respected craftsman for he is known to have had apprentices from as far away as Cheshire! Sadly, he lost his only daughter when she was in her teens. William worked in the town for well over 50 years and at the turn of the 20th century he went into business with his only son (William John Russell) naming his business 'Russell and Son'. He died in Honiton in 1907 aged 88 and his son carried on his father's work until about 1920, by which time he had branched out into cabinet making and upholstering.

Thomas Dyson Austen was the town veterinary surgeon who ran his practice from a site which is presently near the railway station car park. His father, another Thomas, had also been a vet and the family ran the veterinary business through three generations. Thomas married his sister-in-law after his brother James died and it was his stepson James who was the last to practise in the town until about 1890. Thomas would have been wise to keep this marriage a secret from the authorities for it would be some 70 years before such marriages to one's brother's widow were legalised! At this time widows were expected to wear black for one year and a day after the death of their husband followed by a period of six months when they were permitted to wear grey. Widows were not expected to remarry, especially to one's dead husband's brother! Thomas Austen's other brother, William, lived a little further down New Street, 4 houses from the corner of King Street, and was a tailor. Another brother, George, set up his own veterinary practice in Chard, Somerset.

Living in the grand old property joined to the right of the building now known as Fensham House (58 New Street) overlooking Summerland Place, lived Brisco M. Gane, the Curate of Honiton. Brisco was born in Shepton Mallet in 1813, the son of a clothier and a former military man. He married Selina Purnell in his home town in 1841. His brother,

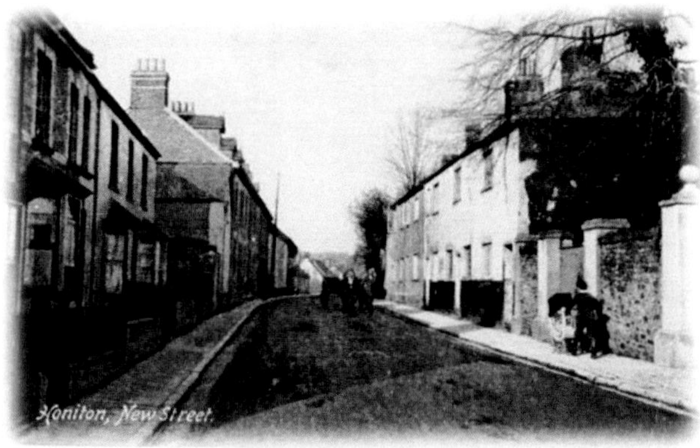

James, followed their father's footsteps into the military and became an army surgeon in Bombay. The couple came to Honiton in the early 1840s and had two daughters called Selina and Rosina. In the 1850s, Brisco moved his family to Stanford le Hope, Essex where he became Curate of the parish, after which they moved to Cowley, Oxfordshire. Selina and Rosina never married and both became private school teachers in Cowley where they lived with their mother until her death in 1902 aged 89.

In the actual property named Fensham House, 60 New Street, lived the Farquharson family. The house in which the family lived had once belonged to Pearce Roger Nesbitt who had inherited the property from his father in 1838. Mr. Nesbitt became an M.D. at Edinburgh University and was a Freeman of the Drapers Company; he also wrote several books one titled: 'Our Invalids and how we treat them.' One of his grandchildren was Robert Chancellor Nesbitt, a noted London solicitor and politician who was also distantly related to the wife of Lord Nelson as well as Edith Nesbit, author of 'The Railway Children'. He did not reside in Honiton for long, although two of his children were born here. His mother, however, remained in the family house until her death in 1846 after which the Farquharsons moved in.

The census of the time paints a picture of a respected middle class family. The head of the household was an author and composer of music whose profession supported his wife and two young children, as well as allowing the employment of a cook and two housemaids; however, beneath this idealic setting lay stories of scandal, death and betrayal: possibly one of the most colourful families Honiton has ever seen!

Archibald William Stuart Farquharson, among other aliases, was the head of the family; this was thought to be his real name, although he went by several others throughout his life. He was born in 1814 in Lynn, Norfolk and was thought to be the illegitimate son of a gentleman from Aberdeenshire. His father is believed to be Archibald Farquharson (1793-1841) of Finzean who was a wealthy landowner and who ironically died without an heir. It seems that his illegitimate child resented his illegitimacy for over the following years he pursued many illegal avenues to grant himself the wealth his father had never left him. He even went so far as to enter in the official register an entry of marriage between his parents which never actually took place. This even involved erasing a precious legitimate marriage entry so that the numbers of the entries matched! The forgery was discovered some 30 years later and accordingly amended, although the authorities could not be sure as to whether it was actually Mr. Farquharson who had committed the crime. Mr. Farquharson was not clearly identified as the perpetrator until 2009, some 200 years later, when one of his descendants compared handwriting samples from personal letters and the forged document and found they matched! This crime was 'small potatoes' though, compared to Mr. F's other ventures...

In his early life he seemed to have conducted himself respectfully and was described as having had a 'liberal education', becoming a clerk in a bank in Lynn, Norfolk. In 1836 he married Honiton born Sarah Amelia Smarke Pople in London, the daughter of a Honiton merchant. As Sarah came from a respected and wealthy family, he managed to get a position in the civil service at Somerset House where he is thought to have gained access to the Marriage Register. Whilst in this position he enrolled on a professorship of Natural Philosophy course at London University, which he never completed, but still gave himself the title of 'Doctor'. He gained entry to the 'Antiquarian Society' and "procured a commission as major in the Aberdeenshire Militaria" with the aid of a stolen uniform. On leaving the forces in 1844, he moved with his young family to Honiton where he wrote several pieces of music, including 'The Dove' which was described thus:

"The composer is particularly happy in treating ballad of this character. With an illustrated title, it is in every respect fit to grace the table of pianoforte-and forms a most suitable trifle as a souvenir for young persons-pure and unexceptional"

He also wrote lyrics for music composed by local musician Edwin Flood and wrote many more "ballads for Italian Music". His most notable publication was a collection of poems titled 'The Pleasures of Home; or the Domestic Scenes and Affections of the Circle Round the Hearth.' The work paints a "lovely picture of the common incidents of domestic life, in the happy rural home of cultivated middle-life, gladdened by the voice of childhood, and elevated by refined sediment and kindly social feelings" and was decribed in a review of the time as "pure" and "elegantly versed".

These numerous artistic works were quite respected and well received but did no favours to their author's finances. It was then, at some point in the early 1850s, that he abandoned his family in Honiton and returned to London where he was said to have "lived for a time in some extravagance at other people's expense", perhaps after he was acquitted of an assault charge in 1852.

In 1853 he swindled a Mr. Furrain out of £250 on the pretence that he could provide him with "a Government situation" and gave Mr. Furrain a "note of hand purporting to be signed by a person named Greenwood and Major Fortescue, of the Royal Artillery." The Major himself soon announced the note to be a fake and Mr. Furrain pursued Farquharson to Hounslow, where he discovered he was now going by the name of Greenwood, and recovered his money. He later pulled a similar stunt with a Mr. Price, this time obtaining £100, as well as fooling many other individuals by proclaiming he could get them foreign diplomas, all of which were later found to be forged.

On another occasion when he had, through false documentation, procured a position as curate to the Vicar of Chacombe, he forged several bank notes which swindled not only the local bank but the Vicar himself!

When he was finally caught, a whole string of offences were produced from throughout the 1840s and 50s. He was said to have obtained nearly

£800 from various assurance companies, in some cases giving, unbeknown to them, sureties of his wife's mother and his own mother which, of course, were all forged! Travelling to Lincoln at one point he had portrayed himself as a single man, telling people his wife was dead and on another occasion he was thought to have been orchestrating a scam involving documents containing forged signatures of both the Bishop of Oxford and Peterborough.

He was sentenced to 12 years penal service and was transported to Bermuda for several years. He later died in Dartmoor Prison in 1864 aged 50 of stomach cancer. Mr. Farquharson was lucky in the leniency of his punishment for a publication of the time wrote that "Perhaps, however, nothing did so much to excite the public feeling on the subject of capital punishments as the frequency of executions for forgery"!

Meanwhile his long suffering wife Sarah remained in Honiton where she was left financially comfortable from bequests from her parents, but sadly lost one of her two sons - Donald, aged 16 - in January 1862 when, in Honiton, he was accidently shot. Apparently, two children had somehow got hold of a musket and whilst playing with it, accidentally fired it and killed him.

Archibald Farquharson had died a criminal, losing all the respect and social standing from his former legitimate works. Apart from his ballads and poetry, Archibald Farquharson had left the world with nothing more than an estranged wife, a lot of out of pocket individuals and a son who would go on to continue the family disgrace, as well as draft a publication that Honiton would respect and applaud.

Richard Archibald Farquharson was born in Chelsea in 1840 and at the age of 18 enrolled in The South Wales, Borderers - 24th Regiment of Foot. It is during his time in the army he is thought to have met his first wife Henrietta Janet Buckley. Henrietta came from a good Derbyshire home: her father was the Rector of Hartshorne and she was educated with her two sisters by a French governess. Lord Barrington was once quoted to have said, whilst looking at a portrait of Henrietta's older sister that "the virtues and the traditionary beauty of the female branch of which, are represented in the subject of, the portrait now before us."

It does not seem, though, that Richard viewed his young bride with such enthusiasm. The couple were married in 1859 when Richard was 19 and Henrietta was 20 and within two weeks of the marriage Richard had been promoted to Lieutenant. Yet within one year of the marriage Henrietta had petitioned to divorce her husband. Divorce in 1860 - it probably does not need to be said - was exceptionally rare, especially at the instigation of the woman, and it had only been 3 years prior to her petition that divorce could only be completed by a private Act of Parliament! By 1857, only 322 divorces had been approved in Britain and that number had only risen to 369 by 1890: the majority of these were almost certainly petitioned by the husbands and not the wives. This was a time when a man could have his wife arrested and imprisoned or returned to him if she left him and women could not divorce their husbands on the sole grounds of adultery. If a married woman of this period wanted to divorce her partner she had to prove cruelty had been involved in the marriage and Richard Farquharson certainly gave his wife good grounds for that. According to the divorce petition, Richard had been adulterous with a number of prostitutes in Cork and Portsmouth and had visited at least four in the Haymarket area of London. He had also contracted gonorrhoea, which he had knowingly and willingly passed on to his wife who, at the time, had been several months pregnant with their first and only child. Their daughter was unsurprisingly born premature and died shortly afterwards. The divorce was successful and was undoubtedly an almost unprecedented event. The freedom from her adulterous and cruel husband did not bring Henrietta happiness for long: she remarried, had two further children, one of whom died at a few months old, and she herself sadly died in 1873 aged 39 when a ball gown she was wearing caught fire. However, her grandson, by her only surviving son, John Henry Revel Homfray, went on to become a Commander in the Royal Navy and was awarded an OBE in 1942.

Richard Archibald Farquharson, after his divorce, remarried 5 years later in 1865 to a Jessie Hooper, the daughter of a prosperous Exeter poulterer; by her he had 10 children and for a time in the 1860s moved back to Honiton where he lived with his mother. It was there in 1868 that he published his well-known local history book 'The History of Honiton' to which nearly every history book since concerning the town, makes reference. The book became a famous local work and this author would strongly recommend reading it, if a copy can be found, as it is quite a rare publication today. Mr. Farquharson remained married to his second wife for the rest of his days and seems to have enjoyed a comfortable and quiet existence, being the one surviving son and heir to his mother's fortune. He died in Surrey in 1912 aged 72. It is interesting, however, that despite devoting his 1868 publication to Miss Peggy Marsh, his "dear old friend", among the numerous bequests made to the people of the town, Richard's name was nowhere to be found in Miss Marsh's Will!

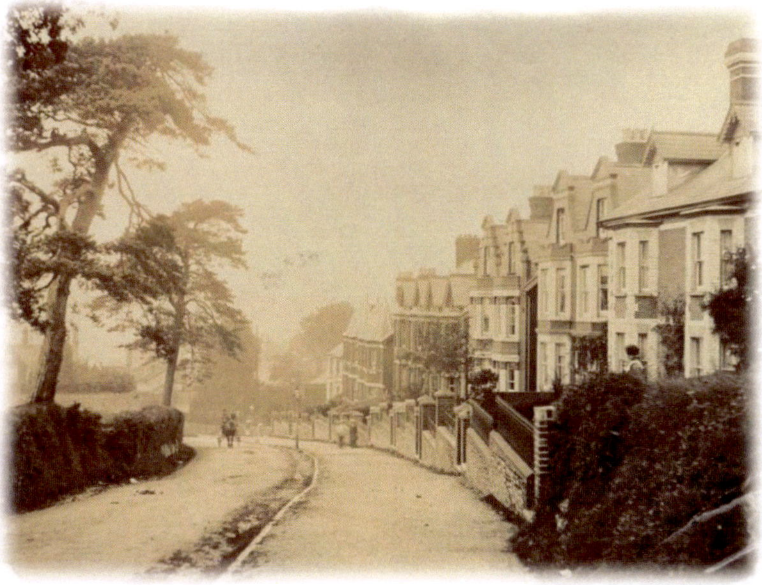

An early view looking down from Church Hill

Chapter 3
Silver Street, Northcote Lane & Dowell Street

"Smaller routes off the main highway.
Less main roads, more rural byways."
The Author

Silver Street

Silver Street, at this time, was a much less affluent area of the town. It was where a small group of artisans and general workers lived and died. A narrow lane, which up until the early 19th century was relatively rural, running a parallel tangent to the High Street and joining with Northcote Lane, many of the properties had only 3 or 4 rooms within them and yet they housed, in several cases, up to nine people! Farquharson described Silver Street as a "back slum" and wrote about the origins of its name...

"nearly every town in England has its Silver Street which is always the lowest quarters why this should be so remains unexplained."

Maria Clapp lived in Silver Street with her four children and elderly mother. Maria's maiden name was Pearcey and she had married her 76 year old husband when she was 22! Maria and her husband, Richard Clapp, who was a thatcher, were one of the first couples to marry in Honiton under the new Civil Registration laws. The couple had three sons and a daughter but poor Richard sadly died of old age before his last son, George, was even born. At the time of his death in 1845, Richard was, in fact, 11 years older than Maria's own mother, who by 1851 was lodging with them. The family presumably had a relatively poor existence after the death of Richard and Maria struggled to make a living as a lacemaker with four young children and a mother, aged nearly 80, who could no longer manage her former occupation as a laundress.

Sarah Hopping was an elderly widow living in Silver Street in 1851 and was listed in the census as a 'pauper', as was her elderly lodger. Previously there had been several Hopping families living next to each other. Sarah herself had married a William Hopping, a carpenter, but since his death finances became hard and by 1861 she was living solely on rent from lodgers. She died in 1865 aged 81.

Samuel Wood was born in Honiton in 1814 and for the majority of his life was a gardener. His wife, Elizabeth, was from Gittisham and worked as a servant. I mention this couple as two of their daughters, Lucy and Harriet, attended a lace school in the town and although it is known that young girls of the town attended such establishments, putting a name to the fact is rather rare. Samuel was born in Honiton, had ten children and died here in 1889. Eleanor, his eldest child, married a shoemaker and coincidentally set up home in King Street next door to a former childhood neighbour from Silver Street, Mr. Truman. His lacemaker daughter, Lucy, married a commissionaire and moved with him to London where they lived comfortably in Kensington.

Philip Wood, unknown whether related to the above family, was the youngest 'head of household' in town at the time at only 19 years old. He had probably been forced into marrying his bride, Ann Pratt, as she was already pregnant. His wife died in 1855, aged only 30, and four years later he remarried to Mary Ann Hunt. He supported his growing family as a shoemaker; however, he died at only 49, leaving his wife with seven young children.

William Rice was the only listed 'silver maker' in the town, ironically and appropriately living in Silver Street! William, maybe jealous of his neighbour Richard Clapp, also married a young girl 40 years his junior in 1841: William was 66 and his young bride was 26. He had already had eight children by his first wife, Ann, yet it seems that after her death he wished for a younger model! The marriage produced two children, a son Richard and a daughter Elizabeth, and as one may probably be able to guess, old age got the better of William and when his children were very young he died, in 1852. Even more sadly for his children was that their mother, Eliza, died only 6 years later in 1858. Richard, as a young man, was known to have got lodgings in Queen Street and became a brick maker. His younger sister, however, was not so fortunate; being only ten when both her parents had died, she ended up in the Union Workhouse.

In total there were 26 families living in Silver Street and including the above mentioned there was a total of 4 general labourers, a straw bonnet maker, 20 lace- makers, 2 paupers, 6 masons, 3 gardeners, 6 dressmakers and needlewomen, 4 laundresses, 5 bootmakers, 3 painters and glaciers, 3 carpenters, a coach painter, a slipper maker, a rope maker, a school mistress, 8 tailors, a silver maker, 2 housemaids, 2 butchers and 1 milliner. There was also a tannery that was founded in the mid 19th century run originally by brothers Martin and Edward Ashley, sons of a currier of Modbury. Martin died in 1852 and Edward, with his other brother John, ran the tannery for nearly 50 years. The Ashleys lived in the property that was once the bank of 'Flood & Lott' (107 High Street) and are believed to have moved in there after its failure. The family also owned 'The Glen' and, prior to Mr. Lilley, they had also offered the land to the local authorities, a proposal that was rejected over fears of high maintenance costs. The tannery was later demolished, presumably after the brothers died, and used as the site for the present day 'Newlands' which was built by Mr. E. A. Dodd. An old water wheel, once believed to have been used at the tannery, is currently located at Tracey Trout Farm after the old owners reclaimed it.

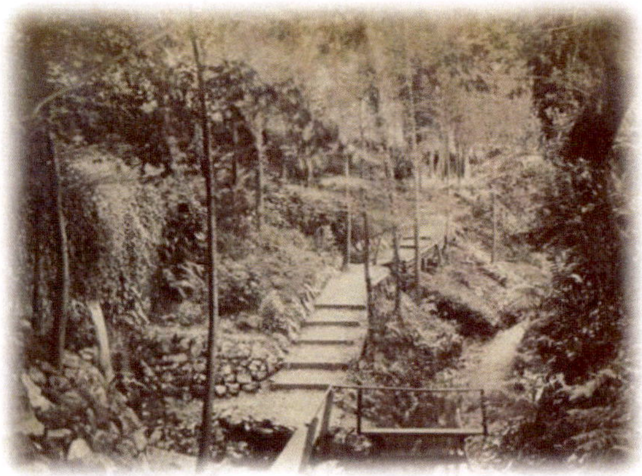

The Glen

Northcote Lane

Northcote Lane originally made up a crossroads in the middle of town: New Street led to London and Northcote lane ran to Cullompton. It was still a road accessible to cars right up until the early 1970s when it was pedestrianised. The road was named after the Northcote family who built a house on the south-east corner of Northcote Lane in 1720 and were once a very prominent family in the town. This property is now occupied by 'W. H. Smiths' and prior to its construction, Northcote Lane was obviously much wider. The last member of the family to reside in this property was a draper called Richard Northcote who was known locally as 'tenpenny dick' as "he held that was a fair days pay for a working man". The lane was also known to have been called 'Cowley Road' for a period in the late 19th century.

At the time, this lane was very short of residential lettings as the town technically ended at Cowley Farm which was once located at the Silver Street/Northcote Lane junction. Apart from Cowley Farm there were four aged families living here whose occupations included washerwomen, tin plate workers and lace-makers. *(For more on Cowley Farm see 'Farms and Fields').*

Dowell Street

Dowell Street, as with Northcote Lane, was named after a once- prominent Honiton family and was also similar to Northcote Lane in that it did not house many people. This road was also, as it is today, another exit from the town, heading towards Cullompton. A small collection of artisans, as well as some more affluent families, resided here.

John Rice was a postman living in Dowell Street with his wife and family. The existence on a postman's wages must have been hard for by 1851 one of his sons William, then 12, had been sent to work on Lowman's Farm, Honiton and another son, Joseph, aged 10, worked on a farm in Farway as a plough boy. As a plough boy, young Joseph could have expected to earn about one shilling a week! Joseph's life did, however, improve: he later joined the navy and sailed on HMS Iron Duke, experienced reasonable promotion and later married and became a railway signalman in Exeter. It seems from the records that John and his wife Hannah had the financial need to send most, if not all, of their children to work when they came of age; another child, Sarah Jane, worked as a servant in the butcher's shop (Hooks) that once stood on Dowell Street corner. This shop would be a butchers for the next hundred years or so until it was demolished as part of the road widening for Dowell Street.
At some point in the 1860s, John Rice had, unfortunately, become crippled yet still continued to work until his death aged 86, probably more through necessity than choice!

Nathaniel Pine lived next door to the Rices and was, by trade, an 'artificial fly maker'- a profession which involved making fishing tackle. He and his wife were certainly inventive when it came to their children's names: amongst their nine children was a Luke Hogarth Pine, a Thomas Youatt Pine and a Horatio Nelson Pine (Nathaniel must have been a fan!) Horatio certainly lived up to his name as far as travelling was concerned for he emigrated to New Zealand in the 1870s with his Honiton born wife, Mary Ann. Nathaniel's uncle was William Youatt (1776-1847) who was a Unitarian Minister at Honiton and a veterinary surgeon. Mr. Youatt became editor of the 'Vetinarian', a once popular journal, and wrote several works specifically on the dog but also the horse, ox and pig, which were held in high esteem and became text books for students of the day. Charles Darwin once said of him: "I have generally found Youatt an

accurate man, & a very sagacious man, for I knew him personally." He sadly died of a self -administered poison overdose in 1847.
The whole 'Pine' family had been established in Honiton for a number of generations and on Nathaniel's branch, the family had not moved more than 6 miles from Honiton since the 1400s.

The Pines' next door neighbour was a Thomas Carslake, a carpenter who unfortunately, like an earlier- mentioned individual, was disabled. In total, he and his wife had 13 children and miraculously his last child, Agnes, was born when his wife was 52! IVF was certainly not needed in those days! All the above individuals lived in a small 'cul-de-sac' type group of houses: a collection of 9 cottages in an L shape with gardens in front of their properties. These houses were situated literally opposite the old National School (now Honiton 1st Scout Group Headquarters). These cottages still stand today and rather than the once communal garden setup, each property now has their own. All these homes were once owned by Amy Lee, an elderly, wealthy resident of the town. Amy Lee was thought to have been the lady known to many as 'Nancy Lee' who was born into a wealthy Cotleigh family and at a young age ran away with the gypsies, touring the country fairs and living a life of travel and merriment. She was also said to have lived under the protection of the Prince of Wales, who took a shine to her "great beauty". On her return to Honiton she was said to have become mistress of 'The School of Industry' that was once located in a small cottage not far from Summerland Place. She died in Honiton in 1848 aged 86.

At the top of Dowell Street, on the corner of New Street, stood a butchers shop (in which Mr. Rice's daughter once worked). The rear of this property, consisting, in part, of the slaughter house, extended into Dowell Street and was demolished in the 20th century in the interest of widening the road. In the early 1990s, one could see a brightly coloured fish painted on one of the existing walls where this shop once stood. This fish was painted by Honiton Primary School pupils in the early 1990s but has long since disappeared.

Living in the property to the left of the 'blue plaqued' police station lived Charles Golesworthy. Mr. Golesworthy was the senior member of a family of stonemasons who had resided in Honiton for several generations. A few doors down from him (at what is now 16 Dowell Street) lived one of his sons, Joseph, who was also a stonemason: he was the last of four generations to work as a stonemason from this address. This cottage can easily be found - a stone plaque situated on the front reads 'Golesworthy' (fitted about 1840): this property is still known as 'Golesworthy Cottage'. Another member of the family, another Charles, worked from a thatched cottage near to the old police station: the cottage in question was demolished when the present police station was built.

The Golesworthys worked in the town throughout the 19th century: many started as masons but diversified later in life, with one becoming a bricklayer, another a plasterer and one even becoming Sexton of St. Michael's - he lived in the cottage not far from the Lynch Gate. The family are known to have worked on Lord Sidmouth's house at Upottery and Monkton Village Church. The last Golesworthy known to practise as a stone mason in the town was Joseph's son, William Harward Golesworthy, who was still working in Dowell Street until about 1910.

The town 'Relieving Officer' of the day also lived in Dowell Street. This gentleman was called William Gayler and he would have been responsible for all applications for poor relief and was the issuer of orders for those to be admitted to the workhouse. A rather precarious place to be living, I would presume, considering the majority of Dowell Street's inhabitants were poorly paid workers such as washerwomen and bricklayers. Mr. Gayler could have expected to earn about £61 a year, which was a moderate wage for the time, probably putting him in the lower/ middle class bracket.

His son James, who once worked at the Union Workhouse as a porter, went on to continue in his father's position until the late 1870s.

The police house was situated in Dowell Street at this time and the town's only policeman was John Treby. John had started his working life as a blacksmith and then became a police superintendant at Honiton in the late 1840s. The property that was once the police house can easily be found with the blue plaque attached to the front. The studded door to the right of the property used to lead to the cells. Mr. Treby was only in the town for a short time but spent the rest of his life as a police officer. His children lived colourful lives: his son, Robert, emigrated to America where he became a farmer, another son, Thomas, first emigrated to Australia and then, in 1913, to Canada and thence to America. His youngest son, Samuel, also emigrated to America where he lived with brother Robert for a short time; he later became a teacher, a lawyer and then an instructor at a Seattle branch of the Y.M.C.A. John's last child, Henry, was the only one who stayed in the country and followed in his father's footsteps: he went on to become an Inspector in London.

Chapter 4
King Street, Queen Street & Summerland Place

"Roads named after a Royal visit of yore
But were not so regal, those homes of the poor."
The Author

King Street

Two of Honiton's back streets, King Street and Queen Street, were named in honour of the visit of King George III and his wife in 1789; however, on maps around that time, King Street was named 'Hind Street' or 'Back Lane'. This was literally because of its position in relation to the town. It would have probably have been built in medieval times as a separation of the rear of the properties of the High Street and the farmlands beyond allowing access to the fields for farmers. King Street was a kind of industrial estate, typical of the town at this time, and probably due to its parallel course with the Gissage. Along its stretch there were breweries, working blacksmiths, masons and carpenters, a tannery, the gas works, a brick makers and the iron foundry.

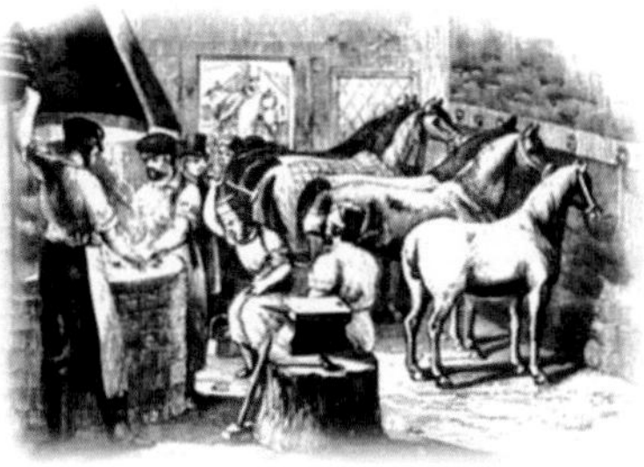

William Letten was a carpenter and builder with several employees and was another of the town's well known builders who built 'Letten's Buildings'- today 'St John's Close'. His workshop once stood on a site situated to the right of the present day 'Homelace House'.

William Holway was one of King Street's three maltsters. The process of beer making was exceptionally important to rural communities at this time, as William Cobbett wrote in 'Cottage Economy' in 1826:

"In former times, to set about to show Englishmen that it was good for them to brew beer in their houses would have been as impertinent as gravely to insist, that they ought to endeavour not to lose their breath; for those times (only forty years ago), to have a [house] and not to brew was a rare thing indeed. Mr. Ellman, an old man and a large farmer, in Sussex, has recently given in evidence, before a Committee of the House of Commons, this fact: that, [forty years ago], there was not a labourer in his

parish that did not [brew his own beer]; and that now, there is [not one that does it], except by chance the malt be given to him...These have quite changed the customs of the English people as to their drink. They still drink beer, but, in general, it is brewing of [common brewers], and in public houses, of which the common brewers have become the owners, and have...obtained a [monopoly] in the supplying of the great body of the people with one of those things, which to a hard-working man, is almost a necessity of life."

William Holway's son, John, remained loyal to the family's love of alcohol (!) by becoming landlord of the Anchor Inn for some 20 years

John Thorn was another of the town's maltsters, working from a site right behind the present day cottages of Crown Court. From this locality, it is highly probable he was the supplier of beer to the old 'Crown and Sceptre Inn' which once stood at the bottom of Crown Court. One son, William, went on to become a groom in the Royal Artillery.

Charles Materface was the town's only listed 'gun smith' and 'bell hanger'; he was born in Taunton and moved to Honiton with his parents at some point before 1823. Charles was also a member of the 1st Exeter and South Devon Volunteer Rifle Corps from 1853. His father, John, was a whitesmith and in an early directory was listed as a 'smoke jack & oven manufacturer'. John Materface lived and worked in the High Street; sadly for him, next door to the Inland Revenue Officer! Charles himself lived and worked in the town for some 30 years, providing guns for the local farmers and country gentry until his death in 1874.

James Marshall and his family lived in a small cottage, long since demolished, that once stood at the base of the hill now leading to Millhead Road (opposite the top of Mill Lane). Before his death, James was an agricultural labourer and his wife Elizabeth was a midwife. The couple's daughter, another Elizabeth, married a local man called Richard Brown and with her husband had twelve children. Richard and Elizabeth remained with the elderly Mrs. Marshall until she died and later moved to Crown Court. Interestingly, which obviously modern day health and safety would not permit, Richard Brown's oldest son, at the age of ten, was working in the iron foundry as an apprentice 'iron moulder'!

Richard Copplestone Wheaton also worked at the iron foundry and was the son of the former landlord of the Golden Lion, previously one of

Honiton's most premier inns. Richard would later go on to move his family to Exeter where he, in later life, became a clerk: strange occupation change from his former career.

Richer residents of King Street were James and Jane Minifie, who were the parents of the aforementioned Richard Minifie (the baker) and Jane Lee (wife of William Lee the builder). After James' death, Jane inherited her husband's properties, a total of 6 cottages, and lived off the rent she received with her widowed daughter, Elizabeth Channon. After Jane's death Elizabeth moved to Kensington with her daughter where she died aged 94. Elizabeth's daughter, Mary Elizabeth Channon, graduated from the South Kensington School of Art and went on to teach the subject at The National Art Training School, one of only two females to have accomplished this at the time. Mary herself never married and resided with her mother until she died; she then lodged with friends in Kensington, where she died in 1900. The name Minifie is a rare name, originating from the West Country, first recorded as this spelling in Honiton in 1563. The name is thought to have been derived from one of the estimated 8,000 villages which were lost in England through land clearance during the 11th and 12th century.

Tanning was one of the main businesses in King Street during this period and the street's tanners were, in 1851, William Carter and Richard P. Harrison. Mr. Carter's wife was one of the town's only listed 'stay maker' or corset maker. Corsets were one of the Victorian ladies' most important items of clothing as the tight fitting fashions of the era demanded as thin a waistline as possible. Some women were so conscious of this that there were known examples of bodices being as small as 17 inches!
The large tan works that once covered over ¼ of an acre, on the corner of Mill Street, had been run earlier by Thomas Beed and Mr. Darke, currently occupied, partly, by 'Halse of Honiton'. Richard Harrison was the new manager of the tannery by the early 1850s and ran it for the next 30 years and was known, at one point, to have had 9 employees.
Tanning was a messy, laborious process; it started with the washing of the skin to remove the blood, which would have discoloured the finished leather. This would have probably been undertaken in the Gissage. The hide then had to be left somewhere warm so that the remaining hair and flesh would rot, after which it would be immersed in a solution of lime in order to loosen the offending material. After the solution had done its work a 'beamsman' would stretch the skin over a beam and remove the loosened flesh from the hide with a sharp knife. Nothing from this process

would be wasted; the hair would be sold to upholsterers and the flesh would be made into glue. The hide would then be 'clean' but would still be full of lime and although some hides could simply be washed and wrung, some, such as kid hides, were too delicate for this which led to one of the most unpleasant parts of the processing...

"the absorption of the lime in the afore-mentioned process makes the skins hard and thick; to render them supple, and prepare them for receiving the tan liquor, they are thrown into a pit called the poke, or mastering-pit, which contains a quantity of putrescent dung diffused in water: the dung of dogs, pigeons, or sea-fowl, is preferred for this purpose, that from cows and horses not being sufficiently powerful...When the skins have become perfectly soft, they are taken out of the putrescent pit, and cleansed on the beam, when they are ready for tanning."

It was only now that the process of 'tanning' could begin: ground oak bark was soaked in a water solution for various lengths of time, up to several weeks in some cases, in order to make a variety of different strength tanning solutions. The limed, dunged hides would then be placed in the solutions in a progression from the weakest to strongest solution of tanning. This was the final part of the process that could take anything up to nine months to complete. The skins would then be washed, rubbed (to remove any bloom), and then oiled to prevent drying, finally being passed on to the 'currier'.

Apart from Mr. Harrison, there was only one currier residing in King Street. "The business of the currier [was] to prepare hides which have been under the hands of the tanner, for the use of the shoe-makers, coach makers, saddlers, bookbinders, &c." This highly skilled job required a steady hand in 'skiving' the hide with an exceptionally sharp blade to reduce the overall thickness of the leather, as was required for its proposed usage, without, of course, piercing it. The currier's task also entailed polishing, softening and oiling the finished product before it went to its prospective buyers.

There was believed to be a tannery in Honiton, pre-dating the above mentioned, which was run by a John Saunders, as early as 1736. All that is known of this tannery is that the gentleman in question did much business with many local families and obtained the wood, for the tanning process, from Penscombe Woods, located near Wolford Lodge.

There were also many employees of Mr. Ward's coach building business living in this road; there were six in total, including a coach wheeler, two coach smiths, a coach builder and a coach spring maker who had one employee.

Queen Street

Described in the late 1700's as a 'back slum' it, like King Street, was named in honour of George III and his Queen's visit to the town. Ironically, this street has little reason to be named so, for George III was never brought down this usual route for travellers from London (from the Copper Castle, down what is now Pine Park Road and into Queen Street) as due to its poor reputation, the King was escorted down what is now Kings Road instead. Prior to being called Queen Street it was, in fact, called Warwick Lane, possibly due to its locality on the old Fosse Way which ran to Warwick, but the real reasons are unknown.
Mainly consisting of late 18th century houses, Queen Street was indeed a poor area of the town; the people residing here were poor labourers, washerwomen and a handful of artisans.

The Hooper family were a good example of this poor existence: Charles Hooper was an 86 year old former mason who was now deemed a pauper due to his inability to work, despite the fact he had worked well into his 70s. Charles died in poverty at the age of 88 and his widow, after her husband's death, still had the responsibility of a young daughter. George Hooper, their son, moved to a property near his elderly mother and supported his growing family as a 'scavenger', which was a road cleaner - not much better than it sounds!

Samuel Lake was a 52 year old agricultural labourer from Colyton living with his wife Elizabeth, a laundress, and his children. Samuel Lake was the grandfather of Joseph Lake, the first in a long line of Honiton's Town Criers. Samuel's son, John, worked as a gardener in the town and lived in King Street and it was his son, Joseph Lake, who was the first to hold the local title. Joseph Lake was Honiton Town Crier from 1903 until the time of his death in 1926. His son, Joseph John Lake, then succeeded him in 1927. Joseph John resigned in 1962 due to ill heath and subsequently died 5 years later in 1966. From then on Joseph's son, 'Tommy' Lake, held the position until 1975 after which, Joe's other son, and Tommy's brother, Samuel Joseph John (Joe) Lake, held the title until he reluctantly retired in 1996 due to heart problems. Joe Lake had hoped his own son would continue the tradition but having since moved away from the town the 'glove' finally fell from the Lake family's hands after nearly a century! Since Mr. Lake's retirement the position of Town Crier has been held by local man, David Retter. Samuel (Joe) Lake, himself, died in 1998 aged 71.

A very politically un-correct entry in the census return of Queen Street appears in the household of John Maddock, an ostler, and his family. His son, Francis Maddock was a 24 year old man whose occupation was listed as "nothing/weak of intellect"!

Queen Street was also the residence of Honiton's only listed 'colt breaker': a man who would tame young horses to enable them to pull carts or coaches.

Roughly where 'The Old Saddlery' now is, stood a small group of seven houses called 'Queen Square', owned by Robert Aberdein, which backed onto his home and offices in New Street. The present group of newly built houses, now situated on this spot, coincidently closely resembles the original property plan: prior to the current houses stood a small group of industrial units, including a garage.
Between Queen Square and Summerland Place stood the extensive gardens of Mr. Woodgates' Academy.
Queen Street was probably the poorest part of Honiton, for in this collection of fifty three families there were 10 'paupers' and 4 handicapped individuals, leading to an almost 1:4 ratio of people unable to work through either physical/mental incapacity or simply being too old. This was a much higher proportion per household than any other part of the town at the time.

<u>Summerland Place</u>
Summerland Place, built in 1839 on the site of the old workhouse, was a collection of eight affluent households situated off the oppositely poor residents of Queen Street.
The following lived in the properties of Summerland in 1851:

1. John Porter; an auctioneer, his wife, daughter and a house servant lived in No. 1 Summerland which had formerly been the residence of Richard Pople, father-in-law of Archibald W. S. Farquharson. One of his daughters married a solicitor's clerk, John Downton, and in 1851 they lived next to Ruth Tooze. The couple later moved to London where John became a civil servant in the Indian Office.
2. Sarah Kenward; a widow living with her daughter, son-in-law and servant. Her son-in-law was William Hann Pine, the father of Nathaniel Pine of Dowell Street.

3. An elderly widow called Charlotte Hill, who was a retired farmer's wife from Milton Damerell, who lived there with a 74 year old relative who was an annuitant.
4. Empty
5. Empty
6. Empty
7. Peter Richards; an 84 year old retired farmer, who had formerly run Little Hale Farm, living with his wife and two unmarried daughters.
8. Thomas Guppy; a bank accountant living with his young family and two house servants. This property stands just off New Street and the small private road that connects New Street to Queen Street now runs through the former garden of this property.

Thomas Guppy was the son of the former headmaster of the British School and was a member of the Independent Chapel Congregation, becoming the treasurer in 1852. Despite his affluent career, this could not stop tragedy falling upon him in 1855 when he lost all three of his children, all under the age of five, in a space of only six days; "each burial taking place before the next death." Maybe not surprisingly, he left Honiton shortly afterwards and moved to Barnstaple where he became an alderman and JP; he died there in 1890. Thomas went on to have three more children - Marietta, Henry and Alice: Marietta married the Baptist Minister of Chard, Henry remained in Barnstaple where he married and followed in his father's footsteps into the bank and Alice never married and lived with her mother until her death in 1906. Thomas Guppy's brother, Alfred Guppy, was once a solicitor in New Street (already mentioned).

Shortly past Summerland place, going up Queen Street, roughly opposite the present Railway Inn, the road once broke into two branches: the main road continued up what is now Pine Park Road toward the Copper Castle and subsequently London and the second continued extending south, through the property now called 'Rose Cottage', into a footpath which led to the Old Rectory (now 'Old Rectory Farm'). This footpath ran through two fields; the first called 'Goyle' and the second 'Madam Fords Close'. The footpath would later have the railway go straight through the middle of it but managed to survive and later became 'The Glen'. Today this pleasant, wooded walk is quite different from its original open country atmosphere, now being an enclosed, wooded narrow park sandwiched between housing estates.

Chapter 5
The Lanes

"Collections of cottages, these hidden thoroughfares.
Would thoust notice them, unless thou lived there?"
The Author

Like many country towns, Honiton had many lanes that housed poor workers and labourers. This is a list and breakdown of the lanes that were in Honiton in mid 19th century:

- *Channons Court*: a small collection of 10 cottages that still stand today on the north side of the High Street, not far from the Gissage. The head of household occupations include: labourers, shoemakers, tailors, masons and carpenters.
- *Diggories Lane*: at this time it was only occupied by one family whose head profession was a bricklayer. It still exists today but has enlarged since the mid 19th century. It is to be found near the Gissage, once again.
- *Wonds Court*: a collection of 9 cottages that once stood on the site now occupied by 'Halse of Honiton', next to 'Minifies Court'. Both Minifies and Wonds Court stood opposite the entrance to Channons Court. This court was once the home of the first Honiton iron founder, James White.
- *Minifies Court*: it also once stood on the site now occupied by 'Halse of Honiton': a small court of 5 cottages which once backed onto Wonds Court. They obtained their name from their owner's family, James Minifie of King Street (previously mentioned). Within the court lived a couple called James and Amelia Livermore, who had strangely adopted a baby girl Emma Berry. Strange, because the couple were both 71 at the time of her adoption. It is, sadly, believed that the entire family had passed away by 1861.
- *Bonds College/Bonds Court*: now known as 'Bonds Cottages' which runs down an alleyway next to the present day Honiton Conservative Club. It consisted of 9 properties occupied by, once again, poor labourers
- *Floods Court*: used to stand behind what is now 'Lees Buildings': a small collection of cottages which were named after their owner Harriet Flood, an elderly woman who lived just off the Court.

- *Jennings College*: once situated virtually opposite the site of the old Crown and Sceptre Inn. The 'college' of three cottages had disappeared by the 1850s and was named after its owner, a Samuel Jennings, who lived in the court and was a blacksmith.
- *Banfields College*: a small court next to Jennings College and was owned by a John 'Banfield'.
- *Porters College*: once again located right next to the above two mentioned lanes; owned by a James 'Porter' who was then the landlord and owner of the Lamb Inn. No records exist of this lane post 1844.
- *Stamps College*: a group of houses owned by Edmund Stamp, the attorney, the lane was once located between the fourth and fifth properties west of Dowell Street. This lane ceased to appear on any records after the 1840s.
- Long Acre: little is known about this back street. It was home to some 8 families and stood somewhere between the old Crown and Sceptre and Fountain Inn on King Street. It had disappeared from the records by 1851.
- *Crown and Sceptre Yard*: also known as 'Crown and Sceptre Court' and 'Crown Passage' this row of workers' cottages, believed to be made of 'cob', were named after the old Crown and Sceptre Inn that stood at the top of the alley. The Court still exists today, now known as simply 'Crown Court'; originally consisting of 11 houses, all of which were owned by the pub's owner, James Churchill (previously mentioned), now only a handful remain with many of the former premises now being the site of a carpark and new developments.
- *Lees Buildings*: the lane itself still exists but the 20 properties that once stood there do not. Originally, these were a row of small, front gardened cottages, '2 up, 2 down', named and once owned by the Lee family (one of whom built St Paul's Church) who constructed them. There was also once a 'Lees Court' located not far from 'Minifies Court'.
- *Kerslakes Court*: formerly known as 'Bussells' and 'Glanvilles', it came into the possession of Robert Kerslake in 1766 and thus obtained its present name. His son, Thomas, had a soap boiling factory here which later became the malthouse of Albion Davey. The majority of the court was once the home and gardens of the Kerslakes; however, a few tenements were inhabited by other individuals. At the bottom of the court there was one property

called 'Mystle Cottage'. Later sections of the court were bought off and rebuilt which was said to have "destroyed the pretty old world enclosure" of the court. Due to its previously "isolated" and "hidden" location, it was a meeting point for members of the Whig party prior to elections and, up until about 1870, there was a passage from the court that led to the High Street - this was lost in the reconstruction. This was not a poor area: in 1851 only retired individuals lived here.

- *Fountains Yard*: a collection of 4 homes behind the old Fountain Inn, all of which were owned by the Fountain's landlady, Eleanor Newton.
- *Swan Yard*: another collection of homes behind one of Honiton's pubs: the yard still exists, though is now developed. The pub, sadly, does not.
- *Vine Passage*: still in existence today, this passage runs down to the present day Vine Inn. In the 1850s there were 8 properties besides The Vine itself.
- *Black Lion Drang*: this was the former name of 'Chapel Street' before the construction of the Methodist chapel from which the lane got its current name. 'Drang' is an old Devonian name for 'lane' and within this 'drang' stood 9 properties, the majority of which ran parallel to New Street. It was named after 'Black Lion Field', on which the properties were built, and the field was, presumably, named after the Black Lion Inn. It is likely, yet not confirmed, that the Inn owned the original field.
- *Angel Yard*: once stood behind the old Angel Hotel and has now been developed into 'Angel Mews'. It was home to only one family in 1851.
- *Lettens Buildings*: now known as 'St John's Court', the earlier buildings here were built by the Lettens, a local family.
- *Kings Arms Yard*: 6 houses that stood behind the old Kings Arms Inn and now known as 'Kings Arms Cottages'. All of these properties were owned by Christopher Flood. Opposite these houses were once the old Kings Arms stables and gardens.
- *Darkes Passage*: presently the small alley that stands next to the Independent Chapel and which leads to the Carlton Inn and adjacent properties' car park. These 6 cottages were collectively owned by James Darke, from whom they got their name. James Darke himself occupied the site now known as 'Honiton Antique Toys' as well as a small dwelling at the top of Darkes Passage,

which has long since been demolished. The passage continued beyond the houses to a small plot which the residents used for gardens and is now occupied by the flats of 'Westcott Way'. James Darke is thought to have been a brother of Peter Darke, the potter. Incidentally, 'The Orchard', near Westcott Way, is thought to have got its name from an orchard that once stood behind the Independent Chapel.

- *Clapper Lane:* this lane, back in the mid 19th century, was significantly smaller than today. Named after 'Clapper Bridge' which in more ancient times would have been a primitive crossing of no more than several long slabs of stone.

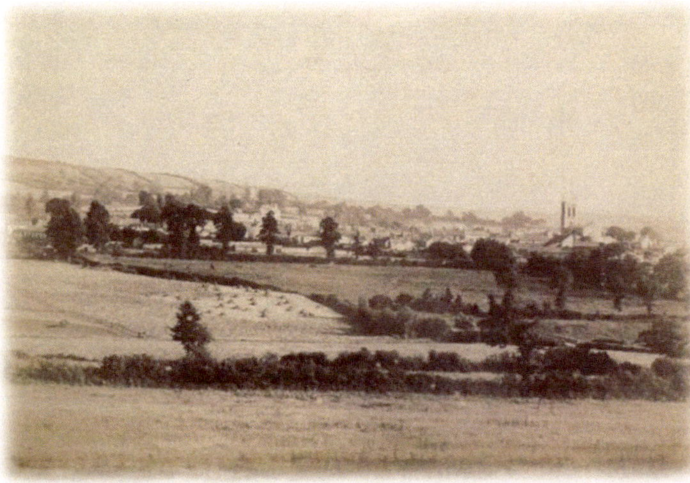

View of Honiton, including Clapper Lane, from the Combe Raleigh Road. The field opposite the one containing haystacks is now part of the site of Honiton Primary School.

In total there were only three properties. Elm Terrace was built in the 1880s which increased the number of residents in this once rural lane.

- *Banfields Passage:* a small court, just off the top of Clapper Lane, which was home to a mere two separate properties. The majority of the homes on these two lanes were on long term leases from Honiton Manor to Christopher Flood, the local banker.

Chapter 6
Town's Ends

"The end of town, beyond which open countryside lay
Where weary travellers view grazing sheep and stacks of hay."
The Author

Kings Road

The High Street ended with Bramble Hill to the west and Holyshute House to the East; Kings Road, only later, consisted of several, rurally situated 'villas' and there were a small number of large homes for the richer members of Honiton society situated in the surrounding town outskirts. This section looks at the dwellings where the more affluent residents of the town lived, retired and worked.

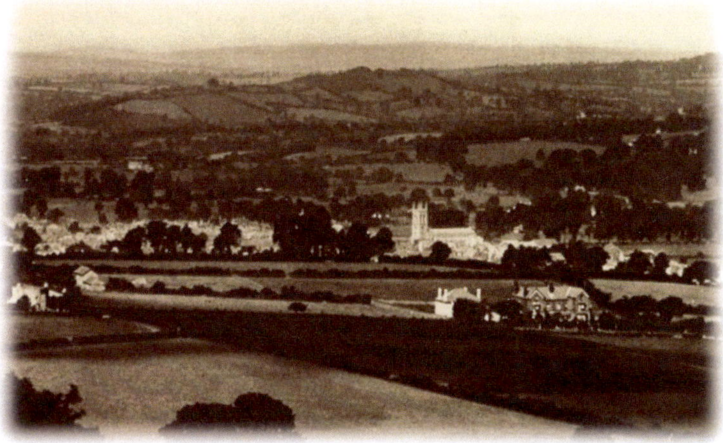

Kings Road prior to twentieth century developments. The two properties (central right) are today 'Adelaide Lodge' and Sunningdale House'.

Holyshute House: a regal Georgian building that was named after the 'Holyshute Spring' located not far from the building. The spring itself was once a long established site frequented by invalids for its alleged medicinal powers. In the 1840s this house was situated in over ¾ acre of grounds surrounded by about 15 acres of fields that also belonged to the owner. There was also a sizeable lake situated behind the house, which was

presumably used for boating. The house still retains much of its own grounds but the surrounding fields have all been built on and are now occupied by 'Langford Road' and 'The Chase'.
One of the building's earliest residents was a Mr. Elliott, a landowner and gentleman. He lived there for well over 20 years up until the 1860s when it was bought by a retired army Captain, John Swann. From the 1880s, the house was owned by a local solicitor, William Every, who was an early partner in 'Everys' solicitors of today. Mr. Every lived there until his death in 1906 when it was then bought by Henry Leslie Rundle, a partner in another local law firm 'Dunning, Rundle & Stamp.' Mr. Rundle remained at Holyshute until his death in 1942. Hoylshute today is still a private residence located on Monkton Road.

Marwood House: built by the son of the famous Honitonian doctor who was physician to Elizabeth I. Thomas Marwood, who died in 1617 aged 105, left four children, two sons and two daughters. It was his second eldest son, John, who, in 1619, built this "pleasant Jacobean mansion" where Charles I twice stayed whilst on a journey to and from Exeter in 1644. Thomas Marwood rose to eminence after curing the Earl of Essex from an illness, after which Elizabeth I granted him an estate near Honiton. John Marwood built Marwood House, originally called 'The Great House', for his son on a plot of land he had bought from a gentleman from Monkton in 1616.

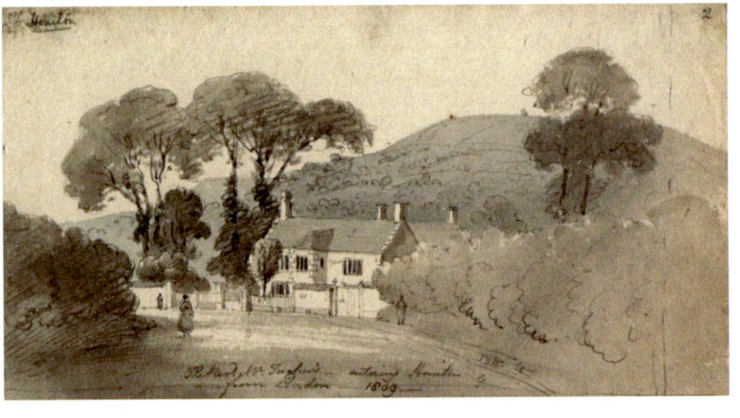

Over the large oak door in the porch once stood a marble tablet reading 'Thomas Marwood, Physician to Queen Elizabeth'. Another Latin texted stone panel, presiding over the mantel in the dining room, read 'John Marwood, Physician to King James'.

From the time Thomas Marwood settled in Honiton, in the late 16th century, his descendants would establish themselves as members of a respectable and wealthy local family; at the time of this book's setting, they had branched out into several of the surrounding parishes...

"The Devon Marwoods descend from a line which includes Dr Thomas Marwood of Honiton who lived from c.1512 to 1617 and gained great repute locally as a physician as well as practising for a time at the court of Elizabeth I. His grandson, also Thomas, was also an eminent physician and between them they founded a family which was sufficiently affluent to establish themselves as landed proprietors of substance in the Honiton and Colyton areas of Devon. The Marwood estates were partitioned in 1811 between the sisters (or their heirs) of James Thomas Benedictus Marwood, great great grandson of the first Dr Thomas, who died without issue. One of these sisters, Frances, had married Edward Elton, and her son, James Marwood Elton, inherited both her portion of the Marwood estates and a portion of the Elton estates. His son, Edward, who assumed the name Marwood Elton and was created a baronet in 1838, acquired the manor of Widworthy, part of the original Marwood holdings, from a descendant of another of the sisters of James Thomas Benedictus Marwood, and concentrated on building up the Widworthy estate in the parishes of Widworthy, Offwell and Dalwood."

Edward Marwood-Elton's seat was Widworthy Court, on the outskirts of Offwell, which today is a complex of luxury apartments. Edward bought Widworthy Manor (Widworthy Court) from the Rev. Harry Far Yeatman and his wife Sarah in 1833 and for the rest of his life expanded and consolidated the Widworthy Court Estate. He held the office of Deputy Lieutenant (D.L.), was invested as a Queen's Counsel (Q.C.) and held the office of High Sheriff of Devon in 1858. On Edward's death in 1884, being one of four unmarried brothers, all of whom pre-deceased him, his baronetcy became extinct.

By the 18th century, Marwood House had come into the possession of James Marwood, who consequently sold the property to his nephew, John William Tucker, for the grand sum of £356 19s. J. W. Tucker is the gentleman already mentioned who was a relative of Edward Ford. This Mr. Marwood died in 1830, aged 88, and childless, the house finally slipped out of the family's hands.

By the 1840s, the house was owned by Herman James Lott who was a Honiton banker. The house had several owners over the next few decades, including a curate of the town, the Rev. Thomas Izod, who resided there in 1878. After Mr. Izod, the Stevens family acquired the property. Widowed Deborah Stevens had moved her family to Honiton in the late 1870s where she lived with her three unmarried daughters, and for a time, another married daughter and her family.

Mr. And Mrs. Charles Stevens had previously been missionaries who were part of a group of people, led by the once well known Rev. John Williams, who set out, in 1838, for the Polynesian Islands to spread the word of God; in fact the Stevens' first son was born whilst they were sea bound. The couple's first child died and Charles' health also failed, forcing the young couple back to England less than three years later. Mr. Stevens' poor health, quite possibly and ironically, saved his life for his leader, Rev. Williams and a fellow missionary, were captured and eaten by cannibals in 1839! Mr. Stevens himself later became a 'general merchant' before his health finally got the better of him.

In 1881, Mrs. Stevens, residing in Honiton, had a total of 11 children and grandchildren living with her, as well as three servants! Charles' and Deborah's family were certainly of some substance: one of their children, John Foster Stevens, who had gone into the colonial army, went on to be knighted and was awarded the Knight Commander of the Star of India. Another son, Charles Cecil Stevens, studied at the University of Melbourne where he, interestingly, became the seventeenth person to matriculate in the colony of Victoria! After obtaining an education, he also went into the Colonial Army where he achieved similar success to his brother, being appointed Chief Secretary to the Bengal Government and finally Lieutenant-Governor of Bengal in 1897-8. Charles also briefly lived in Honiton at Broomhills House, now St Ritas.

The remainder of Mrs. Stevens' children led more down to earth lives. One son, Frederick H. Stevens, graduated from Oxford University and became a maths teacher at Bristol where he co-wrote several mathematical text books, one of which, titled "A School Arithmetic", was reprinted 17 times between 1908 and 1961; some of my readers may remember studying from it!

Daughter, Hannah, married a Robert Cornish who, incidentally, was the actual owner of Marwood House, leasing it to his mother-in-law on an annual basis. Robert lived in Axminster and was a Justice of the Peace.

After Deborah died in 1908, her unmarried daughters continued to live at the house until the oldest sister, Fanny Stevens, died in 1927, by which

time the house had been home to the family for some 45 years. On Fanny's death the house was bought by a Mr. Francis Cottrell.
There was, apparently, once a secret passage in the house that Mrs. Stevens had bricked up for the safety of her grandchildren: two of her granddaughters, during their stays there, claimed to have been visited by a ghostly figure - that of a small boy who was well known to many residents of the town!
It is known that the house was restored at least once in 1828 and was later "modernised" in 1930. When bought by a Mr. Hawkins in 1948, for £8,500, it was listed as having a total of three acres of land, two of which were paddocks. The old stables were where the antique centre now is. This Grade II* listed house stands at the bottom of Kings Road and is still a private residence.
The large property opposite Marwood House, 'Crosslyn', was built to replicate this ancient dwelling by local builder, Mr. Dodd, in the early twentieth century.
There was once a 300 year old cork tree in the grounds which was rumoured to have been planted by Sir Walter Raleigh! This tree was sadly lost in a storm on February 28th 1937.

Adelaide Lodge: built towards the end of the 19th century, this house was originally known as 'The Hill House' and later 'Kingslea'. The property's first resident was thought to be Henry Leslie Rundle before he moved to 'Holyshute'. By 1906 it had come into the possession of Cyril Neville Tweed, the town clerk and solicitor. By the 1920s, one of the Matthews brothers, of the town's ironmongers, was residing there. It later became the two star 'Kingslea Hotel' and in 1995 became the care home of 'Adelaide Lodge' (presently located in Kings Road).

Sunningdale House: also built in the late 19th century. One of the house's earliest residents was Charles Harding who ran a drapery and tailoring business in the shop now occupied by Specsavers (121 High Street). The house was originally known as 'Oak Lodge' and after Mr. Harding left, it became the home of Rev. Richard Seymour, son of the Vicar of Barnstaple, who was curate of St Paul's and Chaplain to the Union Workhouse. Mr. Seymour was also a great grandson of Hugh Fortescue, 1st Earl Fortescue (1753-1841). The house, just like Kingslea, later became a six bedroom hotel and then a nursing home called Sunningdale House (presently located in Kings Road).

Dowell Street

Elmfield House: in this Grade II listed Georgian property, which was, until recently, Honiton Registry Office and the Thelma Hubert gallery, lived the Gidley family.

Lewis Gidley lived here with his wife Frances and their five children. Lewis Gidley was from a highly successful and reputable Devon family who had bought the estate of Gidleigh in Devon in the 17th century. His Gidley ancestors included a Colonel, who had held a commission for the Royalists in the English Civil War, a surgeon to Queen Anne, along with a great uncle, Bartholomew Gidley who had, coincidently, served on the HMS Hampshire with another of Honiton's great heroes, George Blagdon Westcott! Another Bartholomew Gidley, a great grandfather of Lewis, was a godson of William III and there is also strong evidence to suggest the Gidleys of Honiton were descended from a sister of Robert de Mortain, the first Lord of the Manor of Honiton after the Norman Conquest!

Lewis's grandfather, Robert, had been a local solicitor and played a key role in finding and securing the 'Wolford Estate' in Dunkeswell for John Graves Simcoe and, subsequently, the establishment of 'Wolford Lodge' where the entire Simcoe family are interred. If it had not been for Robert Gidley's involvement, Wolford Lodge would have probably never been built! Robert was also highly regarded for his management of 'The Charities of Honiton' which, until his intervention in 1760, had "been much neglected." Robert Gidley married a niece of the Lord of the Manor, Thomas Courtenay, in 1745 and through this marriage managed to secure a piece of the Manor estate, Middle Hills Farm, which was still in the Gidley family until the early 20th century.

Robert's son, and Lewis's father, Courtenay Gidley, carried on Robert's position as steward of The Honiton Charities and became the town clerk. This Mr. Gidley was the gentlemen who had the task of writing to Mr. Courtenay informing him of the damage caused to his property by the great fire of 1765.

Lewis Gidley was also town Portreeve in 1831 and clerk to the Honiton Turnpike Trust. Lewis Gidley died in 1841 and his widow Frances remained at Elmfield House until her death in 1853. The family owned several properties in the town, including Middle Hills Farm and a 2 acre field called 'Streamers Meadow'. Although Streamers Meadows still exists today, it is a small reflection of its former self for it has mostly been built on; that which does remain houses the Honiton Bowling Club and a recreational area but is mainly used as a footpath that runs between the Streamers

Meadows housing estate and Millers Way. The field was named after the 'Streamer' family who were in Honiton in the 16th and 17th century. Elmfield House itself was originally set in nearly an acre of ground and gardens but most of this land has now been developed into 'Dunnings Court' (which was opened in 1990) and the 'Thelma Hubert Gallery' car park.

By the time Frances Gidley died, she had only one surviving male heir who was her son Rev. Lewis Gidley. Rev. Lewis Gidley was born in 1822 in Honiton and was educated at Kings College, Ottery St Mary and later at Exeter College, Oxford and unlike his attorney father, grandfather and great grandfather, he pursued a career in the church and became curate of Combe Raleigh and Sheldon from 1845-50, Gillingham in Dorset between 1850-51, Otterton 1851-59, Gittisham 1859-62 and Branscombe for six years from 1862. He also became chaplain of St. Nicholas' Hospital, Salisbury in 1868 where he stayed until his death. His marriage did not produce any children and all his siblings had died either young or unmarried, thus bringing this line of the Gidley family to an end when he died in 1889.

Another resident of Elmfield House was the family of Alfred Dunning, a well known local solicitor.

Alfred Dunning was born in Throwleigh, Devon, the son of a farmer. He was educated at Exeter and started work as a solicitor's clerk in London. He moved to Honiton and subsequently 'Elmfield' in the late 1880s and later formed a local solicitors firm known as 'Stamp, Dunning & Rundle'. The 'Stamp' partner, William Stamp, grandson of the aforementioned Edmund Stamp, and Mr. Henry Leslie 'Rundle' worked from 'Carlton House' in the High Street before moving to Kings Road at the turn of the century.

Strangely, a great grandfather of Lewis Gidley's had married a 'Dunning' although there is not thought to be any connection to Alfred Dunning. Alfred worked in the town for some 40 years, after which his son Bertrum 'Bobby' Dunning (1892-1983), a once well known local man, inherited his father's position. Both Alfred and his son Bobby lived at Elmfield House and it is from them that the adjacent complex 'Dunning Court', built on an old paddock, got its name. After the Dunnings it was artist, Thelma Hubert, who bought the property and after her death, in 1995, the house was bought by East Devon District Council and is presently a 'shrine' to Ms Hubert's work. The Dunnings had formerly owned the large adjacent field, which today is 'Co-op Car Park'; for a short time before the car park it was a nursery and later allotments.

It may seem hard to imagine but Elmfield House was, at this time, a relatively rural property: to the south of the house was open countryside and between it and the rest of the houses on the east side of Dowell Street, apart from Mr. Wheaton's bowling green, was a long field called 'Dowell Close' on which one may have seen sheep grazing!

Oakmount: this house was a paper mill up until 1840; one of three, in fact, located down old Northcote Lane. There had once been several paper mills in operation in the vicinity but the other mills burnt down in 1828 and 'Oakmount' was the last to survive. After the house was converted to a private dwelling, it was known as Oak or 'Oake' Cottage and was owned by Christopher Flood, who leased it to a tenant. After Christopher Flood's subsequent bankruptcy, it was bought by the Manor of Honiton and among the numerous owners were the Matthew Brothers who ran the ironmongery business in the town. They were resident at the house in the 1920s. When Mr. Matthews died the house was bought by a Dr. Bingley Pullin of Sidmouth who renamed the property 'Rahere'. The house also once had a boating pond which was lost with the construction of the Honiton Bypass in 1966.

Bramble Hill

Before the west end of town was developed, the land to the south of the Exeter Road was known as 'Bramble Hill' whilst the land to the north was known as 'Sion Hill'. However, when buildings started to appear, the whole area was simply

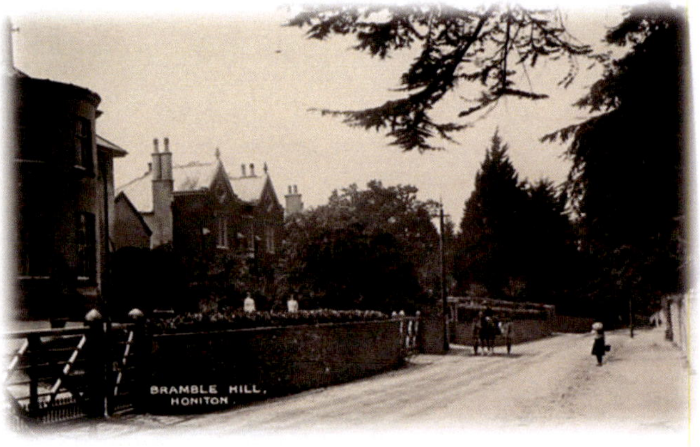

known by the former. Houses were known to have stood in this part of town as early as 1688 and most of the older residencies are today listed buildings.

Ridgeway House: the original name of this house is believed to be 'Ventnor Villa' and is thought to have been named by a surgeon called Harry Barrington Tuttiett who practised at Ventnor, Isle of Wight and died in Honiton in 1878. The records show the earliest owner as a William Pine, who was a maltster; he also owned a malthouse in Mill Street that still stands today. In 1851, Nathanial Read, a retired linen draper, lived in the house. He ran his business with his brother, John, from the shop now occupied by Specsavers (121 High Street) up until the late 1840s. By the 1860s, the house was home to a former Archdeacon of Gibraltar, Edward John Burrow who, interestingly, wrote a number of books, including 'Elements of Conchology, according to the Linnæan System' in 1825, which was last reprinted in 2009, as well as a book on the Elgin Marbles!
By the 1880s, another retired draper and, coincidentally another 'Read', had moved into Ventnor. Charles Read was a nephew of the previously mentioned Nathaniel Read who left the running of the business to him and his brother, another Nathaniel. Nathaniel, the younger, died in 1869 leaving the business solely to his brother Charles. The drapery was very lucrative: in 1861 the brothers had 3 assistants and 3 apprentices. Charles married a daughter of local hop and spirit merchant Thomas Avery, who also had a business in the High Street. Charles remained at Ventnor for the next 30 years, having retired there in his 40s: after his death, one of his daughters remained there for a short time. It was then resided in by a retired butcher called Seabourne Hook who ran his business from the now demolished property on the corner of Dowell Street. By the 1920s, a retired officer from the Indian Army had moved into the house, Major Kenrick Horace Lloyd, who stayed there until his death in 1942. The house today is known as 'Ridgeway House' and is still a private residence.

April Cottage: originally known as 'Ivy Cottage' this small, by comparison, property was in 1851 home to a Mr. Daniel Gould, a solicitor who later moved to Summerland Place. The cottage was once part of the 'Bramble Hill' or 'Rookwood House' estate owned by Mr. Flood. It was also an earlier home of the Rev. Henry Venn, of Monkton House, High Street and in the twentieth century a well known local family, the Icombes. This house was also featured in a painting by famous local artist Alfred Leyman in 1901. It was built in the early 19th century of roughcast stone and became Grade II listed in 1972.

Burwood: this old property was built in the early 19th century and was once known as 'Aspect House', 'St Lawrence Villa' and then, by the 1880s, 'Burwood'. One of the earliest known residents was Dr. James Hill who operated a surgery from the house in the 1840s. By 1851 it was occupied by a John Bridgeman, an attorney, who had formerly been partners with Philip Mules. A later owner was a Mr. Horace De Schmid who was Captain of the Honiton Constabulary and was the gentleman who named the house Burwood. Mr. De Schmid became the victim of a uranium mine stock scandal in 1891. In the January of 1890, he had purchased 50 shares in a year old company called 'The Uranium Mines Limited' at 17 shillings and 6 pence per share, only to have the company collapse in disgrace one year later. It was described as a 'wretched concern' and 'an unfortunate wreck' by the business journal *'The Financial Critic'*. The mining firm had apparently swindled investors with a bogus prospectus and post-dated the actual discovery of uranium at its Cornwall premises, formerly a tin mine. His son, Eric, went on to be the Chief Constable of Carlisle in 1917. Mr. De Schmid lived at Burwood until the late 1900s when Charles Harding, the draper, bought the house, and his family lived there until around the 1940s.

Ernsborough Lodge: this large house at Honiton's 'West End' has a long and colourful history with many different owners and residents.
The earliest known owners and residents were Philip Mules and his wife Elizabeth. Philip Mules was the son of the Vicar of Ilminster and settled in Honiton where he worked as an attorney and was "a long known and respected" member of the "neighbourhood". The house of Ernsborough was named after the ancient family seat of the Mules family in Swimbridge, near Barnstaple, Devon. The manor house of Swimbridge has long since disappeared but was called 'Ernsborough Manor'. Mr. Mules also had an office in the property situated next to the Gissage (180 High Street) for a time in the 1840s.
Despite the fact that Philip had a respectable and well paid profession, his life in Honiton was not kind to him! Philip and Elizabeth had 10 children; however, most of them died young. Their daughter, Sarah Ann, died at the age of one, another daughter, Elizabeth Vibrant Mules, died at the age of 13, Juliana Harriet Mules passed away in 1839, aged 18, son William Marwood Mules joined the colonial army where he was posted to Bombay and was killed aged 33 in the Indian Mutiny of 1858. Another daughter, Ellen, perished at the age of 34 and a further two children are thought to have also died at a young age. One son called Henry Charles Mules

became a barrister in Suffolk, and for a time was clerk to the Poor Law Commissioners at Somerset House, London; however, he, too, died young. There were, in fact, thought to only be three of the original ten who survived to relatively good ages. John Hawkes Mules, born 1813, married a daughter of Charles Gordon of Wiscombe Park who was also a great niece of the last Thomas Putt of Gittisham. He followed a career in the church and became the curate of Yarcombe and later the Rector of Moulton St. Michael, Norfolk. Philip Mules Jr., born 1812, held the post of the Chaplain of Belvoir Castle, Lincolnshire for some 30 years. The last surviving child was his son, Horace Vibrant Mules, who remained at his father's home for the remainder of his life. In St. Paul's church, two of the three stained glass windows are devoted to the Mules family; one devoted to Philip Mules himself and the other to his son William, who died in India. After Philip Mules Snr. was widowed in 1829, he lived alone with his son Horace at Ernsborough where they both practised as attorneys and solicitors; however, in late 1840s things started to go sour for them. In 1847 Philip's business was valued at £1500/year which, in part, was made up of stewardships, including among them 'Clerk to the Honiton Turnpike Trust', 'Clerk to the Honiton and Sidmouth Turnpike Trust', 'Clerk to the Commissioners of Taxes' and 'Clerk and Registrar to the Honiton Poor Law Board', all of which were valued at £421/year. In the spring of the same year, an agreement was drafted bringing in a new partner called John Bridgeman Smith, at a cost of £2,300 to the aforementioned. Later, Philip's son, Horace who had only been working at the firm, was also drafted as a partner and the firm was renamed 'Mules, Smith & Mules'. The £500 capital of the firm was held at the local bank 'Flood & Lott' which in November of the same year went into liquidation. It was found that Philip Mules was, in fact, a debtor owing the bank some £5,000 as well as a "greater amount" from a former partnership which amounted to about £400,000 in today's money. The debt was so great that in the January of 1849, Philip Mules left the country leaving his son some serious problems with the dissolving partnership. In the May of the same year, Philip's former partner, Mr. Smith, filed for dissolution of the firm under a clause drafted in the original agreement that forbade any of the partners from abandoning the business without notice on the penalty of forfeiture of the said partnership and an injunction that also forbade the liable parties from practising as solicitors or attorneys in any other firm for 20 years! Mr. Smith was holding both Philip and his son, Horace, liable under other allegations concerning the withholding of monies, clients and business from the said Mr. Smith. This behaviour, by any of the partners, was prohibited by another clause that stated that all partners in the firm had to be included in all business transactions and dealings and failing to do so would result in the same penalty, as previously mentioned. Horace Mules argued his case to the High Court of Chancery where he denied any such allegations and escaped this severe penalty by the skin of his teeth. The court ruled that as Philip Mules had "absconded" he had indeed been guilty of breaking the terms of the original agreement, yet the judge did not find the allegations against Horace Mules substantiated. It was, therefore, ruled that Mr. Smith's dissolution of the partnership, against Horace, was invalid on the basis that he had not broken the clause agreeing to treat Mr. Smith as an equal partner. The partnership was in the end dissolved but had the court ruled in favour of Mr. Smith on both counts, Horace would not have been able to practise as an attorney until 1869!

In 1851, John Bridgeman Smith lived just two doors from Horace and Philip Mules at the house now known as 'Burwood' and remained living and working in Honiton as an attorney for some years after the dissolution of the 'Mules, Smith & Mules' firm.

Horace Mules had lost his father to foreign parts, a man who had had a "natural love and affection" for his son, and he lived alone at Ernsborough for the next 11 years until, in 1860, he married for the first and only time. The couple had only one son, Horace Vibrant Mules Jnr., who died as an infant.

Horace Vibart Mules died in London in 1878 aged 69 and his widow moved away from the town and also died in London in 1894. What became of his father after his departure from the town is unknown. Both Horace, his wife Fanny and their son are buried at St Michael's.

After the death of Horace Mules, the house passed to John Thomas English who was JP for Devon and Cornwall: he did not live here long for by 1883 it was occupied by Oswald Bloxsome who was a great landowner in New South Wales, Australia and son of a famous diarist.

By the turn of the 20th century the house was owned by Philip Ramsbotham, a retired South American Merchant who stayed at the house until the 1920s. After Mr. Ramsbotham, there lived an elderly, "wealthy woman" called Marian Bayden who was said to have kept "a full staff of servants, including two gardeners and a chauffeur". As old age progressed she became bedridden but still kept on the full staff of servants as well as a live-in companion and nurse. The house remained empty for some years after her death in 1931 until it was bought by another solicitor, Cyril Fawcett, who was said to have paid £3,000 for the house and grounds. The house today is a nursing home and sadly lost its ancient name when several years ago it was changed to 'Honiton Manor'.

In the 1840s, the house was situated in nearly 3 acres of land which stretched right back to what is now 'Millhead Road'. This land had formerly been a large field owned by local banker Christopher Flood and was later bought by Mr. Mules in 1859 for £250 and thus became incorporated into the property's grounds. The land has now all been sold off and the "Georgian type houses" that now occupy it are aptly called Ernsborough Gardens. It is somewhat perplexing to find this land has been built on considering a report published by Devon County Council in 1972 clearly stated the gardens and land as an area subject to a "Tree Preservation Order"!

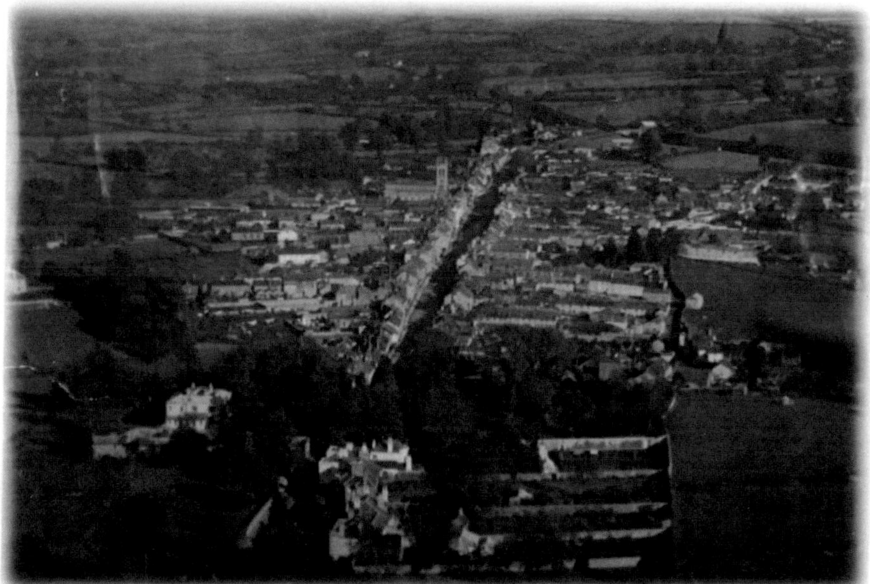

Ariel photo showing Ernsborough Lodge and gardens (centre bottom) and Rookwood House (bottom right) prior to their repective developments.

Rookwood House: possibly one of the most significant houses in the town considering its long history. Rookwood House, originally known as 'Bramble Hill', even though it was originally built on Sion Hill, was built in about 1796 by local attorney and banker Christopher Flood. Christopher Flood was born in New Street in 1759, to the son of another Christopher Flood, a local shoemaker. His father was known as 'King Kester', 'King of

New Street' and 'Kester, King of the Patwallers' due to his great influence over the 'potwallers', a group of voters, at a time when Honiton was described as the most rotten of the rotten boroughs. Young Christopher Flood was first apprenticed to a Mr. James Townsend of Luppitt, the father of another respected Honiton lawyer, James Townsend Jnr., before being 'admitted' an attorney in 1778. Mr. Flood practised in Honiton where he built up a "lucrative business" and originally lived in a house just a few doors west of the old Kings Arms Inn. It was around the time of his marriage that his business had done well enough to enable him to purchase some land at the west end of town and build his fine new abode. His marriage produced two children: a son, Christopher Samuel Flood, and a daughter, Elizabeth Margaret Flood, who married the Rector of Feniton. Christopher Flood Snr. had, a few years before in 1786, founded the Honiton bank 'Flood & Lott in partnership with Samuel Lott. The bank had a fixed issue of around £19,000: it was a subsidiary of 'Lubbock & Co.', London in 1830. Samuel Lott was born in Honiton in 1748, the son of a barber, and started his life as a printer, stationer and post master; he had also been a clerk in the office of Courtney Gidley of Elmfield House. "Mr. Lott was a shrewd man of business and under his management the bank flourished" and along with Mr. Flood they ran the bank as a successful business for over 30 years. Christopher Flood Snr., as an attorney, took a partner in 1810, Philip Mules of Ernsborough Lodge. For some 40 years 'Flood & Mules' were the Tory agents for the borough and for many years the duo had allowed large overdrafts at the bank for voters in order to secure votes for their party's candidates. One man even wrote, in 1816, that Mr. Flood and a Mr. Townsend, another of Mr. Flood's associates, had "entire control of the borough". In 1817, Captain Lord Cochrane, who was MP for the town at the time, openly said "that by paying 10 guineas a vote he had bribed his way into Parliament for Honiton" and was further quoted that Honiton was "where votes were openly, avowedly, and unblushingly sold." Considering C. Flood and Mr. S. Lott had come from humble backgrounds, the sons of a cobbler and barber respectively, it seems correct from Farquharson's comment that "truly politics paid well in those days"!

Samuel Lott died in 1819 aged 71 and the partnership of the bank was inherited by his son, Harry Baines Lott, who sat as MP for Honiton on two occasions. He "served his articles" to Mr. Flood and he himself died in Honiton in 1833 aged 57: his obituary described him as "a gentleman highly respected for his integrity as a public character, and for his urbanity and good feeling in private life." The Lott family home was Tracey House, Awliscombe which the family acquired in about 1828.

Harry Baines Lott's son, Harry Buckland Lott, succeeded his father in the bank. Christopher Flood Snr. died in Honiton in 1843 aged 84 and on the day of his funeral the entire town closed for the day in memory of him. After the death of the two founding fathers of the bank, the business was left in the hands of their respective descendants, Harry Buckland Lott and Christopher Samuel Flood. Although C. S. Flood was described as "a most amicable, easy going man" he and his new partner showed little interest in the bank and spent their time and money on improving and extending their homes. The duo were also quoted to have been "much influenced by Mr. Mules", the attorney and former partner of C. Flood senior, who presumably used the bank as his personal piggy bank, which led to his large outstanding debt when the bank collapsed.

The Honiton bank was, therefore, left in the control of the two clerks called James Player and Herman James Lott, of Marwood House. Not surprisingly, the establishment suffered and in November 1847 it failed with catastrophic consequences. The final blow for the bank was when the Honiton branch of the National Provincial Bank presented a request for a large sum of money which the Honiton Bank could not deliver in cash. A messenger was sent to Exeter to obtain the deficit but when he did not return in time, a letter stating what had happened was written and posted. When the messenger finally arrived it was too late and panic had spread throughout the banks' creditors. The event was so big, in fact, that it was reported in the 'London Gazette'. On November 4th 1847 a meeting was held at Mr. Flood's house to decide the next course of action. Over the proceeding days it was found that the bank had liabilities in excess of £125,359 (about £10 million today) and the two remaining partners were thus declared bankrupt. The outstanding debt was repaid at 5 shillings in the pound and the estates of the two bankrupts, Mr. Lott and Mr. Flood, were sold and both men fled their creditors. Harry Buckland Lott later fled to Brittany, France where he died in 1867 and Christopher S. Flood fled to Exeter where he died, unmarried, at 7 Radnor Place, in 1860. C. S. Flood, who had been the first Borough Mayor in 1847, was replaced by James H. Townsend after his departure. There is a memorial stone to the Lott family at St Michael's Church although Harry Buckland Lott's descendants now reside in France.

The failure of the bank cost the town severely financially and some £15,000 worth of bank notes still in circulation at its collapse, like any bank that failed, were deemed worthless, causing great problems for many of the town's residents. The voters, whom the bank had so favourably looked after, were possibly the worst hit: one story tells of a landlord of one of the town's inns who, coming back from the market with "a pair of fine ducks",

said to a political opponent, holding up the birds, "see how we Tories live". After the collapse of the bank this man was ruined and was forced to spend the rest of his days as a "dilapidated old man" residing in a small cottage and driving a London cab. "Several tradesmen" as well as many "private residents" of the town were also ruined with the failure of the business.
The bank itself was once located in the grand old 18th century building now occupied by the 'Charity Shop for Blind Children' and 'Coral' (107 High Street).

At the time of his death, Mr. Flood Senior was a hugely wealthy man with large sums of land and properties. In 1811, he had obtained the lands and the title of Lord of the Manor of Monkton and at the time of his death owned, in his own right, 114.25 acres of land in Honiton, another 18.5 acres in partnership with Mr. Lott and a further 12.5 acres which he had leasehold from the Manor of Honiton. In total, he owned 69 houses, cottages, shops, inns and gardens in the town including 'The Green Dragon', 'The Anchor', 'The Black Lion', a wheelwright's shop, a butcher's shop and a sawpit as well as numerous other dwellings and premises in the parishes of Luppit, Sheldon, Silverton, Axminster, Awliscombe and Buckland St. Mary, Somerset! Although Christopher Flood lived at Bramble Hill, he also owned Broomhills, a large property further out of town that is today St Rita's. Broomhills is believed to have been built in about 1840 on the site of an earlier dwelling known as 'Sion House'. It was probably fortunate that he died when he did, for witnessing his son lose everything he had worked for, just 4 years later, would probably have killed him!
Rookwood itself was a large, beautiful house situated right next to the Gissage with 20 acres of surrounding land, including yards, gardens, 'pleasure grounds', coach houses, stables and shrubberies. On its sale in 1852 it was described as a "spacious and convenient mansion house...suitable for a Gentleman and his family." The auction of Mr. Flood's properties was conducted by local auctioneer, James Hussey, at the Angel Inn on the 19th September 1852 and was believed to have been purchased by the solicitor, John Bridgeman Smith. The house was sold again in 1859 when it was quoted to have had a drawing room, dining room, library, breakfast room, servant's quarters, and seven bedrooms. There was also once an adjoining "labourer's cottage" which was situated to the east of the mansion. This little cottage had previously been sheds and a "sawpit" which were presumably later converted into a small dwelling.

The house later became the 'new' Rectory, the old one having been situated near the old Church of St. Michael's at what is now 'Old Rectory Farm', in about 1860. John Fielder Mackerness, who later became Bishop of Oxon, was the gentleman who changed the old Flood property into the new town Rectory, an occupation that continued in the property for over a century. In the twentieth century, the rectory was the site of many a local event, including fetes in the summer; however, by the 1970s the house was permanently 'retired'. It seems that this large house, with its many acres of land, including a tennis court, had become too big and expensive for its former purpose and the premises were sold. In 1971 the house was described as "a shell" and its most important feature, a staircase which was "one of the finest examples of its kind in the country", was re-homed in America. Four preservation societies campaigned for the house's preservation but their efforts were in vain. In the late 1970s, the green light was given to local company 'Rush & Tompkins' to develop the site; however, as the building itself was Grade II listed, delays were caused in obtaining permission to demolish the property, which proved problematic for the constructors' deadlines. Luckily, for the developers, an unexpected gas explosion destroyed part of one of the property's walls leaving it structurally unsafe and work was initiated on schedule. The old house and gardens, which were also under preservation orders, were flattened and the flats and residential properties of 'Rookwood Close' were built. The house itself was interestingly, and strangely, only de-listed in 2007, some 30 years after it demolition!
Rookwood got its last name from a large Rookery of birds that nested in the nearby trees and the housing estate, which presently stands on the old site, is still known as 'Rookwood'. After the Rectory's demolition a new, smaller rectory was established nearby where Rectors of Honiton still live to this day.

St. Leonards: another early 19th century property, it was previously known as 'Prospect House' when it was occupied by a Dr. Barker in the 1840s. By the 1860s, local auctioneer, James Hussey, resided here and after him, the widow of the previously mentioned William Rogers. One of the longest residents of the house was Thomas Avery, the son of Thomas Avery who was partner with Capt. Basleigh. He lived at the house, after his retirement in the early 1890s, until his death in 1925.

Oaklands: this house was a later addition to Bramble Hill, thought to have been built in the late 19th century. One of the earliest residents was Douglas Barber, a Honiton Police Superintendent, and by the 1890s,

William Henry Banfield, the retired Dolphin Hotel proprietor, lived there. The house had a variety of owners from the turn of the century until the 1920s when the founder of Moor's Garage, Arthur Percy Moor, had taken up residence. The house today is a B & B known as 'Oaklands Guest House'.

Other Properties

Pine Park House: built in the early 1880s, this property was originally a farm that occupied all the land sandwiched between Queen Street, Church Hill and Parsonage Lane, including the present day 'Glen'. The land and house were sold off in 1884 when Mr. Smith, of the railway, is believed to have bought most of the farmland and the house itself became a private dwelling. The Pines Estate was built in the late 1960s on lands owned by the Smith family. One of the earliest residents of Pine Park was thought to be a Charles Hayward who ran a solicitor's firm in the town.

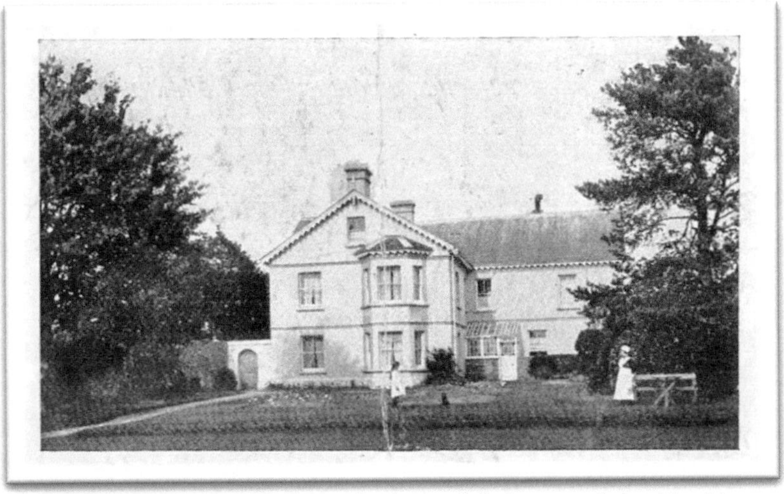

The *Pines* estates of today obviously obtained their names from this old dwelling and this author believes that the house took its name from an early reference relating to 'The Glen' which, around this time, had a large number of pine trees located within it and was also once the only wooded area in the immediate vicinity. The common conception is that the area

was named after the pine trees of Kings Road but these were not present until the early twentieth century.
By the turn of the century it was owned and occupied by John George Hann who ran and owned the old Honiton Brewery in Mill Street. Mr. Hann remained at the house until just after WWI when it was bought by John Tratt, a member of the local farming family. Mr. Tratt spent most of his time in London as a publican and the house remained empty for much of the time. The house later became the residence of Mr. Roy Read of 'Reads Garage'. The Reads moved into Pine Park in about 1931 and Mr. Read became Mayor of Honiton twice in the 1940s/50s. After Mr. Read's death in 1952 his widow lived in the house "in virtual isolation" until she moved to Sidmouth in 1972, when the house was bought by Karl Klampher who owned the Carlton Inn. Today Pine Park House still stands and is a care home for people with learning difficulties. The present day car park was once the farm yard and it is now surrounded by the Pine Park Estate rather than the original farmland.

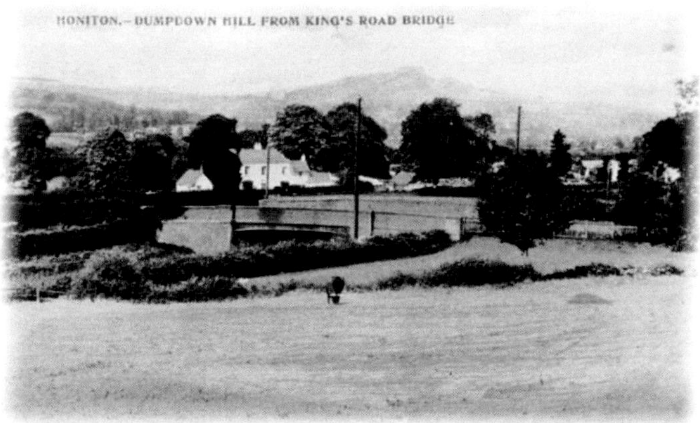

View of Kings Road Railway Bridge before the development of the Pines housing estate. The field, in which the cow is grazing, is now 'Pine Gardens'.

Springfield House: this grand old house was thought to have originally been a farm with 26.5 acres owned and built by a Thomas Denner. Thomas' wife, Charlotte, was a niece of Mr. Wheaton of the Golden Lion. Mr. Denner had farmed Great Hale Farm from the 1830s, a farm that had been in the occupancy of his wife's family in the early 19th century, and by

1844 he was situated at Springfield. At some point between then and 1848, Mr. Denner relocated to Rowley Farm, once occupied by his father, and then back to Springfield again. The occupants of the house, for a part of this period, were the Farquarharson family, already mentioned: the house during the Farquharson's occupancy would have definitely been a residential dwelling. After 1851, Mr. Denner remained at Springfield as a farmer until the late 1860s when he moved to a larger 200 acre farm in Somerset. The house drifted between a private residency and a farm over the next few decades. By the 1870s William Alder, a retired solicitor from Somerset, had bought Springfield and by the 1880s it had reverted back to a farm again, with Samuel Ford as its tenant. From the late 1880s/early 1890s the house became a permanent private residence. In 1891, an elderly widow named Judith Wright, whose husband had been a sub-agent to the Bank of England, lived at the house with her two unmarried daughters: she later moved to April Cottage. The house then changed hands a couple of more times before being bought by John Pawley Bate in the early 1900s. Mr. Bate lived a very successful life; he was born, one of fourteen, the son of a Wesleyan Minister, and later became a teacher at The University of London, a law lecturer and a private tutor at Cambridge University before finally becoming a barrister by 1901. He later retired to Springfield where he translated many foreign works to English, being fluent in German, French and Spanish: he was also a local Justice of the Peace. Mr. Bate is believed to have done much work to Springfield House during his residency; he changed the name to 'Lambpark' and had his last initials (P.B.) inscribed on many of the drain pipes, as well as inscribing on a north facing wall "mihi angulus rider" which roughly translated from Latin reads "my little laughing corner" or "for me this little secluded place smiles". Pawley Bate sold the property in 1920 to a French couple called Currie and he died in London the following year. The Curries changed the name back to Springfield and remained at the property until the 1950s. They were a well known local family and Mrs. Currie played the organ at Offwell Church for many years.

This grand old house, at one time, had 7 bedrooms as well as stables and a tennis court. The tennis court still exists, some distance from the house, but has not been used for upwards of a century.

In 1958, the house was bought by a Mrs. Loud and converted into leased apartments and later, in 1969, Mr. and Mrs. Eyles of 'Manor House School' purchased the house, having outgrown their old site at Seaton. A summerhouse that still stands in the grounds was built from reclaimed panelling from St Michael's Church when it burnt in 1911. Manor House

School, at the time of writing, is due to close due to financial difficulties, although the nursery will remain.

Tracey House: The property of Tracey did, in fact, stand in the parish of Awliscombe but due to its links with Honiton through the Lotts and Traceys, it is worth mentioning here.

Tracey House was anciently the seat of the family of the founder of St. Margarets and the estate later passed to the Chard family by the marriage of the last 'Tracey' heiress. The Chards were related to Thomas Chard, last Abbott of Forde Abbey, and the last male heir of the Chard family, John Chard, left the estate to his sister's son, John Charde Lewis, who was, at the time of Mr. Chard's death, a minor. John Charde Lewis' father, John Lewis, is the gentleman who built Tracey House for his son in the eighteenth century. The older pre-eighteenth century property was said to have once stood on a piece of ground to the south of the house. John Charde Lewis died a bachelor and the house was sold. As already stated, the Lotts obtained the property in about 1828 and spent large sums both extending and improving the dwelling. After the failure of the bank, the house was sold to the Neumann family in about 1860, whose descendants still resided there into the mid-twentieth century. The house had fallen into "a very poor state of repair externally and internally" by 1955 and continued to fall into dereliction over the following decades. In more recent times the house became known locally, specifically to the youth of the town, as 'Freddy's Mansion'; presumably after Freddy Kruger of the film 'A Nightmare on Elm Street', and unsubstantiated rumours of ghostly activity made it a popular socialising spot for youngsters. The continual trespassing and loitering of 'teens within the old property's ruins, led to serious concerns by the local authorities over health and safety and, in 2002, an application was submitted to demolish the dwelling. Much debating ensued but the original plans were later enacted upon and the Grade II listed house was flattened.

The town may have been the commercial centre but in the surrounding countryside stood many isolated farms that supplied much of the parish with both work and food...

PART 3

Outskirts

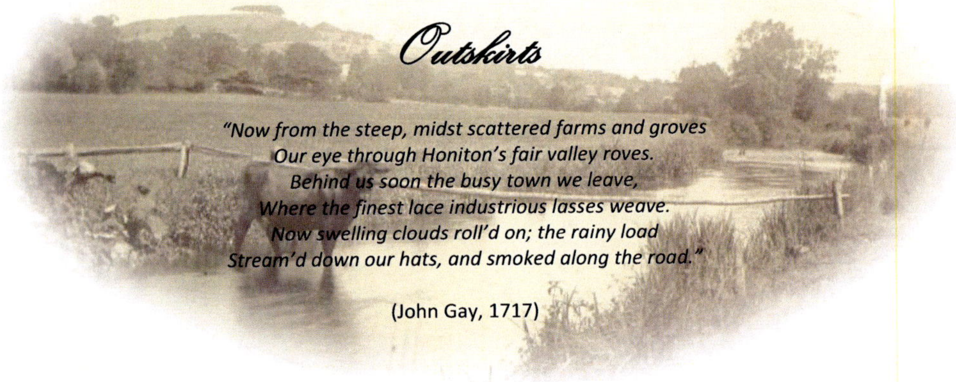

"Now from the steep, midst scattered farms and groves
Our eye through Honiton's fair valley roves.
Behind us soon the busy town we leave,
Where the finest lace industrious lasses weave.
Now swelling clouds roll'd on; the rainy load
Stream'd down our hats, and smoked along the road."

(John Gay, 1717)

Chapter 1:
Farming: A Way of Life

""the red land, which surrounds Exeter, and extends considerably east and west of it; "this soil," we are told "is most natural for pasturing beasts, though it be plentiful furnished with corn.""
(General Description of Devonshire, c.1630)

With just over 3,000 residents, Honiton was roughly a quarter of the size it is today. The town, technically, ended on the east at Marwood House, on the west at Bramble Hill, the north at the workhouse, now the hospital, and the south at Cowley Farm, roughly where the Pit Club now is. Beyond this 'urban' boundary lay a collection of farms, fields, mills, tollhouses and rural country lanes.
Between the end 1919 and 1939, about 18% of all the houses in Britain today were built. The traumatic years of WWI committed the government to provide 'homes fit for [the country's returning] heroes' with more spacious houses that provided basic indoor amenities, such as a toilet and a bathroom, which were scarce in the houses of the previous century. By the end of WWII there were about half a million houses that had either been destroyed or severely damaged by the bombing, putting even more pressure on the space for residential properties. The immediate years after the war also saw a rapidly increasing population, with the 'baby boom' years, and this led to great residential developments throughout the 1960s and 1970s. Honiton took its own part in this period of building and it was, sadly, the numerous farms, fields and smallholdings of the town that were lost to fulfil these post war requirements.
This section looks in more detail at the open countryside surrounding this once small settlement.

In the mid-nineteenth century there were just over 30 farms occupying this small parish. These farms varied dramatically in size, some consisting of many hundreds of acres and some humble smallholdings, maybe of only a few acres. Most have been lost to housing estates and some simply merged with the greater need for land at the turn of the twentieth century.
The majority of the farms themselves can only be traced back, accurately, to the 1600s yet subtle clues hidden in aspects of the construction of the properties - names of the farm's fields and even the names of the farms themselves - suggest that the majority of them have their roots from far earlier than the 17th century and more probably from the middle ages.

Perry Hale Farm's farmhouse deeds, for example, date back to the early 1600s, yet evidence of a medieval trust suggests a much earlier foundation. Many of the other farms, such as 'Coombehayes', 'Thornhayes' and 'Cheneys', take their names from families who were present in the area long before the farm's documentation begins. This name evidence is also prominent in the field names of many of the farms. Medieval West Country farmhouses contained only one main room called 'the hall' in which the fire was located in the centre. This basic house plan had virtually not changed since Saxon times where the house had one main room with a central hearth where cooking, socialising and sleeping was done. At the poorest level of the medieval peasant, the cattle house, where the cows and oxen were kept, formed an integral part of this once open plan home. Prior to horse power, oxen were the primary force used to plough the fields, as well as provide milk and meat, and so were considered the farmers' greatest asset and possession; not to be treated differently from the farmer himself. This setup, with man and beast inhabiting the same four walls, known to be one of the earliest house types in the area, was known as the 'longhouse'. These basic two room dwellings had no chimney and at most there would be a hole in the roof to let the smoke out, with little or no allowance made for times of rain or snow! This primitive setup left very little privacy for the occupants and the lack of a chimney made a second floor impossible. The entire family and farm hands would sleep around the fire in this main room, often on basic mattresses filled with straw or chaff, and infants were thought to be conceived and born in this one communal area, probably meaning that not many farm children would ask their parents 'where babies came from?!' The oldest farmhouses in the area are these single storey properties and it was not until the late 16th and early 17th century that first floors were incorporated into the houses' overall construction. The first major step in the establishment of a first floor came about when chimneys started to become more common: a channelled passage extracting smoke through an orifice in the roof meant one could inhabit the upper part of the house without suffocating. After the construction of a chimney 'the hall' underwent a sealing (ceiling), giving two separate sections to the home: one for living and one for sleeping. This "great rebuilding" or "remodelling" came about from an increased need for privacy and comfort which was initiated by the increased affluence of farmers of the late 16th and early 17th century. Wool and corn had risen vastly in price, whereas the wages of the lowly farm labourer had remained relatively static, meaning a greater bulge in the farmers' back pocket and the desire to show off this new affluence which was reflected in the new setup of the farmhouse. The traditional Devonian farmhouse kitchen floor consisted of blue-slate slabs which were easy to maintain and shed no dust.

"Today the old farmhouse has often become too big and difficult for a farmer's wife, without help of any kind and no servants in the house. The farmer himself runs 200-300 acres with the help of a son or of one man who lives, possibly in a council house, some miles away, and drives to work. So the farmer lives in a bungalow and he is often more of a technician and businessman than a 'husbandman'. The old house has been sold, often to 'foreigners' who fancy an old and elegant house full of character for their retirement, of from whence they may commute; the barns can be converted in to further expensive houses. This development has been brought about largely by technology applied to the working of the farm and to the bringing of once remote areas in touch with urban life. The farmhouse is hardly any longer the home and place of work for a farming family, living largely off the land. This marks an enormous change, the end of a way of life that was centuries, if not millennia old."

(Old Farming Days; Robin Staines)

The county of Devon in 1837 had a total of 1,654,400 acres of land, of which 1,200,000 acres were used for farming. Honiton parish itself consisted of 3,046.5 acres of land, of which some 2,743 acres were used for agricultural purposes. Of this land, 1,770 acres were meadows and pastures, 728 acres were arable land, 142 acres were orchards and gardens and 71 acres were woodland. Meadow and fields that were located near water courses were the most valuable, due to their ability to remain damp in the driest of summers. One visitor to Honiton in 1805 commented on "the fine arable and pasture lands" that surrounded the town. The most widely grown crop was oats followed by barley and wheat: there was virtually three times more oats than wheat grown in 1844. In the same year, barley was the most valuable crop with a price of 8s.11½d. per imperial bushel followed by wheat which was worth about 7s. a bushel and, lastly, oats which were more poorly priced at 2s.9d. per bushel.
This was at a time when land that could not be cultivated was referred to as 'waste' and Dartmoor, one of the most popular tourist destinations in the county today, was then described as "one of the least valuable tracts in the kingdom".
Farming was incredibly important at this time; over the Victorian period, the population of Britain rose from 10 to 40 million and to feed the masses farming had to undergo a revolution which saw the end of traditions and ways of life which had gone unchanged for a millennia.

The average rent of land in Devon in the early 1800s was about fifteen shillings per acre per year.

It was estimated that the total number of farmers in 1837 was 200,000, of which the annual revenue to the country was £30,000,000; the average size of these farms was 136 acres.

The normal term of entry to a farm was Lady-Day (25th March) but entries on Candlemas (2nd February) and Michaelmas (29th September) were also common.

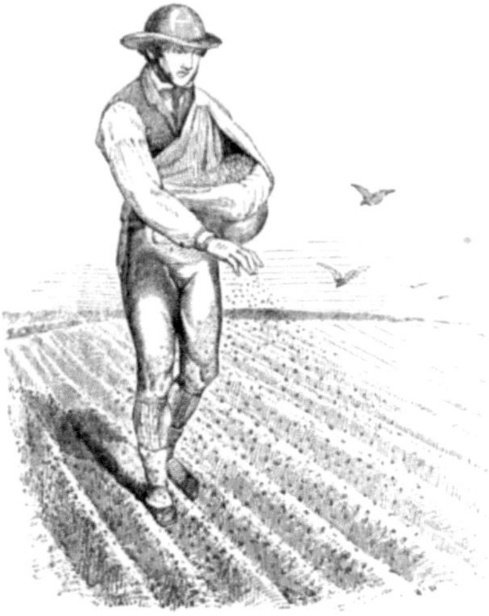

'Broad casting'

The arable farm would first need to be ploughed. Ploughing was an arduous, monotonous task and a farmer would plough an acre a day, walking 11 miles from dawn till dusk. In the 1840s 'Ransomes of Ipswich', a popular plough maker of the day, released the 'Yorkshire Light'; so good was its design it was still being made up until the Second World War.

The field would then need to be harrowed, to break up the ploughed sods, and the seeds then planted. Seeds in the Southwest were planted by hand well into the twentieth century by either 'broadcasting' or using a 'fiddle'. More sophisticated machines such as the 'seed drill', invented by Jethro Tull, were known in Devonshire but many small scale farmers would have found this new machine far too expensive to buy and contractors of the area were known to be "unreliable." Tasks such as seed planting were not often

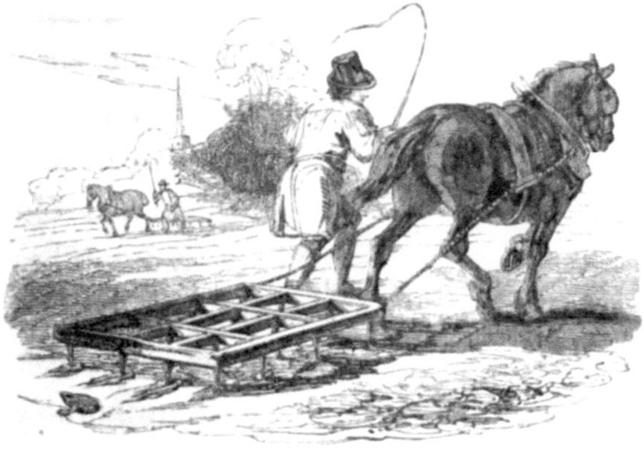

'Harrowing'

performed through scientific measurements but more by estimates of the experienced yeoman or simple rhymes passed down through the ages such as 'One for the rook, one for the crow, one to let rot, one to let grow.'
Once the seed had been planted in September and grown throughout the year the wheat harvest could commence, usually around July 25th to the beginning of August. In the southwest the wheat was not scythed so much as 'bagged' - that is, struck down near the ground with a large heavy hook. It would take 4 men to reap and one to bind an acre a day. The wheat was then left to dry in the field and was ready for collection within about a week or ten days depending, of course, upon the weather.

The 'agricultural revolution' seems to have passed Devon by. Many local farmers alive today still have clear memories of their fathers' ploughing by horse well into the 1950s and cutting crops with scythes well into the 1930s.These primitive practises were common at this time in Honiton and the surrounding area, at a time when mechanisation had been established almost everywhere else some 60 years earlier!
After the harvest itself, followed the much loved harvest festival where drinking and partying would continue well into the night. These celebrations were commonplace well into the 1950s but with the advent of machines replacing workers "the celebration of the harvest is quite gone" today.
The flour produced from the harvest worked out at about 13lb of flour for every 14lb of grain.
Although arable farming was preferable on some farms, it was also more risky and involved more work for a farmer who would need about 50 acres of land to "get by", whereas a dairy farm could make the same income from about one tenth of the land. Honiton farms seemed to have mainly been pastoral, with an emphasis on dairy, as many references of the time talk of large quantities of milk, cream and cheese being sent to London on the newly constructed railway. This new quick and easy way of allowing farmers to send their produce over longer distances assisted men such as John Sainsbury who was one of the first to buy his milk from the incoming trains, when he setup his first shop in 1869. He then was able to sell milk and butter directly to the consumer rather than having to have a resident cow, which had been the practise prior to the railways.
A full half of a farm's arable concern was, however, for the sole purpose of feeding livestock and on many Honiton farms it is seen that a very small proportion of the land was used for the growing of crops. Hay was another important winter feed for animals and a farmer could expect to obtain between 1 to 1.5 tonnes per acre farmed.

The Victorian period was long before the development of fertilisers and pesticides, yet the land was still in need of nutritional help from the farmer, and lime was often used for this purpose. In 1811 it was said "that one half of the lands in Devon require lime in a certain proportion for their effective cultivation...thousands of acres of waste lands could be rendered fertile with profit, if lime were at hand; and that the rent of every estate which is now distant from a limekiln could be increased, if it had the advantages of one brought near to it." The burning of lime was a "new invention" in the 17th century and by burning it, and then applying it on the land, it "produced a plentiful increase of all sorts of grain". Marl was another substance used to aid cultivation of poor soils and was a tradition that dated back to medieval times. Marl contains lime, and its clay consistency provides body to light or poor soils and, unlike clay itself, it did not stick to the shovel. Uncommon in the rest of the South West, its excavation was exclusively practised in East Devon and much evidence points to the extensive use of it in Honiton. There were 6 'old marl pits' that surrounded Great Hale Farm, another two located to the south of Old Rectory Farm, one off Marlpits Hill, three in the vicinity of Gardeners and Roundball Farm, and at least one identified pit at Stout, Rowleigh, Thornhayes, Roebuck and Lowmans Farm. Basically, nearly every farm in the parish at one time dug marl from the ground to aid the fertility and texture of the local soil. The remnants of many of these ancient pits can still be seen in the topography of the Honitonian countryside.

Dung was probably the most favoured substance to fertilise the land. A farmer's or labourer's dung heap, which was often next to the house, was one of their most priced possessions and even had to be legally listed in probate inventories. Virtually everything was thrown on the 'dung heap' including animal excrement, rotten vegetables and even dead livestock. There was even one documented account of a family from Hemyock who, having lost a daughter to plague in 1647, threw her body on their heap!

Horses were, of course, the tractors of their time and produced all the power for the continuation of the farm: it was thought that there was a total of 1,200,000 horses employed in agriculture at this time; this was two- thirds of all the horses in Britain. Horses were, indeed, not a cheap form of power and cost on average about £13 to buy and an additional £30 per year to maintain; they were, however, much cheaper compared to the new steam tractors that had started to pollute the countryside. In the late 1850s a '10hp double cylinder portable steam engine' was £280, a basic 'steam plough' was about £500 and a more powerful and sophisticated '12hp, Steam Cultivating Apparatus' was a whopping £825. Considering a farmer could employ 27 labourers for a year for what the steam plough cost, it is not so surprising that these new machines took a while to catch on! To give you an example of how expensive these early agricultural machines were, at around the same time a steam locomotive was valued at £500! Even with the initial cost, and the average yearly maintenance, a horse was still by far the cheapest form of farm work. The new steam machinery was, however, the way forward and an acre of land, which would take four men a day to reap and bind was reduced to hours with the new innovations hitting the countryside.

Oxen were once the main source of power on the farm and were preferable to horses up until the mid-nineteenth century; there were, in fact, farmers in Payhembury who were still ploughing land with oxen up until 1914. William Youatt, the respected vetinarian previously mentioned, wrote in 1834 "over the Hill to the fruitful vale of Honiton, we do not find oxen so much used here in husbandry. The soil is either cold, hard clay, or its flint would speedily destroy the feet of the oxen."

The numbers of cows throughout Great Britain was virtually fives time that of the horse, with many farms having a dairy concern for the sale of milk, cream, cheese and butter. Milk sold for about 3d-4d a quart whereas cream was much more expensive at 2s.6d. to 3s. a quart.

Sheep were by far the most numerous of agricultural beasts, with an estimated 26 million grazing the fields of England in the mid nineteenth century. As far as livestock went, cows were the most valuable and were valued at about £13 each (compared to the price of around £900 today!), calves were £3, sheep and lambs were priced at £1.10s. each, and pigs at £1.16. The "best herds [of cows] in [the Honiton] district [were] commonly renewed every fourth year, or one fourth yearly". In 1813 a gentleman called Vancouver published a report on farming of the region and within his publication he stated that each cow of the South West counties was capable of producing 140lb of cheese and 206lb of butter every year. He also wrote that a moderately sized farm, containing on average six cows, could produce 1207lb of cheese and 1200lb of butter over the farming season. Even in 1793, some 70 years before the railway arrived in the town, local farmers were known to have sent as much as 5 tons of butter weekly to London markets.

Pigs were also a favourite of the farmer and an integral part of the farm's animal community. It was said that 'a dog looks up to a man, a cat looks down on a man, and a pig looks him straight in the eyes'! Pigs were not scared of their human masters, one of only a handful of farm animals not to be. In some ways pigs were more work than their bovine or equine counterparts. Firstly, they required living facilities free from draught and cold throughout the winter months and if such lodgings in the farm did not exist they would obviously have to be built. They were also known to be dangerous especially to children: one tale talks about a girl who was put into a pigsty as punishment and subsequently forgotten about. Later, when looked for, all that was left of the girl was her nailed boots! Despite their indifferences and tendencies to eat anything, these intelligent creatures were a favourite of the Devonian farmer and were found in most all rural households, from the agricultural labourer's garden to the husbandman's farmyard. A variety of animals on a farmstead was once an essential requirement to run a successful farm. It was believed that a mixture of creatures kept a healthy landscape:

"Beasts alone, nor horses alone, nor sheep alone, will eat a pasture even."

Rabbits, like pheasants, were normally owned by the local land agent, to be used for shooting parties. Tenant farmers were not permitted to shoot these creatures on penalty of being arrested for poaching. However, Honiton farmers had a bit of a luxury as far as this was concerned compared to other parts of the county. Many local farmers owned their own land, others had leasehold rights to the land and, fortunately, the Lord of the Manor, up until the early 1800s, lived at Powderham Castle, some 20 miles away; by the mid 1800s the Lord was still no nearer to home. Those who did own their own land often allowed these furry little rodents to roam free, as money for their meat, or selling the hunting rights, could bring in as much as 15 shillings per acre.

Before the days of cars, couples would have generally met at the annual fair or local market and few travelled far from their home parish: of all the people in Honiton in 1851, over 60% of them were either born there or were from within a 5 mile radius of the town and around 80% of them were from the home county.
Farmers were once very high up on the social scale; in a book by Tristram Risdon of 1811, farmers, or "yeomanry" were ranked third in the social hierarchy, being beaten only by "the gentry" and "merchants", compared to the "labourers" who were last on this list. The men who farmed the land and provided the local community with food and work were the pinnacle of rural societies and were respected members of the country. "Most farmers married farmer's daughters" as the farmer's wife would need to know about the running of a farm, especially as she was in charge of the poultry, dairy and general day- to-day running of the farmhouse. Skills leant from her mother were passed on to her as she moved from one

kitchen to another. Honiton was no exception to this rule; in 1881, of those that can be confirmed, 9 out of 10 of the town's farmers had married women who came from an agricultural background. This inadvertently led to most rural regions having few people not related to the rest of the community. When questioned, in the 1960s, one couple in a Devonian village could number, and name, some 240 relatives, most of whom lived within the local vicinity. It may have become apparent throughout this book that many of Honiton's people of this period were related to each other by either blood or marriage. Farmers were also virtually a society unto themselves; even in the 1930s it was known for almost all of Honiton's farming community to attend the funeral of a fellow farmer or a fellow farmers' relative. This could possibly be because they were related to the other farmers anyway!

Wives worked just as hard as their husbands and one sixteenth century publication stated that "no wife should be idle at no time"!

Farmers would often employ live-in servants or apprentices to assist with the farm work and this led to its own problems. An enquiry of 1840 revealed that farm hands would often sleep three or four to a bed on mattresses made of 'douse' (a leftover product of the threshing machine) and were often housed in the rooms of the farmer's sons and daughters. However, with the farmer's own, and often large, family, the farmhouse often afforded little space for the helpers; at one farm in Bridford there were 21 people living under the farmhouse roof!

Farming became a massive enterprise during the war years of the twentieth century; one man, in 1918, who owned two farms near Honiton, was fined £35 & 20 guineas for allowing his agricultural properties to fall derelict.

Orchards were also once a prominent feature of the Devonian and Honitonian countryside alike. Farms generally brewed their own cider which was given to the farm labourers as part of their pay as well as being consumed by the farmer and his family. Anciently, many people who worked the land paid "their lord's rent with their cyder only." In the early 1790s a gentleman called Sylvanus Urban commented that "cyder made in the adjacent parishes is greater and better than in" Honiton.

In 1877, there were 23,000 acres of orchards in the county as "cider production took place at every farm in Devon and the apple trees were at the heart of the community." This trend lasted well into the twentieth century and even in 1922 Honiton was "noted for its orchards." Victorian labourers were known to have spent one sixth of their wages on this beverage even though, in the 1860s, they were the lowest paid labourers in the country. One acre of orchard could produce about 1,590 gallons of cider (based on a one acre orchard with 60 trees). However, with factors such as mass manufacturing and imports of cheaper cider, along with increased personal affluence, the self sufficiency of the Victorian age came to an abrupt halt and, unfortunately, so did the orchards. By 2009, 60% of the nation's orchards had been lost: 89% of those had once been found in Devon and Honiton was no exception to these statistics. In total, 85% of Honiton's orchards have disappeared since 1844. One such plot, which once stood on Northcote Hill, was appropriately named 'Farewell Orchard'!

In 1868, a meeting was held in the town for proposals to form a 'Chamber of Agriculture'. This was enacted and the 24 original members were charged an annual subscription of 2s.6d. The first president was William Porter of Hembury Fort House.

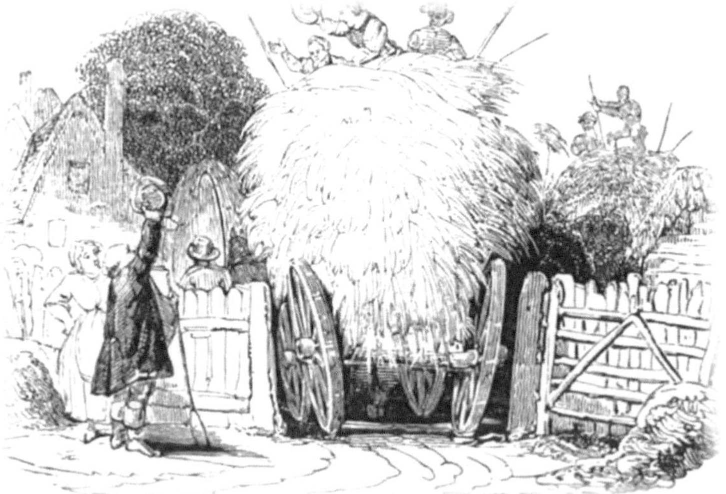

Chapter 2
Farms & Fields

"floating fields from the farm in the cup of the vales"
Dylan Thomas

In the late 1960s/early 1970s, Honiton underwent some big changes. With the post WWII population starting to set up homes of their own and other mitigating factors occurring in the rest of the local area, the town's population was predicted to explode. The M5 was set to be extended to East Devon by 1975; the town was becoming a more desirable retirement location and Exeter was growing as an administrative employment centre meaning Honiton was likely to become a popular home for commuters. All these changes meant increased migration of the populous to Honiton over the following years. The local planning authorities estimated that the population would increase from the then 5,000 people to 10,000 by 1991. These figures were not far wrong as the population of the town doubled between 1971 and 2001. The local changes also coincided with the 'Housing Act' of 1969 which meant new sites for housing and industry were a priority, leading to a massive extension of a town that had hardly changed its boundaries since Victorian times. The need for more homes would, sadly and unavoidably, lead to a drastic drop in the number of farms and farmland, which were once obviously much more ubiquitous outside of the town's urban boundaries.

Fields to the east/southeast of the town were some of the last enclosures in the parish to be 'broken' from their natural state for agricultural usage. By the mid-nineteenth century fields in this vicinity, particularly those on Marlpits Hill and around Honiton Golf Club, were much bigger and of a much more regular shape than the irregularly formed and smaller fields of those in the valley. Many also bore names such as 'Burnt Close' and 'Great Brake', evidence that they were brought into usage relatively recently. Much of these new lands were 'snapped' up by already existing farms as they extended their medieval boundaries and, as can be seen in *Appendix V*, were located some distance from the majority of the farm's original lands. Many of these fields still retain their nineteenth century forms and are worth comparing with those nearer to the town.

Development of new housing estates was concentrated to the south, as the majority of the north of the town, beyond the Honiton Bypass, provoked fears of flooding from the River Otter.

The national trade of farming, once worth about £132 million in the nineteenth century, took a down turn in the successive centuries as social

and financial changes altered the state of the countryside. The following are a list of farms that were in Honiton in Victorian times. There were most probably many farms before and there have indeed been many farms since; however, there were a main few that existed in Honiton for centuries, some of which still exist today.
(an illustration of the old and current town boundaries can be found in Appendix VI)

Barcote Farm: this was a small 10 acre farm located in Littletown on which now stands the old George Blay's Housing Estate. In the 1840s, the land was owned by Harry Buckland Lott, the well known Honiton banker, and was farmed by a Thomas Carter. The farm had disappeared by the 1850s.

Barton Farm: another small farm that once stood somewhere near Bramble Hill, which had also gone from the records by 1850.

Battishorne Farm: The ancient Manor of Battishorne can be dated back to 1253 when it was owned by William de Avenel. The estate was owned by George Younge in 1756 and was bought by John Bowering in 1828. In the mid 1800s the Battishorne estate consisted of some 597 acres of land. The smaller farm estate, which was attached to Battishorne Cottage, consisted of about 40 acres of land and it was Francis Wheaton of the Golden Lion who leased the land and adjoining cottage from Mr. Bowering from 1829. In 1857 some of the farm's land was bought by the railway in order to construct the new line. The old, 4 roomed cottage was demolished in the 1920s and the present house built. In 1952 Edwin Martin purchased the farm and in the late 1980s Mr. Martin's son, Francis, sold much of the land and set up the 'Battishorne Trust'.

Lower Blannicombe: in 1537 the farm, or 'manor' as it was then, was owned by a Agnes Fishmore and at that time consisted of a cottage, garden and some 172 acres of mainly arable land, more than double which existed in the 1840s when it was a 91 acre farm, of which nearly 40 acres was arable land.
One could say this farm was one of the cradles of Honiton's Victorian farmers. At the start of Victoria's reign this farm was occupied by Joan Hartnell; she had four children who, amongst them, would go on to run several of Honiton's farms in the coming years, as well as spawn a famous descendant!
The family originally came from Awliscombe and at some point in the early 1800s the family moved to Clayhidon where Bishop Hartnell, Joan's

husband, died in 1817. Shortly after the death of Bishop Hartnell, his wife moved to the farm of Lower Blannicombe in Honiton. In the 1840s, the farm was occupied by Joan, an unmarried daughter Mary and, amongst others, a farm hand called John Trood. John Trood must have had high ambitions for he later married Mrs. Hartnell's daughter and became the farmer of the land. John farmed the land at Lower Blannicombe for the next 40 years and later retired to the High Street in the late 1880s, dying, aged 81, in 1892. John became a widower in the 1860s and a nephew, from neighbouring Higher Blannicombe, moved into the farm with his young family to assist in the work.
In a sale of the property in 1869, it was said to boast "a newly erected farmhouse, outbuildings" and consisted of "rich meadow, pasture, orchard and arable land" which, at the time, was valued at £116.16.3.
The farm exists today as one of Honiton's only 'ancient' working farms, with much of the land from former, neighbouring farmsteads such as 'Swinesloose' and Higher Blannicombe now incorporated into its boundaries.

Higher Blannicombe: written in text also as 'Blannacombe' both Higher and Lower Blannicombe take their name from Sir Gilbert and Sir Stephen De Blaincomb who were known to have resided in Honiton as early as 1242. The Blannicombe Estates were, at this time, known as 'separate manors' within Honiton Parish: separate from the 'Manor of Honiton' itself. Higher Blannicombe later passed into the hands of the Luttrells and in 1438 consisted of 60 acres of arable, 12 acres of meadow, 20 acres of pasture and 30 acres of heath and furze. In the 16th century, John Northcote purchased the estate from the Luttrells and it later went to the Courtenays, to whom it subsequently belonged in the early 19th century. There were said to have been foundations of former properties in a field that was once an old orchard somewhere to the west of Higher Blannicombe Farm itself; the exact location this author has not been able to identify. These properties were thought to have once been a large hamlet and in an adjoining field there was an old linhay that was said to have once been used as a chapel for Non-Conformists, when non-conformity was illegal. This field's entrance is located at the very end of the track which carries on from where 'Brand Lane' meets 'Stoney Lane', today housing farm buildings; interestingly, the field was once called 'Burnt Close'. It would have certainly been a good settlement for a secret, non-conformist community, for even today this location is isolated. The track was thought to have once continued through the field to the hamlet in question, whereas today it simply leads to Lower Blannicombe Farm.

Some other fields located on the farm worth mentioning are those oddly named 'Great' & 'Little Barebones', whose origins are unknown. These fields have, fortunately, not been built on and, although now merged, still exist today. Another two adjoining fields called 'Studely' and 'Little Studely' are thought to originate from an old English word meaning that the fields may have once been used as pasture for horses.
The tenant farmer of the time was George Warren whose son later married a niece of the tenant of Lower Blannicombe, John Trood. At this time the farm consisted of 161 acres, with just under 60 used for arable purposes. In the 1860s it was valued at £165.15.1 and the annual rent was not much less, at £130 10s. Interestingly, it was on the market in 2008 for some 4,100 times its 1860s value with virtually none of its prior lands! The farmhouse still stands today but is now a private house with only 1.5 acres of its original land remaining.

Brand Farm *1: Brand's Farmhouse used to stand on the ground between 'Higher Brand Lane' and 'Weatherill Road' at the 'Honiton Bottom Road' junction. This was one of Honiton's smaller farms, most of which has since been built on. 'Hazelwood Close', 'Briars Close', part of Littletown Primary School and part of 'Gronau Close' now stand on lands that were once part of this farm.
This farmstead consisted of 43 acres, half of which was arable land and the remainder, orchard and meadow. The following is a list of the former names of the fields:

- Orchard
- Home Close
- Yonder Close
- Two Acres
- Yonder Cadhayes
- Hither Cadhayes
- Little Mead
- Church Close
- Lane Orchard
- Six Acres
- Yonder Five Acres
- Lower Six Acres
- Higher Five Acres

Many of these names are self explanatory: 'Six Acres', for example, was a field of six acres. 'Yonder Five Acres', speaks of a 5 acre field that was "near home" but was probably so named as a kind of irony as it was, in fact, the furthest field from the farmhouse, located somewhere off Cuckoodown Lane. 'Home Close' was the nearest field to the farmhouse and the field called 'Little Mead' would often be applied to a small field near water, which was indeed the case here, a 1 acre field standing next to the Gissage. 'Little Mead' still exists today and is the field to one's right coming up Honiton Bottom Road, from Littletown Primary School, towards Weatherill Road. It is, however, larger today having been merged with part of an adjacent field at some point in the last century. Incidentally, 'Lane Orchard' was not an orchard but more a small plot of land which seemed to have had no specific purpose: it once stood on part of the site now occupied by Littletown Primary School. The farm itself was, at this time, run by a Richard Corner who was tenant for at least 20 year and was rented on a long term lease from The Manor of Honiton. The farm itself disappeared in the 1870s. A nearby cottage, which had once been a part of Combehayes Farm, along with the old farmhouse of Brand, later became labourers' cottages known as 'Brand Cottages' which long outlived the farm itself.

Brand Cottage: one of the above mentioned properties that in the 1850s was a smallholding of 9 acres. It later became an agricultural labourer's dwelling which consisted of only 3 interior rooms and has long since been demolished to make way for modern housing.

Cheneys: also known as Chenhayes, Chenehayes and Chamhays, it takes its name from "the noble family of Cheney" who held "great estates" in Devon and Wiltshire and whose roots can be traced back to the Normans. The Cheneys or Cheyneys were once a very prominent family in the West Country and there were many members of the family who, at differing times throughout the 14th and 15th centuries, held the titles of 'Sheriff' of Devon, Dorset and Wiltshire. Cecily Cheney, daughter of Sir John Cheney, married into

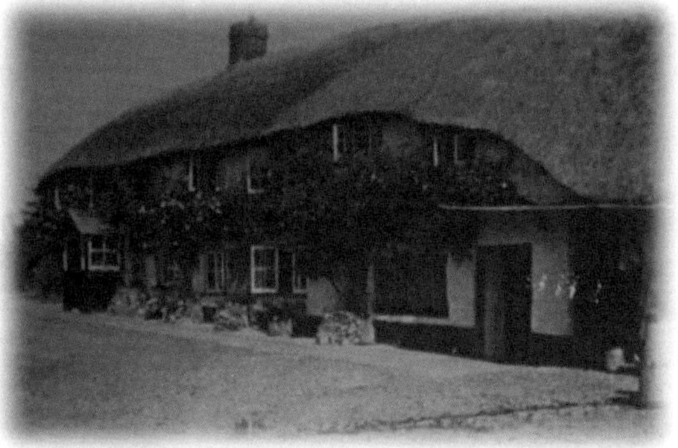

the Courtenay family in the late 1400s. The Cheneys also held the Manor of Upottery in the 13th century. Although the farmhouse itself has only been traced back through the records to the 1600s, the roots from the farm's name suggest a much earlier establishment.

In the 1840s, the farm was once owned by Francis Baring, 3rd Baron Ashburton and its tenants of the time were the Gosling family. Samuel Gosling was resident in 1841 and after his death, his wife Rebecca, and later his son William, took over the farm. William spent the majority of his life on the farm from the 1830s right through to his death in 1901; however, by the end of the 19th century, William had become an invalid so his daughter and his son-in-law, Charles and Susan Lock, continued the work of the farm. The Locks were succeeded by their son, another William, who stayed at Cheneys until the 1950s, when the Nichols took it over. Mr. Nichols purchased the farm in 1951 for £10,000, a sizable sum for the time, which many local people apparently thought was "mad" considering the farm's dilapidated state!
The present farm kitchen was lowered several inches as one of the Nichols was well over 6 foot and consequently found it difficult to manoeuvre around inside! The farm had its own cider barn which is now used as a holiday let: originally this picturesque little farm was 50 acres in size and later grew to 92 acres. When the last of the Nichols departed from the farm in 1999, the land was split up and sold off to different buyers, leaving the present owners of the farm with just over 22 acres. The last of the farm's orchards was also lost in the 1950s when the old, rotted trees were cleared.
Still a working farm today, with added accommodation for travellers, this farm stands just a few miles from Honiton, off Langford Road.

Claylands Farm: a 55 acre farm that was once located in Littletown. It was known to have existed in the town from at least 1686 when its resident was John Prying. The farm got its name from the high clay content of the surrounding soil: there were once at least two "old clay pits" located near the farmhouse. By the 19th century it was owned by Harry Buckland Lott, a local attorney previously mentioned, and had at least one labourer's cottage attached to it. The labourer's cottage was a small property of only 4 rooms which would have included bedrooms, kitchen etc. Claylands later merged with Roundball Farm, which was also owned by Mr. Lott. The farmhouse itself once stood approximately on a site between what is now 'Banfield Way' and 'Wren Close' and standing on the former farmland are now the housing estates of 'Yallop Way' and 'Willow Walk'. Despite its land, it was not thought to have been a working farm in its own right in the early Victorian period, for it appeared on no maps of the time and all references to its inhabitants referred to them as 'farm labourers' rather than the status of 'farmer'. With the losses sustained by the Lott family, after the failure of the bank, the farm came into the possession of the Honiton Manor. During the 1880s and 1890s, Claylands House became "Honiton Small-Pox Hospital" for the benefit of people suffering from the disease as well as other infectious ailments. The old farmhouse remained standing right through to the mid 1960s when it was demolished to make way for the Whitebridges housing estate. In the late 19th century it was used as an agricultural labourer's cottage, along with another adjoining dwelling that was also once part of the farm.

Combehayes Farm: another farm whose name suggests early origins; the farmstead was also known as 'Coombe Hays' and 'Coombhayes'. Both the words 'Combe' and 'Hayes' are Old Saxon words meaning 'valley' and 'dwelling place' respectively, which correctly describes the situation of this farm, standing as it does in "the vale." A Victorian eyewitness noted that in the "farm house was formerly some finely carved oak and the ceiling of one of the rooms was highly decorated, thus suggesting the inference that at one time it was the residence of a person of consequence." The farmhouse was built in the late 16th or early 17th century and was constructed of stone and cob walls.

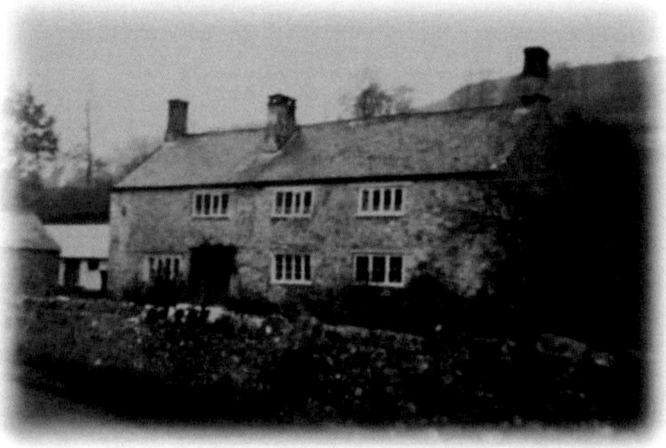

In the early Victorian period, it was a 126 acre farm inhabited by John Veysey and, once again, owned by the Manor of Honiton. At one time, Mr. Veysey had six 'live in' farm hands aged from 10 to 50. The farm was predominantly pastoral with a dairy concern and about a third of the land was dedicated to crop growing. The tenancy later fell into the hands of Joseph Dymond who worked the land for well over 10 years before the long term tenant of Gardeners Farm, John Hartnell, took over in the late 1860s. Later, it would be Thomas and Mary Griffin, the son-in-law and

daughter of the aforementioned Mr. Hartnell, who would work the land. The thatched farmhouse suffered a great fire in January 1935 that "completely gutted" the building.
Combehayes was a working farm until relatively recently, although on a much smaller scale than it once was: the farmhouse itself was converted into three separate houses when the farm was dissolved in 2007.

Cowley Farm *2: the farmhouse was once located at the bottom of Silver Street, where Honiton Cattle Market car park is now located. Cowley was known to have existed in the town as early as Henry VII's time when it was owned by the previously mentioned John Takell.
The once 17.5 acres of land of this dairy farm stood on the site which is now occupied by Honiton Community College. Even in the early twentieth century *"Cowley Farm was quite large and carried quite a large herd of cattle".*

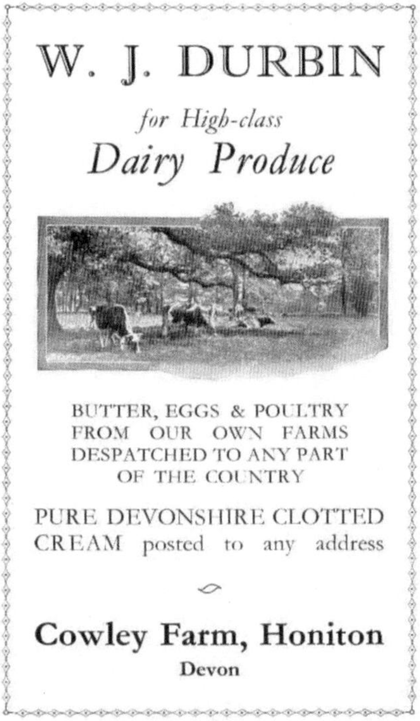

Although the actual origins of the name 'Cowley' are unknown, the old English word 'Cowlay' refers to pasture land for cows and this could very well be from where the farm got its name. The farm comprised of four fields in total which were named: 'Thomas's Field', 'Howells Seven Acres', 'Howells Four Acres' and 'French Nut Close' which were all owned by the local bankers, Christopher S. Flood and Harry B. Lott. There was a family by the name of 'Howell' who were known to have lived in the town in the early 18th century and fields named in this possessive context were often named after former landowners or land tenants. A 'French Nut' was an old West Country name for 'a walnut' but whether this has anything to do with how this field got its name is unconfirmed.

For much of the Victorian era the farm was worked by John Davey, starting there in the 1830s; he later moved to Stout Farm, then Rowley and then went back to Cowley, which is where he died in 1893.
The farm came into the ownership of the Manor after the failures of Mr. Lott and Mr. Flood and when the Manor was put up for sale, in 1868, Mr. Davey purchased the freehold for £2,150.
With the death of Mr. Davey, much of the farm's lands were sold off to separate buyers and the remainder was worked by Seth Durbin as a dairy concern. Two of the Durbin family's sons gave their lives for King and Country in the First World War.
After the Durbins left, the farmhouse and buildings were demolished. The dairy was attached to the old farmhouse and, apart from making products such as clotted cream, the business was also "licensed to sell and deal in game".

Gardeners Farm *3: also spelt 'Gardiners', its name is thought to have been derived from a local family of that name: in the late 14th century there was a Rector of Honiton called Richard Gardiner. This farm was, in the early part of the Victorian period, run by John Hartnell, one of the sons of Joan and Bishop Hartnell of Lower Blannicombe. This idyllic farm was once situated not far from Stoney Lane, originally reached from the 'stoney' track that starts in Higher Brand Lane. The track in question was once called 'Gardiners Lane' and, although still clearly marked on present day maps, this is by no means a vehicular-accessible lane today, for now the old site of Gardeners Farm stands some one quarter of a mile from any public road, making it hard for any passersby or dog walkers to imagine it ever had road access to it.

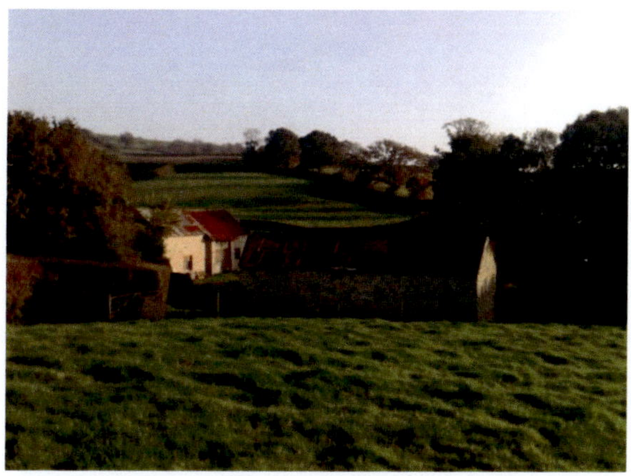

Gardeners Farm as it is today showing the old farmhouse (left) and barn (centre).

The old stone farmhouse and barn still exist today but have not been used for their former purpose for many decades. Today, they simply serve as outbuildings on the land of the present day Lucashayes Farm.
In the 1840s, the farm was a small, 40 acre farm, of which about half was arable. However, by 1868 the farm had doubled in size. The Hartnells managed to acquire another 43 acres of land, most of which had formerly been leased to the Blake family of the Dolphin Inn.
John Hartnell farmed Gardeners until the 1860s when his son, another John, took it over. John Jnr. later moved to 'Bucton Farm' in Sidbury and the farm then fell into the lap of John's sister, Mary, and her husband, Thomas Griffin. The Griffins were, at this time, running Combehayes Farm and with the addition of the new premises the two farms merged. The 1901 census stated that Gardeners farm itself was 'unoccupied' whilst the lands were managed by Thomas and his wife Mary until the early 1900s.
John Hartnell Senior was married twice; his first wife died in 1830 and by her he had three children. However, only one lived beyond the age of 4. His second marriage was to Sarah Western, by whom he had a further six children. After the death of John, his widow Sarah went to live with her in-laws, the Griffins, at Combehayes. In 1881, Sarah was listed as an "annuitant" showing that her late husband must have done well from the years at Gardeners: she died in Honiton aged 93. By the 1880s, the farm was being used as a dairy farm but was later used as a labourer's dwelling for Combehayes Farm. For a short time in the 1930s, the farmhouse was once again used as a dairy but this short lived twentieth century occupation ceased. Today the remaining buildings are sadly a crumbling shadow of their former selves.

Gobsore Farm: a farm that was once located on the Sidmouth Road. The farm is known to have existed in the time of Henry VII when John Takell,who owned land there, made bequests to the town. The estate of Gobsore was later owned by the Searles and by 1727 the lands came into the possession of the Putt family, when Ann Searle, the last of that family, married Raymundo Putt. The majority of the farm was arable and in the mid 19th century it consisted of some 80 acres: from that time it was run, for some 20 years, by James Smith. The farm itself was only 55 acres in size but Mr. Smith rented additional lands from 'The Charity of St. Margaret's' and Christopher Flood, which made up the remainder.
Much of the original farm land has luckily escaped the hands of 20th and 21st century developers. In Victorian times the farmhouse and surrounding land was owned by the Marker family, the nephews of the Putts of

Gittisham who inherited the vast Combe Estate. The old farmhouse still exists as a private residence but the farm itself ceased in the 1970s, with the last tenants being the Hutchings family.

Perrie Hale Farm: Perry/Perrie Hale or Little Hale, as it has been known, was a small farm located at the east end of town. In 1851 it was a 23 acre pastoral farm with 10 separate plots of land surrounding it: the farmer also leased some additional fields near the church of St. Michael's. One field that no longer exists in its own right was called 'Crane Close', believed to be so named because the shape of it resembled a crane's head. In the 1840s the farm was owned by Peter Richards, a farmer who had once farmed the land himself and who later retired to No. 7 Summerland Place. After Mr. Richards retired, for a short time its tenant became Mr. Robert Parker, before passing into the hands of James Snell, who died at the farm aged in his 70s.

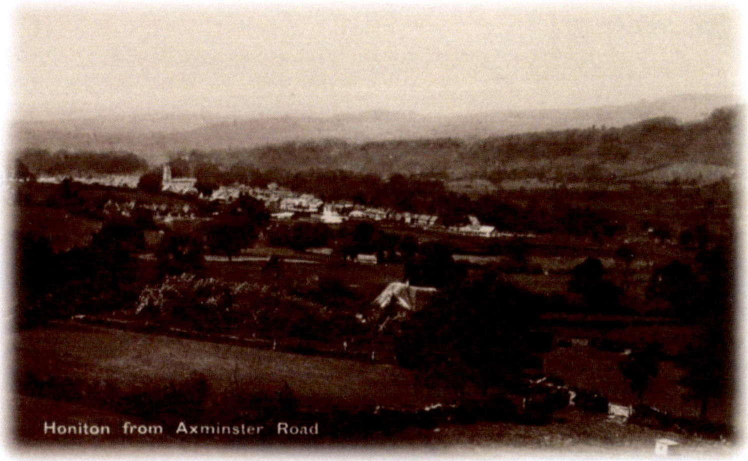

Part of Perrie Hale farm with the old farmhouse situated in the centre.

The farmhouse was built in 1604; however, structural evidence of the property, like other farms of the area, suggests an earlier medieval building. One of the earliest known farmers here was a George Clapp, in 1682. When sold in 1957 it consisted of 27 acres but ceased to be a farm. Perrie Hale was split up in 2006 when the farm house and some 10, of the then 25 acres, were sold off to a private individual. The remaining 15 acres of land was retained by the previous owners as a wholesale nursery, growing and selling trees and shrubs. The family established new offices not far from the old farmhouse and renamed the site 'Perrie Hale Forestry Nursery'.

Great Hale Farm: this farmstead was the big brother to Perrie Hale, with some 150 acres of land and was, in some instances, simply known as 'Hale Farm'. In the early 1800s, the farm was referred to as 'The Great Hale Estate' and was worked by a man called John Wheaton of Woodbury. By the 1840s it was farmed by Thomas Denner, who built Springfield. Thomas Denner had married Charlotte, the granddaughter of the aforementioned John Wheaton, and her uncle was once the proprietor of the Golden Lion. The farm later came into the possession of a Mr. Joseph Perry and by the early 1850s William Collins was resident. William Collins, a man from Stockland, had moved his family to Honiton in 1851 to farm Great Hale and by 1878 his son, Hayman Collins, had succeeded him. The Collins family still reside at the farm today, having cultivated the land for some 160 years! The farm was owned by the Manor of Honiton and at its sale in 1869, the farm was said to have been a few 'roods' short of 148 acres in size and was described as having "a superior farmhouse, with dairyman's house adjoining." The farmhouse was destroyed by a fire in 1850 and was rebuilt with wood from the old army barracks that once stood in Marlpits Lane. Both the 'Hale' Farms are believed to have gotten their name from an ancient family that once resided in the valley. A 14th century gentleman by the name of Sir Ralph de la Hale left all his land at "la hale", in the boundaries of Honiton, to his daughter. The Searles, another old Honiton family, were also once the owners of the estate when the farmhouse was the mansion house of this once rich family. In Farquharson's book he noted that since the destruction of the farmhouse in 1850, there "were no traces" remaining to suggest "that any one of note" ever lived there. The Searles were known to have resided at Hale as early as the reign of Henry VIII and one family member, Priscilla Searle, who owned the Hale estate in the 1500s, was interestingly a great grandmother of two of Great Britain's foremost and famous Prime Ministers. Her great great grandson was William Pitt the Elder and her three times great grandson was William Pitt the Younger, who both ran the country from 1766-1768 and 1783-1801 respectively.

Some of the field names of this farm are worth noting: one field was known as 'Strap' on account of its long narrow shape - it used to run parallel to the A35 but was merged with the two adjoining fields in the mid 1800s. One smaller field was named 'Devil's Acre' and another, with the longer name of 'Blue Marl Pit Wood and Pit', was an 8 acre pasture named after the old marl pits located on the hill. All, apart from the last mentioned, suffered the same fate as 'Strap'. 'Crooked Meadow', which speaks for itself, still stands on Northcote Hill but no longer exists in its own right, having also been merged with adjacent fields.

Heathfield: Heathfield Farm was another estate that was once a seat of the Searle family, being originally a grand home rather than a working farm. The Searles held the lands in the 17th and 18th century and one of the earliest references to their ownership was in the year 1610. The farmhouse itself is known to date from the 16th century. On one of the bedroom windows is engraved the name 'Ann Searle' who was the only daughter of the last Searle to own Heathfield. She later married Raymundo Putt of Gittisham and the estates of Heathfield and Gobsore, another estate owned by them, were acquired by the Putt family and subsequently inherited by the Markers. The last Searle to reside at Heathfield was Ann's father, John, who died in 1727. In the nineteenth century the "old mansion" was described as "the abode of a substantial yeoman or small landowner." The estate later became a tenanted farm and by the 1840s, the 75 acres estate was run by a very capable woman called Susan Cox. Susan was widowed young and managed to run the farm and raise her children there for some 20 years. In a time when farming was primarily a man's job, Mrs. Cox put a dent in the stereotype: in 1841 she had a total of 6 farm workers residing with her. In her later life, her nephew and niece moved to the farm to assist in the work. The farm later became home to Thomas Rolstone who married Jane Davey, a daughter of John Davey of Cowley Farm. The farmland of Heathfield stretched from the old farmhouse as far as Gobsore Farm to the north and Exeter Road to the south. By the twentieth century parts of the farm were lost, first to the army barracks of Heathfield Army Camp and later Heathfield Industrial Estate. When the Honiton Golf Club shut from the early 1900s, there was also a nine-hole golf course established on the farm land, where the

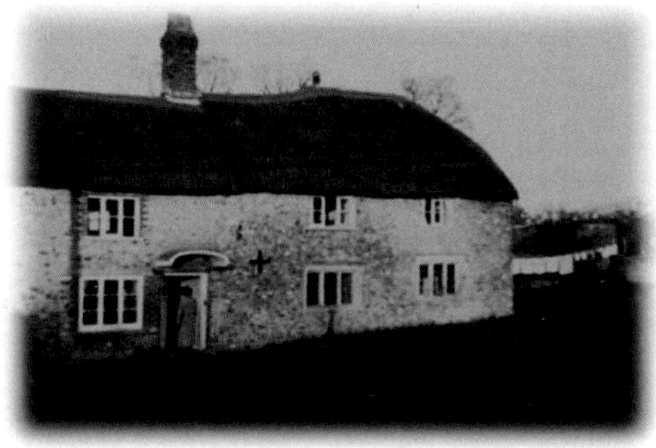

military camp would later reside. The farm had a long history of supporting local military activities, particularly those of the local volunteer army and so it is, maybe, not so surprising that an army camp would later be established there when war was declared. Heathfield Army Camp was established in the early years of WWII and many of the industrial estate's road names remind us of its past. 'Reme Drive', for example, was named after the 'Royal Training Bn. REME' (Royal Electrical Mechanical Engineers). 'Gloucester Crescent' and 'Close' were named after the Gloucester Regiment; Devonshire Road, after the Devonshire Regiment and 'Durham Way' after The Durham Light Infantry, who were also once stationed there. When the shopping complex was built on the old WWII parade ground, it was thought to have been the last remaining example of such in the country.

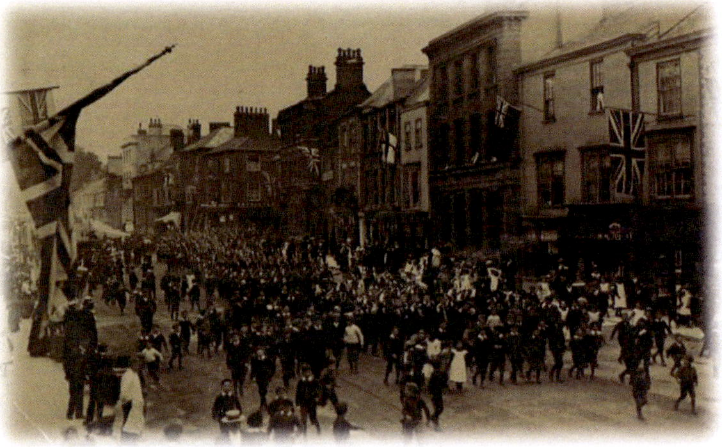

3rd Devon Regiment on their way to Heathfield for their annual training in 1904.

Some 15 years after the War, military spending was cut and the Royal Training Bn. REME were the first to leave the camp in April 1959. The camp slowly shrank and was finally sold to the local council in the 1970s to make way for 'Heathpark Industrial Estate' that is there today. From the late 1970s the old army huts were used as shelters for the homeless until 1988. Originally, the camp stretched all the way to the Sidmouth Road, now partly occupied by St. Peter's Housing Estate, which was built on the site of the old homeless lettings. Roughly where the recreational grounds of St. Peter's are now located, were once a collection of four tennis courts used by the army.

Heathfield is thought to have got its name, prior to the establishment of the building, from an early un-cleared field that would have once supported heather or 'heath'; hence 'heath' 'field'. Two of the farm's fields even had such names - 'Little Heathfield' and 'Long Heathfield'.

The farm, however, remained for some years afterwards but in 1986 the remaining 50 acres of farmland were sold off to make way for the 'Old Elm Road' housing estate that now surrounds it. The plans to construct the housing estate did, in fact, date back to the early 1970s when there were also proposals to build another primary school on the land. The farm's last farmer, Mr. Ford, who had been there since 1955, managed to preserve the ancient listed farmhouse, once known as 'The Barn', within the complex by converting it into a bar which is now a three star, seven bedroomed hotel and restaurant called 'The Heathfield Inn'. The pub was originally intended to be tripled up as a community centre and shop which did not, however, come to pass. In later years there was even a proposal to establish a nightclub within the walls of the old building!

Despite the fact that this ancient seat of the Searles, and hence the prosperous farm that followed, no longer exists today, it is comforting to know that the name of this piece of Honiton history lives on. The building itself is Grade II listed and, interestingly, among its brick chimneys has one made of stone.

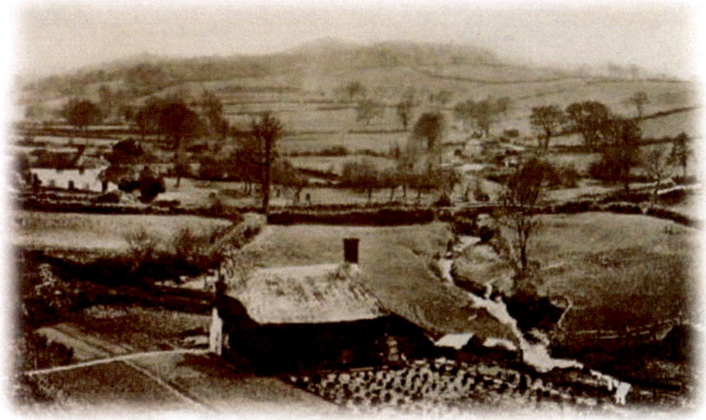

Ivy Cottage in the late 19th century, the surrounding fields were once part of Littletown.

Ivy House/Cottage: this quaint little abode once stood not far from Littletown. In the early Victorian period it was a smallholding farmed by a Mr. Henry Otton. The old cottage and adjoining meadow were owned by the previously mentioned Ruth Tooze and, in total, was 14 acres in size.

Henry resided and worked at this picturesque little dwelling until his death in 1862, aged 77. The cottage has long since disappeared with the construction of the Littletown Housing estates.

Landslide: a smallholding that was farmed by Mr. Thomas Ware in 1850. The dwelling is thought to have only existed a few years.

Littletown: yet another smallholding that was farmed by Chas Budd Musgrove in the 1840s who worked the 2 acres of land for a short time alongside his main career as a thatcher. Mr. Musgrove later went on to become landlord of the Lamb & Flag Inn. The old cottage later became known as 'Pratts' and was once situated in front of an orchard, which stood immediately to the west of the 'Honiton Bottom Road'/'Littletown Junction', now occupied by a pair of semi-detached houses.

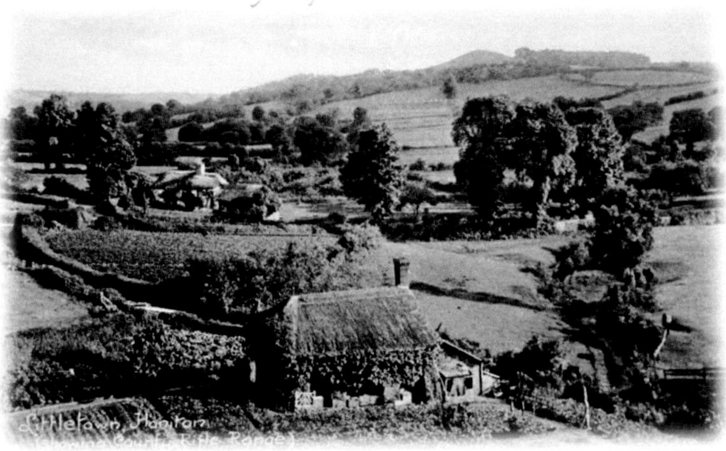

Another later view of Littletown with Ivy Cottage in the foreground. The thatched property in the background was once the farm run by Mr. Musgrove.

Livermore: another of the ancient farms of Honiton. Once known as 'Court Hall', and from its former name and other evidence, is thought to have been at one time a great manor house. In more recent times the old farmhouse was said to have been a "mere cottage" to its former self as a "great proportion" of the pre-dating property had long since been removed. In a field that once stood between Livermore and the church of

St. Michael's was said to have been foundations of numerous buildings, suggesting that a much larger complex was once present there. There is much speculation as to whether this house was, in fact, the ancient Manor House of the town, when the town was thought to be located at Littletown. The farm takes its name from the 'Livermore' family who lived in the area some 500 years ago. One member of this family was buried in St. Michael's in 1694. Due to its close proximity to the church, all parish meetings were originally adjourned to the old farmhouse.

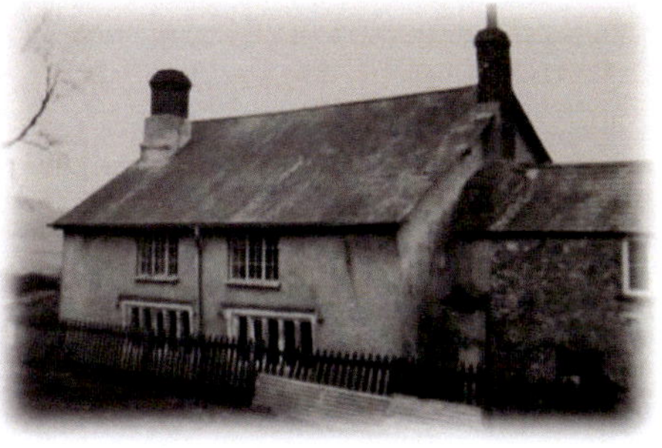

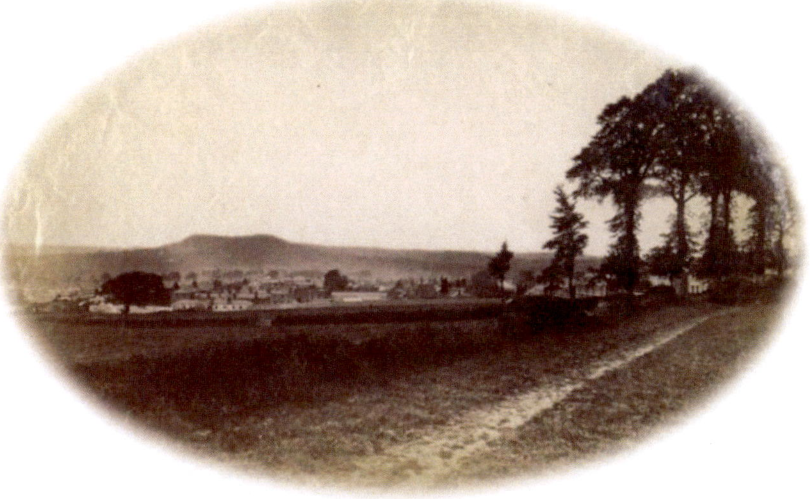

View of Church Hill from one of Livermore Farm's fields (now site of Haydons Park).

The farm's land previously consisted of all that was hemmed in within the triangle formed by the roads of 'Church Hill', 'Lower Brand Lane' and 'Marlpits Lane'. It was a small farm by comparison, totalling about 18 acres.

In the 1840s it was farmed by William Burroughs whose son later went on to farm Old Rectory Farm. On the sale of Honiton Manor in 1869 it was described as "a very compact and desirable farm." The last and most well known farmers who resided there were the Tratt family. The farmhouse, which was once thatched, suffered some structural damage during the war years. A Wellington bomber was returning from a training exercise over Brest, France on July 5th 1944 when it started to experience engine trouble. At about 3 am, the pilot apparently made an attempt to land in one of the farm's fields but, having to narrowly avoid hitting a pylon, the plane crashed into the farmhouse and exploded in one of the adjacent fields. No one in the house was injured but all six of the Canadian crew were killed and a service for them was held in St Michael's Church shortly afterwards. The farmhouse was reconstructed but in 1976, when the then resident farmer William Tratt died, the family were faced with massive death duties of some £170,000, as some years earlier the land had been in dispute over a compulsory purchase order. The family had no choice but to sell up and relocate which they successfully completed in 1978 when they moved to 'Lower Marlpits Farm', just a stone's throw from their former dwelling.

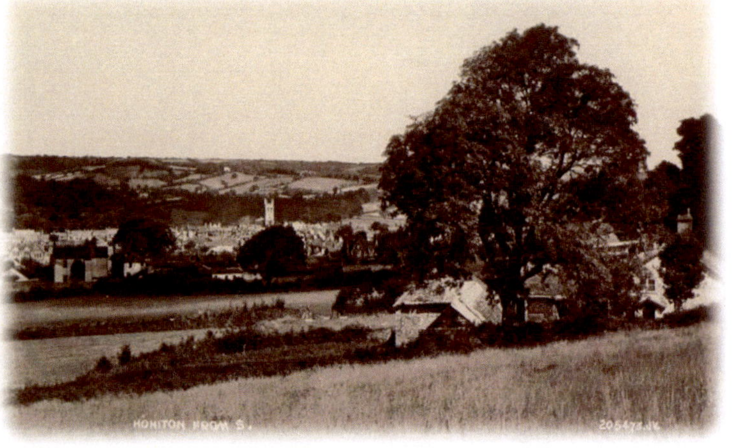

A view overlooking Livermore Farm, with the old farmhouse on the right.

The farmhouse, no longer being of any structural interest due to its former damage, and all of the farmland were sold off to developers and standing there today is the 'Haydons Park' housing estate and an extension of the Honiton Hospital. The old farmhouse once stood in 'Lower Marpits Lane', not far from the 'Weatherill Road' junction.

Lowmans: or 'Lomans' as it was also known. The farm takes its name, and dates from the Lowman family who resided in the town in the 16th century. Lowman was a corruption of the name 'de Lumine', a family who settled in Gittisham.

The farm was once known as 'Down Edge' so described in a document bearing the date 1806. In Victorian times it was a farm of some 75 acres, whereas today it is about 300! This farm was also one of the Honiton tenancies to fall into the hands of the aforementioned Hartnell family. James Hartnell, second eldest son of Bishop and Joan, resided at this farm from 1851 until his death in 1870. James' son, Henry, took over the farm after his father's death and remained there until the 1880s when he moved to Livermore Farm. After Henry's departure, the farm was run by a Walter Clapp until the early twentieth century. The farm is one of the only 'ancient' farms of the town to still exist today and is presently situated down 'Stoney Lane'.

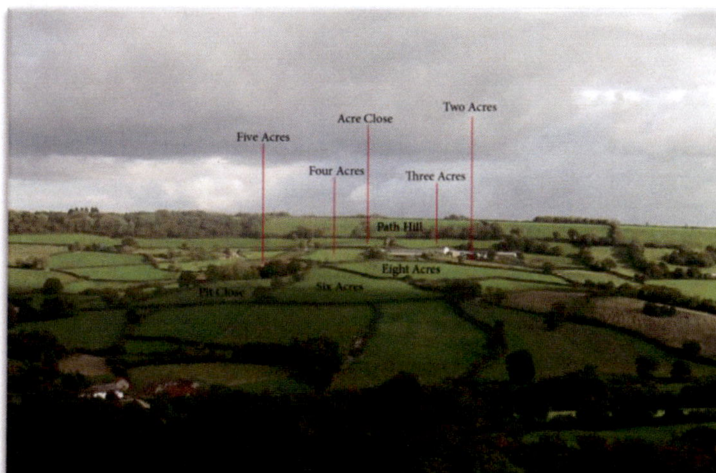

Photo taken from Roundball Hill showing the old field names of Lowmans Farm

Lucerhayes: this was once a 50 acre farm, the lease of which was held by a Margaret Lott from the Honiton Manor and who, in turn, rented it to Samuel Skinner in the 1840s. It has also been referred to as Lucashayne, Lucashayes and Luckerhaws. The farm was later taken over by Samuel Tratt, the son of another Samuel Tratt of Throwhayes. Samuel put about 25 years into the farm before his death in 1876, after which his second wife, Emma, ran the estate. Following Emma's death, her sons jointly ran the farm up until the mid 1930s, after which one of their respective sons, James Henry Tratt, carried on alone. Today the farm is the private residence of one of the town's doctors and still retains some 5 acres of its original land. The property stands in Stoney Lane.

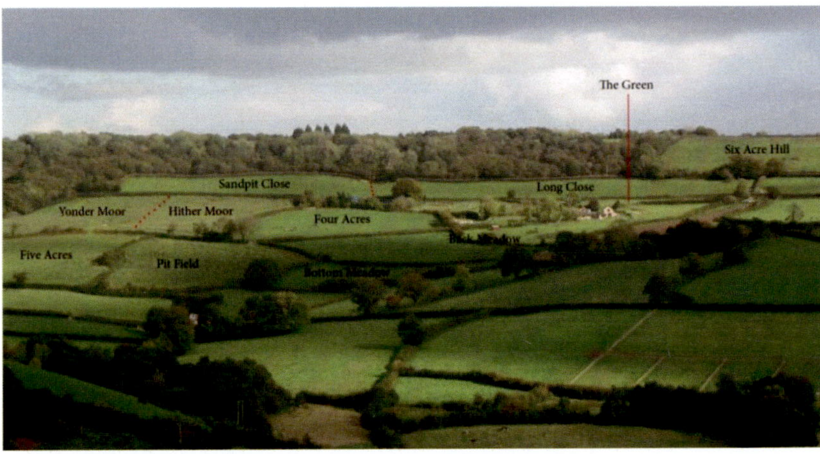

The old fields' names and locations of Lucerhayes Farm.

Middlehills: this was another relatively small farm known to date back to the 17th century. It probably got its name from its location in relation to the surrounding farms, as it was sandwiched in between 5 other estates. The farm was originally a small holding that was part of the Blannicombe estate which was sold for the sum of £300 in 1698 to a Samuel Clapp. The premises from then on was a farm in its own right and consisted of some 30 acres, 20 of which were woodland called 'Popes Wood'. Over the following 140 years, Popes Wood was cleared into fields and was first split into separate wooded plots known as 'Little Popes Wood' and 'Great Popes Wood': these were also later cleared into open fields. The road that today leads to Lower Blannicombe Farm was so named 'Popes Wood Lane/Way'

in 1698. It is likely that this wooded area got its name from the family of 'Pope' who owned lands in Honiton in the 15th century. An orchard, which was once situated by the Gissage, was also cleared and re-located to the field that joined the farmhouse; however, this *newer* orchard has also been lost today. Samuel Clapp left the farm to his wife and after her death, bequeathed the estate to his great nephew, John Clapp; however, owing to a legal technicality in his Will, the land had to be sold and then bought back by the Clapp family.
The farm later came into the possession of the Gidley family of Honiton and by 1844 it was a 23.5 acre farm rented by Thomas Melhuish. Mr. Melhuish spent well over 20 years at the farm until his death in 1867 when the farm then became tenanted by William Hartnell, son of John Hartnell of Gardeners Farm and grandson of Bishop and Joan Hartnell of Lower Blannicombe Farm. The farm still exists today on the outskirts of the town.

Great Northcote: also known as 'Northcott', this was one of the largest of all the Honiton farms in Victorian times. In 1844 it was 185 acres in size, stretching virtually the entire length of Northcote Hill. Northcote was anciently a manor in its own right within the Manor of Honiton and was conveyed by Baldwin de Redvers, then Lord of Honiton Manor, to The Priory of Bromore in Hampshire in the reign of King Stephen, some 900 years ago. The Priory of Bromore was an order of Black Canons under the patronage of the Holy Trinity and St. Michael, which had been originally founded by the de Redvers family. With the dissolution of the Catholic religion in England during the reign of Henry VIII, the estate of Northcote was sold to the Minify family. The Minify (Minifie) family were from Pothill in Kent and a certain Thomas Minify, in the reign of Henry VIII, married a member of the Honiton Stremmers family who gave their name to 'Streamers Meadows'. The Minify family held Northcote until the 17th century when it passed to the Pearce family who, at the same time, were known to have farmed the lands of Blannicombe. After the Pearce family, the estate went to the family of Blagdon who built the old farmhouse, originally known as 'Northcote House'. The Blagdons resided at the house until around 1809 and by the late 19th century the old "mansion" had all but disappeared, apart from a solitary wing which later became the farmhouse. The farm then passed to Mr. Denner, thought to be the father of Thomas Denner of Great Hale, and later Springfield. Mr. Denner later sold the estate and it eventually became the property of Lord Ashburton who owned the estate in Victorian times. When it separated from the Manor of Honiton, at the time Baldwin de Redvers sold it to Bromore, it became a Manor in its own right and a gentleman named Potwhele, writing in 1795, stated that there was once said to have been a hamlet of houses, inhabited by those who served the old manor, some 150 yards from the farmhouse. All of these properties had disappeared by the early 19th century; presumably when the property became a farm. The Manor of Northcote must have been a vast one considering that, as well as the little settlement of houses, it also had a mill linked to the estate which has also long since vanished.

In the early 19th century the farm was run by John Baker who remained tenant until his death in 1878, after which his son, William, took over. When William died, his wife Mary remained there until her son, John, took the reins. John stayed there until the First World War when the farm left the hands of the Baker family after nearly a century. Among the many strangely named fields of Great Northcote Farm were examples of its regal past. Plots of land were so named 'Knights Close', 'Knights Meadow' and 'Lords Close'. As a matter of interest, these three fields were all grouped together around what was once known as 'Northcott Mill', which was once located down the present day 'Langford Road' *(more can be found about Northcott Mill in the next chapter)*. Other fields worth noting are 'Mathews Park', most probably named after the person who cleared the land along with 'Wills Meadow' and 'Wills Moor', where 'moor' would have been a field of poor quality for pasture or crop cultivation. 'Pudding Close' was another interestingly named plot of land basically because of its shape: this field still exists and stands west of, and opposite, Cheneys Farm.

The farm no longer exists today; however, the farmhouse does. Today the farmhouse is surrounded by 'Otter Valley Park' which was built on the orchards of the former estate and are appropriately named 'The Orchard' and 'The Bramleys'. The former was previously a 3 acre orchard once known as 'Barn Orchard'. The farm itself changed its name to 'Lower Northcote' in the twentieth century and disappeared altogether in the 1980s. However, another farm was later established from a small dwelling that was once part of Great Northcote estate. This property was once a small labourer's cottage originally called 'Bishops House', thought to have been so named when the estate was owned by Rev. William Coney of Somerset in the early 19th century, and is now an 80 acres farm known as 'Middle Northcote Farm'. Middle Northcote today is run by a descendant of the Hartnell family.

Northcote Hill: Northcote Hill was a smaller brother to Great Northcote, once run by a gentleman called Benjamin Trim, when it was simply called 'Trims'. Mr. Trim worked the 50 acre farm until the 1850s when he was stated as being "out of business". His lack of luck was inherited by his son, Benjamin Trim Jnr., who ran the 'Green Dragon' in New Street and who was also put out of business when the pub was shut and demolished. The farm still exists today and is now known as 'Higher Northcote'.

Old Rectory Farm: this became a farm after John Fielder Mackarness, Honiton Rector, moved the Rectory from Parsonage Lane to Bramble Hill in 1860. The old rectory then became the farmhouse and the first tenant farmer was James Burrough, a son of a previous farmer of Livermore Farm. Mr. Burrough remained at Old Rectory until the mid 1920s, after some 60 years! When James died, aged well into his 90s, his son William took over, but only for a few years. By the late 1920s a certain Robert Smith became tenant, and his family kept the land until 1982. Today the farm is an 82 acre pastoral farm run by the Davey family who have been resident since the last of the Smiths died. Mrs. Davey was a daughter of the last Smith to run the Railway Inn. The farmhouse was built in the 17th century and has been a listed building since 1949.

Ring in the Mire: this was a farm run for a short time by a son of George Warren of Blannicombe, George Warren Jnr. It was once located somewhere on the western edge of the Honiton parish.

Roebuck: this farmstead is today located right beside the A30 just a stone's throw from Heathpark Industrial Estate. The farmhouse is late 18th century and in Victorian times it was a dwelling of about 80 acres. At this time Roebuck was owned by a Francis Stevens and its lands once stretched across the Exeter road, which is now occupied by part of Heathpark Industrial Estate. In the 1840s the farm was run by James Farrant and later George Hartnell, another son of Joan and Bishop Hartnell of Lower Blannicombe. George Hartnell married a daughter of James Farrant and took over the farm in the 1860s.

Another of James Farrant's children, William, who resided in Ottery St Mary, fell on hard times in 1841 - James was actually ordered by the local Poor Law Authority to pay them two shillings a week to help maintain him! George Hartnell's son, Henry Bishop Hartnell, was born at Roebuck and was sent to work in a London inn at an early age. By 1901 Henry Hartnell had excelled and then owned and ran 'The Crown & Sceptre' in Streatham, Wandsworth; it was here that his son, Sir Norman Bishop Hartnell, was born in 1901. Norman Bishop Hartnell later went on to become the famous and influential fashion designer and dressmaker to HM Queen Elizabeth, the Queen Mother in 1940, and HM Queen Elizabeth II in 1957.

The pub where Norman was born still exists and today is a 'J. D. Wetherspoons'. In the 1950s the farm was 30 acres in size but in 2003 'The Honiton Show' organizers bought lands from the farm for use at the annual event and the farm is subsequently much smaller today.

Roundball *4: previously the largest of all Honiton's farms it was, like many others, once the seat of a "gentleman". One such man who lived there was Sir Henry Hooper. A portion of the old house was pulled down leaving what was once the farmhouse. It took its name from 'Roundball Hill', previously known as 'The Ball', as it "rises like a ball" and was quite possibly spelt 'Round Ball' before becoming one word. The farm's land, at some point in the 19th century, merged with those of 'Claylands' and by 1869 was some 237 acres in size. Among the dozens of fields were a few worth mentioning. One field called 'New Breach', although described as pasture in 1844, would have originally been a field claimed from its wild state for the planting of crops. This field still exists within a larger field to the west of 'Roundball Wood'. Another two fields named 'Higher' and 'Lower Calves Plot' were fields that would have once been used for the new born members of the farm and were, therefore, situated near to the farmhouse so the farmer could keep a close eye. The farmhouse does not exist today but the previously mentioned two fields do *5. Some other curiously named plots of land were 'Duck Plot', 'Lower/Little & Higher Rough Close' and 'Press Meadow'.

In the 1840s the farm was owned by Harry Buckland Lott, of Tracey House, and by the 1850s it was farmed by George Brassey. Mr. Brassey had frequently moved his family around the country before finally settling in Honiton in 1851. Before Honiton, Mr. Brassey had been a gamekeeper in Huntingdon and then a railway contractor in Manningtree, Essex. He was descended from a long established family of landowners from Cheshire and he was a first cousin to Thomas Brassey. Thomas Brassey was a world famous railway engineer who had aided the construction of railways all over the world, including the first railway in the then new Australian state of Queensland. George's eldest son, Richard, moved to Queensland where he became an engine driver. George's well-known cousin died in 1870 leaving an estate worth £5,200,000! To give one an idea of how much this was when he died, the total value of all the current accounts of Britain's 650 banks in 1860 was £41.5 million. The *Oxford Dictionary of National Biography* described Thomas Brassey as "one of the wealthiest of the self-made Victorians".

George Brassey remained at Roundball for well over a decade where he employed 3 full time agricultural labourers; however, when times were busier, which they often were, he gave work to as many as 15 men.
The present day 'Roundball Wood' was also once part of this farm which, in 1844, was a 4 acre area of "pasture and wood" simply named "copse". Today it is a part of East Devon Areas of Outstanding Natural Beauty, being a popular site for walkers and a wildlife haven. 'Roundball Covert' was a much larger area of woodland just south of the farmhouse that covered nearly 30 acres. At the same time this was an unnamed "plantation" probably intended to be used for timber. Roundball Covert still exists today much as it was 160 years ago.
Roundball Farm itself was later run by James Tratt, a son of Samuel and Mary of Thornhayes Farm, and in 1871 there were a total of 18 people residing at the farmhouse, including a 17 year old governess for his children, four "indoor" servants and four lodgers! In the same year the farm had its own separate dairy and dairyman. By the time of Mr. Tratt's tenure, Roundball had merged with the old Claylands Farm: in total the estate had 3 workers' cottages, not including the Claylands farmhouse. Roundball appears to have lost its status as a farm in the late 19th century. By the late 1870s the old dairy had been converted into two labourer's cottages and less than ten years later the farmhouse and cottages were uninhabited. By 1890s the farmhouse itself was inhabited by a gardener with the two cottages occupied by a labourer and a bricklayer and by 1901 all the properties were once again unoccupied. It was later abandoned permanently around the time of World War I, with the establishment of the Roundball rifle range, and whilst much of the original lands remain, the farmhouse was left to rot with its old plot now a part of Combe Estate.
The rifle range consisted of twelve targets that were used by Allhallows O.T. C., the regular army and the Home Guard during WWII. The longest range attempted was stated to be 600 yards but apparently on one occasion Littletown Road, which lay in the shooters' path, had to be closed for target practise that took place from the railway embankment which equated to a 1,000 yard range! The range closed when the authorities decided to build council houses in the area. From aerial photos it is still easy to see the old boundaries of the farmhouse and adjoining orchard, although both are now long gone, as are the two cottages.

Rowleigh: another of the Honiton farms with a bit of an identity crisis! Over the centuries it has been known as Rowleigh, Rowhays, Rowlays, Rowley and Rowlhayes and dates back at least 400 years. As already mentioned, one of its derivatives is from the Saxon word 'hayes' meaning 'dwelling place'. This was another of Honiton's larger farms, totalling 118.25 acres in 1844. The farm was owned by Thomas Denner, the father of Thomas Denner of Springfield, as early as 1811, with his son also at the farm in the 1830s. By the 1870s the farm had its own dairy where a separate dairyman and his family resided. Once again, some of the old field names of the farm give one clues to its past as well as general information, possibly centuries old.

- Home Meadow: this was the nearest meadow to the farmhouse
- Linhay Close: this was a large pastoral field and presumably once had a 'linhay' for cattle.
- Hollow Meadow: so named as it had a dip in its centre
- Strap Moor: defined by its long, narrow shape
- Waggon Linhay Close: a field that once housed a lean-to for wagons.
- Pit Orchard: an orchard that had been planted in an old pit (probably marl).
- Pigs Close: a field near the farmhouse where pigs were presumably once kept
- Home Orchard: the orchard nearest to the farmhouse
- Ten Acre Hill: self explanatory
- Path Hill: so called as it had a path that ran from the farmhouse to 'Farway Common Road' which is still present today.
- Great Brake: this would have been a reference to the point in history when the field was 'broken' from its untamed origins of bracken to a field suitable for crop growing. It was probably called 'Great' Brake due to the huge amount of work taken to bring this 16 acre field into a state suitable for arable land usage.

Rowleigh was bought by the Manor of Honiton at some point in the mid nineteenth century and had its name changed to 'Broadacres' in 1960. The "homestead" was rebuilt in the 1860s and by 1970 it became a small holding, a status it held until recently when it became a private house. The White family were the last to farm the estate until the 1960s when the premises were put on the market. The Whites, not wishing to purchase the lands from Honiton Manor, left much of it to be bought by the Donkey Sanctuary. By the time the old farmhouse was sold to its current residents, it was said to have been in a poor state of repair and a full restoration project was carried out. One such example of the house's former state was that a half-shaft from a tractor was found as a structural substitute for a rotten, weight bearing roof beam!

Stout *6: also referred to as 'Stouts', was a 60 acre farm that was owned by the Manor of Honiton. From the late 1840s it was run by another son of Bishop and Joan of Lower Blannicombe Farm, James Hartnell. The farmhouse must have once been a big dwelling for in 1861 it had 13 people residing there! By 1869 the farm had increased in size to 73 acres and was valued at £83. In 1881 it was not a farm but simply a dwelling for an agricultural labourer. The old farmhouse of Stout was converted into houses when the farm ceased in the late 1980s and the lands were taken on by Lower Blannicombe: quite ironic considering the Hartnell link!

Swinesloose: this was once the most westerly of the farms of the town and doubtless one of the most isolated. It was probably one of the last farms to be established within the parish. There is evidence to suggest that in the early-mid nineteenth century large proportions, or parcels of land, were still being 'broken' from their wild, natural state in this area of the Honiton parish. The lands of the farm were probably 'cut-out' of what is now Gittisham Hill and, prior to their cultivation, would have looked much like the rest of the hill appears today. As can be seen from *Appendix V* many of the existing town farms had already expanded their lands to the very edges of the parish as new ground was cultivated. Swinesloose was, as stated, located on the corner of Gittisham Hill and it is now known as 'Faraway Farm'. In the 1840s this was a farm on leasehold to the previously mentioned Thomas Denner Snr. and owned by Harry Buckland Lott. In the 1840s it was, for a time, run by Samuel Tratt before he moved to Lucashayes. By the 1860s the farm was run by George Warren, a son of George Warren of Higher Blannicombe, who had married a daughter, Hannah, of Samuel and Mary Tratt of Thornhayes. By the late 1800s Hannah had been widowed and she was running the farm with her daughter and son-in-law, Hannah and Frederick Tratt. Hannah Warren's daughter, another Hannah Warren, had married her cousin, Frederick Tratt, the son of Samuel and Emma of Lucashayes Farm. Hannah Warren died in 1891 aged 70 and the farm was then continued by her son-in-law Frederick: Frederick ran the farm up until WWI.

Thornhayes: another of the farms that was once located in 'Honiton Bottom Road'. In the mid nineteenth century it was a farm of around 70 acres and it is here that the Tratt story begins. Samuel Tratt was born in Yarcombe and moved to Thornhayes in the early 19th century. Samuel's wife Mary was from Chardstock and after her husband died in the 1840s, their two sons, James and Thomas, jointly managed the land for some 10 years. James, the youngest child, moved away from the farm in the 1850s and Thomas continued on at Thornhayes until his death in 1890, over which time he managed to increase its boundaries to 103 acres. It was then Thomas' son, William, who jointly farmed both Thornhayes and Higher Blannicombe (where he had been located prior to his father's death).

Samuel and Mary Tratt had 7 children in total - Thomas, Joseph, Hannah, Harriet, Samuel, William and James. Many of them have already been mentioned as they made their own way into the Honiton countryside. William, however, left Honiton to become a farmer at Blamphayne Farm in Colyton. Joseph established a butchers shop in the High Street in the property now occupied by 'Bel-Ami' (138 High Street). He worked there until his death in the 1890s and after him his son Ernest, and later his grandson Edwin, continued the business well into the twentieth century. Thornhayes, like so many others today, no longer exists as a farm and is instead a private house.

(for a map of the majority of the farm's lands see Appendix V)

There was another farm that was situated at the west end of town which was the old Turk's Head Inn. The landlord from the 1840s, William Stroud, appeared to have diversified into farming as well as innkeeping, having some 20 acres at his disposal in 1844. After Mr. Stroud, another landlord also kept a smallholding along with the inn and when the inn closed, the land, along with that of the old Turk's Head Tollhouse, became part of Roebuck estate. In 1921 part of Roebuck Farm, the old tollhouse, and what was left of the inn, was sold off to make a separate farm. This new farm was run by the Cooke family for the following 40 years until the Honiton Bypass arrived in 1966. In 1931 the old inn was sold off to become a roadside cafe and the old tollhouse became known as 'Turk's Head Farm'. Turk's Head Farm was mainly a dairy concern but also kept sheep and raised prize winning 'Hampshires'. With the coming of the bypass, much of the farm's lands were seized under Compulsory Purchase Orders by the Ministry of Transport and over the ensuing years the farmstead ceased. By the 1980s the old tollhouse had fallen into disrepair but was, fortunately, saved from demolition in 1988 when it was refurbished. The name changed to 'Manna House' in 1998 when the premises were opened as a B&B, an occupation it still retains today.

Many of the aforementioned farms had numerous, strangely named fields and plots of land which were often so named in relation to the topography/geography of the land or after early owners or those who cleared them; however, in many cases their sources have been lost in time. Field names appeared to have remained the same throughout the centuries up until Victorian times with many of the farms remaining in the possession of the same landowners, as well as agricultural practises staying constant. By the mid 19th century the Manor of Honiton had been sold several times, having remained in the Courtenay family for centuries, and agricultural practises had also started to change with the coming of the agricultural and industrial revolutions. With such events, many of these ancient field names were lost and newer names were introduced as the next generation of farmers worked and viewed their respective new lands. Apart from those already mentioned, below are some more field names that existed in Honiton in Victorian times that are worth listing here for posterity.

- Willis's Orchard
- Great Lea Moor
- Staggy Gate
- Drunken Parlour
- First Higher Hurslakes
- Baker Dennis's Close
- Little & Great Hooperhayne
- Knackers Plot
- Horse Pond Close
- Poples Plot
- Bareleged Lane
- Farthing Close
- First Broom Park
- Madam Fords Close
- Prattleman's Mead
- Iron Gate Four Acres
- Tiddicks
- Rexey
- The Bowers
- Red Ham
- East Rhodes
- Gribblehayes
- Knappy Field
- Higher & Lower Blacklands
- Great & Little Styles

- Higher Hoggerhaynes
- The Wrangle
- Little Studley
- Buckle Bridge Meadow
- Little Pale Gate Close

Many of the previously smaller fields of Honiton were merged into larger, more manageable plots. This trend was common place throughout the Victorian period as farming underwent a revolution to feed the ever-growing population and as farmers moved away from arable to dairy farming. A farming depression in the 1870s, started by the rise in cheaper corn imports, led to the area's farmers turning their corn fields to grass, and by taking advantage of the new railway, they set up pastoral farmsteads by sending fattened pigs, sheep and cattle to the markets of the east. The victims of all this regeneration were the hedgerows, lying between the ancient, smaller fields, many of which were centuries old. In the years after World War Two, some 150,000 miles of hedgelands were lost with the high farming demands of the post war years. Hedgerows that exist today are thought to be in the region of 600 to 700 years old - there is a simple experiment one can perform to ascertain the age of these ancient land barriers. By taking a 30 metre length of hedgerow, and counting the number of indigenous shrubs, excluding elder and bramble, one can arrive at a rough age by multiplying the number of species by 100.

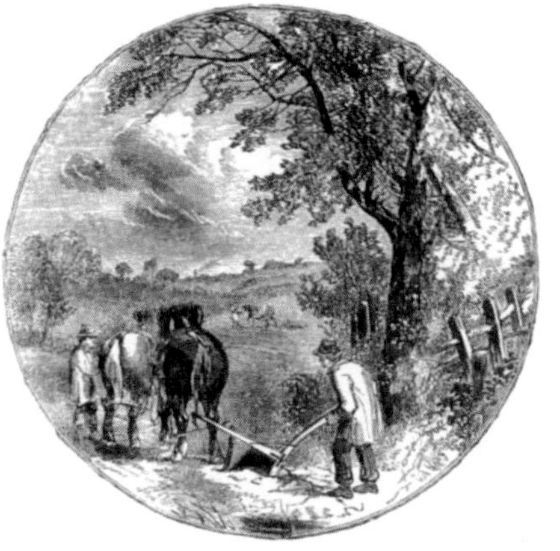

Chapter 3
Town Mills

"And blame not me if you do choose amiss.
The miller was a churl, you well know this"
The Miller's Tale, Geoffrey Chaucer

There has been a mill in Honiton since before the writing of the Domesday Book, some 1,000 years ago. The mills of the town would have been at the heart of the settlement, along with that of the church, as it was the place where farmers would bring their wheat to be ground into flour for their 'daily bread'. One reference, if not the earliest, to an actual miller was regarding a man called 'John of the Mill' and his wife 'Salome' who worked in Honiton in 1309. Like many other tradesmen, many of the Honiton millers took on apprentices who resided with them whilst they learnt the trade.
Some of these mills have gone and some still exist but one thing they all have in common is that none of them are still in working use today.

Manor Mill: the 'Manor Mill' located at Littletown is believed to be the one mentioned in the Domesday Book of 1086. Also known as 'Dungeon Mill' this would have once been the property of the Lord of the Manor, who would have insisted on a proportion of the early settler's bread corn, and by the 1840s the mill was still owned by the Manor of Honiton. In one document dated 1869, the establishment was referred to as 'The Honiton Manor Mills' which had two pairs of working stones. The mill also had a stable, orchard, garden and outbuildings set in 7 acres of land. From the late 1840s the miller was James Plucknett who milled there for over 30 years. He later became the 'Surveyor and Inspector for the Borough of Honiton'. Manor Mill, also known as 'Littletown Mills', was in operation up until the 1960s when the last of the long term tenants, the Smiths, died. The existing Grade II listed building is thought to date from the 18th century, although an earlier building would have most definitely once stood there prior to this time. The wooden machinery, wood and iron water wheel and millstones were all still present when the building became listed: the property was then known as 'Manor Millhouse'.

Perryman's Mills: this mill was located a short distance from 'Littletown Mill'. In the 1840s the mill was run by John Viney who later became a labourer and ended his days in Stockland. The mill building, along with

'Littletown Mill', still exists today. It was fed by a separate leat from the Gissage near to where old Brand Farm once stood.

Langford Mill: little is known about this mill, only the fact that it existed just outside of the town in 1334. It is possible the mill bore the ancient name of 'Northcote Mill' but this is yet to be confirmed.

Northcote Mill *1: as previously mentioned, there was once a mill known as Northcote Mill that existed at the east end of town and is thought to have been a part of the old 'Northcote Manor' as it was once a part of what later became Great Nothcote Farm. The mill was also known as 'Blackallers Mill' which is thought to have come from the 'Blackaller' family who were resident in Honiton in the 1600s and 1700s. It was in operation up until the late 1830s and later became a labourer's cottage for Great Northcote Farm called 'Blackallers House'. The mill was fed by a stream once known as 'Townlake Stream'. The old buildings were once reached by a road that led from what is now 'Langford Road', now the other side of the Honiton Bypass. The old dwelling has gone and its old site is now open countryside. Even after the mill lost its status in the 1830s, the adjacent field continued to retain the name 'Mill Plot'.

The Old Mill: an 'honorary' title the building holds today but was also known as 'Town Mill'. This mill was, and is still, located on the corner of Mill Street. The mill is known to have existed in the late 18th century when it was known as 'Thomas' Mill' and was once owned by both Sir George Younge and The Manor of Honiton. When John Channon took possession of the building in 1782, it

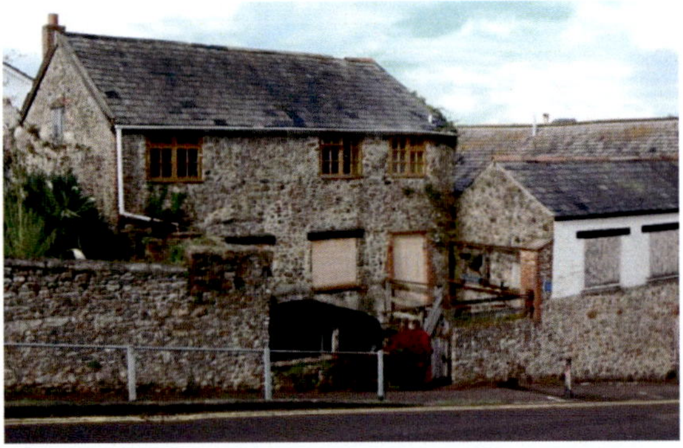

became known as 'Channon's Mill'. It was a working mill until 1968 when a flood destroyed the leat that supplied water to it. The mill was fed by a stream diverted from the Gissage near the old rifle range. The water supply, only a four foot wide channel, after leaving the mill went through the old Honiton Brewery to the iron foundry before rejoining the Gissage's main course. The channel today is no longer in existence "as all the ground it flowed through is now built on." "The unusual gearing for the wheel, still existing, is made from iron and applewood" and the present water wheel was made by Mickleburghs in 1898. By the 1840s the mill was owned by Henry John Tooze, the son of the aforementioned Ruth Tooze, and was run by John Skinner. This section of 'King Street', and hence the town, technically ended at the mill and the old mill garden once stood at what is now the summit of the steep hill leading up to 'Millhead Road'. The building was saved from demolition in 1981 when it was partially restored and still stands in its original location, although is now uninhabited. Many of the road names in the mill's vicinity reflect the old building's past such as 'Mill Street', 'Millhead Road' and 'Millers Way'.

Higher & Lower Grigg's Mill: these were once two water mills that were sited in Dowell Street. Originally corn mills, they were converted into mills for processing animal feed in the 1950s and finally lost their status of working mills in the 1960s. Earlier in time they had been used as mills for the Tracey Estate, from which they later got their more recent name of 'Tracey Mill'.

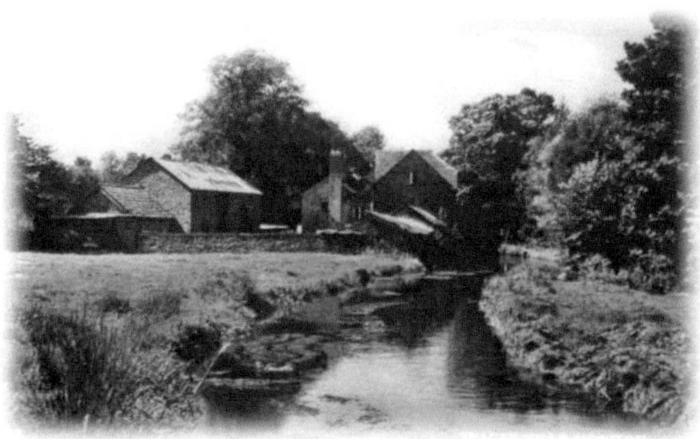

Tracey (Higher Grigg's) Mill

The earliest known occupant of the mill was a Mr. Balston who had the business in 1780. The mills got the name of 'Grigg' from Robert Grigg who was the first of the Grigg family to run the mill in 1787. Higher Grigg Mill survived the test of time whilst Lower Grigg Mill was later converted into a cottage. Fanny Grigg was the last of the family to work Higher Grigg's Mill before she retired to Lower Grigg's Mill in the late 1830s. Lower Grigg's still held the status of a mill but by the time of Fanny's retirement it was simply a dwelling known as 'Mill/Grigg's Cottage'. After Fanny's retirement she leased Higher Grigg's to a Samuel Melhuish who, after his death in the mid

1840s, left the running to his wife Mary who remained there until her death in 1862. When Fanny Grigg died, the mill reverted back to the Manor of Honiton, from whom she leased it, and when the Manor sold it in 1869 it had a "wagon lodge, stable, cow house and other outbuildings" along with 3 acres of land, including an orchard. It was bought by a gentleman for £1,050. In July 1891, an unknown disaster struck the mill leaving its water wheel out of action and the local iron foundry, 'Mickleburghs', were called on to make a new one "quickly". The new water wheel measured 10 feet in diameter and was 14 inches deep.
The old cottage, once Lower Griggs, existed until it was demolished fairly recently. Higher Grigg's Mill, however, still exists today and is known as 'Tracey Mill Trout Farm' and although the mill no longer grinds corn, the water wheel is still present and functional. From the early 1900s the mill was run by the Rounsevells, George and his wife Mary, until their respective deaths in the 1930s. This couple were the parents of Lucy Mary Rounsevell who later married Harry Roy Read, founder of 'Reads Garage'. Mary's brother, George Rounsevell, lived and also worked at the mill for a time and later ran what was once Glen Farm.

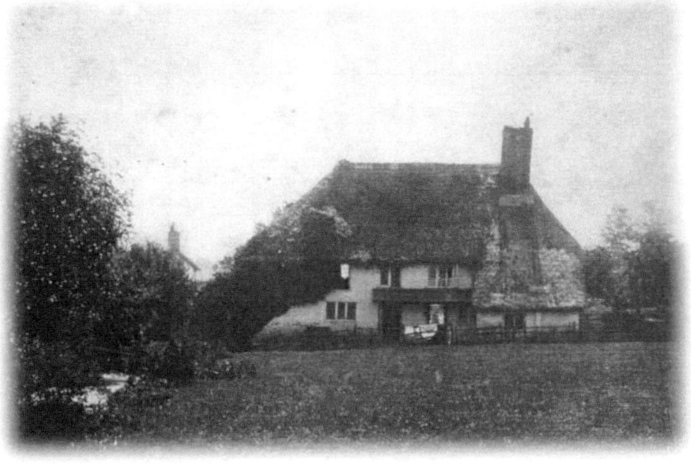

Lower Grigg's Mill, later Mill Cottage prior to its demolition

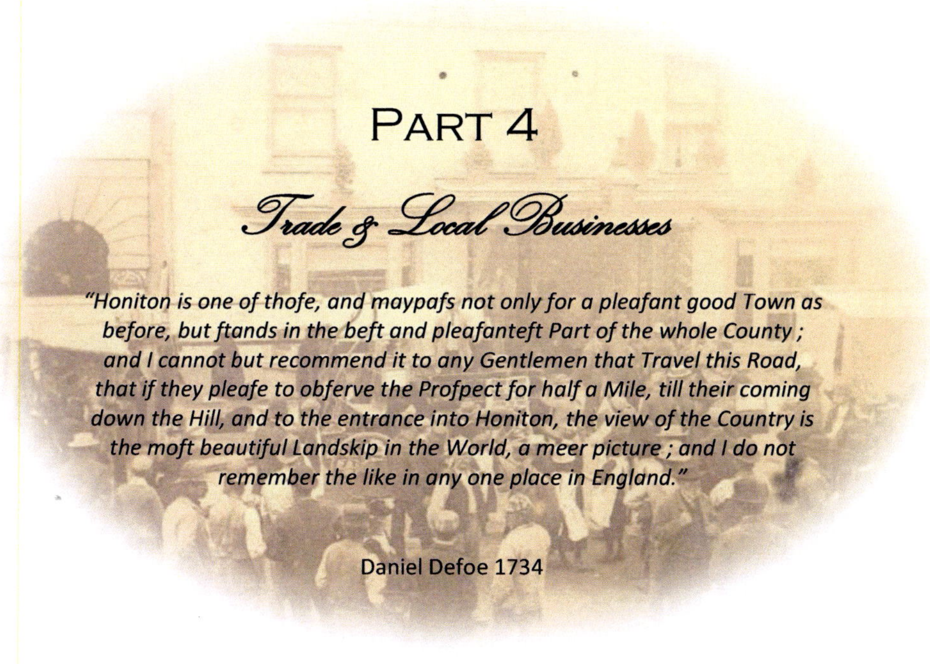

PART 4

Trade & Local Businesses

"Honiton is one of thofe, and maypafs not only for a pleafant good Town as before, but ftands in the beft and pleafanteft Part of the whole County ; and I cannot but recommend it to any Gentlemen that Travel this Road, that if they pleafe to obferve the Profpect for half a Mile, till their coming down the Hill, and to the entrance into Honiton, the view of the Country is the moft beautiful Landskip in the World, a meer picture ; and I do not remember the like in any one place in England."

Daniel Defoe 1734

Chapter 1
Town Trades

"The life so short, the crafts so long to learn"
Hippocrates

Among the many occupations that employed the people of Honiton were a few which had not only been present in the town for centuries but also put Honiton on the map.

Wool Trade

The longest established trade was the Honiton wool trade which has, unfortunately, long since vanished.

The Devonian cloth trade is thought to have originated from Flanders and in order to obtain skilled cloth makers, Edward I granted charters to foreign merchants and manufacturers to settle in England. Edward III, at a time when the majority of English wool was exported in its raw state, established a settlement in the country for several woollen cloth weavers, as well as dyers and fullers, in about 1350. Shortly afterwards, the skill had reached Bristol and Taunton and it is known that a wool staple was fixed in Exeter in 1354. Honiton, at this time, was situated on a major wool trading route which ran from the big cities of Bath, York and London ending at Exeter where wool was shipped abroad to France, Flanders and Spain. Tiverton was known to have been a central town for the industry and even had its Kerseys (coarse cloth) named after it. In 1612, the income derived from this trade, from Tiverton alone, was around £300,000 and there were some 8,000 men, women and children working in or around the town!

Honiton was the first place in Devon, if not England, where wool was made into cloth and the trade dates back to at least the 13th century when, in 1286, "considerable sales" of wool were recorded in accounts of Honiton Manor. One of the earliest examples of how prolific this industry was can be seen from Michaelmas 1395 to Michaelmas 1396 when there were 6 cloth merchants who sold 250 "cloth of assize" between them. "Cloth of assize" was a medieval measurement with one "cloth of assize" being 24 yards long and 2 yards wide, meaning that during this year the Honiton merchants sold 12,000 sq yards of cloth. In 1395, Honiton was also noted to have been the third most important centre for the Devonian wool industry.

Prior to the reign of Edward IV (1442-1483), only coarse plain cloth was manufactured in the region but a man named Anthony Bonvin, an Italian, was said to have taught the methods of producing Kerseys and spinning of wool with a 'distaff'. In 1599, a gentleman by the name of John Hooker, writing about Devon, stated that the main type of cloth being manufactured in the region was "Kersey Cloth" taking its name from the village of Kersey in Suffolk where it, presumably, originated. He went on to state that there was "no market nor village scarse any privat mannes house where in theise clothes be not made." Exeter was another city of great importance to the industry and when a Celia Fiennes visited the town in 1698, she wrote that:

the whole town and surrounding countryside for at least 20 miles round is employed in spinning, weaving, dressing and scouring, fulling and drying of serge's, it turns the most money in a weeke of anything in England.

The methods of production changed very little over the next 400 hundred years, from Bonvin's initial introduction to the eighteenth century, and it is said that "every cottage in the west had a hand loom." One lady working in the Ashburton area in 1866 was said to have purchased wool from the market one week and the next week returned a finished woollen product, for which she received 4 shillings. Farquharson wrote: "the noise made by these looms was deafening; with such poor pay and large families, their owners have enough to sustain life; most of them may be said to be "a hand loom weaver with small children four, and looming in the distance perhaps once more"".

The wool trade took a significant decline throughout the 17th century due to increased competition from cloth imports from the New World and other European countries; however, it managed to remain afloat a little longer due to a Government Act passed in 1678. It stated that no man or woman was to be buried in any other clothing than that made of sheep's wool and that all coffins were only to be lined with woollen cloth. The penalty for ignoring this law was quite severe; failure would result in a fine of £5 not only upon the dead man/woman's estate but also that of the owner of the house where he/she died, the organisers of the funeral and even the parson who performed the ceremony! The Rector of Honiton at the time, Rev Ozias Upcott, even started new burial records to comply with the new law which, in Honiton, was recorded to have been initiated on August 1st 1678.

As a sad example of these entries, I now quote from the parish register as written by Rev Upcott:

"A childe of a stranger; died in our Town, buried in our Church-yard, June 8. 1686. No Affidavit brought to me within the time limited by the Act for burying in Woollen. Which neglect was certified under my hand June 20. 1686. to the present Church-wardens & Overseers."

Many people, apparently, ignored this rule, Honitonians being no exception. Many simply paid the fine in order to bury their loved ones in more attractive and expensive attire. In lots of cases a family member would act as an informer to claim the 'reward' for reporting abuse of the Act, which thus reduced the overall fine. The law was finally repealed in 1814, by which time it was hardly enforced.

There were other earlier laws brought in to protect the English wool trade: in the time of Elizabeth I the taking of live sheep from the country was punishable by forfeiture of the perpetrator's land and goods, followed by a years imprisonment. The punishment for the unlawful exporting of sheep did not end at prison: after completing the penal time, the criminal would have his hand cut off in the market place. The severed limb would then be nailed up somewhere public as a warning to others thinking of setting up an 'international' wool venture! The exporting of wool was also one of the first crimes to be punishable by transportation.

One Spanish gentleman, travelling through Devon in 1836, even stated that "England seems to be the paradise of sheep".

The trade employed numerous numbers of people of the area for "many hands [were] required to supply even a moderate quantity" of wool.

One of the earliest recorded members of the wool trade in Honiton was a Benjamin Powning, a woollen draper who died in Honiton in 1639; another individual called John Hake was a wool weaver who was buried in St. Michael's in 1659. There is also known to have been a 'woollen draper' called Walter Abbott who died in Honiton in 1660. Another early recording, printed in a local newspaper 'The Western Flying Post', gives much more information on the town's trade with relation to a James & Jeremiah Maynard, who lost much of their property in a fire in 1752. This family, at the time, was said to have had as many as 1,000 people working for them, showing what a prominent industry the trade was. In one document it becomes obvious that Mr. Maynard was still active in the trade in 1763 as well as two others, Samuel Newbury and John Snook, who were serge-makers, along with an additional 30 registered names that produced wool. The Maynards were, for generations, "the great wool traders in Honiton"; James Maynard died in about 1786. The Maynard line descended from a Jerom Maynard who was born at Corfe Castle in 1677.

His father had served in Cromwell's army and Jerom was apprenticed to serge-makers, after which he started his business in Axminster. The aforementioned James Maynard was a nephew of Jerom.
Another family, who seemed to be as involved as the Maynards with serge manufacturing in the late 18th century, were the Bamfields (or Banfields) and more particularly Abraham Banfield who took over from the Maynard family in about 1812.

The best period for the Honiton wool trade was between 1768 an 1787, for after 1787 the trade began to decline and by 1822 there were only three serge-makers in the town by the names of John Bamfield and Thomas & Benjamin Isaac. There were also three wool dealers so the trade had not completely died by the early 19th century. The 'knife stabbing' for the local trade was when the coal-fuelled mills of the north flooded the market with mass produced, and hence much cheaper, wool/cotton products.
The property and land once occupied by the previously mentioned Capt. Basliegh were once a row of houses called 'Bickenstaff College' that were solely inhabited by hand loom weavers. These houses disappeared in a fire.

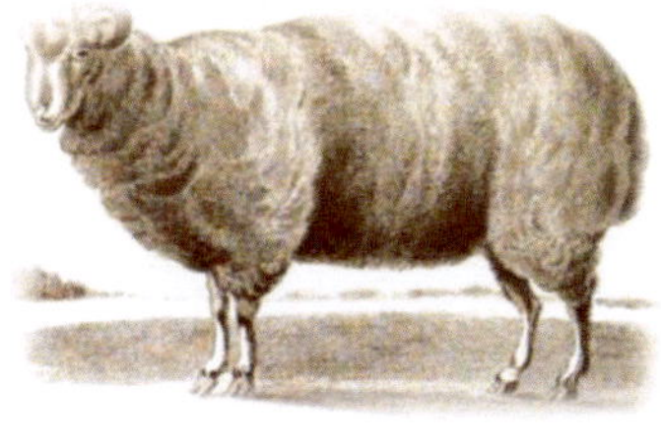

By 1841 Honiton had 3 people working in the industry, as well as one former worker, John Parker, a 75 year old wool comber who was homed in St. Margaret's Alms Houses (and presumably poorly retired). The three gentlemen still working were Abraham Ash and his son James who were listed as 'worsted makers' as well as William Isaac, who was a 30 year old wool comber. At this time Mr. Ash lived next to the pottery, which was run by the Hussey family: ironically, two of the great Honiton industries sitting side by side at this point in history! Ten years later there were only two people working with serge and they were John Isaac, a 78 year old serge-maker, and Susanna Churchill. John was the last of a family of serge-makers and it had been his brothers, Thomas and Benjamin, who had been prominent in the early 19th century. Susanna Churchill was a 66 year old hand loom wool weaver. It is indicative that the business' last breaths were in the 1850s, for by 1851 the only 2 people working with wool were elderly, and no young people had taken up the trade. By 1861 there was now only one serge manufacturer, the aforementioned Abraham Ash who had come out of retirement, probably due to the death of the former two workers of 10 years previously. This indicated that there still must have been a small demand for the product. There were only two other people living in the town in 1861, who were linked with this trade: one was an elderly woman who had given up her former occupation and the other individual was, surprisingly, only 26 years of age but was, unfortunately, in the workhouse, proving that the manufacture of wool was indeed virtually dead by the 1860s. Within the next 20 years the serge and wool manufacturing ceased entirely, for by 1881 there was not one soul in the town working with this ancient material.

Whilst the wool weavers and manufacturers had become extinct, there were still a handful of people, by the end of the nineteenth century, dealing in wool. Mr. Gustavus Gidley was probably the most prominent who was first listed as a 'wool buyer' and later a 'wool dealer' who provided his customers with "real Devonshire serges direct from the mill". Mr. Gidley lived at 'Rose Cottage', Queen Street and after he died in 1906, no one replaced him.

Today the wool trade is, sadly, not even a shadow of its once glorious past. Sheep farmers today must pay £2 for the shearing of each of their sheep and are lucky to be paid 25p for the final fleece.

As an early example of how important a flock of sheep was to its shepherd, I quote a verse painted onto a wall of the old farmhouse of Boycombe, Farway, four miles from Honiton:

"Lent but a year, now in ye month of june
The bale pated Farmer sings his tune:
Go Tom, fetch home ye sheep we will them shear.
This day will make amends for all ye year;
With pleasing labour now he take from his sheep,
His long lent Fleeces in plenteous heap:
Mirth males ye House run round, yet all joys be,
But grateful tributes to the Deity.
1744".

Honiton Pottery

The pottery trade has been in Honiton since at least 1643 - some references suggest as early as 1332 - and up until comparatively recently has been an internationally known industry.

A broadsheet, published in 1763, gives some early names of those employed in the trade - listed as follows:

- Samuel Ford, Master Potter
- Thomas Brooke, Potter
- Charles Denham, Potter
- William Flood, Potter
- Isaac Collins, Potter
- John Linnington, Potter

Some other names are mentioned in a document relating to a James Rogers being called before a Justice of the Peace in 1775. Samuel Ford is mentioned once again, as well as a John Flood, a potter of Honiton. The names of Flood and Ford were very prominent in Honiton pottery for nearly a century. By 1791 it was a Samuel and Humphrey Ford who were listed as town potters: they are two sons of the previously mentioned Samuel Ford of 1763. The Ford family, at this time, owned the pottery and were descended from an Edward Ford who married into the Marwood family in the 17th century. Over the next 40 years, the trade passed into the hands of a Thomas Flood and a Peter Hussey who had gone into partnership. Thomas Flood was a son of the aforementioned John Flood and a brother of another potter, William Flood, who died in 1820. He continued working in the trade until his death in 1850. Thomas Flood came from a long established Honitonian family whose ancestors had been working in the pottery trade since the late 17th century. Thomas was the last of that long line of Flood potters and with his death, a two hundred year family tradition also ended.

In the 1840s it was Peter Hussey who owned the pottery and the adjoining field that now houses 'Pottery Close', as well as a couple of other cottages in the pottery's vicinity. Thomas Flood operated his pottery from another site and his pottery kiln was located very near to the present day 'King's Terrace.' The potteries of this time were so prominent that the tollhouse, now known as 'Holyshute Cottage', was once called 'Potter's Kiln Tollhouse' which was set up by the Honiton Turnpike Trust. After the death of both Thomas Flood and Peter Hussey, Mr. Flood's kiln seems to have gone out, but the pottery of Mr. Hussey was taken over by his widow, Susan, until her death in the 1860s. The pottery Thomas Flood ran seems to have been taken over by a Richard Carpenter who moved away from pottery and into the manufacturing of bricks and tiles.

The 1851 census described Susan Hussey as a 'Red Earthenware Potter' and it was this "coarse and rather primitive type of brown earthenware" that had been used since the industry began in 1643. By 1850, Mrs. Hussey had 8 people working for her, one of whom was a James Greenslade who worked for the pottery from when he was a boy, in the 1840s, right through to the 1890s!

It appears that after Susan Hussey's death, one of her former employees continued her work. This gentleman was Francis Copp, who was taught by the Husseys. He worked as one of the town's only potters until his retirement in the late 1870s.

In 1868, Farquaharson wrote:

"The only manufactories now in Honiton are one for coarse ware and one for bricks and tiles"

The old pottery of Mr. Hussey, and later Mr. Copp, was once found in the road now known as 'Pottery Close' which has long since been redeveloped. It was a James Webber from Rockbeare who established the current pottery shop in 1881. As Mr. Copp retired in the 1870s, and Mr. Webber arrived in the town only a few years later, it can be assumed that it was James Webber who took over the old pottery as well. Mr. Webber started by making simple household items and utensils, such as baking dishes and flower pots. He was said to have gone to Exeter with his products every Saturday, selling them off the street, leaving home early on the Saturday and not returning till 2 or 3am Sunday morning!

James Webber held the pottery until his retirement, at some point in the 1890s, and sold it to two of his former workers called William Hunt and Ellis Forster. Webber's only son, Lewis, could not have had any interest in his father's business for rather than continuing it he moved to London where he became a policeman.

Forster and Hunt continued the establishment until 1918 when it was taken over by a Mr. Charles Collard who went into partnership with his daughter, Joan. Mr. Collard won various international pottery awards, including medals at exhibitions at Turin and Brussels, and ran the pottery until 1947 when he retired aged 73. After his retirement, Mr. Collard continued to make pottery at home but latterly his eyesight failed him and he died in 1969 at the grand old age of 95!

Up until the time of Collard's retirement, the clay used was still excavated from behind the pottery itself. Mr. Collard was the gentleman who took the pottery from its humble, but practical, local fame to an international audience by creating much more decorative pieces of porcelain. He is quoted to have sent his work to "Australia, New Zealand, Canada, America, Malay States, France, Africa, India, China, Denmark, Bermuda, British Columbia, etc" and by the 1930s business was booming with Collard employing around 30 people.

After Collard's retirement he sold the business to Norman Hull and Harry Barrett, two men who came from the Staffordshire potteries. Barrett remained for only one year and sold his share of the business to a couple by the name of Chapplow. Mr. Hull remained with the pottery until 1961 and it was during these post-Collard years that the ancient local red clay was replaced with 'blended white clay' which came from outside the local area.
In 1961, Mr. Hull's widow sold her part of the business to Mr. Paul Redvers and, with Mr. Chapplow's retirement later the same year, the pottery entered a new era of management and saw a new introduction of more modern products such as pub ashtrays, children's money boxes and table lamps.
This fine little piece of Honiton culture, unfortunately, came to a recent, premature end. Demand for these exquisite masterpieces was still high and expansion was necessary for continuation; however, efforts to relocate were unsuccessful. The owners, therefore, sold the franchise in 1991 to 'Dartmouth Pottery' with whom it is today. The current pottery is now simply a showroom and 'milkshake bar', strangely enough, that is located at number 30 High Street Honiton. The old pottery behind the showroom was demolished, and as one may expect, developed into flats!

Lace Trade

Lace making has been recorded as early as the 13th century, meaning that this trade was already centuries old when it arrived in England by the 1500s.
The art of making lace was thought to have been introduced to England by refugees from the Low Countries and Flanders, fleeing the cruel religious persecution by Fernando Álvarez de Toledo, 3rd Duke of Alba. A large number of these 16th century refugees settled in Devon and hence forth established 'pillow' lace. Another theory by many was that lace was brought into the country by Lollards who took refuge here in the 14th century due, once again, to religious persecution in their home country of Germany. There is credence in both these theories: as already mentioned, there were lace -makers as early as the 14th century but many of the Honiton Lace designs followed patterns that would have been credited to those who came to England in the 16th century from the Low Countries rather than the earlier settlers from Germany. It is generally accepted, however, that Honiton lace is descended from the artisans of the 1500s, rather than those of the 1300s.

The making of lace is achieved by the procedure of twisting threaded bobbins around a series of pins set in a cushion, and, after many laborious hours', fine patterns and intricate designs can be accomplished.
There is a quaint story connected with the introduction of lace manufacturing to Brussels.

"a poor young girl named Gertrude was dying for love of a young man whose wealth precluded all hopes of marriage. One night as she sat weeping a lady entered her cottage and without saying a word placed in her lap a cushion with its bobbins filled with thread. The lady then with perfect silence showed her how to work the bobbins and how to make all sorts of delicate patterns and complicated stitches. As daylight approached the maiden had learnt the art and the mysterious visitress disappeared. The price of the maidens lace soon made her rich on account of its valuable patterns and she was able to marry the object of her love. Many years after while living in luxury with her numerous family about her she was startled by the mysterious lady entering her comfortable house. This time not silent but looking stern she said "Here you enjoy peace and comfort while without famine and trouble. I helped you you have not helped your neighbours. The angels weep for you and turn away their faces." So the next day Gertrude went forth with her cushion and bobbins in her hand and going from cottage to cottage she offered to teach the art she had so mysteriously learnt. So they all became such and their country also."

The earliest recorded lace-maker in Devon is thought to be a Mrs. Minifie, a daughter of John Flay, Rector of Buckerell, who mentioned his child in his Will, dated 1614. The earliest lace seller known to have existed in Honiton was a certain James Rodge who died in 1617 and whose tomb is still easily found in St Michael's church yard. Mr. Rodge was thought to have been a valet, who escaped from Brussels and brought "the secret of the finer stitches as used in the Flanders laces of the period" to Honiton where he subsequently made his fortune. James Rodge left £100 to the "poore of Honiton" presumably as a grateful gift to the town that had given him his prosperity. Mr. Rodge left bequests amounting to several hundred pounds, showing that the occupation of lace selling was once quite prosperous. Another early Honiton lace seller was that of John Pring who was mentioned in a document dated 1681. Hontion lace, at this time, was exceedingly expensive; one yard of the material cost £6 in 1698! There are many recorded members of the Honiton lace trade in the 17th century burial registers, with nearly 20 individuals listed with names such as:

Minifie, Cross, Clarke, Pearce, Bishop, Horman, Dark, Stockman, Humphrey and Pulman.

Early examples, written by Honiton visitors and their perception of the then great abundance of lace making, are as follows:

- In 1630 Thomas Westcote wrote: "Here is the abundance of bone lace, a pretty toy now greatly in request."
- In 1669 Cosimo de Medici quoted: "there is not a cottage in all the county nor that of Somerset, where white lace is not made in great quantities so that not only the whole kingdom is supplied with it but it is exported in great abundance."
- In 1698 Celia Fiennes, an English traveller, observed: "here it is they make the fine bone lace in imitation of the Antwerp and Flanders lace, and indeed I think it's as fine, it will only not wash so fine which must be the fault in the thread."
- ...And in 1724 Daniel Defoe wrote: "the valuable manufactures of lace for which the inhabitants of Devon have long been conspicuous are extending now from Exmouth to Torre Bay."

Another quoted text from the mid sixteenth century by T. Fuller is one of the first definitions of the term 'bone-lace':

"Much of this is made in and about Honiton, and weekly returned to London. Some will have it called lace, a lancinia, used as a fringe on the borders of cloth. Bone-lace it is named, because first made with bone (since wooden) bobbins. This it is usual for such utensils, both in the Latin and English names gratefully to retain the memory of the first matter they were made of; cochleare, a spoon (whether made of wood or metal) because cockle-shells were the first used for that purpose. Modern the use thereof in England, not exceeding the middle of the reign of Queen Elizabeth: let it not be condemned for a superfluous wearing, because it doth neither hide nor heat, seeing it doth adorn. Besides, though private persons pay for it, it stands the State in nothing: not expensive in bullion, like other lace, costing nothing save a little thread descanted on by art and industry. Hereby many children, who otherwise would be burdensome to the parish, prove beneficial to their parents. Their fingers, gain a livelihood thereby; not to say that it saveth some thousands of pounds yearly, formerly sent overseas to fetch lace from Flanders."

The term 'bone' lace, therefore, comes from the fact that the bobbins were often once made from bone. Many of these early lace-makers were so poor that they could not afford the pins needed for fastening the lace to the pillow so they improvised by using fish bones and hence the term 'fish bone' was born.

The lace trade spread like wild fire through the town and county and by 1698 there were 1,341 people in Honiton working in the industry. Out of a population of just over 2,000, the lace trade dominated with 56% of the workforce in Honiton and 31% of the Otter Valley. In the same year, a petition was sent to Parliament in protest over a repeal of an Act of the previous year granting the English lace-maker protection from foreign competition. In the same petition the "lace manufacture in England" was described as "the greatest next to the woollen".

By 1763 it is known that a John Stocker was a lace merchant in Honiton, as well as a William Stocker and John Guard. This John Guard was the father of the once well known Lieutenant-General William Guard who was born in Honiton in 1773.

In 1770 an Italian visitor, Joseph Baretti, was passing through Honiton and made the following observations:

"Honiton, where they make a good deal of that lace so much admired by Italian women...I wonder why it is not made everywhere, as those who make it are neither Philosophers nor conjurers, but poor ignorant women"!

Although not exactly complimentary to the poor individuals that made the lace, it does reiterate the fact that this product was internationally known and admired.

The finest thread from which the lace could be made was imported from Antwerp and in 1790 cost £70 for 1lb of the material; there were also some references to it costing as much as £95 for the same amount! The lace-makers, though, would be lucky to see one shilling per yard for their finished product. The shopkeepers, who paid the poor lace-makers, "jealously" prevented the women from becoming

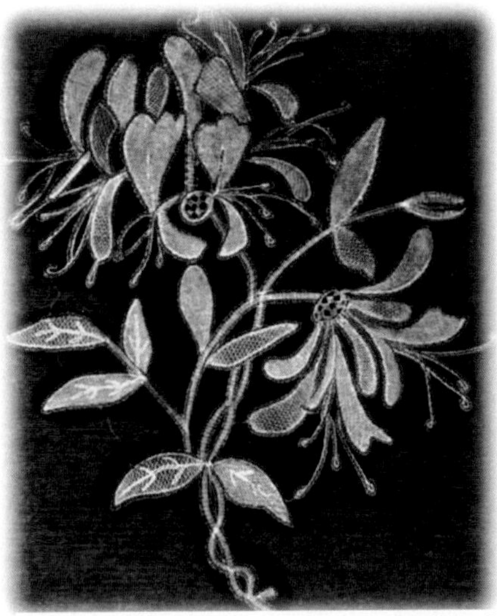

Honeysuckle Sprig of Victorian Honiton Lace

independent by paying them not in money but with a fraction of the profits and, in many cases, with 'goods' such as tea or sugar. Even this form of payment was scrutinised and the women were given the very bare necessities as there were fears they would sell any excess goods, hence giving them more money for their products. Other buyers would give these girls the option of whether to be paid in goods, or money but, if money was preferred, the buyer would expect 7d. worth of lace for only a payment of 6d.

Girls were often sent to "lace schools' to learn the art of this ancient trade. One girl called Harriet Channon was sent as an apprentice to a lace school of 30 girls in Sidmouth at the tender age of 4 where she was taught for up to six hours a day! 5 or 6 were the common ages to start apprenticeships in lace-making and when Harriet had been in attendance for a year, she was able to put "12 hours' work in a day."

Even into the late nineteenth century many people of England were under the false opinion that the famous lace of 'Honiton' was a town in France or Belgium, being quite unaware of its position in the Devon.

The trade took a rather dramatic nose- dive at the turn of the eighteenth century, for in 1760 a gentleman established a factory in Nottingham based on the idea of using machines to make lace. This gentleman was called Hammond Lindley and after his original invention it was not long before the device was revamped and improved by numerous other individuals. By 1810 a newly created 'Point Lace' was produced and rapidly started to take over the industry. This new problem of mechanisation was increased for East Devon lace- makers when a factory at Tiverton, founded by John Heathcoat in about 1810, threatened the local industry. This led to the introduction of mechanisation of the trade in the county, leaving the hundreds of hand spinners destitute. By the early 1800s a local man named Gidley predicted that employment in the industry had fallen by 88% and that most of this fall had happened over the 1810-1820 period. Another blow was the establishment of another such factory at Barnstable, some 15 years later in 1825. These new mass produced lace products cost far less than their handmade counterparts and rapidly started to swallow all the trade's demands. East Devon lace- makers desperately tried to compete with the mechanisation of their trade by 'quickening' the production of the products; however, this proved detrimental to the lace's overall quality, as patterns were simplified and methods of manufacture were hastened. The mid-nineteenth century hand-made lace of the area coined the phrase "rag-lace" and it proved to be yet another nail in the coffin, or dropped stitch, in the local trade! Lacemakers came up with new ideas "out of their own heads" and started to move away from the designs that had once been so desirable. New concepts such as "Turkey tails", "frying pans" and "bullocks' hearts" became common place and "not a leaf, not a flower was copied from nature."

"It is from this neglect in their patterns that Honiton has fallen in public estimation"

The reaction to this new 'rag' was reflected in its price drop. During the Napoleonic Wars, lace from Honiton was reaching anything from 20 to 100 guineas in London; however, by the early 1840s the same items were struggling to be sold for more than 15 guineas. There was, however, a revival - it was a Royal 'kiss of life' that fortunately revamped the floundering lace trade of Devon and, more precisely, Honiton. When Queen Victoria commissioned the local women to make her wedding dress in 1839, she gave the industry a boost. Victoria's wedding dress and veil cost £1,000 and started the trend of women marrying in white. The following year, the Queen asked for a christening robe to be made for her first child, Princess Victoria, which is still worn by Royal babies today. Victoria also ordered a shawl to be made of black lace, which was not only very rare but was exceedingly hard to work with. Later, when the Queen started to appear in Honiton lace, the fashion was copied by the ladies of her court and a new status symbol was thus established. By 1848 there was a written account of a veil of Honiton lace that was bought from 'Howell & James', London for 15 guineas which was said to have been "very cheap at that money". Royal approval was not, however, a new thing to the local area. In 1830, Queen Adelaide, wife of William IV, had granted a Royal Warrant to the previously mentioned Amy Lathy. Queen Victoria later granted a similar Warrant in 1882 and in 1901, the wife of Edward VII, Queen Alexandra, issued another. In 1904 a further Warrant was issued by the then Princess of Wales.
Honiton lace was displayed at the Great Exhibition of 1851 and the then Mayor of Honiton stated...

"That it is desirable that an effective representation of the Honiton lace manufacture should be secured in the Exhibition of 1851 as tending to revive the trade of the town by exciting attention to the surpassing beauty and excellence of the fabric."

Royal patronage did, indeed, help the local trade but only achieved in postponing its demise. Lace-makers' earnings had, in the early part of Victoria's reign, been relatively good: in 1841 such a woman could expect to earn as much as 10 shillings a week, 3 times more than the average labourer. However, throughout the ensuing decades, earnings plummeted and in the years just after the First World War the same women were earning half that of their grandmothers. By comparison, the typical labourers' wage of that time was nearly 10 times that of the lace- maker. This trend was reflected in the number of those working in the industry. The 1840s, as already mentioned, saw a slight revival and the number of Honiton workers tripled to over 350 in those ten years but the numbers slowly ebbed once again and by 1881 there were less than 60 working in the town. Throughout the East Devon area the number of workers fell from 4 figures in 1870 to single figures at the start of the Second World War. Despite the problems that the Honiton lace industry faced in the late 19th century, the craft did continue and after Miss Lathy, it was Mrs. Ann Fowler who received the Royal Warrants. She originally had her shop near 'Manor House' and in 1926 moved further up the High Street to where 'The Bird's Nest' currently stands.

Even as late as 1947, a cocktail tray mounted with Honiton lace was presented to Princess Elizabeth, later Elizabeth II, for her 21st birthday and, in 1951, Her Majesty was graciously presented with another sample of Honiton lace which a Mrs. Dowell of Branscombe had worked on her ninetieth birthday.

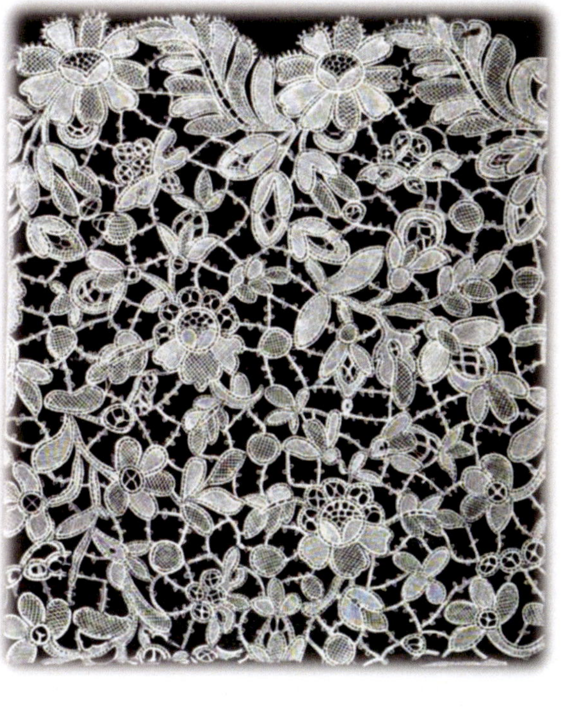

Lace making by the early/mid twentieth century had become a hobby more than an occupation and there are still a select few who continue to carry on the ancient skill today.

Honiton Guipure Lace

Chapter 2
Local Businesses

"To open a shop is easy, to keep it open is an art"
Chinese Proverb

Among the numerous businesses that have come and gone in Honiton, there are a select few that not only had their roots in Victorian Honiton but also managed to survive in the town well into the twentieth century, and in some cases beyond. Here are a few of those businesses that long established members of Honiton will undoubtedly remember, with a small history for those who do not!

C. Harding & Sons

The business has existed in the town since the early 1800s but not always under the name of Harding. From the early 1800s, the shop that was once located in the present day 'Specsavers' was run by Nathaniel Read, a linen draper from Dorset, who located to the shop in the early 1840s and previously ran his business further up the High Street. Nathaniel died without children and it was his brother, John Read, who continued the business after his death in the 1850s. John already had his own drapery business in the town. After John died, his sons, Nathaniel and Charles, ran two drapery businesses side by side from what is now Spec Savers and

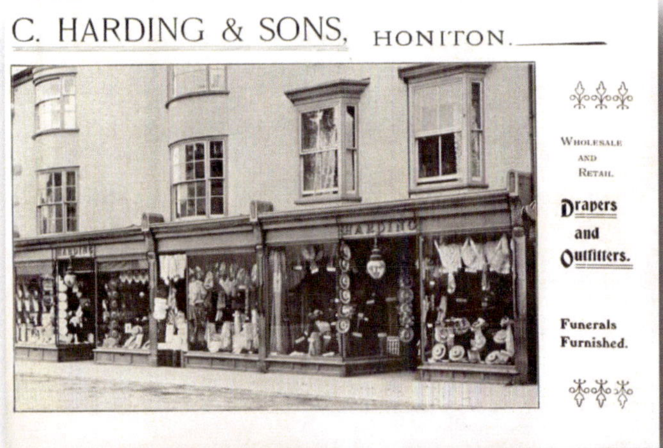

Boots. By the 1870s, Nathaniel had left the business to a young farmer's son from Branscombe, Charles Harding, whilst Charles Read remained next door. Charles Read's son, Herbert, went on in life to achieve great eminence and was later knighted.

By 1881, Charles Harding employed six assistants and two servants. The business became 'Charles Harding & Sons' at the turn of the twentieth century and Charles himself died in Honiton in 1927, aged 84. From the early 1920s his son, Frank, became the proprietor of his father's drapery, tailoring and millinery business, whilst another son, Percy, set up his own "outfitters" in what is now 'Complete Meats' and 'Cafe 102' (100-102 High Street). By the start of World War Two, Frank's store extended across three premises (121-125 High Street). 'C. Harding and Sons' was a wholesale and retail establishment as well as being agents of the Devon and Exeter Savings Bank. When Frank Harding retired, in the 1960s, the premises were split up with one of the shops continuing as a gentleman's outfitters shop known as 'Foster Brothers' whilst the remainder became the 'Co-op'. When Percy Harding retired, his premises were split into 'The Honiton China Shop'- now 'Complete Meats'- and 'Horseshoe Cafe'- now 'Cafe 102'.

A. Dimond & Co.

This long established Honiton business was started by Robert Dimond in the late 19th century; Robert came from a very poor background and establishing his own successful business was an admirable achievement. Robert Dimond was born in Honiton in 1848 to James and Susan Dimond. In 1851 the family were living in Claylands Cottage where James supported his family as an agricultural labourer. James, however, died in 1857 and left his young wife to raise 3 young children, working as a poorly paid seamstress. Robert was forced to work as a basket maker from a young age to support his two younger brothers. By the 1870s, money was even tighter and the family were forced to reside with Susan's widowed mother in Lees Buildings; however, Robert had already started on the road to his future career as a printer. Robert married a local lace- maker, Eliza Connett, in 1878 and established his printing firm, which he took over from Mr. John Knight, at their longstanding High Street address ten years later in 1888. Robert Dimond died in 1902, aged 53, and after his death his widow continued the business, as well as raising their 5 children. Mrs. Dimond ran the stationers and printing establishment until the early 1920s when it became known as 'Dimond & Co.' It was taken over by Robert and Eliza's son, Archie Dimond, then their grandson, Arthur and finally Anthony who closed the old High Street shop in 2008, relocating to smaller premises nearby.

In 1934 the business extended it premises with a new printing works behind the old shop which, although still in existence today, is now empty.

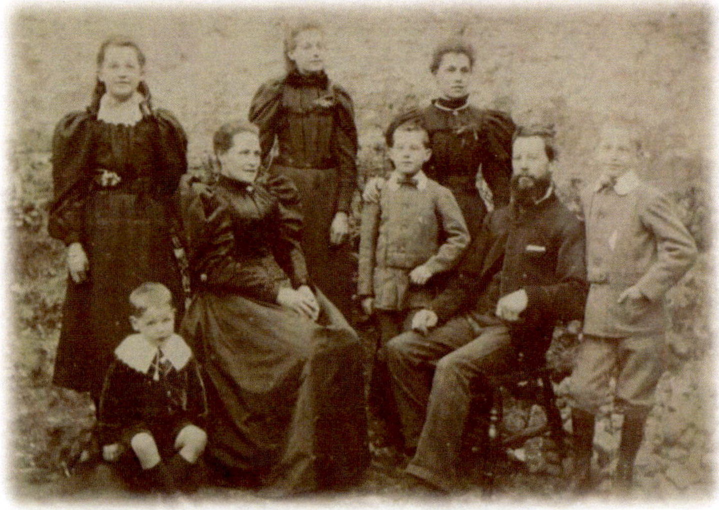

Robert Dimond and Family

Ironically, in the early 1840s Robert's mother, Susan, was a servant to the printer, John Knight, with whom it is believed her son, Robert, undertook his apprenticeship. Victorian printers would have a tool known as a 'stick' in which they would arrange the letters of each word to be printed. The letters were usually embossed onto a metal cube and were divided into two separate sections. An 'upper case' would hold all the capital letters whilst a 'lower case' would contain all the small letters. It was important for apprentices, such as the young Robert Dimond, to construct each word on their stick from left to right rather than right to left. If they did the latter the word would appear backwards on the finished product which wasted precious ink and paper; it was therefore imperative that the trainees did not "get the wrong end of the stick" – hence the saying.

Dyers Chemists

Edward Henry Dyer, the youngest son of a baker, was born in Corfe and came to Honiton in 1883. He set up his pharmaceutical business from the property now occupied by 'Greenslade Taylor Hunt Estate Agency' (111 High Street). Later diversifying into photographic needs, Mr. Dyer remained at his premises until his premature death in 1897, after which his widow continued the business for the next 20 years. Edward's son, Bernard, took over the business after his mother and ran it until around the time of his death in 1957 when the premises were taken over by 'Hinton Lake'. During a later refurbishment of the property, hundreds of old Victorian drugs and bottles were allegedly found in the property's basement!

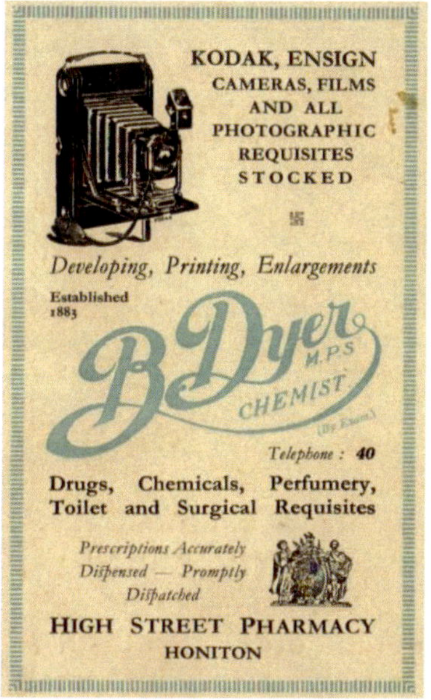

The Victorian chemist catered for the majority of the nation's sick, with higher skilled physicians and doctors being too expensive for the average family. Many of their recipes, tonics and remedies dated back centuries and had their origins in the practises of medieval herbalists. Until 1837 anyone could be a pharmacist, even grocers, and these numerous individuals had a wide range of weird and wacky concoctions to cure virtually any ailment one may suffer from. A mixture of oil of almond and garlic applied with cotton to the ear was said to cure deafness. Cough mixtures which may have contained anything from arsenic, laudanum and cannabis, were sure- fire solutions to a tickle in one's throat and a belladonna solution for eye diseases! Freckles could also be removed from one's skin with frequent application of a tonic containing hydrochloric acid. This 'harmless' acid could also be added to warm water to "deodorize foul feet". Mercury, mixed with sarsaparilla, would be administered to cure syphilis. One would have also probably been able to find many oddly named tonics in Mr. Dyer's shop such as 'Daffy's Elixir',

'Cabbage Paper', 'Hudson's Cold Cream' and 'Grains of Paradise', which was used as a medicine for cattle.

E. A. Dodd & Son

Ernest Albert Dodd was born in Silverton, Devon in 1877. He was the son of Richard Dodd, a former carpenter and later a Sergeant in the Devon Constabulary. The family moved to Honiton in the late 1890s when Richard retired and it was there that his son, Ernest, started work as a carpenter and joiner. By 1906, Mr. Dodd was working as a builder and decorator but in the early 1920s, he concentrated solely on building. His business grew and by 1930s Mr. Dodd was a contractor, builder and undertaker. Ernest's son, Derek, continued the business after his father's death in 1948. The family builders were responsible for many of the houses built in the town. All the properties from the bottom of Kings Road to the railway bridge were built by them, including Newlands, which is thought to have been named by Ernest after his childhood address of 'Newland', Landkey (nr. Barnstaple). Many of the houses in Exeter and Sidmouth Road, as well as many others in the town, were constructed by the Dodds. Derek Dodd had two premises, one for the undertaking branch which was, and still is, located in King Street and the building branch which was once located in Silver Street. After Mr. Dodd retired he sold the building firm to his long term manager Antony Grigg who, unfortunately, died only a few years later. The undertaking business still exists today and is located in King Street. Derek Dodd died in 2005.

George Blay

George Blay was a 5 acre timber yard located in Marlpits Lane; although known as George Blay, the original founder was called Buckingham. Frederick Buckingham was born in Oxfordshire, the son of a baker and corn dealer, and it was this trade in which he first started. He then became a mason and later started a timber business in Gillingham, Dorset in the 1870s. It was not until the early 1880s that he moved his family to Honiton where he set up business on a site that it would occupy for the next century. The last of the Buckinghams retired in 1917 and it was then a man called George Blay took over the establishment which, at that time, was known as 'South Western Saw Mills'. When Mr. Blay took over the firm, all the machinery was steam powered and haulage was supplied by the company's 26 horses which used to graze in fields once located near 'Streamers Meadows'. In the early 1930s, Mr. Blay converted the mill from

the old steam powered machinery to electric and renamed it 'George Blay': by 1936 he had made it a public limited company and the name thus changed to 'George Blay Ltd'.
In the 1930s the company was making all manner of items including garages, poultry huts, greenhouses, kennels, portable stables, gates, steel buildings, huts and even bungalows. The factory suffered a great fire in September 1941, due to an electrical fault, in which the entire premises were consumed. However, the inferno allowed the business to start afresh and install new modern machinery which, in the years after WWII, earned it the title of "one of the most up-to-date saw mills in the country". For many years the company was referred to as "The Electric Sawmills Honiton". John Maeer was the company's managing director for many years until his son, Jack, succeeded him in 1970. Jack Maeer later retired in 1986 after having served the firm for over 50 years. John Maeer built and lived in the property connected to the present day 'Small Animal Clinic' called 'Woodstock'. The property's floor was constructed from wood for a ship George Blay were commissioned to build but never actually completed.
The old factory turned its machinery off for the last time in 1998; hit by a recession in the timber industry, the mill closed and its 30 workers lost their jobs. The site remained unoccupied for 6 months before it was demolished and the site was converted into 'Crosscut Way' housing estate in 1999. Many of the present day road names pay a tribute to the area's former industrial past.

Hoskins & Co.

The well known, successful clothes shop that was situated on the corner of New Street for many years had a founder who came from a very humble background.
James Hoskin was born and grew up with his widowed mother and four brothers in St Ives, Cornwall and started his working life as a copper miner, which he did for at least 10 years. He later moved to Honiton where he married a local woman, Jane Parsons, and worked at first in the town as a travelling draper or 'hawker'. By the turn of the twentieth century, Mr. Hoskin moved into the site of Hoskins & Co. which, prior to his arrival, had been a grocery shop. The building itself was thought to have been constructed in the 18th century. The shop was originally known as 'J. Hoskin' and in 1909 one could buy a suit made to measure for thirty shillings! James remained in business there for over 20 years until the mid 1920s when he retired to Church Hill. Having no surviving children, he left

the business in the capable hands of a proprietor named Frederick G. Pollard.

A local woman who worked at Hoskins & Co., in the 1930s gives an interesting insight into how the shop operated (extracted from S. P. Nielson's book 'Honiton Memories', 2003):

"We started at half past eight in the morning and the shop usually closed for lunch and we had an hour. Then we worked until 7 o' clock...we daren't shut the shop 'til the last customer had gone and until the church clock had struck the hour.

When we went home at night, especially the juniors, you had to cover the clothes that were on stand and things with these drapes to keep the dust from getting on them.

We didn't sell ladies hats. There were plenty of men's felt hats and of course sold by the size. The men mostly did that. I was given the job of looking after the men's shirt department. That was after i had been there a while. All the men's shirts were without collars, whether it was working shirt or a best shirt. They wore stiff collars around them so that you didn't change them – you just changed the collar when it got dirty.

We sold clergyman's collars as well

Mr Scanning had a workshop out the back and he used to sit on a table and wax his thread – one piece round his foot and the other in his mouth and his hands going to and fro to do the waxing. The thread was sued for sewing on the buttons.

No man did the lot. Another man did the trousers and another would do the waistcoats – what they called vests.

Well now another busy time was February. That was the month when there were more deaths and a funeral was a real big thing, especially among the farmers. They would buy black suits and the bearers would have to have black diamonds stitched onto their jackets and other clothing. The whole of Honiton had to know if you had a death in the family... It all had to be paid for. It was only people with money showing off.

In the drapery department we actually sold everything; cotton, needles and pins and lots of stockings, hosiery, underwear – nice underwear, Kayser Bondor, I think – that was kept in a glass cabinet.

We were paid in the beginning 5/- a week and the second year it went up to 7/6-. This was while we were still apprentice learning. The third year, when you qualified it was up to one pound.

Oh yes we sold materials by the yard - all kinds – not a lot of fancy goods. Butter muslin which we used for straining the milk on the farms was one thing we sold a lot of.

On the top shelf was a pair of stays or old corsets that had been there for years. Nobody would throw them away or write them off. We used to hand them down from the shelf and have a good old giggle about it. They were there long after I left. Whether they were there at the end of the closing down, I don't know.

Oh men wore bibs and brace overalls in their work then, there were breeches and cord trousers and leggings that the farmers used to wear. They didn't use Wellington boot like they do now. They've completely taken over, Wellington boots have, and seldom do you see these nice leather leggings on Saturday time or fair time"!

But on the whole we couldn't have worked for better people. We had a week's holiday every year."

'Dorset Place' in New Street was once the rear entrance to the shop and was where the stables, hay loft, store sheds and coal store were located. This yard was formerly cobbled and accessed from New Street by a large pair of doors. This was also the point from which deliveries were made and, when horses became second hand news, the store employed a Model-T Ford van for the purpose.

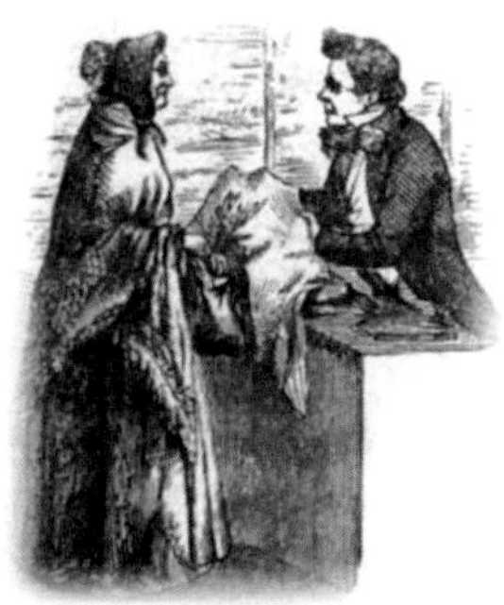

The shop remained in business for over a century, but in 1981 the large building was sold to developers and turned into several individual premises. Whilst Hoskins & Co. retained a small part of the new development, and became known as 'Hoskins of Honiton', it was not long afterwards that it closed down. Today the original shop has been split into a travel agents and a jewellery shop.

<u>Matthews Brothers</u>

This was once a long established Honiton business that remained in the town for nearly a century. The Matthews Brothers were ironmongers and their business was once located where 'W. H. Smiths' now stands. The aforementioned premises was an ironmongers before the Matthews family moved to the town and was run by a gentleman called William Wheaton. The firm was originally founded by a Robert Hunt Matthews, the son of a Colyton grocer, who moved to Honiton in the mid 1850s. Mr. Matthews originally started in business with Walter Miller, who later teamed up with Mr. Lilley. By the 1880s Robert's two sons, Robert Henry and Edmund

Walter Matthews, had taken over the business. The brothers "had a large iron store" at the rear of their High Street premises and kept a small brick shed, once located near the railway bank, in Kings Road where they made their own gun cartridges. Matthews Brothers supplied all the local blacksmiths in both the town and surrounding rural area and also had two other shops in Axminster. When the family retired it was taken over by three local tradesmen: Roy Read (of Read's Garage), Mr. Yates and John Maeer (who was once manager of George Blays Saw Mills). Robert and

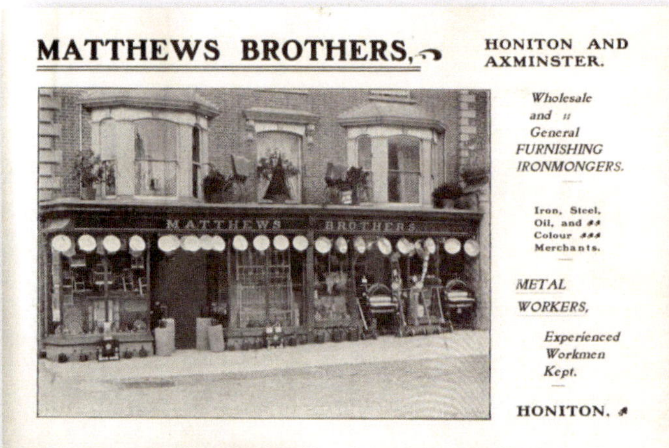

Edmund died in 1922 and 1938 respectively and the business was eventually sold to the World Stores. The shop later became 'NSS Newsagents', 'Key Markers', 'Forbuoys Newsagents' and currently W. H. Smiths.

<u>Mickelburgh Iron Foundry</u>

Although this famous local business was always known locally as Mickelburgh's, the foundry had its roots in Honiton long before Mr. Mickelburgh arrived at Honiton.

The foundry was known to have existed in Honiton as early as 1843 and the first to run it was a Mr Robert White who had started his working life as a whitesmith in Colyton. Mr. White ran the foundry for some 30 years and, having only one son who became a banker, he had no one to continue the business so after his retirement, in the late 1870s, it was taken over by a William Huxtable. At this point the foundry was making agricultural implements for the numerous farms of the region. Mr. Huxtable was not at the foundry for very long and later moved to Colyton where he completely changed professions becoming an "aerated water manufacturer"!

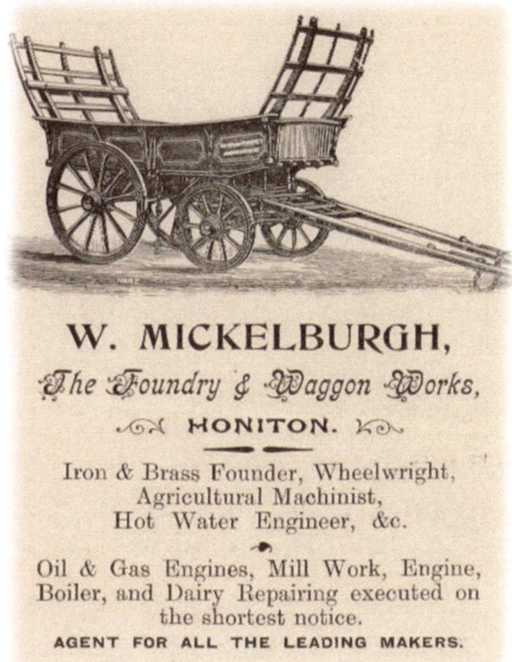

By 1889, Mr. Mickelburgh had taken the reins at the foundry starting a whole new and long chapter in Honiton history. Walter Mickelburgh was born in Ottery St Mary in 1857 and before running the foundry had been a silversmith in London. His father, Richard, was a solicitor and had been an influential figure locally: not only was he the agent for Lord Coleridge, he also became clerk to the Court of Exeter as well as being honorary Chief Constable of Ottery St Mary.

Walter Mickelburgh had two daughters and remained in Honiton for the next 60 odd years making agricultural tools, wagons and other items. One gentleman who remembers him is a Mr. Upton who recalls memories of his great uncle, and the foundry, during the war years:

"At the outbreak of WW2 my mother with my sister and myself were evacuated to the foundry in Honiton. The house was run by Norah Snell - known to us as Cousin Nell. She was his daughter who had been widowed in the First World War. Walter, then 82, was more or less retired, the foundry being run by a manager. However Walter did go into the office

(across the yard) every day. He also went up to the caravan which acted as a market office on market days. All business was conducted face to face and in longhand (no telephone or typewriter) I believe he still attended Masonic meetings in the hotel at the top of the town.
My chief memories are of the foundry. This consisted of a blast furnace, fed from the top, an engineering shop, a smithy and a carpenters shop. All the machinery was powered by a central waterwheel. I was allowed the run of the place provided that I did not get in the way. The event of the week was the lighting of the blast furnace. When, in due time the plug at the base was pierced the molten iron poured into a ladle held by two men. It was then poured into hand crafted sand moulds, mostly of ploughshares but also of other castings depending on customers' orders. The man who spent most of his week preparing the moulds was Fred Flood. The carpenter's shop was presided over by Fred Fairclough - a superb craftsman. While I was there he made, among other things, a haywain entirely out of wood apart from the metal "tyres" on the wheels. I remember no plans being referred to, all dimensions seemingly in Fred's head. A third Fred was the blacksmith; another skilled operative who, to my ten year old eyes, could magic anything out of iron."

Quite hard to believe that such a large establishment was still powered by water, even in the mid twentieth century, and that the furnaces were obviously so powerful they had to remain lit all week!
Walter Mickelburgh died in 1951 at the grand old age of 94. After his retirement, the foundry site was taken over by John Halse and later went on to become 'Halse of Honiton', which it still is today. There are remnants of the great foundry still to be seen in the town. The old iron trough that runs along the pavement of the High Street, in which the river Crystal used to flow, was made there and also a number of drain covers outside premises toward the west end of town still clearly bear the name 'Mickelburgh'.

Miller & Lilley

Henry Eaden Lilley was the son of a Cambridgeshire farmer who started his working life as a draper in Basingstoke. The family moved to Honiton in the mid 1870s and it was here that Mr. Lilley went into partnership with Walter Miller.

The company was based in New Street and they started as brick and tile manufacturers as well agricultural merchants, selling seeds and other farm

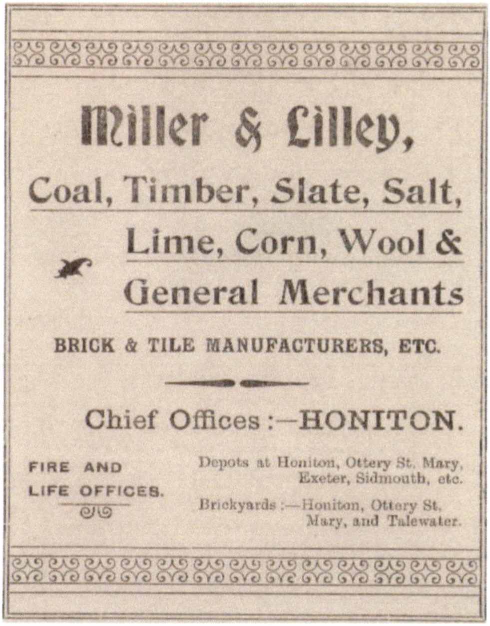

implements. In 1878 they were recorded to have branches at 'Sidmouth Junction' (Feniton), Ottery, Sidmouth and Whimple railway stations'. By the later Victorian era the company had branched into suppliers of coal. One advertisement from the turn of the century describes them as thus: "Timber, Slate, Salt, Lime, Corn, Agricultural Manure, oil cake, General Merchants"!

Henry Eaden Lilley died in his 70s in 1903 and his son, Henry Herbert Lilley, continued the business after his father's death. The business ceased brick manufacturing in the 1930s when they were still dealing in coal and general supplies: it was also at this time that they became a public limited company.

Miller & Lilley had one premises for many years at the building now occupied by 'Sue Ryder Charity Shop' and what was recently 'Conway Electrical Store', as well as having a store at the Honiton Railway Station. The site's main offices were Laurel House, also in New Street. It was said that "Miller & Lilley were the biggest concern" at the train station, reiterating how huge the company once was. The site of the present day Honiton Library was the company's stores and repair shops and was formerly the gardens of Mr. Woodgates, the schoolmaster.

Miller & Lilley remained in business for nearly a century and were finally taken over by Bradfords, who merged with them. Bradfords can still be found right next to Honiton train station.

H. H. Lilley aka (Henry Herbert Lilley) was the gentleman who donated 'The Glen' to the town in 1937 in commemoration of the Coronation of King

George VI and, rightfully so, had the recently developed 'Lilley Walk', near the Glen, named after him. Lilley Walk was originally another field where the company grazed their horses before the construction of their showrooms and stores. When Mr Lilley died, Laurel House became the offices of the East Devon Water Board and was later purchased by the solicitors 'Every & Philips'.

S. Shute & Sons

This local business was started by William Shute, a Honiton man, who was the son of a humble agricultural labourer. William founded the business in 1842 and started out as a plumber and glazier. William's son, Sidney, by his second marriage, took over the business in the 1880s and was assisted by his brother, another William. By 1910 William Shute Jnr. had left the business and Sidney was running it alone. It was Sidney who gave the company its name of 'S. Shute & Sons' in the mid 1920s. The business had always been located in New Street and by the 1950s they were listed as "builders, plumbers and decorators" based at number 29. The business was later taken over by William Duncan and after he retired in the 1980s local builder, John Boland, bought out the premises and the businesses were thus merged. They were later converted into what is now 'Kings Court Shopping Centre'. William Shute's other son, Alf, started his own business in the High Street.

Slades Countrywise Ltd.

Charles Slade was born in 1854 to the son of an agricultural labourer of Tedburn St. Mary and came to Honiton in the late 1870s. He married a daughter of an already established grocer and corn and flour merchant, James Parsons, who had been in business in the town since 1860. Mr. Slade joined forces with Mr. Parsons and ran the successful business which became known as 'James Parsons & Co.'. By the late 1900s Mr. Slade's eldest son, Charles Parsons Slade (1884-1948), started his own business as an iron founder and wagon builder/repairer in Northcote Lane and by the start of WWI had relocated to a new site in Kings Road. At the end of WWI, James Parsons & Co. had expanded to merchants of "corn, seed, cake, salt, manure & coal". Charles P. Slade lived in Plympton House, now 'Anthony James Antiques', and by the mid 1930s had converted his business to motor repairs. C. P. Slade also presented one of the 'new' bells to the town church. By the late 1930s 'James Parsons & Co', which had formerly been run as a partnership between a Mr Bernard J. Yates and

Charles Slade Snr's second son, James Henry Slade, had been dissolved. Mr. Yates had founded his own business at 93 High Street (now Dalzell Distributors Ltd.) and James Slade had started his own corn merchant business under the name of 'J. H. Slade'. James Slade started his business in the left hand side of the old Assembly Rooms and later relocated to a shop now occupied by 'Soft Options': his storage facilities were at the old Butter Factory at Littletown. Slade's Countrywise was established at its present site in 1983 when they moved to the site of the old Turks Head Road House. Interestingly, four large petrol containers, filled with concrete, still remain under ground at the present Slade's site from when the premises were a coach halting and fuelling station.
At the time of writing Slades is due to close and an Aldi Superstore to be put in its place.

Chapter 3
Inns, Hotels & Taverns

"It is abundantly certain that the labouring classes consume at this moment ten times more malt liquor than their ancestors ever did in either the fifteenth or the sixteenth century."
(A Statistical Account of the British Empire, 1837)

The term 'public house' has only been in existence since the 18th century; before that alcoholic drinks were served in licenced inns and alehouses. Many were merely a room in a private house where the owner/occupant could earn some extra money from the venture.
The origin of tavern signs began with the Romans who portrayed such an establishment to its illiterate population with a symbol illustrating a trail of vine leaves. After the Romans left England, its inhabitants adopted the symbol of a bush instead but it was not until 1393 that a law was passed making it compulsory for all drinking houses to show a symbol on a signboard. One, if not the earliest, record of an inn in Honiton was in 1385 when a sum of 350 marks was stolen from John de Montford, Duke of Brittany, at an inn run by Simon de Carselake, who was held responsible for the theft, and was referred to as "Carselake's Inn".
'Beer Houses' were also a popular invention of the Victorian period and Honiton was no exception. Gin consumption by the end of the 18th century had reached critical levels: in 1742 a population one-tenth of that today consumed ten times as much spirit and the Government was called upon to do something about this "mother's ruin". In 1830 the Government passed the 'Beer Act' which was intended to portray beer as more 'wholesome' than the evils of gin. The Act allowed any householder with a 2 guinea licence to sell ale and porter, but not wine or spirits. The plan, however, worked too well and beer houses exploded all over England: by the 1870s alcohol consumption peaked at an astonishing 344 gallons of beer per person per year. This is the equivalent to nearly 8 pints of beer a day, proving that "Booze Britain" was not a 21st century invention! The 'Beer Act' was when pubs started becoming a central part in working class communities; Honiton itself had several beer houses, some of which can be found in the list below.
There have probably been hundreds of pubs which have come and gone in Honiton over the centuries. Today the town possesses numerous establishments where one can quench his/her thirst, including 11 public houses, 7 social clubs, 2 hotels (including Honiton Motel) and 1 night club (sometimes 2!). In 1851 there were a total of 5 malt houses and an

additional 32 places to have an alcoholic beverage, 21 of which were in the High Street alone but within less than 20 years, 8 of these had closed. Over 80 different public houses have been identified that were open at one time or another.
Among those 80, the following are the ones that have been identified:

The Ackland Arms: this pub was located in King Street and was in business as early as 1870 and as late as 1917.

The Anchor: recorded as early as 1749, this inn was situated where the current pub 'The Holt' stands. Although one may think this tavern took its name from a nautical derivative, it actually originated from the Bible. Taken from 'Letter to the Hebrews (6:19)' "We have this as a sure and steadfast anchor of the soul, a hope." The pub's grounds originally stretched back onto King Street, which was once the garden. Today the old gardens are a part of 'Halse of Honiton'. After the closure of the pub in 1913 it became known as 'The Anchor Dairy', then 'The Anchor Cafe' and after 1954, when it was referred to as 'The Heathfield Cafe & Guest House', it became a private house but was still referred to as 'The Old Anchor Dairy.' Before it became 'Dominoes' in 1984 it had lain empty for some ten years, prior to which it had been called the 'Old Cauldron Cafe'. The restoration cost, prior to its opening as Dominoes, was £60,000 and although now renamed 'The Holt' it is still a restaurant/bar. When closed, in 1913, it was described as a "small" establishment where "sanitation was bad." Situated right next to the Gissage, this inn was run by Mary Ann Pope in 1850. The pub's last landlord to open its doors as 'The Anchor' was Mrs. Holway.

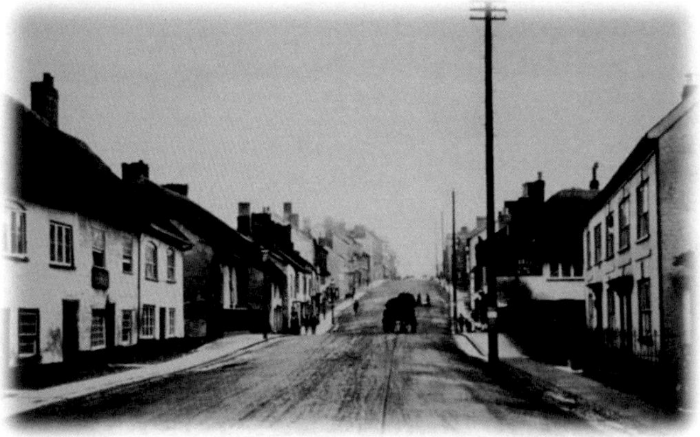

The old Anchor inn to the right of the horse and cart.

The Angel: first recorded in the town as early as 1605, it was one of the many coaching inns that had sprung up during the 18th century. It was engulfed in the terrible fire of 1747 and was badly damaged in the inferno of 1765 but was rebuilt and was one of the last old Honiton inns to close.

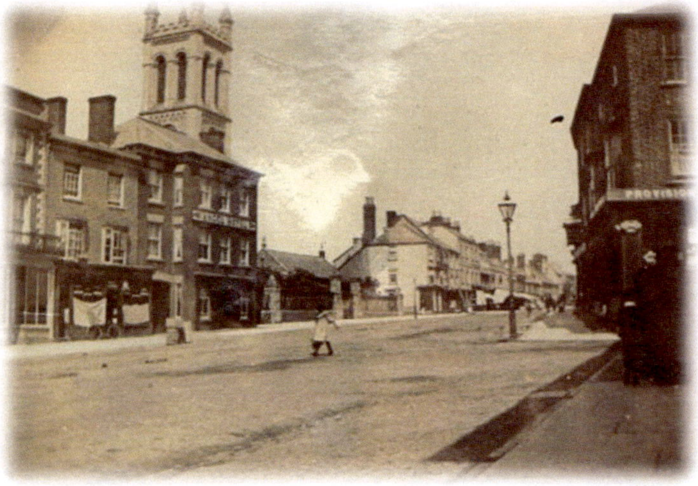

A view of The Angel c.1900

In 1860 it underwent a big refurbishment and was enlarged with the front being rebuilt and another storey added (originally only being 2 storeys) so that another 4 bedrooms could be accommodated. In one Victorian document, the 'Angel Commercial Inn' boasted 'families & co. Supplied with strong beers and ales.' In 1851 the landlady was a certain Elizabeth Lee, widow of the late William Lee (not to be confused with the man who built St. Paul's) who had held the licence since 1832 (in 1841 there were a total of six William Lees residing in the town!) Elizabeth ran the hotel after her husband's death until the 1870s. After her retirement, Elizabeth lived with her unmarried son, William, who was a chemist and later left Honiton and moved to Essex to live with her widowed daughter. The house they lived in was ironically called 'Devonshire Villa'. She died in 1906 aged 92. There was once a well known tale that a son of William and Elizabeth fell in love and eloped with the daughter of the landlord of the Fountain Inn. The evidence, however, suggests this to be false and it is believed that it was, in fact, William himself who married the daughter of the Fountain's landlord.

Over the decades the site has also been an Inland Revenue office (in the 1890s), a garage and the home of the town fire brigade. At its peak it was a 10 bedroom hotel but was later reduced to 5. Ralph Durbin Sprake, a 31 year old man, took over the hotel in 1916. Mr. Sprake had his family roots in Honiton but he was born in Suffolk. He had problems with St. Paul's Church, in the 1930s, for the hourly chimes through the nights apparently kept his guests awake, with many of them refusing to return. He petitioned to have the nightly chimes stopped, which was later upheld. Ralph Sprake also ran a garage, repair shop and taxi service in the old yard: the town fire engine was also housed there when he was Captain of the Brigade. This popular local man ran the hotel until his sudden death from a heart attack in 1956, after which his wife succeeded him until her retirement in 1965. Its closure was prevented when a Mr. Davidson took it over from the Bass Charrington brewery in 1973. However, on his retirement in 1989, the inn closed its doors for the last time. The old stables and upper floors were converted into private residencies and the lower section into a shop (Threshers) from 1995-2009. During the reconstruction, a large number of clay pipe fragments were found which had presumably been discarded by the many number of patrons who once drank there. Today this ancient inn is easily found as the building still retains the sign 'The Angel' above the shop doorway and is located next to St. Paul's Church in the High Street.

Apothecaries Arms: a 17th century inn known to have existed in 1663. Its landlord William Derby was an apothecary, an early chemist, who died in 1682.

The Bakers Arms: mentioned in 1766, it was located where Retail Therapy now stands and later changed its name, in 1824, to 'The King's Arms'. It was one time owned by local attorney Christopher Flood who lived only several doors away.

Beer Houses: there were several of these in town at different times. Two were located in Queen Street; one had its licence revoked due to being a disorderly house and the other, recorded as early as 1844, lasted for around 20 years and was run by a Francis Hooper who was also a stone mason. He apparently ran the premises until old age got the better of him and he and his wife ended their days in St. Margaret's Alms Houses. Another stood at the east end of the High Street (north side) and was open in 1883. Another was located in the High Street and was run by a Frederick Cowley in 1893. There are probably many more yet to be identified.

The Bell Inn: recorded from 1675 to about 1850 it was located where the current entrance to 'Lace Walk' is. Its last landlady was Elizabeth Richards when the property covered a quarter of an acre of land.

Bird in Hand: the name refers to falconry. This 18th century inn was located on the north side of the High Street, at the east end of town and was, sadly, once again destroyed by fire some point in the later 1700s.

The Black Horse: possibly more than one inn by this name. One was documented in 1681 and 1746; however, there was no record post 1844. One was located on the south side of the High Street and Farquharson stated that there was another one, by this name, at the east end of the High Street but was not open for long.

The Black Lion: this inn was in Honiton as early as 1663 and was thought to have once been called the New Inn. It was located on the corner of New Street but after the council purchased it, was sadly demolished in 1967 to give easier access to New Street which had, prior to its demolition, been controlled by traffic lights due to the narrowness of the road. In its heyday the Black Lion boasted 7 bedrooms for guests and stabling for up to 17 horses. An iron statue of a black lion that was housed with the pub still stands in Black Lion Court. In 1851 it was run by Charles Sanders with his wife, Harriet.

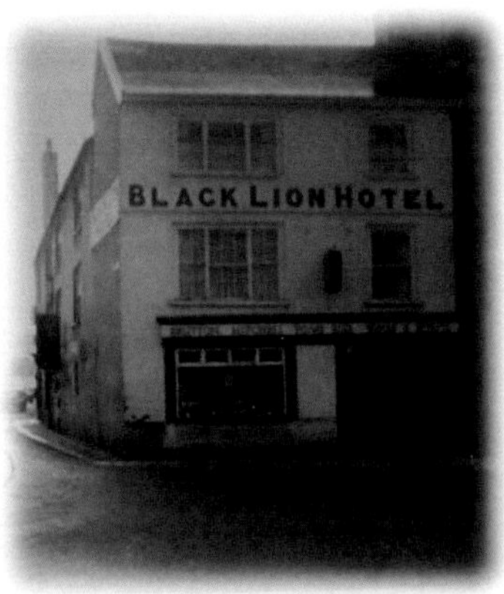

The Blacksmiths Arms: sometimes referred to as the 'Smiths Arms.' It was situated opposite The Anchor, right next to the river, in a small thatched cottage. It had fallen victim to the great fire of 1765 but was still in business well into the 19th century. The inn closed 1843/44 and its last landlord was a Thomas Woodland whose day job was a farrier. There was another Blacksmith Arms located close to the old Kings Arms Inn but this was destroyed in the fire of 1765.

The Blue Ball: located in Northcote Lane, its licence was forfeited in the late 18th century.

Browns Wine Cellar: a drinking establishment known to have been run in 1774 by a certain Arthur Brown - no more is known.

The Bull Inn: a little inn located in the High Street. It closed at some point between 1844 and 1850 and after its closure became a private residence, finally becoming part of the modern day Red Cow when an extension incorporated the two adjacent cottages. Its last landlord was a Mr. Joseph Clarke who was also a shoemaker.

The Butchers Arms: mentioned in 1766 and had the alias of 'Lott's Wine Cellar' in 1808. Its exact location is unknown but stood at a central position in the High Street and closed at some point between 1808 and 1844.

Carpenters Arms: a very old inn that has had several names in its past. In its early life the site was used for a prison as early as 1675. It then became the Carpenters Arms, then 'The Compass', then the 'Bakers Arms' and was rebuilt in 1852 after a fire, when it was raised a storey and renamed 'The Globe Inn'. The Globe closed its doors in 1971 after the Gloucester Regiment, the pub's biggest customers, was relocated from Honiton to Germany. The old inn then became a private residence, a meeting place for the 'Society of Friends', an antique centre called 'Globe Antiques' and latterly an amusement arcade. This listed building can currently be found on the corner of Dowell Street. In 1850 its landlord was yet another William Lee! - by 1851 his widow, Elizabeth, had taken the reins.

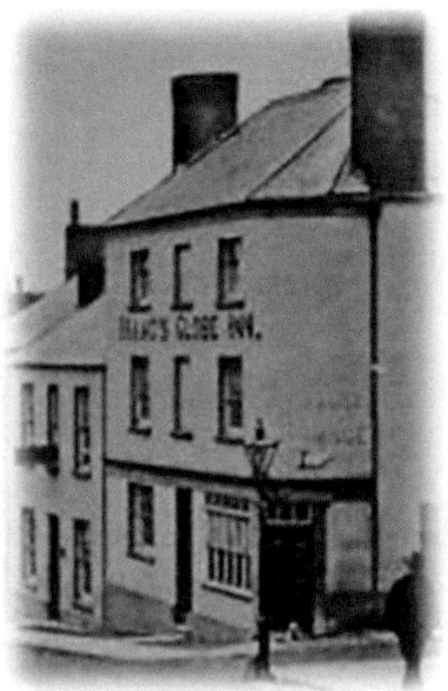

The Chopping Knife: it was known to be open in 1774, when it was called the 'Rolling Pin' and closed in 1890. It was located in the old Honiton Lace Shop which today is the 'Birds Nest' Chinese Restaurant (44 High Street).

Opening hours of this pub were good for the devout drinker: in a court observation of 1849 it was noted that 2 geese stealers went into this pub at 9.30am on a January morning for a 'pint of cider'! It suffered a fire in 1862 which, fortunately, for the 'cider' drinkers did not result in its closure! In 1851 it was run by a John Holway who, as well as running the pub, was also a butcher. The building has fortunately retained its early 19th century doorcase and is today a Grade II listed building.

The Clarence: named after the Duke of Clarence, one of Queen Victoria's sons. This inn was a 'commercial inn and posting house' in 1857. Its landlord was Benjamin Ward, formerly a coach builder, and it was located in the present day 'Abingdon House', which at present is an antique centre (136 High Street), where Mr. Ward had formerly run his coach building business. It was open for about 10 years, from about 1851.

The Coach and Horses: was recorded in the town in 1773 but had closed long before the 1840s. It was thought to have been near the old Oxford Inn on the south side of the High Street.

Cock Ale House: also known as the 'Cock Inn' it was noted in Honiton in 1741 and closed about 1770. Located on the north side of the High Street very near to Marwood House and was latterly home to the independent pastor.

The Compass (also known as 'The Three Compasses'): see The Globe

The Crown and Sceptre: previously this inn was to be found in Northcote Lane and was originally called 'The Knackers Hole' and later, in about 1796, 'The Mermaid'. The inn was celebrated for its 'hipe suppers.' When its landlady died, it was moved into the High Street at some point before 1823 and was renamed 'The New Mermaid' and then later 'The Crown and Sceptre.' The Inn was located in the property at the top of Crown Court and, at the time, the landlord owned the inn as well as all of the Court's properties. The name of the 'The Crown and Sceptre' has its origins in the time of the restoration of the monarchy in 1661. Its last landlord was William Proll and it went out of business in 1905. It is now 'Bennetts of Honiton' at 162 High Street.

Curriers Arms: named after a process of the tannery trade. Thought to have been located in the fourth house up New Street from the Queen Street junction. Known to have existed as early as 1780, it was apparently closed in the early 19th century by a local solicitor, Mr. Aberdein, as it was too near his offices! The inn was also thought to have had an earlier name of 'The Woolcombers Arms'.

The Dolphin Inn: known to have existed as early as 1656 and is reported to stand on the site of the town Manor House of the Courtenay family, dating from 1377 when Sir Phillip Courtenay inherited the title. It was said that a common fate of an old mansion was to become an inn and in The Dolphin's case this seems to be applicable. A life sized dolphin figure carved from wood hung outside the inn up until around 1860 when the inn was enlarged.

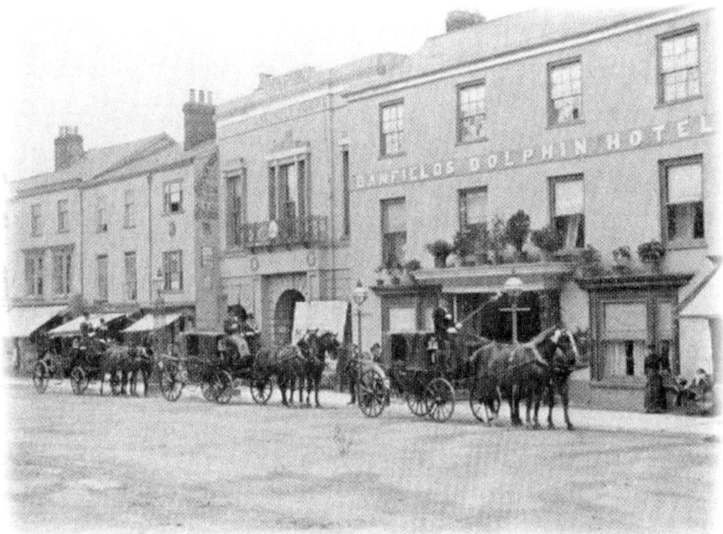

It takes its name from the Courtenay's Coat of Arms, on which there was a dolphin, said to represent 'swiftness, diligence and love'. This ancient hotel was once the heart of the town's social calling: nearly all recorded references of meetings, lectures and performances were held at this establishment. Princess Victoria, later Queen Victoria, paid a visit to the inn on August 7th 1833 when the coach driving her and her mother halted to change horses. The inn was severely damaged in the fire of 1797 and was not completely repaired until 1799. It was local builders, John and William Lee, who rebuilt the hotel at a cost of £1,530. The Blake family ran the inn from at least the end of the eighteenth century and was then run by a Richard Blake from 1813 until his death in 1845. Mr. Blake was known locally as 'Guinea Blake' as he was always pestering people for change of one guinea. When Richard died in his 70s his son, John Denner Blake, took over and ran the inn until he retired at some point around 1860: he died in 1861.

The inn then came into the possession of the Banfield family, more specifically William Henry Banfield, a farmer's son from Awliscombe. He ran the inn until he retired in the early 1890s when his son, Harry, became landlord; Harry was also a town alderman. Harry Banfield held the reins at the Dolphin until his retirement in 1921 when his services included funeral cars, motor car repairs, coaches and supplier of wine & spirits.

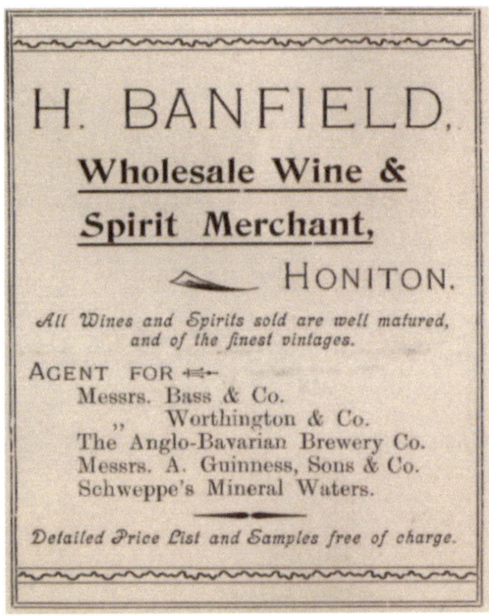

In an account book from 1892 it is found that a bottle of Mr. Banfield's 'best brandy' was 6 shillings a quart and his 'best gin' was 3 shillings per quart, today about 93p and 43p per litre respectively. In 1922 Harold Fitch spent a large sum of money on the hotel when he added a new ballroom with eight more bedrooms above it. Prior to the construction of the new ballroom, town dances and concerts were held upstairs in the Pannier Market - the site of the ballroom had been the old hotel stables. Mr. Fitch also had a plot of land where George Street now stands. He had a tennis court built for the use of his guests. In 1959 Mr. Eric Hall, who also owned the Fortfield Hotel in Sidmouth, spent £45,000 on a massive refurbishment of the hotel. It was reopened in April of the same year when it was renamed 'The New Dolphin Hotel'. Originally a 30 bedroom hotel, the inn had half its property sold off to developers in 1982, including the majority of the bedrooms, former kitchen, restaurant and ballroom (which is now 'Market Carpets' and 'Dolphin Court'). The remainder of the building was refurbished. 'The Orange Tree' was once known as 'Bill's Bar' after the then owner William 'Bill' Reece. A later owner, William Tyson, converted 'Bill's Bar' into 'Liberties,' an American themed bar, by moving the bar into a central position and in doing so, did away with the old skittle alley. Mr. Tyson later sold the hotel to the Brewery 'Punch Taverns'. In the earlier days of the inn, the proprietors used to have their own bakery and the ancient brick ovens were still present in the old kitchens when they were sold off in the early 1980s. More recently, in 2009, The Dolphin lost its 450 year identity when its name was changed to 'Montgomery's Hotel'.

Dolphin Tap: a small bar frequented by older members of the town, especially cribbers in the interwar period. It stood in the present day Dolphin Court and latterly became the hotel kitchens. It was sold off in the 1980s along with other parts of the hotel for redevelopment.

The Dove: was demolished in 1835 to make way for the new parish church of St Paul's.

Duke Williams Head: was located in New Street in the property that is now 'House of Hair' (17 New Street).

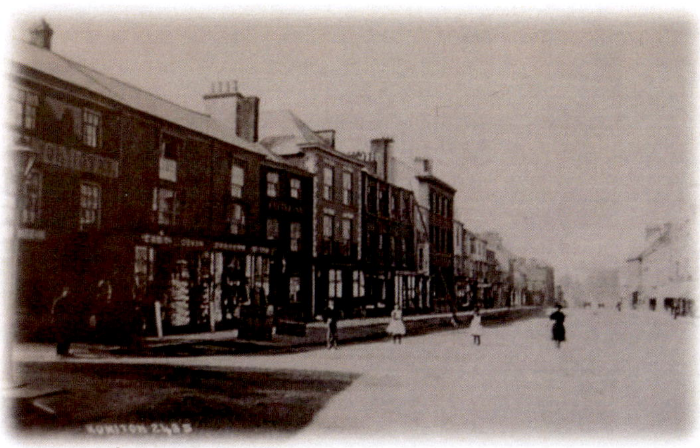

The old Black Lion is on the left and the Exeter Inn is located three properties to the right.

The Exeter Inn: once called 'The White Hart' it was open as early as 1757 and remained in business until 1965 when the outbuildings were later developed into what is now 'Black Lion Court'. 'Perfect Pittas' (84 High Street) now stands on the site. In 1851 its landlord was John Bromfield.

The Farriers Arms: situated in New Street. It later became 'The Temperance Hotel' and was, until recently, a clothes shop called 'Leos'.

The Five Bells: stood at the bottom of New Street in 1737. It closed in the early 1790s at which time it was owned by Christopher Flood, the local banker.

The Fountain Inn: was open in 1780 and was named after the town fountain that once stood nearby. It is currently an antique shop appropriately named 'Fountain Antique Centre' (132 High Street). In the 18th century it was a coaching inn and the stables can still be seen at the rear of the building. It was open until 1975 and its last landlords were Mr and Mrs Bill Cox who had run the inn 25 years prior to its closure. Interestingly, Mrs. Cox's parents once ran the White Lion and Mr. Cox was twice 'World Conker Champion'!

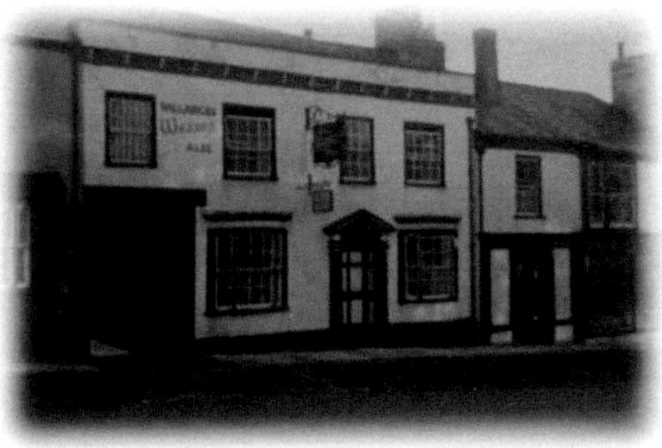

The George: probably named after St. George, it was recorded in 1661 and was previously next to The Swan Inn. In 1786 the landlord was a Mr. Redstone and the inn formerly had accommodation for travellers. It closed about 1840.

The Globe: *see Carpenters Arms*

The Golden Fleece: 17th century inn, the name is probably derived from the former prominence of the wool trade.

The Golden Lion: the name was thought to have been derived from the Lion of Flanders and is probably the biggest and most important tavern in Honiton's history. It was the setting of many of Honiton's events and both Horatio Nelson and Charles Dickens stayed here. During the last years of its life it was party headquarters for the Whig Party. A life-sized gilt, carved wooden lion stood outside the second storey, resting one foot on a ball. Originally it was said to have been "of blue flint with free stone mullions" but was later covered in plaster: another storey was added to the building at the same time. Although it was the biggest inn in Honiton, when the Dean of Exeter visited it in 1767 he described it as a "bad inn." The year of 1790 was not a good one for the inn; a terrible fire broke out in the stables in which 26 horses were burnt to death, including 5 belonging to soldiers and 17 to the postal service. As awful an example as this is, the fire does give some idea of how large an establishment this inn once was, with stabling facilities for at least 26 horses! In the mid 1800s the Golden Lion was one of only two inns situated in the town that provided private hire of horses and vehicles, the other inn being The Dolphin. This inn was also the meeting place of the freemasons from 1806 to 1811, after which they moved to the Baker's Arms. In 1830 one guest's over night bill came to a total of £1.0s.4d with 2s.6d for dinner, 1s.6d for the bed, 2s for breakfast and 9d for the chamber maid. This grand old building could have also taken its name from the Redver's family, whose 'cognisance was a lion rampant'. The inn closed in 1851; its longstanding landlord, of some 20 years, Francis Drake Waldron Wheaton, died in 1849 and his wife continued for the last two. The inn then became the town post office. Mr. Wheaton had started life as a farmer before moving into the hotel trade but during his tenancy at the inn he still rented several fields around the town for agricultural purposes. He was also one of the town's 'potwallers'. Before Mr. Wheaton, the landlords had been a Mr. and Mrs. Mitchell. When the inn was later sold in the 1860s it was converted into private lettings and the old stables were turned into cottages, once known as 'Manor Place' and, more recently, Co-op car park. This old Grade II* listed building currently stands in the High Street and is named 'Manor House.'

The Greyhound: thought to have been at least two by this name, one of which was in New Street. The other stood where the old Pannier Market now stands. It was in Honiton in 1718 but was destroyed by fire sometime before 1820. Inns named after the greyhound find their roots from the badge of the Tudors

The Green Dragon: this tavern was in the town for at least 70 years and was open until at least 1851 after which it was pulled down. It later became a timber yard and 'The Sue Ryder Shop' (13 New Street) now stands on the site. The inn's last landlord was Benjamin Trim Jr., son of Benjamin Trim Snr. who ran a farm on Northcote Hill.

Half Moon: more than one of these existed. One was known to have existed up until the mid 1820s and was later demolished along with another 10 houses in preparation for the new parish church in 1835. Its exact location is thought to be under the forecourt and gardens of St. Paul's.

The Hare and Hounds: recorded as early as 1737, thought to have once stood on the site of the old residence of Dr Terry and Catherine Glanvill, now 'Grove Antique Centre' (55 High Street). The house was originally built in 1679 and later rebuilt by a George Darke. It closed in the late 1780s/early 1790s.

Hat and Feathers: an inn known to have been in Honiton in the 17th century. The sign resembled a low crowned hat with a feather.

The Head and Arms: located in a small cottage at the east end of town.

The Head and Horns: recorded as being in town between 1761 and 1784 shortly after which it was closed. It was originally in a cottage at the east end of town on the south side of the High Street.

The King's Arms: another coaching inn of the town. It is currently located where 'Retail Therapy' (56 High Street) now stands. Once it was from where hot pennies were thrown on fair day and was previously known as the Bakers Arms. This inn was known in the 1840s to have been where Justices of the Petty Sessions District held their meetings. For this the landlord of the time received £1 per annum. During an extension, in 1973, a small room was found

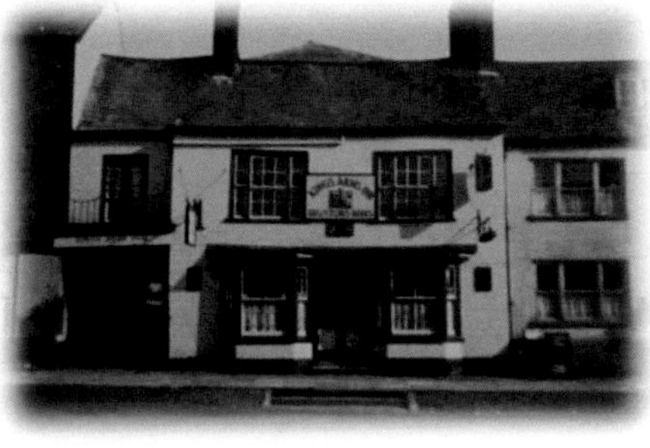

which was not known to have existed. Inside the room a Victorian candle-powered film projector and film was discovered, which one assumes were once used by a previous landlord as a sideline for his more amorous drinkers! It closed in 1975 after which it became an antique shop named appropriately 'Kings Arms Antiques' and is presently a clothes shop. There was also another Kings Arms located in the same area on the other side of the High Street.

Kings Head: stood somewhere near Clapper Lane. The inn had a bad reputation and the licence was forfeited after which it was destroyed by fire in 1790. Its last owner was Thomas Issac.

The Knackers Hole: this 17th century pub was so named as it was situated next to the knacker's yard in Northcote Lane where the town's horses were slaughtered. It must have been a lucrative inn for when one of its landlords died in 1677 he left gifts in excess of £550! The inn's name was changed to 'The Mermaid' in 1790 and later 'The Crown and Sceptre.'

Lamb and Flag: known to have existed in 1741, this coaching inn was latterly known as simply 'The Lamb.' The Lamb and Flag, and other so called pubs, takes its name from the Gospel of John "Behold the Lamb of God, which taketh away the sins of the world." The Lamb is seen carrying a flag (usually of St. George). It was located where 'Honeybees' used to be and is currently a branch of William Hill (110 High Street). The inn's last landlord was local man Les Ackland who took the inn over from his mother, interestingly, a lifelong teetotaller! This 7 bedroom inn closed in 1975. One local gentleman, apparently, enquired about salvaging the curved glass Victorian frontage of this inn after its closure but unfortunately was unsuccessful as it was destroyed during its reconstruction.

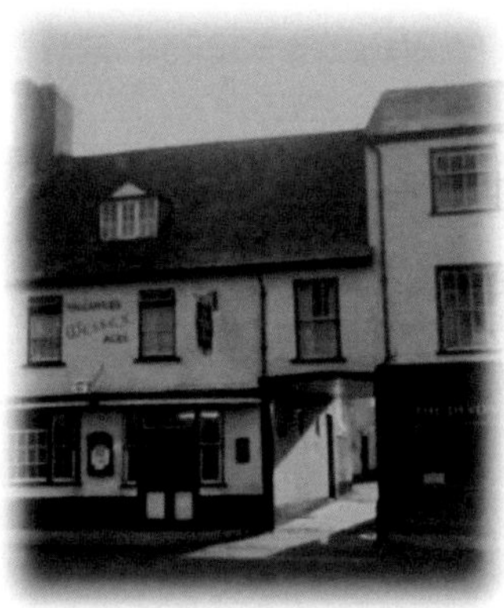

Lion Inn: another 17th century inn which was known to have once stood in Queen Street.

London Inn: once again there were at least two of these. One was located at the east end of the High Street which is now Merchant House Antiques (19 High Street) and was described in 1843 as "London Inn and Coachmakers". This London inn was burnt down in 1871. The other London Inn was located on the corner of Queen Street, so named due to its position on the London road. It is now the site of a second hand furniture store. In 1851 the landlord was a Daniel Newton who was also a butcher.

Magpye: once stood on the north side of the High Street, somewhere near the middle of town, between 1739 and 1822; its earliest known landlord was Elizabeth Draper.

Malthouses: although not public houses, these establishments were the predecessors of breweries and nearly every English village/town had at least one. There is known to have been a malthouse run by a Mr. Golesworthy in 1835; however, there were many more located in Honiton around this time and in 1843 there were at least 4. One was located behind one of the cottages between the Gissage and Dowell Street on the north side of the High Street, the second was behind the property, two houses up from the 'Crown & Sceptre', the third was believed to be in the vicinity of the old 'Kings Arms' and the fourth was directly behind the property four houses from the old 'White Horse' - appropriately all within a short distance of an inn!

Maltsters Arms: an inn known to have existed in the 18th century but had closed by the turn of the 19th century.

The Mermaid: when first opened it was called 'The New Mermaid': *see 'Crown and Sceptre'*.

The New Inn: one of the already mentioned taverns was previously called by this name. Pubs by this name are usually some of the oldest in the area, having mostly been built on the site of an older premise. The actual New Inn was not in town itself but was situated on the Axminster road (now the A35). The building still stands and is now a private residence called 'High View'; it is the large white house which backs onto the A35 between the Copper Castle and the Devil's Elbow. Recorded in 1700, it was undoubtedly a popular inn with travellers from London. Its last known landlord was a gentleman oddly named 'Page Turner' who was landlord from about 1906. Possibly due to the changing form of transportation, he was not landlord long and, from about 1910, lived at the inn as a mason until his death in the late 1920s.

The Oxford Inn: stood on the site of the present 'White Lion' whose licence was forfeited in 1790 due to its disorderly conduct. Its last owner was a Mr. Benjamin Issac.

Phoenix: believed to have once stood next to the Bell Inn.

Plough: little is known about this inn. Its name may seem self explanatory for a country parish such as Honiton, but some pubs by this name also have links to 'The Plough' constellation which consists of seven stars. It was located on the south side of the High Street and was said to have only been open a short time.

Sydenham's Pott House: also simply known as 'Pott House' once existed in Clapper Lane

Pressing Iron and Shears: was located in New Street as early as 1667 but was converted into houses by 1781.

The Queens Arms: this little pub stood in Northcote Lane on a site near that of the current 'Pit Club.' It was only open for a couple of years, sometime between 1841 and 1844. It was run by a silversmith by the name of John Jennings who had the inn as an extension off his workshop.

The Railway Inn: built in 1860 when the railway finally arrived in Honiton. Previous owners have had some interesting sidelines, as attached to the pub was a fighting club along with workshops, as well as, at some point, a funeral directors. The inn's first landlord seems to have run the pub more as a 'beer house' than as a public house for he was described in most all the records as having his main occupation as a wheelwright with beer retailing as a secondary source of income.
The landlord, William Smith who owned the premises, was, in fact, over the decades, described as a wheelwright, carpenter, coachbuilder and builder; only later, when in his 70s, did he seem to settle into the sole occupation of innkeeper.

The inn remained as a beer house, only selling beer and cider, until the end of WWII. William made a "small fortune" selling emergency building supplies to railway engineers when topographic problems occurred. In 1893 the inn was "gutted" by a great fire that started in an outbuilding. The fire engulfed the workshops and contents, including an unfortunate terrier dog and a tame fox! The inferno, fuelled by wind, soon spread to the inn itself and every room was "broken down". One would have thought the local fire brigade would have been quick off the mark, with the events of the previous century still in people's minds, yet they did not appear on the scene until some forty minutes after the alarm was raised!

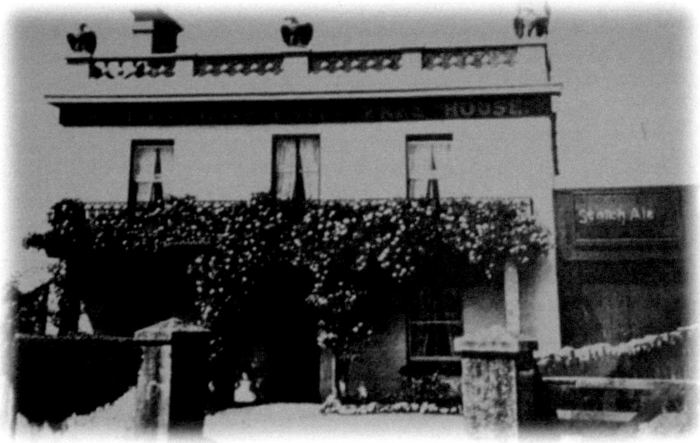

Mr. Smith ran the inn for over 63 years and died in the mid 1920s, aged well into his 90s. His sons, William, and later Herbert Smith, ran The Railway up until the end of WWII. One of William Smith Snr's daughters, unfortunately, perished at the inn having falling down the steep stone stairs. During the War Years, soldiers frequented and slept at the pub for the purposes of surveillance of the railway line. Some were even said to have been given straw mattresses to sleep in the yard. When the Smith family sold the inn to a brewery in 1945, William Smith Jnr said that he had been at the inn for "70 years". From 1977 it was renamed 'The Lazy Landlord' but reverted back to its original name in 1986 having being shut for some 4 years. The Railway has changed much since its early days when it was an ornate building with fruit gardens but fortunately has stood the test of time by surviving into the 21st century. The inn recently underwent a large restoration and is currently a restaurant and bar: it can be visited in Queen Street.

The Red Cow: one of the few inns that still exists today. Originally a single, two-storey cottage that dates from at least 1795, it was enlarged in the 1930s, incorporating the two cottages next door. It was apparently a popular haunt of gypsies and at fair time it was customary to go up to the inn to "watch the gypsy men fighting and the gypsy ladies arrive in their velvet and feather." It currently stands at 43-47 High Street. In 1851 its landlord was a Mr R. Parker and around this time also had a 'brewhouse'.

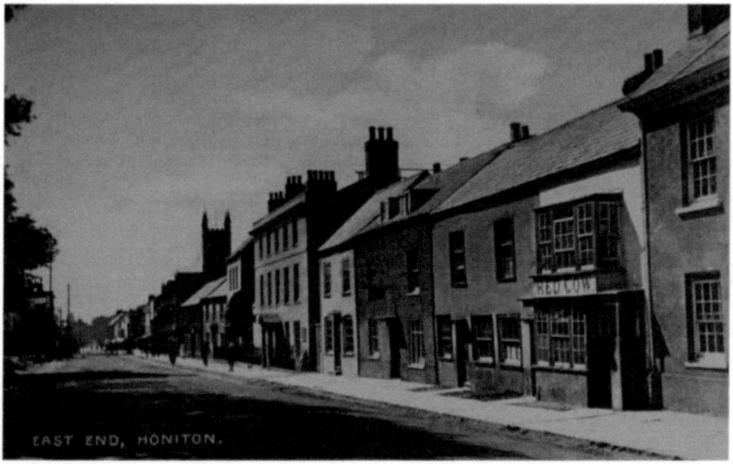

The Red Cow before its extension.

The Red Hart: this little tavern was situated in a cottage opposite Summerland Place in New Street. It was open as early as 1774 and was engulfed in the New Street fire of 1887 that destroyed all but one of the Tudor cottages that once stood there.

The Red Lion: thought to have opened in the 1780s, it probably obtained its name from a local coat of arms on which many red lions appeared. Ended its days in another fire, about 1820, and later became a house. Was once situated in New Street.

The Rolling Pin: see The Chopping Knife

The Rose and Crown: an old inn that was once where the mail horses were stabled. It was recorded in 1691. Pubs so named derive their name from the Monarchy and more specifically the Wars of the Roses. In a newspaper report of 1762 it was said to be "for the reception of gentlemen, ladies & [co.] There are several Stall-Stables, and others very convenient for a large Number of Horses, and all other conveniences for coaches or Chaise, the court yard being now very much enlarged, and every other Thing convenient for an inn." It is believed to have been located where until recently, Oxfam (98 High Street) once stood. Closed in 1796.

The Royal Oak: taking its name from the celebrated story of the young Charles II hiding from Parliamentary soldiers in an oak tree in Bishops Wood, Staffordshire. The inn was recorded in Honiton in 1774 and from the origins of its name one can assume it was founded no earlier than 1651. The inn was to be found in Queen Street and lost its licence at some point in the early 1800s.

Sachell's inn: another 17th century inn known only from a token issued in its name.

Salter's Arms: also named 'The Three Cups' this 17th century pub was housed in a cottage near the Gissage and was destroyed when the new Honiton Cinema was built, although the inn itself had closed long before the 19th century.

Smiths Arms: see 'Blacksmiths Arms'

The Star: yet another one of the lucky few inns to survive the wrath of time. The 18th century building suffered, like so many other buildings in the town, from a fire in 1824. In the mid 1840s the inn owned a quarter of an acre plot of which most has been sold off over the years; one part, which was once the gardens, is now King Street car park and public toilets. The most recent example of the sale of some of its land is in 2008, for residential housing. It is located in New Street on the corner of King Street. This inn has been confused, in some records, with 'The Seven Stars'. Presently one of only two inns in the town owned freehold, the other being The Vine. Whether the inn will, in time, become brewery owned or converted to flats, hangs in the balance.

The Sun & Anchor: this inn was known to have existed in the town in the late 18th century, at which time it was owned by the Maynard family. It disappeared in the early 1790s.

The Swan: this coaching inn stood next to 'The George' and was known to have been in the town as early as 1529. The original Swan Inn stood on the site where the Baptist Chapel now is. This plot became vacant when the inn was destroyed by fire. The Swan was rebuilt to the east of the Chapel, which is now 'Cats Protection League Charity Shop'. It had over ¼ acre of land; its old stable yard is still in existence and is now residential housing known as 'Swan Yard.' The old pub finally closed in 1881 and with a business spanning over 400 years, it is probably the longest running tavern in Honiton on record.

The Temperance Hotel: one of Honiton's only lodging establishments where alcohol was definitely not sold. Thought to have opened in the late 1850s/early 1860s, it was founded by John Marshall, a farmer from Northleigh. He ran the "eating" and "refreshment" business until his death in 1872 and it was then carried on by his wife Ann. Ann ran the hotel until the late 1870s when she swapped the hotel for a dairy a little further up New Street, after which it closed. It was located in New Street in what is currently a clothes shop named 'Leos'. Another Temperance Hotel was at one time in the High Street. Believed to have opened in the 1890s the hotel went through a number of proprietors. It finally closed in the early 1930s and was located somewhere near the vicinity of the present police station.

The Three Compasses: (name has association with carpenters) *see Carpenters Arms.*

The Three Cups: located in the town as early as 1664 when the landlord was a Thomas Ash. Coxhead wrote that the inn once stood where the old Honiton cinema once was. It closed in 1790.

The Three Tuns: another one of the only old pubs still existing in Honiton today. Dating from at least 1774 and today is a Grade II listed building.

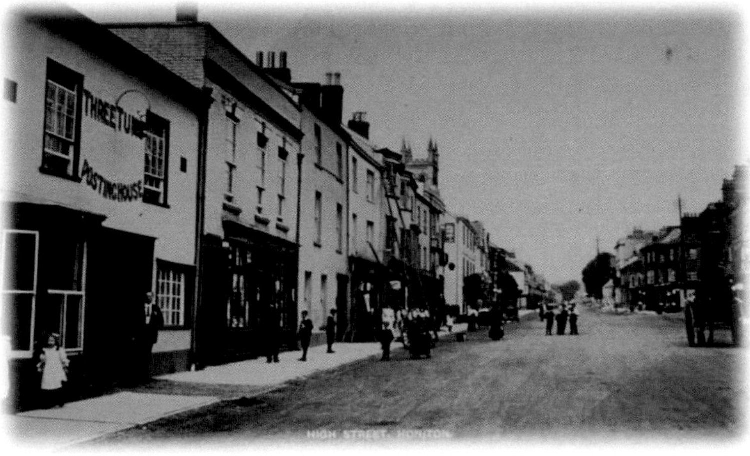

The Turks Head Inn: this once thatched inn was located on the present site of 'Slades Countrywise.' The surrounding area was named 'Turk's Head' for many years before the inn was founded. It is thought to have taken its name from the crusaders who fought against the Turks and also, presumably, its close location to St. Margaret's Chapel, whose founder fought in the crusades. The inn closed in 1887. The site of the inn became 'The Turk's Head Road House' for coaches and travellers in the 1930s: its 'branch' facility in town was once 'The Carlton Cafe'. After the bypass was built in 1966, trade fell and the owner sold it to Noel Walmsley-Kastner who ran a garage. 'Kastners' sold it to 'Munfords' in 1973 and 'Slades Countrywise' moved in in 1983. At the time of writing the closure of Slades is imminent in preparation for a new superstore.

The Unicorn: the name was taken from the Royal Coat of Arms of James I.

The Union: was a small inn situated in a cottage somewhere in New Street. It was only open for a short time and was pulled down in 1860. It was presumably not a pub for the 'inmates' of the workhouse!

The Valiant Soldier: an early 18th century inn of which nothing else is known.

The Vine: a quaint little pub located down Vine Passage. The building dates from 1540; however, the cellar beneath the property long predates it. Originally it was a smokehouse and the current bar is situated where the chimney once stood. There was once a vineyard in what is now the car park, which is where the pub is thought to have got its name. In 1710 it became a cider house and subsequently a pub with three bedrooms for weary travellers and, apart from falling to the Honitonian contagion of being damaged by fire in 1841, it is one of the only older Honiton inns that is still in business today. In the 1920s it was also known as the 'Vine Tree Inn'. The large cellar beneath once used to flood near to "the brim" and the town fire engine was known to have pumped out the water "several times".

The Volunteer: now the only thatched inn in Honiton. It was once located in a row of thatched properties that have since been demolished. The inn changed its name for a short time to the 'Pig and Barrow' in 1996 but has since resumed its original identity. The building, at the west end of town, is Grade II listed and is still open for business. The name has military roots.

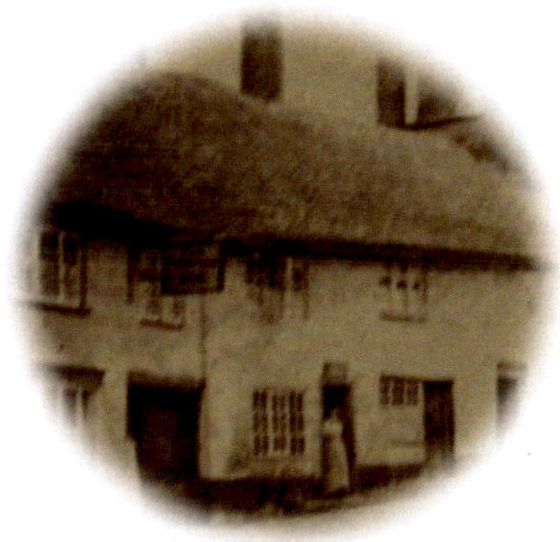

Vintners Arms: another of the short lived Victorian drinking houses; the name is derived from wine production. It was open as early as 1876 and seems to have been more of a beer house than a pub. Its landlord was, by day, a grocer but the pub lost its licence in 1913 when the local police protested at the number of drinking establishments in the town. It stood where what is now 'Shauls Bakery' (76 High Street) and its last landlord was Walter Willey Harris who ran a wine and spirit business from the same premises.

Wine Cellar and Vaults: mentioned in one report and was thought to have been near the old Honiton Shambles.

The White Hart: the symbol is synonymous with Richard II who used the white hart as his emblem. There were at least two other inns that have gone by this name.

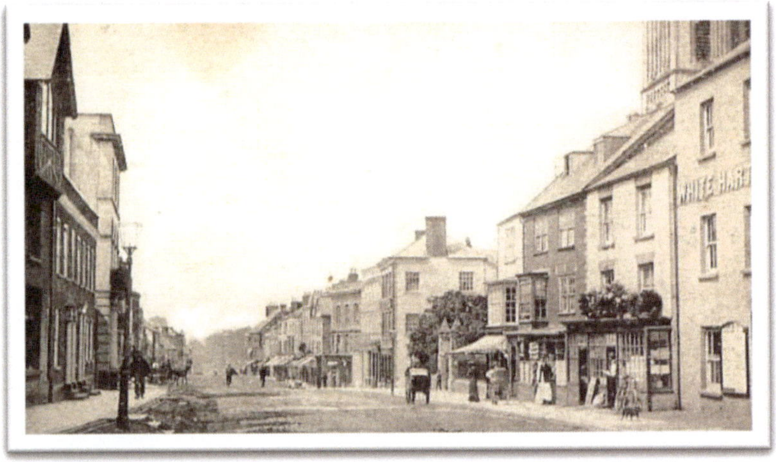

The White Hart can be seen on the right.

One was located in the premises that is now 'Creature Comforts' and 'Soft Options' (91 High Street); known to have been in town as early as 1728, it closed in 1913. The last landlady was Kitty Cheeseworth and for a time, before its closure, it was a 'Temperance Hotel'. After its closure it became incorporated into Allhallows School when it was known as 'Baronial Hall'. Another pub, by the same name, was thought to have been located behind the old Black Lion Inn in 1737 which would have been demolished along with the Black Lion itself.

The White Horse: recorded as early as 1666 when the landlord was a George Humphreye, a great-great-grandfather of the well known painter Ozias Humphrey. The 'white horse' represented the Kings of Wessex. It was once located at the top of Silver Street in the property now at 76 High Street. This inn was lastly run by Henry Parsons Hann and after his retirement in 1937 the inn closed.

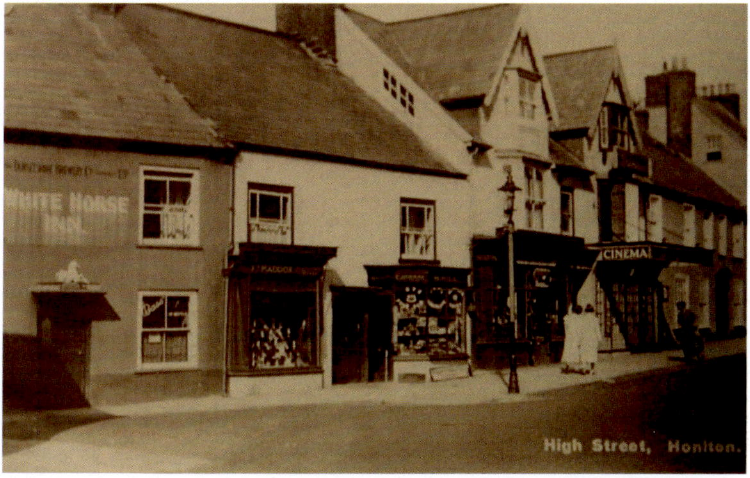

The White Lion: stands on the site of the old 'Oxford Inn' and is still open today at the west end of town. It was originally located on the other side of the road and whilst there, was called 'The Bottle' then 'The Anchor' and was twice destroyed by fire. There was a story that when the inn burnt for the second time, some inhabitants of the town rescued the beer and cider within and drank it in the street! The inn was moved to its present location in about 1798 when a local businessman, Christopher Flood, intervened as he disliked it being too near his new abode on Bramble Hill! The inn was run by the Gould family from the early 1890s until 1937 when the last of the family retired. William Gould, the first of the family to run the inn, was the son of a Honiton labourer and started his working life as a butler at Hembury Fort House. The 'White Lion' appeared on the badge of Edward IV. This listed building still stands in the town but the inn shut and at the time of writing is being turned into three residential dwellings along with an additional three homes to be constructed on the the old car park.

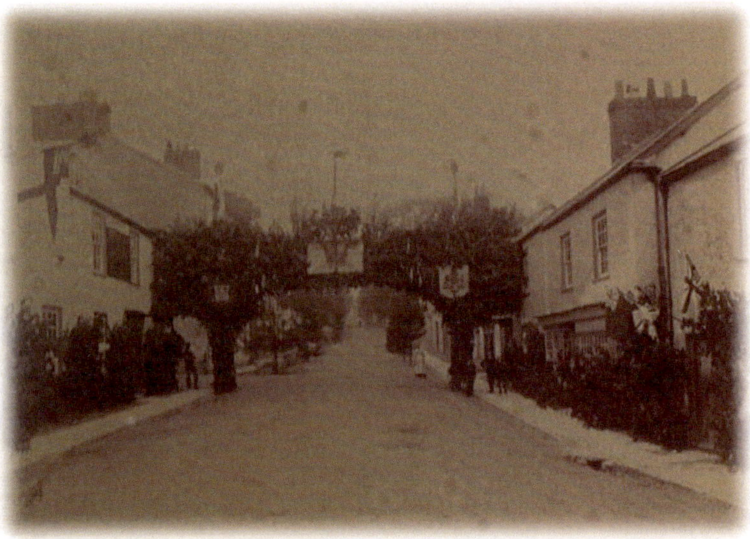

A Royal celebration depicting the decorated White Lion on the right.

Of these 80 odd recognised inns, established before 1900, only 7 of them are still open today! There have, however, been new additions to the town's drinking establishments, ensuring a steady flow of alcohol for Honitonians for many years to come...hopefully! Among the new establishments are 'The Wine Bar', 'Cafe 102', 'The Heathfield', The Carlton/Top Bar (now closed), 'Pit Club' (also now closed), 'The Orange Tree', as well as a number of local social clubs.

A couple of Temperance Hotels have already been mentioned but there was another one, located roughly where 'Bests of Honiton' is now located, at the turn of the twentieth century. It was run by a tea dealer called John Purse and his brother Harry. The business did not last long before John reverted back to a solo shopkeeper.

Virtually all the pubs in Honiton, in the Victorian era, had skittle alleys where the drinkers played for liquor and as the winners usually won more than they could drink, metal checks were issued which could be redeemed at a later date.

Honiton also had at least two breweries at one time; one was once located in Mill Street. There has been a brewery in one shape or form in Mill Street since at least the early 1800s. William Hann Pine ran a malthouse from a building that still exists in Mill Street today until he was declared bankrupt in 1848.

'The Honiton Brewery' is thought to date from the late 1840s/early 1850s and prior to its establishment the site was a part of the White Lion Inn's gardens. From the 1850s till the late 1870s the brewery was run by a Yarcombe man called John Grabham. By the 1870s Mr. Grabham had retired and the brewery was managed by James Cuddon who, in 1881, employed 7 men.

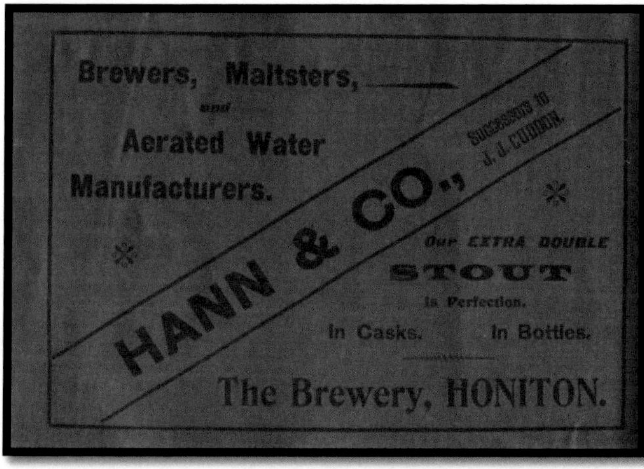

When John George Hann, a timber merchant from Coylton, took over the business at the turn of the twentieth century, it became known as 'Hann & Co. Ltd'. John's son, Lewis, became the brewery manager and the family were known to have owned at least a dozen licenced premises in Honiton and the surrounding area, including the Black Lion. It was later sold to 'Dorsetshire Brewery Co.' of Sherborne in 1927 who subsequently closed the business and sold the property to Devon County Council. The Council used the premises as repair shops and an overnight storage facility for their steam wagons. Until recently, the sign of the brewery could be seen clearly on the side of the property. The old building still exists today and is located at number 7 Mill Street but is now a private residence. The premises also once had an Oast House attached which, when sold to Dorsetshire Brewery Co., became a furniture store. It is somewhat ironic that some 150 years before, in 1780, there was a William Hann in Honiton who ran a malthouse: there is not believed to be any connection to this Mr. Hann and the aforementioned John George and Lewis Hann.

Part 5

Roads and Rail

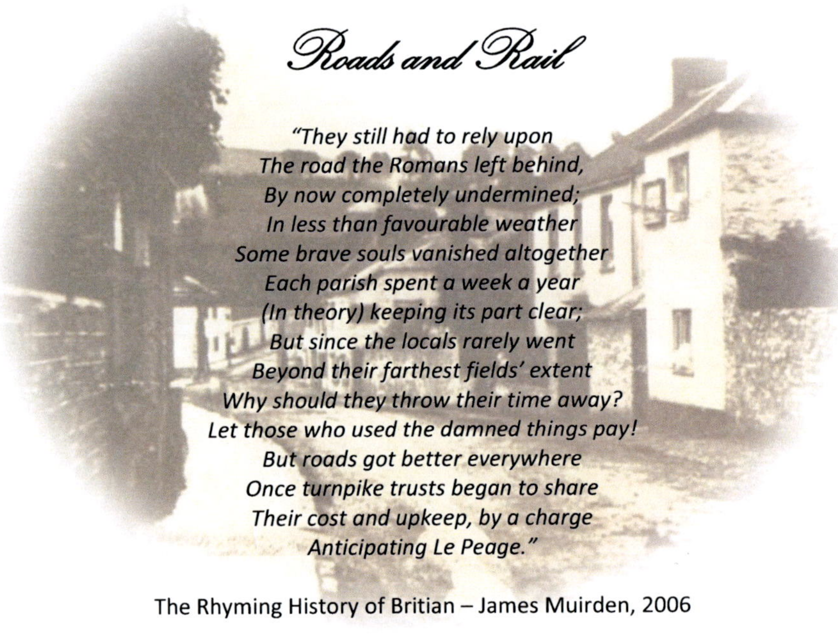

"They still had to rely upon
The road the Romans left behind,
By now completely undermined;
In less than favourable weather
Some brave souls vanished altogether
Each parish spent a week a year
(In theory) keeping its part clear;
But since the locals rarely went
Beyond their farthest fields' extent
Why should they throw their time away?
Let those who used the damned things pay!
But roads got better everywhere
Once turnpike trusts began to share
Their cost and upkeep, by a charge
Anticipating Le Peage."

The Rhyming History of Britian – James Muirden, 2006

Chapter 1
Highways & Byways

"There are more miles of roads in Devon than in any other county, with a bewildering network of lanes leading to farmsteads, isolated hamlets, and remote manor houses."
Rosemary Launder

Many of the roads within the town itself have already been mentioned in earlier chapters; however, many of the roads which exist today in bustling housing estates and as important connector roads were, in Victorian times, mere country lanes used by a handful of people who lived on them. It is understandable that as the town has grown, these country lanes have become incorporated into town boundaries. Honiton's road network has generally not changed that much since Victorian times, or the centuries before; however, with growth of residential and industrial estates, many new roads have been built and many older roads changed. It is somewhat ironic that many of the older main roads have today been reduced to poorly maintained country lanes, and in some cases disappeared all together, whereas many more rural roads of the 19th century have now become main, and more frequented, routes. This chapter looks at the history and development of the road network in and around Honiton in an attempt to show how the town's infrastructure has changed over the last two centuries.

Kings Road, now part of the A35, is today one of the main roads out of Honiton, connecting the town with several major cities on the south coast and finally ending at Southampton. A couple of hundred years ago, until relatively recently, it was this road that was the main route to London rather than the modern passage of Monkton Road and onto the A303. If you were an 18th century individual travelling from, say, the Dolphin Hotel in Honiton to London, you would have embarked on to a stagecoach outside your inn that would have then travelled up New Street, into Queen Street, up what is now Pine Park Road and turned right at the Copper Castle, onto the A35, after halting to pay the toll! The coach would then have climbed the hill and, originally, ran up the right fork to what is now Manor House School, not continuing on the modern A35 that was constructed much later. The reason for this unusual route, by modern standards, was because Kings Road did not exist until 1795. Originally, from the Copper Castle to Hale Lane there was no more than a "narrow passage" called Shipley Lane and from Hale Lane to Marwood House there was simply a field called Shipley Close. Shipley Lane was later extended and widened so that it met with Honiton High Street. It was named Kings Road after the visit of George III, only a few years before. It is probably for this reason that many of the old inns of Honiton were located at the west of the town for there was not much traveller traffic east of New Street prior to Kings Roads construction.

The original route of the A35, carrying on into Springfield Road (towards Manor House School), was changed in 1807 when it was becoming clear that the steep incline was too much for coach horses, paving the way for the foundations of the modern A35. By the 1840s, Springfield Road and the A35 were appropriately named 'Old London Road' and 'New London Road' respectively. There was also once a milestone on the present A35 located not far from the old New Inn which read 'Honiton, 1 mile' and 'Axminster, 8 Miles' *1.

Farquarharson wrote that:

> *"On the south side of the parish, there were formerly large commons + some exist still. To the east and south of Springfield was an extensive open space covered with gorse; fields now occupy the site. The traveller of today has little idea of the highways travelled by his ancestors. Before the advent of Macadam in 1817 the roads were such as we now see running across the commons that are left."*

There was once a road which ran from Higher Northcote Farm, 'Northcote Hill', to Hutgate Road which today is simply a public footpath.

Beggars Lane is also a relatively new addition to the town's road network, built in the early 19th century as a cut through for travellers travelling from Exeter to Sidmouth and was said to have once been part of 'the great western road.' Originally, and until very recently known as St. Margaret's Road, it formed a crossroads with Sidmouth Road and Rosemount Lane; this crossroads was once known as Starcross. Beggars Lane took its present name from the activities of people travelling to the Union Workhouse who were known to have left valuables in the hedgerows and rabbit holes along the lane so as not to have them confiscated on arrival at their formidable destination.

The old route to Taunton was originally along Clapper Lane where travellers would cross the River Otter and travel through Combe Raleigh, Luppit, Smeatharpe and Churchstanton, a complex and confusing route to the uninitiated traveller! The route later changed to that via Monkton, which was set up by the Turnpike Acts of 1828 and 1829.

Marlpits Lane has had a number of different names over the past two centuries. At one point in the 19th century it was known as 'Barracks Lane', when there was a small retained army garrison located in the vicinity of Littletown, in fear of Napoleonic invasion. The barracks were said to have been located in Marlpits Lane "where the road winds round to Littletown and faced Streamers Meadow." The soldiers were disbanded in 1816, when peace was proclaimed and the barracks were dismantled and partially destroyed in 1820. That which was left of the settlement was finally removed in 1850 and used to reconstruct the burnt farmhouse of Hale Farm. In the mid 19th century Barracks Lane had changed to 'Love Lane' and some years after the construction of the Workhouse it changed again to 'Union Lane' (after the Honiton 'Union' Workhouse).

The road network between the Copper Castle and the present day Tesco Superstore has changed dramatically since Victorian times and although the majority of the old road network still exists in some way, many are not in use today. To give you an example of what the old road network of the south end of town was once like, I shall endeavour to guide you along these roads and explain where the modern day, seemingly 'defunct', roads are now sited. Originally, the only road connecting Pine Park Road with St. Michael's Church was Parsonage Lane and, today, is a good example of what an old lane of the town once looked like. 'Waterleat Avenue' was built much later; once one had travelled down Parsonage Lane, so named as it was the road home to the original rectory (Old Rectory Farm), one would come out at St. Michael's, as you would today. The traveller would then proceed down the modern day Weatherill Road and shortly past the church, he/she would come to a fork in the road; one branch proceeds down Lower Brand Lane and the other up, what is now, an inclined public footpath *1. This public footpath was the route of the original road and at the top the traveller would come to a junction *2. At this point one could either take the south turning or continue down what is now Higher Brand Lane. Higher Brand Lane was the original main road before Weatherill Road was built and was simply known as 'Brand' or 'Bran Lane' due to its proximity to the old Brand Farm. Higher Brand Lane comes out into Honiton Bottom Road, which is where this journey ends; we now go back to the aforementioned 'south turning' at the top of the footpath (*2). Today, this left turning is nothing but a rough, stony track, but was originally a fully operational connecting country road called 'Gardiners Lane' and is probably the best modern day example of what the unpaved, rural roads surrounding Honiton were like. Originally, the track ran for about ½ mile to yet another junction*3: Gardiners Lane continued onto Gardeners Farm but this section of the route, today, no longer exists and is now a gated field. At the aforementioned junction (*3), the road veered off to the left down what was known as 'Magpye Lane'. 'Magpie Lane' is still listed on present day maps but until recently was nothing more than a hedgerow between the two adjacent fields, being completely reclaimed by nature after a century of dereliction. Magpie Lane connected Gardiners Lane with 'Stoney Lane' and it was probably named after the adjacent field (Magpie Hill). Today it has been partially cleared and is a small footpath used by horse riders and walkers.

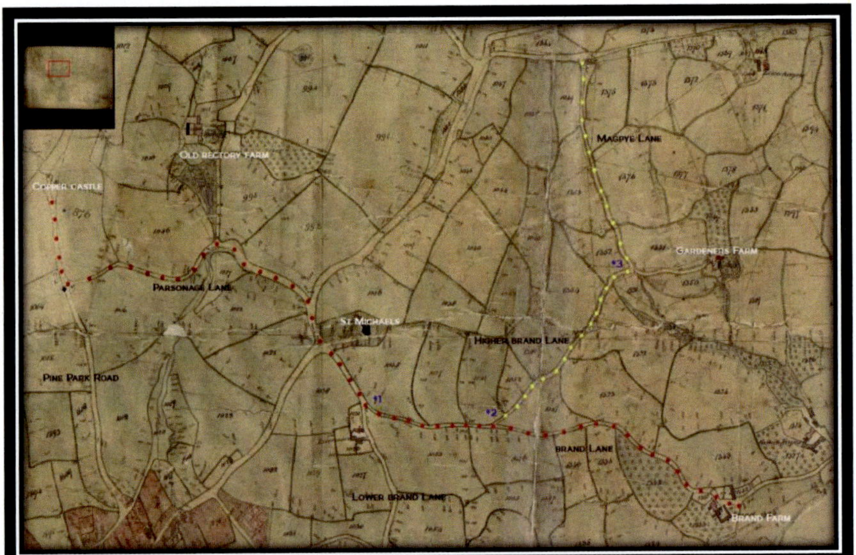

Illustrated depiction of the above mentioned routes as seen on a map of the town from 1844.

Waterleat Avenue was eventually extended to meet Weatherill Road when the land of the old 'Glen Farm' was built on in the late 1990s, the first uninterrupted straight road connecting both ends of the town since the High Street was built. Many of these new residential roads in this extended section also reflect the land's former past, including 'Glen Farm Crescent' and 'Durbin Close': the Durbins were a local family who used to own and run the old farm.

'Targets Lane', which ran from *4 to*5, was once a footpath that ran from Whitebridges to the old rifle range on Roundball Hill (*5 is where the targets used to be and the path thus ended). The entire surrounding land has long since been built on but still technically exists as a suburban footpath through the housing estate of Willow Walk.

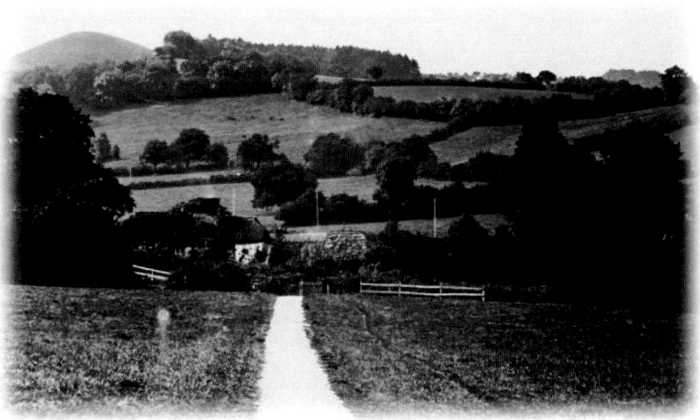

A peep at a smallholding in Littletown with Roundball Hill in the background.

'Duck Path' is thought to have been constructed in about 1860, after the arrival of the railway. Where it got its strange name from is unknown, but it has always provided a vital pedestrian connection with Pine Park Road and New Street.

Originally 'Honiton Bottom Road' joined 'Littletown Road' forming a staggered crossroads. Littletown Road/Rosemount Lane still follow their original courses but opposite Honiton Bottom Road, roughly where Livermore Road now is, was a track that curved west where it followed the Gissage, technically ending just above Kings Road where it joined the river. This road was lost and rerouted in the construction of present housing estates of the area.

Streamers Meadows was originally a footpath before the construction of the housing estate in the 1930s. It ran through a field called 'Streamers Meadow' and continued under the railway line, where it joined with the present day 'Littletown Road': the section of the footpath, beyond the railway bridge, became Livermore Road with the rest of 'Streamer Meadows' being continued when the houses were built. The field, through which the footpath led, was once owned by 'George Blays Sawmills' and was once pasture for their horses. However, when motor cars started to displace the equines, the land was sold off for the housing estate, which would be constructed by a building firm from Tiverton. For a long time, Streamers Meadows only contained two stone houses and a tannery. The tannery, in 1925, became a laundry called 'Vanity Fair' which closed in the 1980s and today is the site of 'Meadows Crescent'.

In the 1840s, the road from the bottom of Mill Street to Rosemount Lane was originally a track that ran up a section of King Street, into Millers Way and round in to 'Highfield' where it ended at a field. It was not until the late 19th century that 'Millhead Road' was built, which was then little more than a footpath known as 'Mill Head Path' surrounded by farmland. By the mid twentieth century, the land all belonged to a Mr. Connett, whose farmhouse was where 'Bithrey Holding Ltd' now stands. After his retirement, in the early 1950s, Mr. Connett sold the land to a local man, Mr. Walden, who, latterly made an agreement to sell the land to local builder Derek Dodd only to later sell the land to 'Wimpy' in the late '50s, for over ten times what he had paid only several years before! It was when Wimpy constructed the housing estate that the modern day road network of 'Millhead Road' was established.

Rosemount Lane has not changed its route over the centuries but has changed its name. In the late 19th century it was known as Brickyard Lane, after a Brick Works owned by 'Miller & Lilley' that once stood there. The brickyard shut in the early 1930s and became the scrap yard of Kenneth Kirten, which closed shortly after WWII. In August 1925, a new concrete bridge, over the Gissage at Littletown, replaced an old wooden, carthorse bridge that had become unstable with the increased amount of traffic on the road. The first car to pass over the bridge was driven by Mrs. Juanita Phillips who took the Mayor, Mr. H. R. Harris, as a passenger. After the brickyard vacated the lane it became known as Rosemount Lane. Branching off Littletown Road is 'Higher Brand Lane' that was once called 'Livermore Road' after the farm that stood not far from it.

'Wadmore Lane' originally used to connect 'Northleigh Hill Road' with 'Farway Common Road' but was closed in the late 19th century. It stood on the southern edge of the Honiton parish and had a boundary marker at each end of it and later, therefore, became the parish boundary for Honiton and Farway. The road still exists as a footpath/track that runs through the present day Golf Course and ends at the entrance to the Farway Common Donkey Sanctuary farm. It was named after 'Wad Moor', a wooded area to the south of the old road *6.

Dowell Street has also had some changes made to it since Victorian times. Apart from being widened where it meets the High Street, it originally ran to meet Northcote Lane. The original road to Awliscombe was the now disconnected road in which 'Tracey Mill Trout Farm' stands. When the Honiton Bypass was built, in 1966, it cut straight through the old road so it was decided to 'bend' Northcote Lane Back on itself to meet Dowell Street, where the 'British Legion' now stands, disconnecting it with Tracey Road. The bypass also led to the loss of one of Honiton's ancient bridges: 'Stoney /Tracey Bridge'. This bridge was called 'Stoney' for the simple reason that a new 'stone' bridge replaced the much older wooden one. The wooden

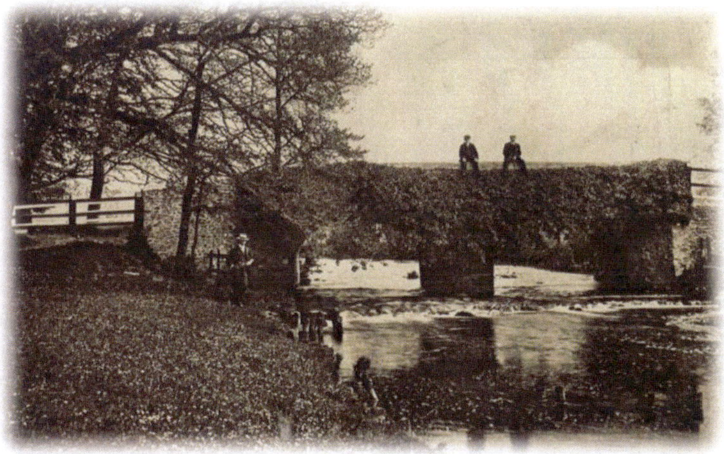

Stoney Bridge

bridge was in place for foot passengers whilst vehicles passed through a ford. There was also once a road that ran from this bridge, parallel to the river, which led to Combe Raleigh; this was, however, 'stopped up' in the early 19th century.

With the increasing popularity of the motor car, traffic through the town became more and more of a problem and by the early 1950s things had reached ridiculous levels. In the height of summer it was known to take a motorist at least an hour to reach Honiton from the old 'Stopgate Services' on the A303, just past the B3170 turning to Taunton and it was also quoted that "going through Honiton was purgatory"! It was also quoted to take "four hours from Monkton to Torquay on a Saturday"! The problem was finally addressed in 1966 when the Honiton Bypass was opened directing traffic away from the town centre. The Turk's Head Cafe was one business

that suffered greatly at the significant reduction in passing travellers and it closed shortly afterwards.
A County Council report of 1972 stated that "the whole town suffers from the intrusion of the motor vehicle" and to remedy this imbalance, several dramatic proposals introducing 'pedestrianised' areas and a radical reform of the town's road networks were drawn up. It was proposed, though, fortunately, not inaugurated, that Silver Street and New Street become pedestrianised and that a one-way system be introduced for traffic through King Street and Mill Street. These plans were obviously never acted upon and if they had been they could have brought the town to a 'grinding halt'!

The bed of the Gissage was also once used as a connecting road. The route led from Stoney/Tracey Bridge to the town and was once known as 'Watery Lane'. It was known to have been used by pack horses and people delivering flour to the town from Griggs Mill (now Tracey Trout Farm).

School Lane was another road that has changed both its route and usage since ancient times. The lane originally was a muddy farm track that proceeded on from its current end to a stream that flowed parallel to the Otter known as 'Mill Leat' and later 'Mill Race'.

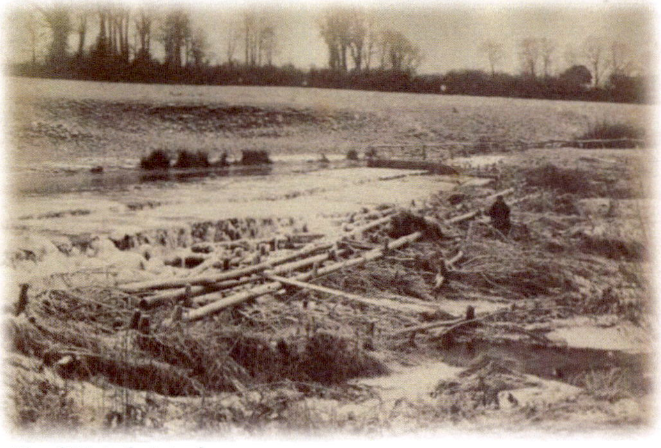

Head Weir (winter).

The lane would have once been used to drive cattle to the river but was also used by local people to reach a bathing spot known as 'Head Weir'. In the early twentieth century it was known as 'Durbin Lane'.
There were also once a number of other footpaths that surrounded old Honiton which were all closed in the 19th century and the land through which they once ran now built on.

- One was located in a field behind the old Kings Arms Inn which ran to Chapel Street; this was closed by Issac Cox.
- Another stretched from old Claylands Farm to Mill Street and ran along the Gissage; this was lost as a consequence of the railway.
- There was a passage from New Street to Winkleigh Court which, owing to the fact it ran through his garden, was closed by Mr. Aberdein.
- The last known footpath was one that ran beside the Gissage, not far from Mill Lane, and finished at the old Stoney Bridge (Tracey Bridge before it was knocked down for the bypass). This path was 2,365 feet long and was closed by local banker Mr. Flood in 1825; once again, as it ran through his land!

Chapter 2
The Honiton Turnpike Trust & Early Travel

"Outside the inn, proud horses take their rest.
The waiting post coach bears a royal crest.
Another day begins, infused with life and sound.
Along the Roman stretch of this fair market town."
Lyn Darrant, 2008

The last clerk to the Exeter Turnpike Trust wrote in 1885 that "until the middle of the last century, the condition of the Highways had remained almost without change since Mediaeval time." There are a number of witnesses prior to the Turnpike Trusts' formation who corroborate this statement.

In 1630, one gentleman wrote that the roads of the district were "exceedingly bad" and that they were *"painful for man and horse, as they can best witness, who have made trail thereof. For be they never so well mounted upon horses out of other countries, which they have travelled one journey in these parts , they can, in respect of ease of travel, forbear a second."*

He went on to say that "Specimens of what the roads formerly were are yet visible in many places" and concluded that "the roads of the county cannot be commended" and even though some of the main highways were "pretty good" overall, most of the "district [were] bad."

In 1723 a doctor, travelling from Chard to Honiton, wrote that the highway was a "very bad road of stones and sand over brooks, spring heads and barren downs." One gentleman observed in 1801 that "the roads [were] so dreadful that the difficulty of getting there is scarcely repaid by a view of so charming a county and thus the inhabitants seem as if they were in voluntary exile."

The roads of the county, up until the mid eighteenth century, were oceans of mud in winter and dust bowls in the summer, leaving travelling times, and journey comfort, incredibly difficult for visitors, locals and travellers. The weather was a far greater obstacle and risk than it is today for in bad conditions coaches were forced to a halt. In 1745 the mail was delayed for several hours due to the water level of a river between Honiton and Crookhorn (Hampshire) being higher than "in the memory of man."

The poor conditions of roads made the whole area very inaccessible and popular tourist retreats of today, such as "the mountains" of Dartmoor, were described as nothing more than "wide barren" tracts "between Exeter and the border of Cornwall" that consisted "of naked rushy marshes, and bleak rocky hills" which served no other purpose than "for the pasturage of sheep."

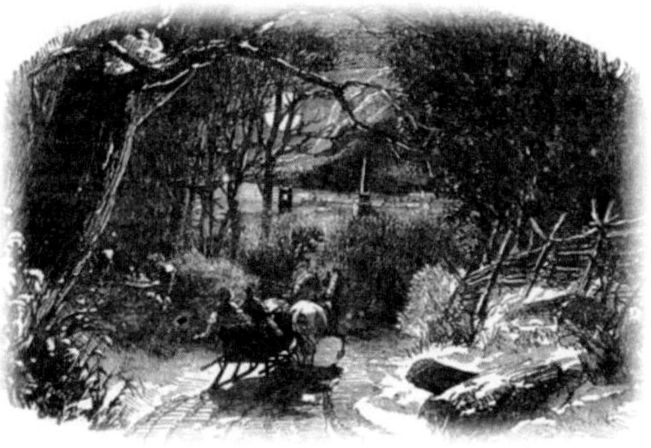

Travelling in the 17th and 18th century was a long, arduous and dangerous task for those bold enough to undertake it. In the 1650s, a trip from Liverpool to London would take 10 days in summer and 2 weeks in winter. In the 1750s, London to Edinburgh was a trip one would have to set aside a fortnight for and an aspiring student travelling from London to Cambridge would have to allow for a 2 day journey. Even a journey from Exeter to Honiton would take several hours: in 1789 the 'horse express', the fastest way to send letters from the city to the town, took 2 ¼ hours.

In the summer of 1725, a Mrs. Manley undertook the journey from London to Exeter. Leaving on a Friday, the journey was expected to take 5 days, with four of them being on the road - Sunday was spent at Salisbury, as no stage coach travelled on the 'day of rest'. The coach started from each stop at 3 in the morning and after 12 hours solid travelling, rested at 3 in the afternoon. Prior to the introduction of turnpikes, many attempts were made to reduce this 'never-ending' journey and 1740 stage coaches had started to travel by moonlight. To ensure no collisions occurred on these treacherous night runs, the coaches would ring bells to signal to any other coaches coming in the opposite direction. Any wagon travelling in the opposing direction would, therefore, halt at the sound of the bells to allow the approaching coach to pass without incident.

It was for these reasons that people travelled large distances very seldomly. One Honiton woman, who died in 1854 aged 90, remembered travelling to London in about 1780, which was her one and only trip to the capital, the journey still taking between five and six days.

If journey by road was too much for you in the eighteenth century, you could always embark on a boat trip to London. The 'Steam Packet Express' left Topsham every Saturday and arrived at St. Katherine's Dock, London 3 days later; the return trip was on Wednesday.

A trip to London, from Honiton today, would have been the equivalent to a trip to Exeter for the people of nineteenth century Honiton and an excursion to London would have been the equivalent of a trip to outer-Mongolia today! Victorian Honitonians travelled to Exeter between once or twice a year and maybe the occasional "jaunt to Sidmouth"; however, the limited spare time and money of the average family simply did not permit them to partake of long journeys. All trips were, therefore, few and far between and long ones were often not undertaken at all; travel was a luxury of the rich.

Despite the poor highway conditions, 18th century road traffic was heavy: on the roads of Tiverton there were recorded to be 22 wagons and carts, 10 coaches and 2,975 horses over a two week period in November of 1757, an average of 215 journeys per day!

The journey time from Honiton to London fell dramatically over the centuries with improved travel routes. A journey in 1660 on the 'Exeter Carrier' would take 10 days; by the eighteenth century it had been cut to only a few days, then to 33 hours and finally 16 hours.

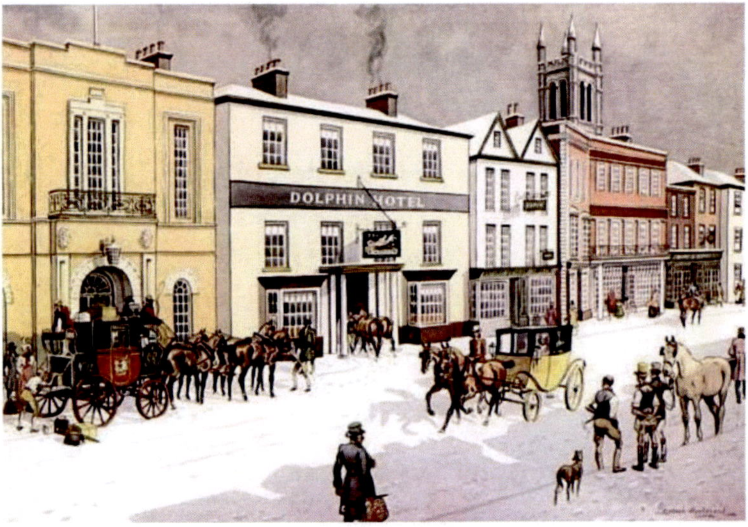

THE DOLPHIN HOTEL, HONITON, DEVON painted by JOSEPH APPLEYARD for "HOLLY LEAVES" 1951

The improvements of the roads, inaugurated by the Turnpike Trusts, reduced journeys to hours rather than days or even weeks; for example, a coach bound for Cambridge from London, leaving at 10am could arrive by teatime. The Turnpike roads had started to allow travellers passage to their destinations within one day, which was revolutionary at the time. In 1814 one gentleman even described the Bristol mail coach as "the quickest in the kingdom" with its average speed of 8 miles an hour "stoppages included": an incredible perception by today's travel speeds!

With increased movement of people and goods on the mail coaches and a road system that had not been updated for over a millennia, it became obvious to the people of the country that a toll system would be needed to generate the necessary revenue for improving the nation's defunct infrastructure.

Tolls had originally been introduced in the early eighteenth century to pay for the repairs and maintenance of bridges, such as in Bideford in 1722. However, many travellers simply raced past the toll booths and hence got away with paying, so 'Turnpikes' were introduced. Turnpikes were defensive barriers of pikes fastened to a frame that stretched across the road, forcing travellers to stop and pay the required toll before they were permitted to pass.

By 1700 there were several Acts which had been passed authorising turnpike trusts, and by 1750 there were 143 trusts responsible for some 3,386 miles of road; however, not one yard of these roads was in Devon or Cornwall. It was not until 1770, when 389 trusts regulating 14,065 miles of road, that the counties of the West Country were included.

Honiton Turnpike Trust was formed in 1765 as a trust from the Second District of the 'Devon and Dorset Turnpike Trust' which consisted of Penn Hill to Honiton, Cullompton and Whimple, and was itself formed as part of the 'Askerswell Hill Act' of 1754. The management was complicated, having to deal with the Commissioners of the Honiton Paving Act who were responsible solely for the town's streets.

Through the Act, the local authorities were permitted to levy a fee of 6p in the pound to the inhabitants of Honiton to help pay for and maintain the Trust.

At the height of the Turnpike Trusts, in the 1830s, there were some 1,000 individual Trusts administering over 30,000 miles of roads with almost 8,000 tollhouses.

In 1790 an Act was passed allowing the authorities of Honiton to erect tollhouses and turnpikes around the town and by 1792 the town was granted £7,000, raised from tolls, to pave and generally improve the town. By 1855 there were over 15 tollhouses and 51 ½ miles of turnpike roads within the Honiton Trust. The following are some of the identified tollhouses:

1. The Copper Castle: (also known as 'Kings Road Gate') located in Kings Road and covering the road from Honiton to Axminster*1

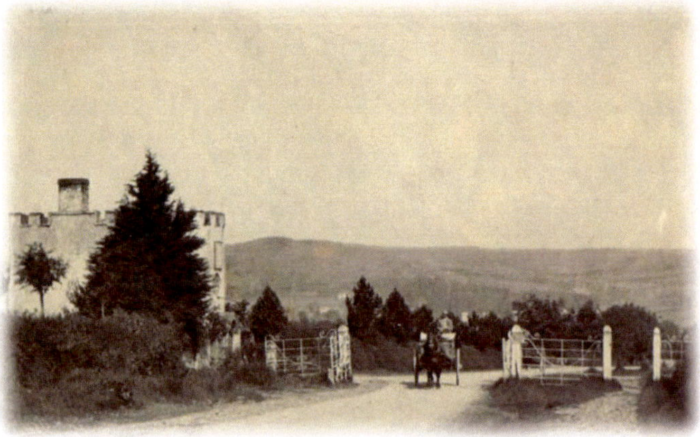

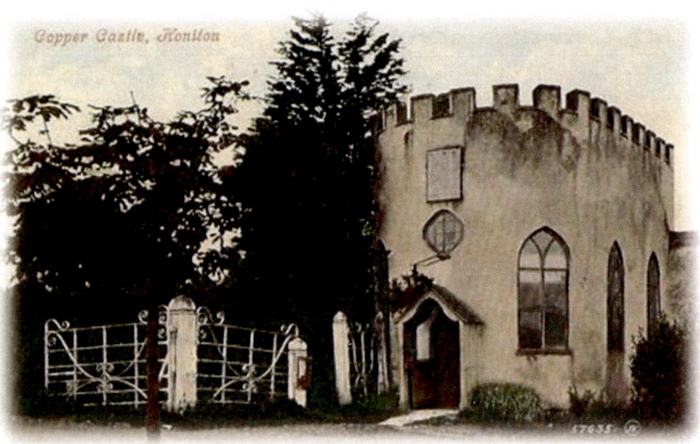

2. Cheeseway Ash Gate: covering the road from Honiton to Chard, was located in Hutgate Road*2
3. Clapper Lane: situated in Clapper lane and took payment for travellers from Honiton to Dunkeswell *3

4. Hayne Lane: collected monies from people going from Awliscombe to Sidmouth
5. Lower Marlepits Gate: also known as 'Marlepits 1st Gate', it was a 4 roomed cottage that served those journeying from Honiton to Sidmouth *4
6. Higher Marlepits Gate: the 2nd gate on Marlpits Hill located near the Honiton Golf Club *5
7. Gobsore Gate: once again for the road from Honiton to Sidmouth *6

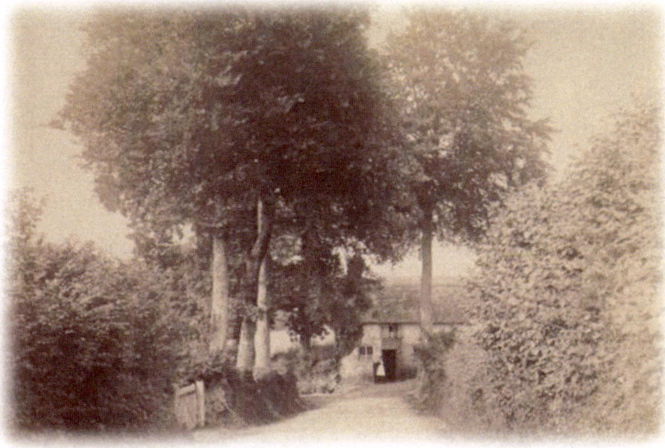

8. Red Lane: Honiton to Churchstanton which used to be located on the Upottery Road at the Red Lane Crossroads.
9. Churchingford: located out of the Honiton parish.
10. Trafalgar Bridge (bridge near the Otter Inn): the road from Weston to Buckerell: (also known as Weston Gate) for *7

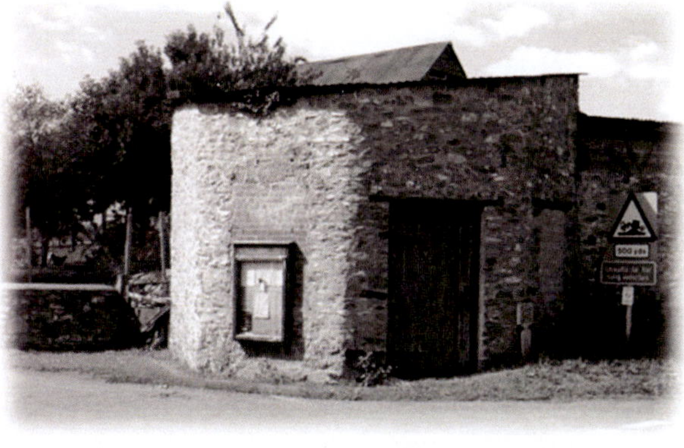

11. Smeath Harpe: Honiton to Churchstanton road
12. Appledoor Gate: once located in old Wadmore Lane *8
13. Holyshute: (also known as 'Potters Kiln Gate') Honiton to Taunton road, now Holyshute Cottage *9

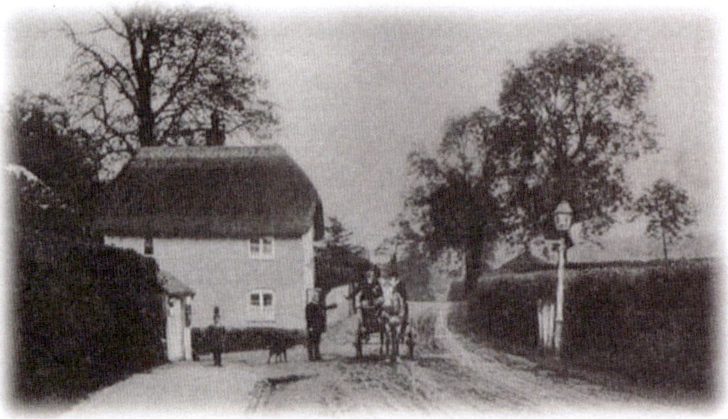

14. Stoneyford Bridge: Honiton to Cullompton *10
15. Cullompton: a tollhouse that was located on the outskirts of Cullompton
16. Turks Head Gate: this gate also once had a 'weigh-bridge' to ensure carts were not over the permitted limits. Honiton to Exeter road, now Manna House *11
17. Newdown Lane: road from Honiton to Churchstanton.
18. Hut Gate: for travellers from Honiton to Axminster *12
19. Round Ball: located near to Gobsore Hill Gate
20. Bramble Hill: once simply a small hut occupied by the toll collector located on Bramble Hill.

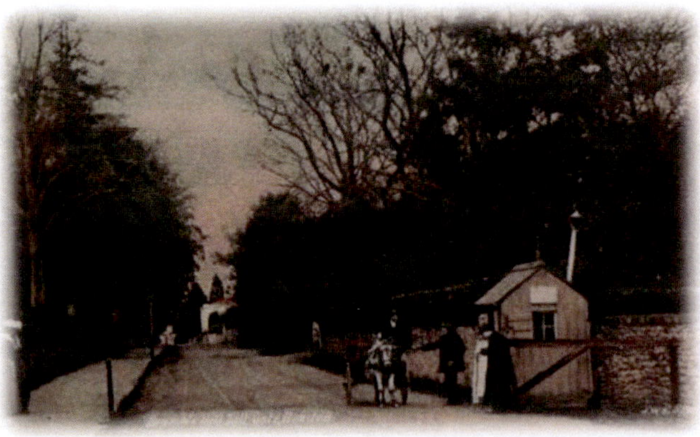

The tollhouse on the Exeter road, now known as 'Manna House', was by far the most profitable, noted to have taken £1,500 a year at the peak of the coaching era.
Today, only three of the tollhouses in the town survive, which include 'The Copper Castle', 'Holyshute Cottage', and 'Manna House'. The Copper Castle is generally thought to have got its name from the fact a 'copper' was charged for passage but a less well known, and much more likely, theory is that the building was said to have originally had a copper roof. On the north side of the building one can see a bricked up window, presumably done during the years of the unpopular 'Window Tax Act' of 1766. The premises today are a private residence and, until relatively recently, was a striking shade of pink, giving it the unofficial local name of 'The Pink Castle'. The old tollgates still stand, continually open to the many motorists using the A35. Both the house and gates are Grade II listed today. Holyshute Cottage stands on the junction of 'Monkton Road' and 'Langford Avenue' and, like the Copper Castle, is today a private house. Manna House, which was once called 'Turk's Head Gate', stands at the end of the 'Exeter Road' and is today a Bed and Breakfast.

The following are the roads that were in the Honiton Turnpike Trust:

- Cullompton Road; A373 from the old Cowley Farm, Honiton through Awliscombe to Cullompton (about 9 miles stretch of road)
- Awliscombe Road; road from old A30 at Weston, past the present day Otter Inn, over Trafalgar Bridge and through to Awliscombe (about 1 mile)
- Cuckoodown Lane; road from the Potter's Kilns Gate (Langford bridge), Honiton to Cheeseway which is now Tower Cross, and from thence to Cuckoodown Lane on Honiton Hill (approximately 1 mile stretch of road)
- Roncombe Gurt Road; the road running south from St. Michael's Church by the Marlepitts Gates, past the Golf Course over Farway Common to the Lyme Turnpike Road near Roncombe Gurt; (about 4 miles)
- Gittisham Hill Road; lane that ran from Rosemount Lane/Sidmouth Road junction in Honiton, over Gittisham Hill towards Sidmouth, to the old Lyme Turnpike Road; about 3 miles in length.

- Smeatharpe Road; road from Potter's Kilns Turnpike, by Langford Bridge, over Luppitt Common through Smeatharpe, crossing over to Somerset where it joined the Upottery Road near Churchstanton; this was about 12 miles long.
- St. Cyres Hill Road; lane off A373 at old Stoney Bridge, Honiton, through Tracey to Saint Cyres Hill, thought to have linked with Churchstanton Road, about 1 mile; (this was removed under an 1854 Act)
- Upottery Road; A30 from Cheeseway Ash Road, through Monkton to Rawridge, then branched NW on road through Upottery to Whitewall Corner (believed to be at junction with Churchstanton Road across Somerset border) about 12 miles.
- Combe Raleigh Road; road from Clapper Lane, Honiton, through Combe Raleigh, and joined the Churchstanton Road, approx 1.5 miles.
- Straighthead Road; A30 from Beggar's Lane, Honiton, through to Fenny Bridges and Whimple to join with the Exeter Turnpike Road, about 9 miles in length.

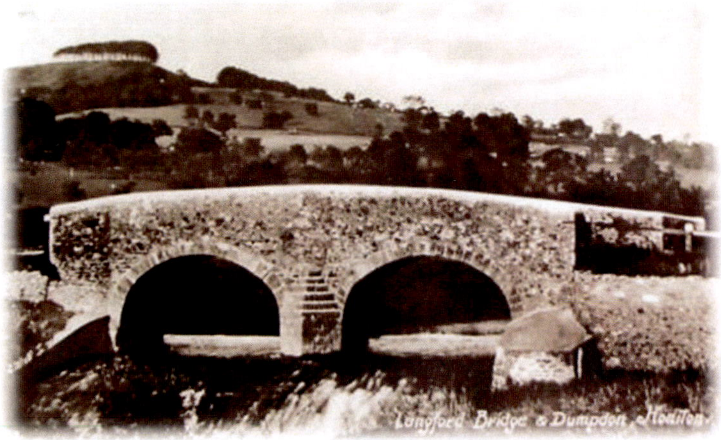

The rates charged at Honiton in 1825 were as follows:

- For every horse, mare, gelding, or other beast drawing a coach, chariot, barouche (four wheeled coach with two seats), chaise (single occupant hooded coach), curricle (similar to a chaise), landau (generally a carriage with facing seats over a dropped footwell), berlin (a covered coach), calash (similar to the barouche), hearse or other carriage, the charge was 4 ½d; therefore, a typical stage coach with four horses would be charged 1s.6d
- For every other horse, mare, gelding or beast drawing simply, or alone, any carriage of any other description whatsoever was charged 4d.
- For every horse, mare, gelding, or other beast drawing any wagon, wain, cart, or other such carriage drawn by two horses or beasts or draught or more, the sum of 3d was asked.
- For all other working animals, laden or unladen and not drawing anything, 1d was the fee.
- In Totnes in 1835, the charge for any horseless, steam powered vehicle was 5 shillings.

The rates were known to have been doubled through winter months, when the roads were more at risk from the colder conditions, and fees were also known to have varied from Trust to Trust and year to year.
There was a small list of lucky travellers exempt from paying any charges which included; mail coaches, the military, those in the King's service, farm implements, clergymen and those going to vote or pray. Tolls were not charged within four miles of a previous gate and travellers were given a ticket so they would only have to pay once per day. The return journey was permitted from midnight to midnight. If the passerby refused to pay, the toll collector was permitted to confiscate the animal(s).

The new roads were vigorously guarded from damage and a whole new set of rules were introduced to ensure their protection. No one was permitted to allow blood from slaughter houses to spill onto the roads, no bonfires or fireworks were permitted; in fact, no fires were allowed within 80 feet of any turnpike roads. Football and other such games were banned from the highway and no one living beside the road was permitted to have any door or shop front that opened out onto the roadway. Such strict rules, as those governing roads, were not as revolutionary as many may think.

There had been equally strict laws in preserving and protecting the roads of mediaeval England and those, such as forbidding animal effluent and entrails from being cast onto the roads, were comparatively similar to those introduced in the fourteenth and fifteenth centuries.
The imposed tolls were about as popular as car tax is today and there were probably lots of ways that local travellers attempted to avoid the charges, such as travelling through farmland, with or without the farmer's permission, to reach a point in the turnpike road that was out of town but most importantly beyond the toll gates. One such commuter, who was a farmer from Awliscombe, stumbled upon an ingenious idea to travel down the course of the Gissage, as it was technically a right of way, but no tolls gates were situated on the a river bed. This gentleman frequently drove cattle he had bought from the market up to where the river meets Littletown, which was outside the toll area. He was then able to ramble down the west side of town back to Awliscombe without passing any toll gates and hence got away without paying a single penny!

Prior to the Paving Act, the High Street had been impeded by the presence of the shambles and houses that were located in the middle of the road, known as 'Mid Street.' Farquharson so described the High Street before the Paving Act:

"From opposite the Dolphin westward extended two rows of shambles occupying the centre of the street at the east end of them was the market cross at the west end a few houses called mid street. Opposite Allhallows where St Paul's now stands were dwelling houses in the middle of the highway facing west with a narrow road on their south side connecting the streets on their east and west."

The latterly described houses were burnt in the fire of 1745 and 'Mid Street' was pulled down in 1790 as a consequence of the Paving Act; however, the shambles remained for several more decades.
The shambles had had a variety of uses in its lifetime, such as the sale of meat and vegetables, a polling station and a prison during the civil war, but by the late 18th century, its presence was proving to be an impediment to traffic and aesthetically displeasing to the town as a whole. In 1805, one traveller stated that the "shambles" was "never judiciously placed", that it had had to be repaired a number of times because of its age and it was "an absolute nuisance to the place".

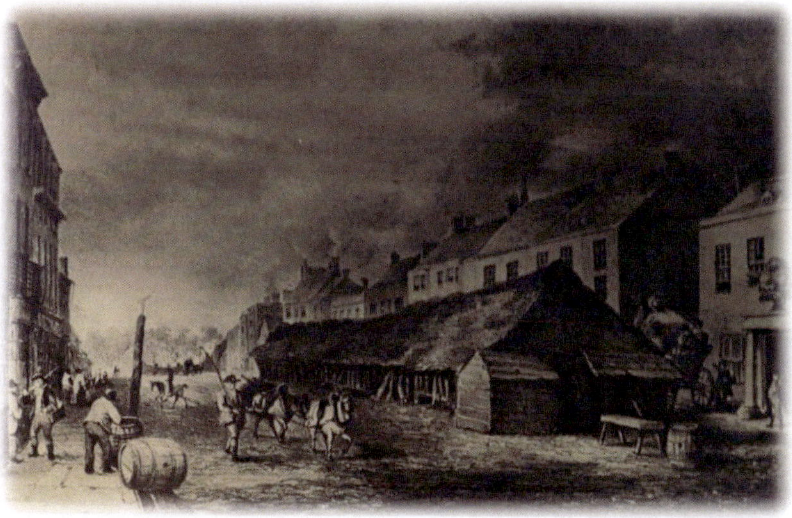

An 18th century view of the old shambles. Note the pillared building on the right hand side thought to be the Dolphin Inn.

Thirteen years later another traveller noted that if the "tottering shambles" was to be "shouldered down", it "would heighten the beauty of the place."

Surprisingly, in 1813, a jury, acting on behalf of the Paving Trust, valued the shambles at £2,400, about £124,000 today! The shambles was described as a low, long structure with a thatched roof supported by wooden poles. The problem with removing the structure was the fact that an elderly man had been granted the right to live there for the duration of his life and that on his death, it would be removed. The shambles was finally demolished in 1823 having plagued the centre of the High Street for at least 243 years. The shambles was known to have existed in the town as early as 1580 as it was mentioned in a Will of the same year.

'Shambles' were historically also known to have been the sites of meat markets where animals were butchered and the Honiton shambles could quite possible have been used for this purpose.

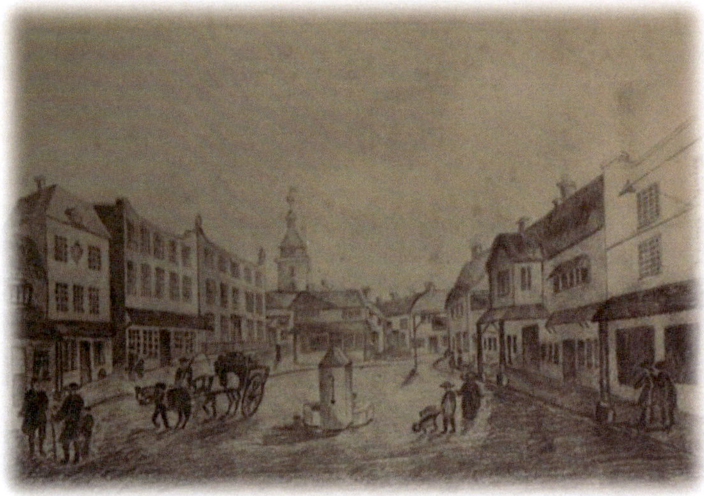

View of Honiton High Street in 1745 showing the old town fountain (foreground) and in the background, midstreet and the old Allhallows Chapel.

After the removal of the shambles, the market suffered and the number of weekly visitors was said to have "decreased". This was later compensated by the construction of the new 'Market House' (Assembly Rooms) which was built by the 'Paving Trust Commissioners' to replace the shambles' former purpose of the selling of goods on market day. It was opened on November 5th 1824 and was celebrated by a public dinner and celebrations. Many towns had Assembly Rooms constructed to provide a place for the younger, richer members of the area to dance.
To the east of the shambles once stood the market cross and the town fountain, both of which were removed around the same time as the shambles. This was a point in the street, "directly opposite the Dolphin", where local farmers pitched their sacks of corn for sale and the section of road inherited the unofficial title of "Cornhill".

Before tarmacing, the High Street was frequently rolled flat by a steam roller but was still basically just dirt, proving a great problem in the wet winters and dry summers. The final improvement to Honiton's main highway came in 1920 when the council finally tarmaced the road for the

sole reason that the old water spraying cart, used to clear the dust, had broken down.
Minor roads, like the main highways, consisted basically of mud and it was the local authorities, rather than the Turnpike Trusts, that were responsible for their repairs. The repairs of these minor roads were not always completed to a high standard, as the following story shows. At the end of May 1896, repairs were undertaken to the road leading from St. Michael's Church to Littletown, today a section of 'Weatherill Road', 'Lower Brand Lane' and 'Littletown Road'. The problem was that the local authorities had used soil from St. Michael's churchyard and, on closer inspection, it was discovered that the remains of some former Honiton residents were now paving the highway! Amongst the earth that had been deposited on the road, bones and parts of coffins were discovered, much to the shock of local residents. A summer shower shortly afterwards left the newly spread marl with "a corpse-like, faint sickly smell" and several people who lived in the vicinity became sick. The then tenant of Livermore Farm suffered losses in his cattle, which had also fallen ill from drinking contaminated drinking water. The run-off of this earth had made its way to Littletown and people feared it had infected the local water supply. An inquest was held before town magistrates and among the human remains, a jaw bone with 3 teeth was presented as evidence. One of the labourers who had been employed to shift the 40 odd cart loads of soil was also taken sick but his superior had accused him of being drunk and forbade him to leave! He later consulted a local doctor and was told he had probably "frightened himself sick" and was prescribed a bottle of "sugar and water"! It was revealed that the soil had been excavated from beneath St. Michael's Church and the magistrates promptly instructed it to be returned. The human remains were not ancient; one date plaque found on the highway bore the date 1856, only some 40 years prior. Despite the public health risk this incident could have caused, no one was prosecuted and the case was dropped.

In 1835, the Devonshire Turnpike Trusts was the 7th greatest generator of revenue in the country, earning over £12,000 for the treasurer's pocket. Honiton, in the same year, had raised £1,081.11s.1d from tolls. The treasurer of the Trust was Christopher Flood and the clerk was Mr. Courtenay Gidley.

Although many of the roads were improved by this Act, many remained in their former state and of a dangerous nature. By 1821, over 22,000 miles of English roads had become turnpikes but only 10% of the highways in

Devon fell into this category. Charles Vancouver, writing in 1808, stated thus:

"the turnpike-roads have by no means that width prescribed scribed by law, and required for the accommodation of the public—so essential to the giving a proper form, and afterwards keeping them in sufficient repair. The consequence is, that these narrow ways are raised so high in the middle, that without sides or bulwark to support them, they are, in a short time, by the traffic of the limecarts, bilged, and forced out upon their sides, when the only passage remaining is confined to a narrow ridge on the top of the road, but which, from the excessive coarseness of the materials of which it is made, is soon broken into so many holes and unevennesses, as very much to endanger the knees of the horse, and the neck of its rider. It is truly surprizing, however, to see with what speed and security the native horses of the country will pass over these rough and broken places, whether burthened or otherwise...
The parish roads are extremely various, some corresponding with, and even worse than those above described; but where the black gravel before noticed occurs, they are usually self-made, and with a little levelling, could not be surpassed by any in the kingdom."

The roads surrounding Honiton lived up to Mr. Vancouver's expectations but it was obvious to him that the equivalent 'b' roads were not of this description...

"The public roads round Exeter, Axminster, Honiton, and many other large towns in the county, cannot be excelled for goodness in any part of England; but the parish roads generally, and particularly through the red loamy district, are very indifferent; nay, bad indeed."

This was the opinion of many a traveller, even as late as 1849 when one gentleman, travelling on the rural roads surrounding Honiton wrote:

"The roads are exceedingly uneven, and in some cases almost impracticable... They (rivers) frequently intersect the roads—when they have to be forded, bridges being but rare conveniences in the district. Sometimes, after heavy rains, they render the roads impassable for hours. You are scarcely a mile from Honiton, ere you enter this lonely and sequestered region. Your road leads you now to the hill top, now to the bottom of the valley, and then to the hill top again. The rough and stony track which you pursue is generally flanked by high and crumbling banks,

overspread with the ivy, the young oak, the holly, the fern, and the bramble. In short, it is difficult to believe yourself any longer in busy and enterprising England—so sudden and so complete is the transition from one of its main thoroughfares to this lonely and secluded district."

The mail coaches travelling to and from London generally had a team of 16 horses which were changed every 10 miles; the coachman was relieved every 30 miles, when he was paid one shilling, whilst the guard was on for the duration and was subsequently paid 2s.6d.
A typical coach driver was described by a gentleman travelling in 1820 saying that he was often "swelled by frequent portions of malt liquor, and his bulk [was] still further increased, by a multiplicity of coats in which he [was] buried like a cauliflower. He was said to have worn "a broad rimmed low crowned hat, a large roll of coloured handkerchief about his neck" and a waistcoat "of some light colour, striped, and his small clothes [extended] far below the knees to meet a pair of jockey boots which [reached] about halfway up his legs." The coachman was also said to have enjoyed "great consequence and consideration along the road" and was known to have a good understanding with every bright eyed young country lass."!
The drivers of these coaches were highly skilled individuals; one such driver, travelling from Ilminster to Honiton in 1821, was known to have killed a partridge with a solitary lash of his whip when a flock of them flew in front of the coach from a hedgerow!
There was one interesting story about a coach leaving Honiton in 1836, written by a Spanish gentleman.

"I have reason to remember this town, as our lives were endangered here by the misconduct of the inn-keeper. There was a demur about procuring horses for us; a pair were fetched from the field, as we afterwards discovered, who had either never been in harness before, or so long out of it as to have become completely unmanageable. As soon as we were shut in, and the driver shook the reins, they ran off—a danger which had been apprehended; for a number of persons had collected round the inn door to see what would be the issue. The driver, who deserved whatever harm could happen to him, for having exposed himself and us to so much danger, had no command whatever over the frightened beasts ; he lost his seat presently, and was thrown upon the pole between the horses ; still he kept the reins, and almost miraculously prevented himself from falling under the wheels, till the horses were stopped at a time when we momently expected that he would be run over and the chaise overturned."

There were some 130,000 horses once employed to ensure the Queen's mail arrived on time; however, the life and treatment of these horses was a short, arduous and cruel one - the above quoted gentleman went on to note his sympathies for these poor beasts:

"the poor horses, instead of being suffered to rest, weary as they were, for they had just returned from Exeter, were immediately put to for another journey. One of them had been rubbed raw by the harness. I was in pain the whole way, and could not but consider myself as accessary to an act of cruelty; at every stroke of the whip my conscience upbraided me, and the driver was not sparing of it. It was luckily a short stage of only two leagues and a quarter.

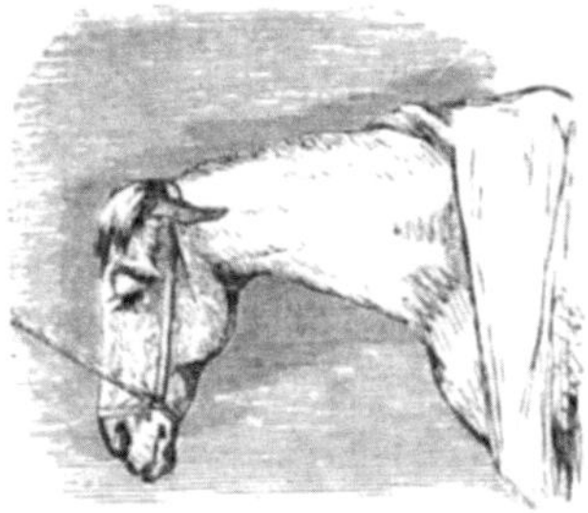

English travelling, you see, has its evils and its dangers. The life of a post-horse is truly wretched;—there will be cruel individuals in all countries, but cruelty here is a matter of calculation: the post-masters find it more profitable to overwork their beasts, and kill them by hard labour in two or three years, than to let them do half the work and live out their natural length of life. In commerce, even more than in war, both men and beasts are considered merely as machines, and sacrificed with even less compunction."

There was another written account in 1837 that commented on the treatment of such horses in Devon.

"Horses, a small compact breed ; but they are said to be less attended to and worse treated in this than any other English County"

Cruelty of their horses was the last of the coachman's and the coach operator's concerns. The emphasis was to get their paying passengers to their destinations as quickly as possible and with the improved road network it became a very competitive business.

The stage coach had been established during the reign of Charles I and had flourished during the reign of Charles II when they were known as 'hackney coaches.' The first "conveyance" that passed through Honiton, on its trip from London to Exeter, was in 1766 and the first mail coach to pass

through Honiton, on the route from London to Exeter, was on October 25th 1785. A single letter from Honiton to London cost 10d in 1835 and the mail coaches soon became a common sight on the new roads. In 1810 the mail arrived at Honiton at 6.45pm and left for the capital the following morning at 7.15am.
With the improved road system, journey times were significantly reduced and the fastest stage coach to London from Exeter was the 'Telegraph'. It left Exeter at 5am and arrived at the capital by 10pm, a journey time of 17 hours that was incredibly fast for the time. As stated before, journeys of great distances were being completed within one working day. Two other slower alternatives included the 'Subscription' and the 'Defiance' which completed the trip in 18 hours. The 'Defiance' was driven by 'four greys' and its coachman, at one time, was James Cossins, a well known local Exeter man. The journey was not cheap though: the fare on the fast coach was 35 shillings outside and £3.10s. on the inside. If this was too expensive, one could partake of the slower coaches which were much more reasonable at 25 shillings outside and 35 shillings inside! For most people these fares were well beyond their means; a journey outside, in all weathers, on the slow coach was over two week's wages of the average man! A typical coach in 1775 could carry 8 passengers inside and another 10 outside.
Coach traffic through the town could be hazardous to other road users and pedestrians. When the Exeter Stage Coach was driving through Honiton in December 1767, one man was thrown from his horse and run over by the wheels of the coach, dying on the spot. It was noted that it was "wished" that stage coaches "would drive less quick" to prevent any such accidents from happening again. This could very well have been Honiton's first death by speeding or dangerous driving!

The coaching era generated massive business and industry and the coaching routes were the equivalent of the motorways of today. 'The Deptford Inn', which once stood "where the great Western Road crossed that from Bristol to Portsmouth", was one of the largest posting houses in the south of England. With stabling for over 240 horses, it was the main resting point for travellers from London to Exeter, Bristol and Portsmouth. It was written that "the weary travellers were only too glad to alight there and cleanse themselves of the white dust which a journey across the chalky downs had plentifully bespeckled them". This inn stood on the western edge of Salisbury Plain and was the eighteenth century equivalent of today's 'Lakeside' or 'Bluewater'.

There were 13 coaches travelling through Honiton daily in 1830, three were the mail coaches - the 'Defiance', 'Subscription' and 'Telegraph' and the remaining were named 'Vivid', 'Balloon', 'Eclipse', 'Traveller', 'Clarence', 'Regulator', 'Portsmouth Coach', 'Bath and Bristol Coach', 'Barnstable Coach' and the 'Sidmouth to Taunton Coach'. Two of these coaches ran every Tuesday and Friday from The Dolphin and the 'Clarence' to Exeter, leaving about 8am and returning from the city at 7pm. There was also a daily return coach to Cullompton.

Travellers on these coaches could have told how far they were from the town by the variety of milestones that once stood on the settlement's outskirts and of those, here are some identified examples:

- There was one located on the A35 which has previously been mentioned.
- Another identified milestone once stood on Lower Marlpits Hill, not far up from the 'Cuckoodown Lane junction' reading 'Honiton, 1 Mile'.
- A milestone once stood between 'Roebuck Farm' and 'Manna House', on the southside of the highway, once again indicating Honiton was only 1 mile away.
- At the end of the old track that once led to Heathfield farm from the Sidmouth Road, stood another stone stating 'Honiton, 1 Mile' and 'Sidmouth, 8 miles'.
- There was another milestone in Clapper Lane, some 4 miles from the town.

By 1850, the only coach passing through the town daily was 'The Coronet', travelling from Exeter to Weymouth. The coaches had begun to decline with the approach of the railway and the last mail coach to go through Honiton was in 1846; the last ever coach was 'The Coronet' which was made redundant in 1860, the year the railway arrived. By the end of the nineteenth century, stage coaches were a relic of the past and Farquharson wrote, around that time, that there "are few now living who travelled" on such vehicles. It was not just the stage coaches that suffered at the arrival of the railway; by the second half of the nineteenth century the Turnpike Trusts were approaching financial ruin, with the massive decrease in traffic and hence monies collected. In 1877, the majority of the Honiton toll houses were sold off and by 1885 all turnpikes had been abandoned; however, the tolls remained in many places. Even though it was not until the 1870s that the tollhouses of Honiton were officially sold, many of the collection points had not been used for their original purpose for a number of years. By 1871, 'Turk's Head Gate' was inhabited by a tailor, 'Gobsore' and 'Lower Marlpits Gate' had become the homes of agricultural labourers and 'Higher Marlpits Gate' had completely vanished. These old houses continued the trend of becoming the homes of poorly paid workers for the remainder of the 19th century and although 'Hut Gate' still stood, by the turn of the twentieth century it was no longer inhabited. Lower Marlpit's Gate was a very old cottage that was once inhabited by a man who died in the Monmouth Rebellions of 1685: his ghost was once said to haunt the hill. (*For more information about this see 'Fun, Fairs and Folklore' section*). This cottage survived until its last occupant, an elderly widow called Mrs. Gaydon, died there in 1928, having resided there for some 50 years. Mrs. Gaydon, having outlived her only son and husband, had no family and the property remained empty for several years. When the elements brought it into a state of disrepair, it was demolished and the recovered stones from the house were used to repair buildings of Combe Estate.

The old wooden hut that was once used as the tollhouse in Northcote Lane was later used as a tool shed for council workers before it also disappeared altogether.

In Totnes, in 1881, the toll gates were taken down to be publicly burnt and on June 2nd 1910 the toll charges at Honiton were finally abolished. There was said to have been public "rejoicing" and "public entertainment" at the removal of these hugely unpopular charges. Honiton was, in fact, thought to be the last town to have had an active tollhouse; most other West Country tolls, not including bridges, ended in April 1924 and the Road Traffic Act of 1930 finally brought a unanimous end to all the remaining tolls gates.

In the years between the end of the stage coaches and the arrival of the motor car, the roads were a desolate and lonely place. In 1886, a James Hissey who was travelling on a summer's morning on what is now the A30, wrote what he witnessed on his journey from Honiton to Exeter: *"we met not a soul, we saw no one, not a solitary farmer, nor a stray shepherd, not even the ubiquitous bicyclist".*

If only Mr. Hissey could see that road today!

The town's inns and taverns were the other victims of these changes for as the coaches ceased, so did the dozens of pubs that had sprung up throughout the 18th century to accommodate the tired travellers. There was even an inn 3 miles from Honiton on the road to Stockland known as

'The Bell Inn' which had been a 'halting' point for coach users. This tavern has long disappeared into history.
Farquharson wrote the following about the loss of the coaching era;

"In many places the grass is growing on the old highways once beaten bare by the horses hooves, many an inn that of yore stood with open portals to welcome the weary traveller has disappeared, and we know it no more, no longer do we hear the guard's horse, proclaiming the arrival of the coach and the many melody of the bells on the horses of the stage wagons is hushed."

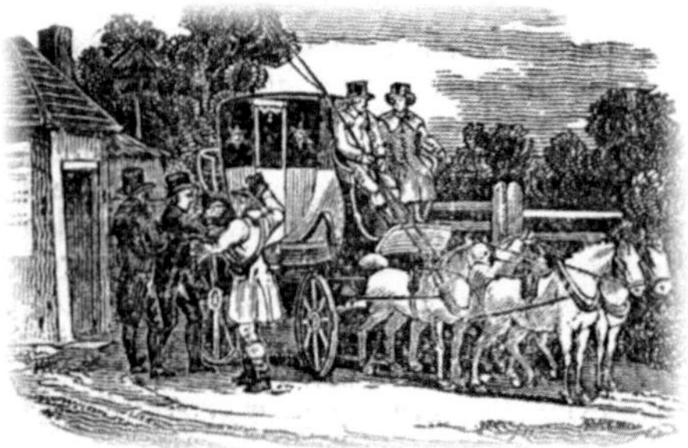

As many enthusiasts and people of today may reminisce and discuss the pre-Beeching years of the railways, so once did the Victorians of the age of the coaching era as, once again, James Hissey went onto describe:

"At Honiton it was our good fortune to come across another old-world coaching inn, for in past days this town was a famous centre of travel, and its hostelries were in good repute. In our hotel yard here we discovered in the course of our investigations sundry quaint vehicles, cumbrous and heavy, all of the olden time, relics of a bygone age ; these contrasted strangely with our modern phaeton. If any eccentric individual were to have one of these curious conveyances copied, and drive about the country therein, what a sensation he would make ; almost as incongruous he would appear as a man walking down Regent Street in a suit of armour. Amongst these nondescript creations on wheels was one of a more recent date than the others, but ancient still, rejoicing in a vigorous old age, and actually in daily use to convey her majesty's mails to rural outlying parts beyond... This antique two-wheeled affair interested us much ; as if it could only have related to us its life history, it would, I feel sure, an eventful one.... The body of the conveyance, by a most ingenious contrivance, slid backwards and forwards at the will of the driver, controlled by a lever ; we tried the, to

us, novel arrangement, and found it to work well and easily. Thus the position of the load was varied, according to the up or down hill gradients of the road, thereby easing the horse, and allowing him to make hest of his powers, adding moreover considerably to the safety of the driver. This appeared to me to be a simple and excellent device, and we wondered it has not ere this been rediscovered and reintroduced in two-wheeled vehicles for hilly countries. In spite of the cleverness of our age, some old ideas are worth reviving."

The train had cut the once revolutionary time of 16 hours to London into pieces with the journey only occupying 4 ½ hours from 1860. The real 'horse power' of the stage coaches simply could not compete with the brute horsepower of the locomotive and with the coaching era over, only the relics of this once great age were left to rot in the yards of the taverns their former masters had once resided in. The railway, although the killer of one way of life, started another: a new, bolder and famous era of transportation that would go on to carry the world into the twentieth century.

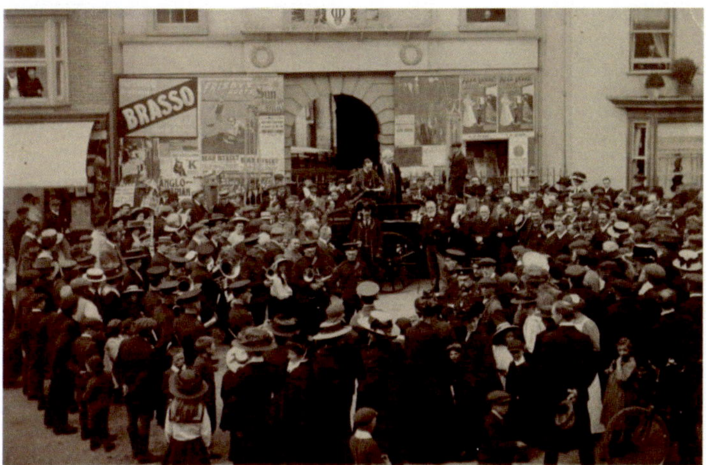

Honiton Toll Abolition Celebrations, June 2nd, 1910.

Chapter 3
Honiton Railway Station

"I do not believe the introduction of motor cars will ever affect the riding of horses; the prophecies that have been made are likely to be falsified as have those made when the railways were introduced"
(Mr. Scott-Montagu, 1903)

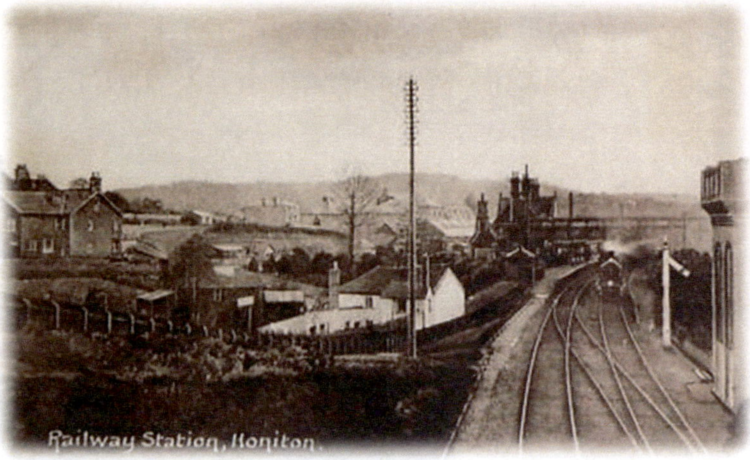

When Victoria came to the throne in 1837, there was not one girder or sleeper in the entire of Devon. The first train to arrive in the county was on May 1st 1844 when the first journey from Paddington to Exeter was completed in exactly 5 hours: 194 miles at an average speed of 39 mph. By 1850, there were only three railway lines in the whole of the South West: the line connecting Plymouth and Exeter to Bristol and two short, local lines, one from Bodmin and one from Truro. The railway was not welcomed by everyone: the Duke of Wellington feared the new mode of transport as it would "encourage the lower classes to move about"!
By the 1850s, the establishment of a railway station at Honiton was a regular debate amongst developers and the government. Several proposals had been put forward but had come to nothing. It was the Admiralty, requiring improved access between the naval ports of Portsmouth and Devonport who, among others, put considerable pressure upon Parliament to extend the railway line.

Joseph Locke, MP and Lord of the Manor of Honiton, was another individual who extensively campaigned for a Central Line during the mid 19th century. Joseph Locke had been an engineer of South Western Railway from 1837-1840 and his efforts were finally rewarded when a single track was laid from Yeovil Junction to Exeter St. David's, passing straight through Honiton. 'The London and South Western Exeter Extension Act' of 1856 paved the way for the construction of the railway through the town. The Honiton Railway station was opened on July 18th 1860 and was enthusiastically welcomed by local people. Supervision of the line's construction fell to John Errington, Locke's successor. The earthworks, tunnel construction and the laying of the permanent way were contracted to a Mr. James Taylor. Taylor employed several thousand men, known as navvies, and hundreds of horses in creating the largest civil engineering feat the area had ever seen. The tunnel, just outside of Honiton, was constructed through 1,350 yards of "green sand" that is a substance "so fine that it will run through a silk pocket handkerchief." Mr. Taylor supplied the eleven million bricks used to build the tunnel and it cost £70,000 to complete.
The then Mayor of Honiton, Mr Jerrard, read an address at the opening ceremony and stated that...

"We look upon this railway not only as an accommodation and boon to ourselves and the whole line of the country through which it passes, but as a great national advantage."

As the first train left Honiton station it was bid a fond farewell with "the hearty cheers of thousands."
The railway was to bring a whole new era of industry to Honiton and the surrounding area. Journey times became a fraction of their former duration and local farmers were able to specialise and extend their produce to the larger national cities like London: many texts written after the opening of the railway comment on 'large quantities' of 'butter' and 'cream' being sent from Honiton to the capital. Traffic on the line became immense over the following years; in 1867 one train that arrived at Honiton was carrying 16 goods wagons, two passenger carriages and a goods break van. Considering this was the era of steam and not diesel, one can appreciate what a feat these early locomotives achieved. The line's traffic became so great that the line from Axminster was doubled on July 31st 1860 and the line to Whimple doubled by August 1861. In fact, three of the biggest businesses located at Honiton station - Miller & Lilley, George Blays and Parsons and Co. - were all established within 20 years of

the station arriving in the town showing how much influence this new form of transportation had on the local area. A train traveller writing in 1869 wrote of a "neat little station, on the edge of a neat little country town, of Honiton".

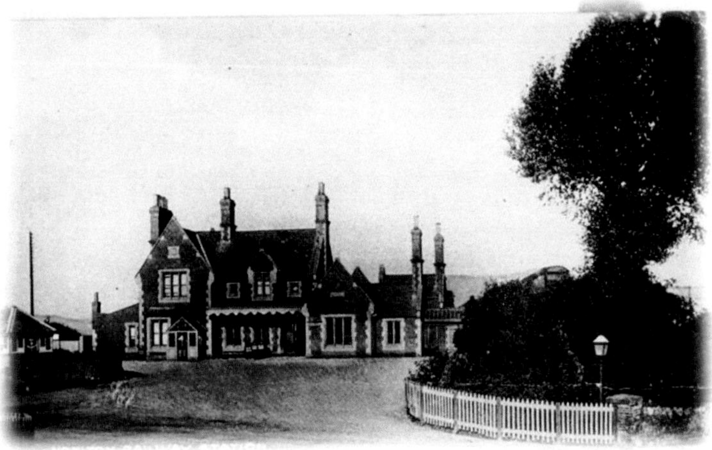

The old Honiton Victorian Stationhouse prior to its demolition

The original station house, like many others on the Yeovil line, was designed by Sir William Tite whose greatest achievement was the Royal Exchange, as well as co-designing the London & Westminster Bank. The station house was thus described in the 1950s...

"Most of the station house was built with two storeys, the porch at the west end providing the entrance to the stationmaster's house, which occupied the upper storey, with station offices in the remainder of the ground floor. No less than five chimneystacks, the largest with five chimneypots, were provided for at least eleven fireplaces inside."

The remainder of the station was so described...

"For pedestrians there were steps direct up to the cab yard. Here was a Southern Railway enamelled "Honiton Station" sign next to the stationmaster's small fenced garden. Here was an extensive cab yard with two sets of gates giving access to the goods yard, and up to the station house. There was a small awning to shelter passengers entering the booking hall, where they were able to buy tickets from the booking office

window or collect or deliver parcels from the parcels office. Moving out to the down platform there was a wide, flat awning the length of the station house and access to the ladies and waiting rooms, and toilets. Under the awning were the covered steps to the footbridge...Proceeding down the platform there were two small wooden buildings with slated roofs and chimneys, looking like small South Western signal cabins, used as an office and a porters room...West of the main building there was a small fence then the short dock siding, where a couple of vans could be loaded from the platform side. At the end of the down platform was a locomotive water column, and the first signal box until its replacement in 1957...On the up platform there was a standard Tite waiting shed, but no platform awning. A footpath ran from here down a slope to New Street...At the west end was the lamp room and at the east end...a little further up the line a large brick-built pump house and tower topped with a large iron water tank from where water gravitated to the station house, goods yard, and locomotive water columns. The water supply came from a small stream which ran along the down side of the line, and opposite the water tower filled two covered tanks 13 ft long, 7 ft wide and 7 ft deep...Water was pumped from here to the top of the water tower; for many years a small steam engine was used but later this was replace by an electric pump."

In the immediate years after Honiton Station opened alighting travellors were conveyed to their respective destinations by 'old-fashioned' type stage coaches which, in some instances, could cram up to sixteen passengers within them.

The first stationmaster of Honiton was thought to be George Hill, a gentleman from Bath. Mr. Hill was raised by his aunt and uncle, of whom the latter was a Railway Superintendant at Southampton. George Hill remained living with his aunt, after his uncle's death, until her death. He was only station master of Honiton for a few years, later becoming stationmaster of Richmond and by the 1880s, after the death of his wife, settled into a clerical position, where he ironically lived 2 doors from 'The Railway Hotel' in Twickenham.

The second stationmaster of Honiton was James McLees from Glasgow. He was thought to have got the job in about 1866 and remained in the town for nearly 30 years, until his death in 1894. In 1874 he requested that two of his daughters work alongside him as a booking clerk and telegraphist but for some unknown reason, his request was declined.

After McLees died, William H. Smith from Exeter became the third master: he had formerly been the stationmaster of Bridgestowe, Devon. Mr. Smith lived at the stationhouse with his only daughter, Florence, until about the start of WWI. From then on the stationmasters were as follows (list incomplete):

- William Thomas Smith: circa 1911-1923
- Frederick T. Perry: 1923-1927
- Mr. W. G. Kail: 1930-1936
- Mr. Hayter: 1937
- Mr. S. S. Towler: 1939
- Mr. W. Piper: 1948
- Mr. H. Wood
- Mr. Ronald Foster: 1955

Mr. Foster was the last station master of Honiton and was made redundant as a result of the changes in the early 1960s.

A footbridge for passengers was installed in 1885 which was built from recovered girders from Rockley Viaduct near Hamworthy. The footbridge, which cost £210, until recently carried a plate inscribed "L&SWR Wimbledon Works 1885." The first signal box for Honiton was constructed in 1875 and a presumably pioneering 'electric' repeater signal was installed in 1868. For a short time there was a second station in the town, opened in September 1906, about half a mile from the main station. It was built to allow soldiers to reach the old rifle range at Roundball Hill. Known as 'Roundball Halt', it was once located in the present day vicinity of the railway bridge on Rosemount Lane, presumably giving alighting soldiers access to the old 'Targets Lane'. It was not known to have been advertised in timetables, though did appear in some maps, and was demolished in early 1921.

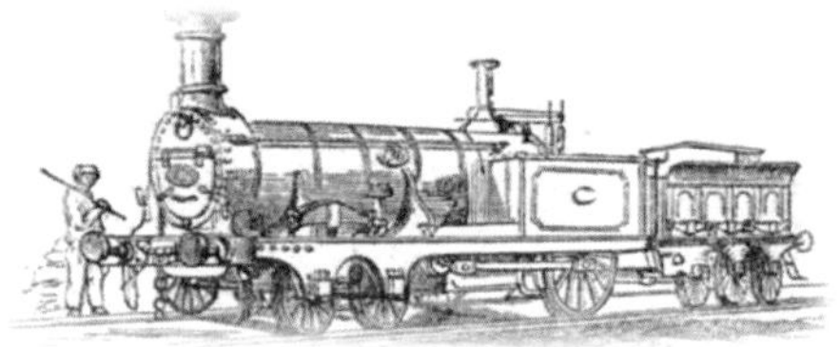

By the twentieth century business and traffic at Honiton railway had grown even greater. As mentioned earlier, milk was a large commodity and in 1928, when Ambrosia opened a processing factory at Lapford, transportation increased dramatically: by 1932 Lapford station received 191,304 gallons of milk, most of which came from Honiton. In 1933 a single fare to London Waterloo from the town was 19s.5d. for 3rd class and 32s.4d. for a 1st class ticket.

The goods yard was just as busy; one of the main businesses, with its headquarters at Honiton, was Miller & Lilley who had their own private lettered wagons. Coal was one of the company's biggest products but the shipping of fertiliser and animal feed, which came from local mills to be transported to their other branches at the stations of Ottery St. Mary, Sidmouth and Exmouth, was just as common. Messrs Silcocks and Bibbys both also had premises at the railway station and due to an absence of staff, all work was carried out by the stations' workers. Even Lyon's Tea had a depot at Honiton station. 'Halse & Board & Sons' had numerous agricultural equipment delivered by rail and George Blay's Saw Mills, located only feet from the station's goods yard, was known to have transported 'considerable quantities' of sawn timber and whole tree trucks, much of which was cut locally. It was not just large commercial products sent on the railway; foodstuffs such as pies, fish, meat etc. were delivered to Honiton by freight and then delivered to local shops and businesses. Everyday household items such as calor gas, paraffin and tyres were also all delivered to the town by rail. Honiton Pottery also 'forwarded considerable output' via the station; even blood samples were transported by train from Honiton Hospital to Exeter for analysis. In the 1950s there was room for 148 wagons and the station was so busy that if any remained there longer than 24 hours, the respective owners were fined 9 shillings per day until removed.

This huge amount of work required a large staff; in the 1940s no less than 22 people worked at the Honiton branch, including the stationmaster, two booking clerks, two signalmen and three porters and in the goods yard there was a chief clerk, a junior clerk, a checker, two goods porters, a porter signalman, 5 lorry delivery drivers, two mechanics and a permanently retained team of platelayers responsible for track maintenance.

However, these 'boom' days of Honiton railway were soon to come to an end with both economic and social changes taking place in the post war years. The railway had reached its peak just after WWI when there were some 23,440 miles of track throughout Britain. After a minor slump in the inter-war years, the usage of the railways picked up much more during WWII when transportation of troops and goods became top priorities. However, by the 1950s, with the abolition of fuel rationing and the opening of the first motorway in 1959, the car was beginning to seriously compete with the train, especially as the rail network was in a poor state, with little investment and maintenance during the war years. Ironically, the car had had a cold reception in its infancy: the Locomotive Act of 1865 (or the 'Red Flag Act') stated that any such 'horseless carriages' should not only be operated by no less than 3 men but also a maximum speed of 2 mph in towns and 4 mph in the open countryside should not be exceeded.

All such vehicles should also "stop instantly if a horse rider or driver of a horse-drawn carriage raised their hand." This law was not repealed until 1896 when the speed limit was raised to a generous 14 mph! Local journeys, before the car, were still very much restricted to walking distances, for even a bicycle cost anything between £4 and £5 in the 1880s.

The government of the early 1950s planned major modernisation of the newly nationalised railway to keep up with the ever increasing number of motor cars. This plan was never inaugurated for labour costs rose much faster than inflation and by 1962 the railway was the equivalent of £1.6 billion in deficit. Harold MacMillion's transport minister, Ernest Marples, was prepared for 'radical' action to bring the railways back into profit by stating that "the future lay with roads, [and] that railways were a relic of the Victorian past." The infamous Dr. Richard Beeching was then appointed Chairman of the British Railway Board and was instructed to find a way to reduce the deficit and did so by massive closures and cut backs. Honiton itself had seen little investment after the war: gas lighting was still in operation up until the 1960s and the Beeching years saw an end to decades of trade, commerce and a way of life. In 1950 there were 21,000 miles of track and 6,000 stations in Britain; by 1975 (after the Beeching Reports) nearly half of all British Railway lines had been made redundant and two thirds of all stations had been closed. Dr. Beeching did away with hundreds of wayside goods depots and some 300,000 freight wagons. Although the Honiton branch remained open, the station saw massive changes as its former business slumped with the closure of so many of its tributary lines. The goods yard was closed on May 8th 1967 and the railway line singled for the first time since 1861. All the station buildings were demolished along with the regal Victorian Stationhouse. There was no longer a need for the stationmaster's accommodation as the position no longer existed. Also the maintenance costs of such a large establishment for a now much smaller station was unnecessary. The old stationhouse was 'replaced by a ghastly modern building', as written by Edgar Pulman in 1989, which now houses the booking office and waiting room. The 'Beeching Axe' was a failure, saving only a quarter of the predicted £30 million and car ownership doubled over the course of the 1960s, paving the way for a new era of congestion. It seems ironic that the government of the 1960s created the massive dependence upon the motor car but only 40 years later the pressure is now for the motorist to use the train and leave the car at home!

The station underwent a £65,000 refurbishment in 1994 to improve access, parking facilities and the building's overall appearance.

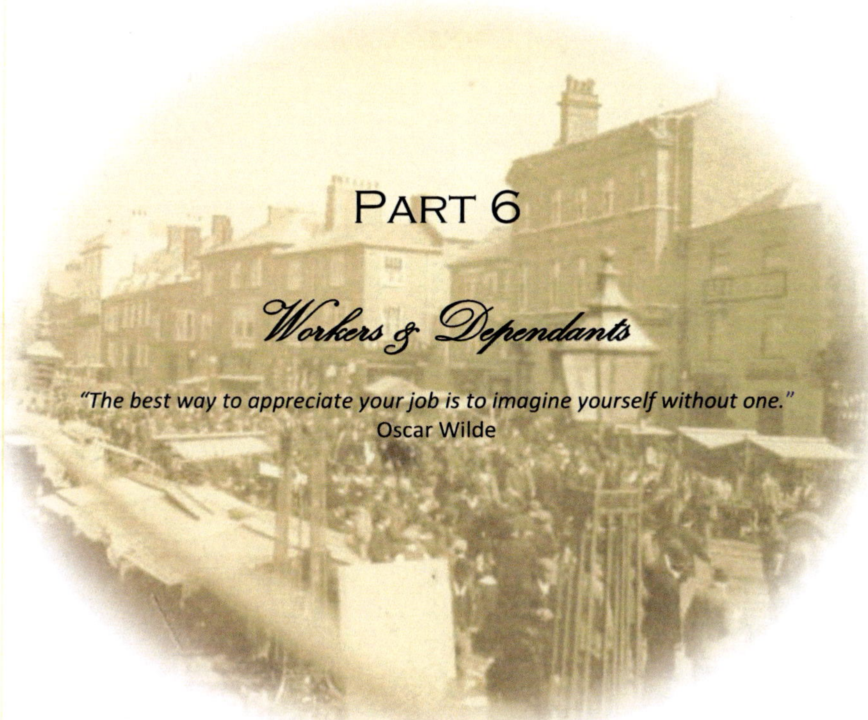

Part 6

Workers & Dependants

"The best way to appreciate your job is to imagine yourself without one."
Oscar Wilde

Chapter 1
The Working Population

"Who first invented work and bound the free
And holiday-rejoicing spirit down?"
Charles Lamb

In Victorian England the gap between the rich and the poor was much greater than today and there were also a lot more poor people in the country than rich. There were many reasons for being on the breadline, so to speak, either from illness, death, old age or too many dependants; however, if the bread winner came from a poor home himself, it was unlikely he would be able to better himself by getting a trade such as a blacksmith or mason. Poverty would, therefore, pass from one generation to the next and with such large families, the poor's meagre earnings were stretched to the limits.
When one spent a lifetime in the lower paid careers such as agricultural labourers, laundresses and charwomen, the only time one could stop working was when death called. When many people of this time reached old age, their bodies simply could not endure the continuation of work, and with every penny earned in earlier life spent to support themselves and their families, many had little alternative but to go to the workhouse or take shelter with a relative. In Honiton, in 1851, there were only 35 people over the age of 80 living in the town and, of those who can be confirmed, over 40% of them were still working; a lucky 27% of them were either retired or living on dividends and the remaining 33% were either on parish relief or in the Union Workhouse.

There were a large number of occupations in Victorian Honiton, many of which have long vanished.

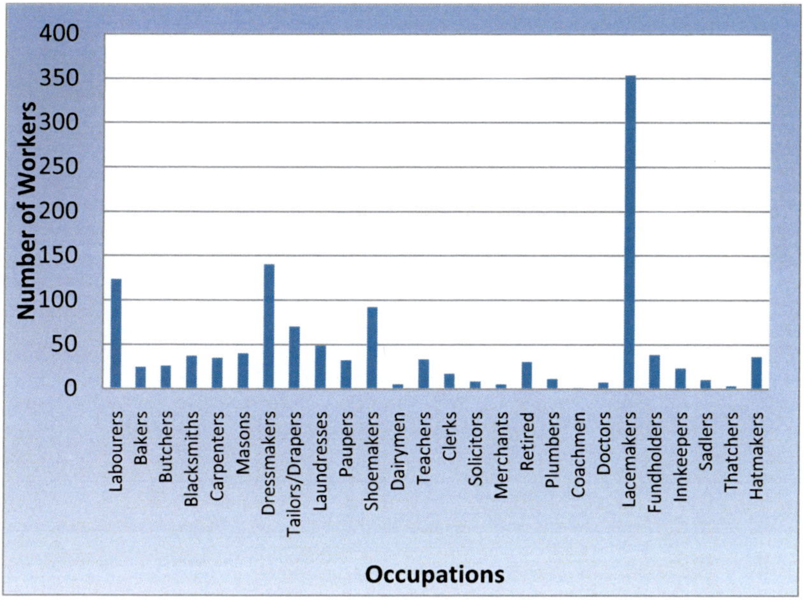

Above: Cross section of number of Honiton workers in a variety of trades, in 1851.

It is obvious from the graph that the most common occupations were also the poorest paid. Directories of the time can be deceptive when dealing with trades of a location. Although Whites Directory of 1850 states that there were only 10 tailors/drapers in the town, there were, in fact, 70 people working as tailors/drapers; the directories only listing the registered head of each business which did not include the vast number of staff working within each respective business or those working from home. As an example of what drapers may have supplied and what one may have expected to pay for said items, here is an extract from an order, from 1892, to Mr. Charles Harding, who ran a drapery shop where Specsavers now stands.

Item	Cost (per yard, unless otherwise stated)
Blue Skipe	6 ¾d
Serge	8 ¾d
Cambury	7 ½d
Calico (bleached/unbleached/fine)	4d/ 3 ½d/ 3d
Cheak	7 ½d
Lindsey Woolsey	1s, 4 ¾
Stay Cloth	6d
Fustian	1s, 4 ½d
Bed Tick	7 ¾d
Flannel	11 ¼d
Linen Sheeting	2s, 6d
Coverlids	2s, 8 ½d
Worsted (dark speckled/black)	1s, 7 ½d/1s, 6 ½d
Men's & Women's Handkerchiefs	5s, 11d per dozen
Coarse & Fine Barrus	5d/8 ¾d

The most prolific form of work in the town was lace- making followed, maybe not so surprisingly, by dressmaking. Dressmaking was such a demanding business in the Victorian era because the fashionable clothing for women of the time "was closely fitted and intricately cut". It was, therefore, necessary for a large number of dressmakers to craft every dress to the buyer's specific measurements. Dressmaking also went hand in hand with the lace-making industry that was so prominent in the town at the time.

Agricultural labourers are surprisingly the third most prevalent form of employment, leaving Honiton with a female dominated workforce! As of 2001, agriculture accounted for less than 3% of Honiton's working population, with most people being employed in the wholesale/retail trade. Although dressmaking was a relatively low paid occupation, it was mainly a small additional form of income for the housewife on top of the meagre earnings of the man of the household. Dressmakers who took on apprentices could, however, lead a prosperous life and earn upwards of £70 a year; this would only be in established premises though, not a poor labourers' wife working from a small rural cottage.

Servitude was a good occupation for a woman to enter into for she would be provided with bed and board, allowing her time to build up some savings - the life was hard though. The humble housemaid would rise at

5.30am to make breakfast for the senior staff by 6.30am and would be expected to not only clean up after the master and mistress but also the servants above her: bed was at 9pm. Entering into the service of a private house would also enable a poorer girl to escape the poverty of home. The need for employment of live-in servants slowly died away with the coming of the new machines and technologies of the twentieth century that could do much of the former servants' work. In 1851 there were 251 live-in servants in Honiton, of which 92% were born in the West Country, 82% being born in Devon. This shows that although many local people moved to the cities for this type of work, those employed locally did not travel far. The older trades and craftsmen of the 19th century lasted well into the twentieth century. In a Honiton Guide of the 1930s there were quoted to be "a good number of cunning craftsmen, hedgers, thatchers, saddlers, shoeing smiths, coopers and so forth."

Those who were fortunate enough to be presented with apprenticeship opportunities would, after several years training, have a trade that would earn them a respectable wage. An apprenticeship would usually be set up by the father of the individual and would often involve a legally binding contract, as well as a fee to be paid to the master who was to teach the child. This is why it was generally only the more affluent who could allow their children this privilege. An apprenticeship was, however, a long and arduous learning curve that took many years to complete. An example of such is that of William Porter, son of William Porter, a saddler of Honiton. In 1822, Mr. Porter apprenticed his son to Samuel Stocker, a brazier of Exeter. The apprenticeship was to last 7 years during which time William Porter Jnr. was to obey Mr. Stocker's "lawful command" and "his secrets keep". The working hours were long though: from November to February he was to work from 7am until 8pm, six days a week, with half an hour for breakfast, one hour for dinner and twenty minutes for "tea". Between March and October the hours were 6am until 8pm with the same allowances for meals. For the first year of his apprenticeship he was to be paid only one shilling a week which increased to 1s.6d in the second year, 2s. in the third year, 2s.6d in the fourth year, 3s. in the fifth, 3s.6d for the sixth and four shillings in his seventh and final year. Mr. Stocker was required to provide young William with "sufficient table beer or cider to drink" and to allow him 3 days at Easter, six days at Christmas and another unspecified 3 days of holiday. The terms of the agreement did not, however, include any allowances for being ill, for "to be sick or incapable of working" Mr. Stocker would not be required to "pay the said weekly sums of wages during such times."

When Mr. Porter qualified in 1829 he would be an artisan and could expect to earn over £1 a week which, at the time, was considered to be a comfortable wage.

Such individuals who were able to gain apprenticeships were deemed the aristocracy of the working classes. Becoming qualified by 20 and marrying in their mid to late twenties was of sufficient time for both the man and his new wife to have saved money. They would "have a carpet in the front room" and would be of the newly developing middle class.

Further education was, however, generally only a venture for the rich, and whilst the higher paid artisan may have been able to send his children into apprenticeships, secondary and tertiary educations were exclusively for the upper classes. Books were excessively expensive: a hard bound novel, in three volumes, cost over 31 shillings and with little schooling, illiteracy was common, meaning the poor were trapped in their poverty. A university education would require a father to put aside £150 a year from birth.

Children of poorer families had no real opportunities; before 1870 school was not compulsory and all children would be expected to work as soon as possible to bring money into the home. Ten years after marriage was probably the worst time for a poor couple as they would generally have several dependant children under the age of ten who would be too young to work. Even in 1870, when schooling became compulsory, the leaving age was only 10 and few children were expected to attend school during the busy harvest times. There was some government intervention for the protection of children early in Victoria's reign for in 1844 a law was passed forbidding children under the age of 13 from working the full 48 hours a week! There would, therefore, be no, or little, time or money for a child from a poor family to further themselves anymore than their parents.

The average wage for a man in the 1850s was 11 shillings a week and the majority of working men were not even earning this.

Chapter 2
Life of Labourers & the Poor

"Go forth to thine work, til' ends light of day.
Go hence to the fields, and bring in ye hay.
Go thence to thy Master, for weeks meagre pay.
Go Mad if thoust will, be no other way."
The Author

Working the land was one of the most dominant forms of employment in Victorian Honiton: over 20% of the entire working male population worked as labourers and this was reflected in the rest of the country with over one quarter of all males being employed in agriculture in 1851. The life of a labourer was a long and hard one for very little money and many labourers' children were sent to neighbouring farms for extra money. One woman, Mary Puddicombe of Bridford, told her story about her early years as a labourer's apprentice in the early 19th century. She was sent to a farm for her apprenticeship when she was 9, where she shared a bed with 3 others. Her days were spent out in the fields driving bullocks, bedding the animals, washing potatoes, pulling root vegetables, leading bullocks and horses to plough and milking. She rose at five or six in the morning except on market days when it was three: bedtime was at half past nine. Mary went on to become a washer woman which, she stated, was "harder than working in the fields"!
The treatment of these child labourers/apprentices was poor and beatings were commonplace: Mary stated that she was "beat black and blue" and when complaining to her parents about it she was told to be "a better maiden next time"! She stated that the "apprentices were treated worse": one woman had her arm cut to the bone when she was hit with a stick from a hedgerow for not harrowing properly!
Treatment of workers was poor and the majority simply had to endure the life, although some such punishments proved too much. In 1799, a 16 year old girl, apprenticed to a milliner, had been "reprimanded" for "misconduct in her business"; she was apparently so affected by the course of events that she threw herself into the River Otter and drowned.

Labourers were not held in high regard by those who could witness and write about them. Charles Vancouver, in his book titled 'General View of Agriculture of the County of Devon' (1808), wrote...

"Even in summer when at day-work, the labourer is frequently seen on his way home with his tools upon his back thus early in the evening. This does not arise so much from absolute idleness"

The 'idle' labourer usually worked from 7am until 12pm when an hour was given for lunch and then 1pm until 5/6pm, with much longer hours worked in the summer, and was expected to complete so much work per day. If labourers were thrashing wheat, they would be expected to get through 5 bundles @ 28lb each, if harvesting barley no less that 12 35lb bundles were expected by the end of the day and if he/she was working with oats, the master would expect each worker to produce 16 40lb bundles by sun down.

For all their hard work, the labourer and his family could expect "a score perches of dunged land" for the cultivation of their own crops; this was often rented at between 6d-8d per perch.

There was a lot of tension between labourers and farmers which often led to crimes, such as arson and burglary. "Devonshire farmers as a class were not noted for their generosity towards their workers" and many of these workers were tied to a specific cottage which came with their job. This led to virtually complete dependency upon the tenant farmer or Lord of the Manor and considering the conditions of most of the houses in which they lived, these tensions were easy to understand.

The picture that many of us may have of a typical Devonian village, of a florally enriched, serene setting where little white, thatched cottages stand in disorganised harmony, could not be further from the truth to the actual state in which many of these little settlements once existed.

Poor living conditions were all too common in rural Devon and the "chronic shortage" of cottages left many workers living in semi- derelict properties. "Such cottages as existed were all too often horrible, dark damp places where a man and his wife were crippled with rheumatism before they were forty."

A travelling writer, visiting East Devon in 1849, wrote a letter to 'The Morning Chronicle' about the poor state in which agricultural labourers lived. Although his detailed account did not include Honiton, he stated that "of all the cottages" he visited in the region, Honiton exampled "the most wretched specimens". ..

"In traversing both counties, more especially Devonshire, I was particularly struck with the utter absence of new cottages. Along the highways and by ways their absence is observable; and not only this—but in many places

there are abundant evidences that cottages, which a few years ago were tenanted, are now, if not altogether untenantable, going rapidly into decay. Many are so rickety and ruined, that to inhabit them any longer is impossible; whilst, as regards others, the process of demolition or decomposition has only commenced— confining the wretched tenants, who had formerly two rooms, to the only apartment which remains, and which they can with difficulty keep together. In search of these, one has not to go into remote and sequestered parts, where things are done which would not be exposed in the neighbourhood of the highways. I have seen specimens of cottages in this state along the line from Exeter to Honiton, and in the district traversed by the high road to London. One in particular struck my attention, from its dilapidated appearance, and the discomforts to which it obviously subjected its inmates. The upper part of one of the end walls was entirely away, exposing the crazy anatomy of the roof, and laying the whole of what used to form the sleeping apartment of the family bare to every tempest that swept around their miserable house. I entered this fragment of a cottage, and found the family to consist of seven. The dilapidated wall had, for some years, shown signs of weakness; but no effort was make to repair it. At length it became so shaken that the only resource left appeared to be to pull down its upper part, and leave the lower and sounder portion standing. This was done, but nothing—not even a boarding—was put to supply its place, so that the family were driven to occupy the lower apartment only, unless they could contrive to sleep in a room exposed on one whole side to the elements. The lower room, which was about 16 feet square, with a mouldering brick floor, served as kitchen, sitting-room, and bed-room for seven people. The ceiling, which was rickety, bulged downwards, as if oppressed with its own weight—whilst through the gaping beams, with which it was replete, trickled the rain, whenever it was driven by the wind into the dismantled room above. The approaching winter will be the second spent by them in this wretched ruin."

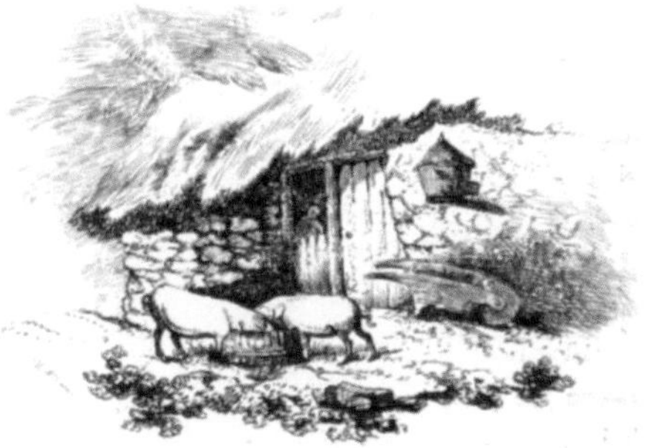

The following is this gentleman's account of the residences of the poor who lived and worked in the parish of Southleigh, only 6 miles from the "most wretched specimens" of Honiton. This gentleman's first encounter, on descending into Southleigh, was with a woman aged about 50. In attempting to engage her in conversation he found she had refused payment of rent to her landlord for "twal'month". When the gentleman enquired as to the reason behind this the woman replied ...

""Because the house isn't fit for a pig to live in,
let alone a Christian,"... with great indignation.""

The man asked how long she had been resident there to which she told him it had been a total of twenty year "in this piggery"!
The gentlemen then investigated her hovel and in turn several others in the village...

""We had by this time gained the house, but before entering I thought it as well to examine its exterior. It was a cottage, containing, like too many others, but two rooms ; the walls were of mud, or rather of what is called " cob "—a kind of mixture of mud and small stones. The roof was of thatch, and had been recently repaired in parts. Each room had but one window; that in the upper room, which was in the gable end of the cottage, being extremely small. On three sides of the house there were great cracks or fissures in the walls, all of which added to its discomforts, and one of which positively endangered its stability : it was in the front of the cottage, near one of the corners, and ran from the thatch to the ground, occasioned by the end wall having fallen considerably from the perpendicular. I asked her if she was not afraid that the house would come down about her ears. She replied to the effect that her apprehensions had been blunted, as they had been excited by the same cause for the last ten years. I then entered the hovel.
Bad and unprepossessing as was its exterior, it did not half prepare me for what I witnessed inside. The chimney stalk was at the side of the door, and its side formed with the wall a small passage, about five feet long, at the end of which was another door, suspended upon one hinge, which opened into the lower apartment. In the recess formed by the other side of the chimney stalk and the opposite wall was the window, so small and so situated that it threw but a shabby twilight into about one-half of the room. The other half was equally lighted when the door was open; but when it was shut it was in such a gloom that it was scarcely possible to discern the objects which it contained. I requested her to leave the door open, that I might see to more advantage, but chiefly—although I did not

tell her so—that I might have the, benefit of the fresh air, to counteract the sour and sickening smells which were rife within. The ceiling, which was blackened with smoke, was so low that it was only between the small rafters that I could stand erect with my hat on. The fire-place was of an enormous size; but although the day was cold and raw, there was not at the time a spark of fire upon the hearth. There were a few chairs and some tripods, in the shape of stools ; about and within the ample fireplace was a bit of log, supported on four rude legs, which formed a kind of bench, on which about three could sit at a time, sheltered by the chimneystalk, in which they sat, from the drafts which pervaded the room in every direction. At one corner was an empty barrel, which answered the purposes of a table, and close to it an old deal chest, over which were two or three shelves full of crockery of all shapes, colours, and devices, and in all stages of fracture. Hard by was a large black-looking tub, in which there was a quantity of flour which had recently been sifted from the bran. In the centre of the room was the moiety of an old round table, at which the family partook of their meals. What these were will be afterwards mentioned. In the deep recess occupied by the window sat the eldest daughter of my guide, working hard at the lace-cushion, taking that position as the one which afforded her most light in the room ..The floor of the hovel was of mud. It had never known the covering of quicklime and sand, which frequently forms the flooring of the cottages, and which is to be seen in some of those in the village. Towards the fire-place it descended so as to form a tolerably deep hole, in which water not unfrequently collects, and which has been prevented from deepening still further by a species of rough causeway work with which it is lined. With this exception, you trod nothing, whilst in the lower room, but the cold clay which formed the uneven flooring. I hesitated ere I ventured up stairs. The family was not large, as most of the children were grown up, and were afloat on the world for themselves. But there were still five at home—the father and mother, a young man of 21 years of age, a girl of about l8, and another girl of about 13. The five slept in the room above. In this instance it was more the chamber itself than its furniture that was at fault. It was wretchedly lighted, and the room seemed, in places, to be falling in. To ventilation it was an utter stranger. The crazy floor shook and creaked under me as I paced it. The bedroom was approached by a few broken steps, which rose to it out of a dark recess opposite the door, and in which were stowed away a few pots and pans, some small bundles of faggots, pieces of broken furniture, and a few implements of labour.

"What do you think of it now ?" asked my guide, after I had emerged into the light and fresh air; " is it fit for a pig to live in ?" With its cracked walls,

its clay floor, its imperfect light, and unwholesome atmosphere, I certainly could not say that it was fit to be the abode of a human being. "What rent do you pay ?" I asked. "A shilling a week," she replied—a rent for which, in many places, the labourer has a very comfortable home.

The next cottage which I inspected was situated directly opposite the one described. As in that case, the walls were of cob-work, and the roof of thatch. It was one of two cottages which were attached together. The door was in the gable end, which faced the main road. Like that just visited, it had but two apartments, one above and the other below. What struck me before entering was the condition of the window designed to admit light into the lower room. The aperture in the wall was about two feet high and about fifteen inches wide. This was occupied by a leaden window frame, with small diamond-shaped panes. Some of them were filled with glass, some with brown paper, and others with rags—whilst a large piece of rusty sheet-iron occupied the place of several of them which had been broken. It was difficult to recognize it as a window. Small as it was, only about one-half of it was serviceable for the admission of light, the only purpose to which the other half was applied being the exclusion of fresh air. I entered the cottage, and on my eyes becoming accustomed to the twilight within, I found myself in the presence of five small children and a woman who appeared to be their mother. The floor, as in the other case, was of clay, and the ceiling so low that I had to stoop to walk about. The cottage was, in every way, as wretched in its appearance and accommodation as that which I had just quitted—whilst the general condition of its inmates as much worse than in the other case, seeing that the family was comparatively large, and all the children of so tender an age that they could not work. I asked to be shown up stairs, and groped my way to where I supposed the staircase to be. But instead of a flight of steps, no matter how rude or unsteady, I came in contact with what seemed to be a perpendicular ladder, which led through a hole in the ceiling. On inquiring if this was the only means of communication with the upper apartment, I was informed that it was. It was up and down this that children of two and three year of age had to climb up daily, to get to and from their miserable dormitory. The poor woman observed that she was in daily dread of some accident happening, especially to the younger children, in their ascents and descents. It was not an uncommon thing for them to tumble, especially on endeavouring to descend; but hitherto such mishaps had not been attended with any serious consequences, for the clay floor on which they fell was generally moist and soft. As for herself she did not much care about it, having become accustomed to it; but it was rather a difficult job to go up and down when she had a child at the breast. She had not the means herself of improving her staircase or repairing her window, nor was her landlord disposed to aid her in so doing.

The cottage attached to this had rather a sad story connected with it. It was built of precisely the same materials as its neighbour, and was of about the same dimensions. The end looking upon the hill behind the village had been overgrown with ivy, which had been cut down, as it was supposed that it rendered the cottage damp. The dead wood of the mutilated parasite was still thickly imbedded in the wall, as it could not be pulled out without endangering the stability of the edifice. On scanning the wall closely, one could see near the angle of the roof a square hole, in which there was a casement with four panes of glass. The whole window did not look more than fifteen inches square, yet it was all the means by which light was admitted into the upper chamber of the hovel. There was no tenant occupying it at the time, the door being locked—nor is it likely that it will ever be opened again for the admission of another occupant. In the course of a few more years, it will be another cottage blotted from the face of England. As the last occupant had died about a month before. She had been long an invalid, and was removed, shortly before her last struggles, to a cot not far distant, that she might not die alone. About the close of last year, as I was informed by some of the villagers, she was frequently visited by the lady of the vicar of the parish, of both of whom they all spoke in terms of the greatest kindness and affection. Her malady was increasing, and she was then confined to her bed in the upper room of the cottage. On the occasion of her first visit to the invalid, this lady is reported to have said to her, " Betty, do you not feel this room too cold for your" " Yes," she replied, "I do; but you see there is no glass in the window, and it has been so for a long time." It was as she represented. There was not a single pane in the casement. The temperature without was consequently that within. The wind rushed in whenever there was any stirring; the rain, when it fell, encroached upon the floor, and sometimes upon the very bed; and on stormy winter days, when the snow was driven before the blast, it would enter at the open casement, and form tiny wreaths upon the floor. "And was it allowed to remain open I" I asked my informant. "It would have been, sir, but that the vicar had it glassed at his own expense," was the answer. And who was she whose last sickness was thus aggravated by the cruel discomforts of her home. One who for five-and-twenty years of her life had been a faithful servant to the squire! Her reward, on becoming superannuated in the service, was the liberty to occupy this doomed cottage rent free. We hear of horses which have served their owners long and faithfully been pensioned off upon the best pastures for life. Dining my peregrinations through Oxfordshire I was told of the case of one horse which had served its master so long and well that, after he could no longer eat grass, he had it fed on slops, and finally on sugar, to prolong its existence. It died at last in a comfortable stall. But there was no such sympathy in store for poor "Betty" in the day of her extremity. I was anxious to see the room in which this forlorn invalid had lain bed-ridden for so many months; but I could not do so, as the door was locked, and all entrance prevented. I could, however, see into the lower apartment through the window—it was like the rest, "not fit for a pig, let alone a Christian, to live in."

I crossed the road, and entered another hut, which overlooked the churchyard. It had two apartments below, and but one, I believe, above. The outer of the two lower apartments seemed to be abandoned by the inmates, and looked as if it would have been applied to the purposes of a storehouse, had there been anything to store away in it. I passed through it to get to the inner apartment. Everything was grim and black, the ceiling being low, and the floor composed of earth. The water was trickling in different directions about it and no wonder. The aperture which contained the window was divided into three parts, something like a Venetian window, by two perpendicular pieces of wood, which formed the staple of the casement. There was neither glass nor sash in the middle portion, nor had there been since it was tenanted by its present occupants, which it had been for many years. It was open and summer, except when they chose to close it up with some opaque substance, which they seldom did, as they would be thereby deprived of light.

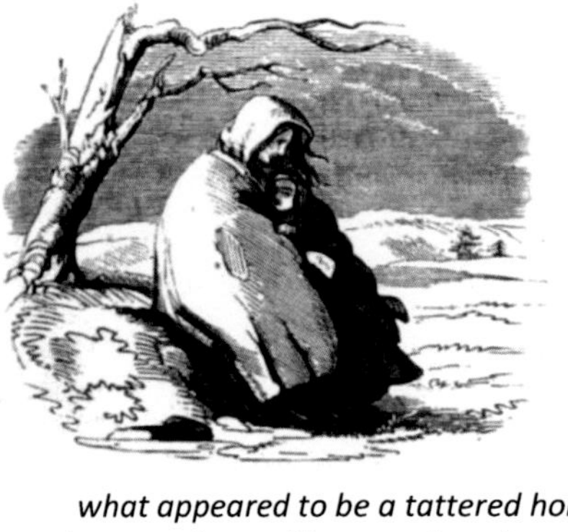

One winter it was intensely cold, and they had it boarded up. It remained so, however, but for a very short time, for the board was soon taken down to be burnt as firewood. Immediately below the open window was a cradle, in which an infant was being rocked. It was nothing but a black greasy box, shattered a little on one side, and placed upon a couple of rough rockers. The child was covered by what appeared to be a tattered horsecloth. Only a few days before, I had inspected a workhouse, where I was shown the apartment which served as a nursery for the children. What a contrast did their comfortable circumstances present to the wretched accommodation of this child of

honest and industrious parents! I remained below whilst one of the family went up stairs to show me the state of the ceiling. There was scarcely a plank but seemed to yield under her feet, whilst the seams which extended along the floor at one corner were so broad as to expose to those above everything going on below. The first thing which meets the squire's eye on coming from church is this ruinous hovel with its ever open window. He certainly cannot plead ignorance of the condition of his tenants...

My next visit was to a small tenement divided into two dwellings...On entering I found the floor paved with small stones, after the fashion of a rough and irregular causeway, with a kind of gutter in the centre to let the water run off", for the house lay low and was very damp. Passing through this, which seemed to serve the purposes of a lumberroom, I entered the "day-room" of the family. It was more comfortably furnished than I expected to find it, especially as I had been informed that the tenant had been disabled for some time by rheumatism from working. How a rheumatic patient could expect ever to recover in such a place was to me a mystery, for the earthern floor was quite damp and cold after the rains which had recently fallen. His wife was seated at the lace-cushion by the window, working very industriously, but complaining of her head. Beside her sat a young girl, also with a lace-cushion before her, engaged in making large sprigs, which were to form part of a bridal scarf and veil for some fair lady who was about to be led to the altar. There was still another in the room—an old man, who sat in a corner by the window, sewing a piece of flannel. He was about sixty, but looked older. A few grey hairs still clung to the sides of his head, just above his ears, but all the rest was bald. He had on the top of his head a scar, which was partly hidden by a piece of dirty sticking plaster. He continued his work, but in a most unworkmanlike manner, apparently taking no heed of anything passing around him. I stepped up to him, and asked what he was about, to which he replied that, having nothing to do out of doors, he was employing himself by "doing a bit of tailoring." The whole picture was a curious one: the rheumatic invalid seated by the feeble fire, his wife and daughter working busily over their lace-cushions at the window, and the old man making a waistcoat for himself in a way which plainly showed that "tailoring" was not his vocation. Had the accommodation been better, it would not have been, on the whole, an unpleasing one—but the cottage was one of the worst description, although everything in it in the shape of furniture was neat and clean.

The dwelling adjoining it had a better entrance, but the accommodation which it afforded was not a whit better. Here, also, the lace-cushion was in requisition, and the inmates were subject to rheumatism, from the dampness of the floor, which, like that of most of the other houses, was of earth. A part of it looked as if it had been recently under water. On inquiry, I found that it had been so—as it was more or less, indeed, after every heavy rain. In these cases the water was removed by soaking cloths in it, and wringing them dry out of doors.

These last-mentioned cottages, with one or two others, occupied the lowest ground covered by the village. Until recently their unwholesomeness and other discomfort! were greatly aggravated by a broad stagnant open ditch, which exposed its putrescent contents on the other side of the road. The offensive smells which used to emanate from this hotbed of pestilence were spoken of by the inmates as something incapable of description. "You should have tried them, sir," said a woman who had waxed eloquent on the subject. I told her that I could fancy what they were, and would content myself therewith. Yet, bad and pestiferous as was the malaria engendered by this reeking abomination, it was never removed until the vicar took the matter up.

After visiting a hovel situated in the midst of some copsewood, a little distance up the slope of the opposite bank, and in which the inmates were obliged, whilst working at the lace-cushion, to place boards under their feet to protect them from the cold wet floor, I betook myself to the residence of one of the farmers of the neighbourhood. In this part of Devonshire the number of "small farmers" is very large. This gives rise to many evils, some of which will be alluded to in a subsequent communication. How far they retard the progress of the agricultural labourer may be inferred from the simple fact, that in many cases they are contented with house accommodation little if at all better than that of the labourer who is so badly housed. The person in question was one of this class. He was an elderly man, of rough exterior and stem character. During the war, an endeavour was made to force him into the militia; but having no taste for military glory, he put a stop to all the persuasions of the authorities, and to the suggestions of patriotism, by chopping off a part of the forefinger of his right hand. This disabled him from manipulating a musket, but it did not prevent him from handling the plough. He has ever since farmed in the neighbourhood on a small scale, in doing which he has amassed a little money. His house was some distance up the hill; but although it might have been well and easily drained, it was scarcely drained at all; for at one end, and partly in front of it, filthy solutions had accumulated to a disgusting extent. They were powerfully impregnated with an infusion of a rotten dung-heap, which supported itself against the gable end of the house. His wife was ill of a mortal disease. She was able to sit up, and was accompanied by her sister, who had come from some distance to see her. They were both seated within the huge chimney stalk, at the back of which burnt a more ample fire than I had seen in any of the other houses. Behind them, and as it were on one side of the stalk, was a window, which lighted up the huge fire-place. On my suggesting that such was hardly the place for an invalid, I was told that it was selected as the most comfortable part of the room. Every now and then a puff of wind would come suddenly down the chimney, and envelope the invalid and her companion in smoke. The house was in no respect better than that of many an agricultural labourer of the class not the most comfortably housed; but it was in some respects superior to most of those in the village below. The lower room had, for instance, two windows, instead of one; its floor was of lime and clay, which kept it hard and dry, and there was a little more room between it and the floor of the upper chamber. It also contained more furniture; that which it had being cleaner and less mutilated than the furniture in the other houses, but in all other respects—in size, in general appearance, and in style and design, and in its external accompaniments—it would have been difficult to distinguish it from the rest. It was anything but what one would picture to oneself as an English farmer's home.

A little lower down the hill was the residence of another farmer, who cultivated on a somewhat larger scale. It also contained an invalid, a young man, who was just recovering from an acute rheumatic fever. When I entered he was expecting a visit from the clergyman, who also acted the part of physician to his flock. The house was a degree better than that last alluded to. There was a spacious yard in front, surrounded by a number of out-houses. In the midst of it was a filthy pond, surrounded with manure and garbage of every kind, from which proceeded an atmosphere which it weakened one in every joint to inhale. When farmers themselves are contented with such hovels, it is no wonder that they think the agricultural labourer sufficiently well off in his den, or that the landlord—perhaps taking the farmer's notions of comfort as his standard—does nothing towards ameliorating the condition of his humbler tenantry. For all the hovels described—as well as for others of which they may serve as specimens—rents are paid. In amount the rents vary but little from each other, and they are in general far too high. For the same rent that is paid for these cottages, accommodations on a much better scale are enjoyed by the labourer even in Wiltshire. But few of the cottagers at Southleigh have gardens attached to their houses. Most of them have small field allotments, which are supplied to them by the vicar, at a reasonable rent. In these they raise cabbages and turnips, and, but to a small extent now, potatoes. The failure of the potatoes for several successive years has occasioned the people to lose their former faith in them. They regret, however, not having planted more this year, seeing that the crop has been, generally speaking, both abundant and good, and that they find it difficult to make up for the want of them, turnips being but a poor substitute. The average rent of the cottages is about 50s. a year. The name of the landlord whose tenantry are so deplorably circumstanced is, as I have already stated, Gordon. It is now many years since he came into possession of the property, which he did by purchase, I was given to understand that there was not a cottage in the parish then which was not in a far better state than it is now. They have been gradually going to wreck and ruin—but little, if any effort having been made to save them; and all this time, as already stated, the population has been increasing—so much so, indeed, as to require a large addition to be made to the parish church. The cottages have been getting more and more crowded every year, and the whole condition of their inmates more and more wretched. The mansion of the proprietor is about a mile from the village, and is known as Wiscombe Park. For several years after he took possession he resided at the Park—a course which had a very sensible effect upon the employment and comforts of the villagers, But for many years past he has chiefly lived in the neighbourhood of Exeter. His son, however, has recently been residing for some months at the Park and his presence was of considerable advantage to the poor people. Mr. Gordon has lately revisited Wiscombe; but, should he leave, and his son not re-occupy the house, the condition of the poor will be one of extreme privation during the winter. For some time past, in their hour of difficulty and sickness, they have had none to whom to look for advice and relief but the resident clergyman and his family. The living is but a small one, and it is very hard that the incumbent should be called upon to bear unaided so grave a responsibility and so heavy a burden.

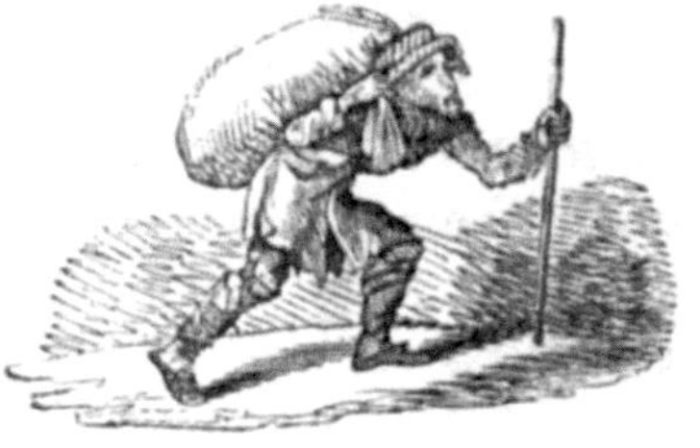

I mention this case in all its circumstances, because it is one of the most striking that has presented itself to me, and because it illustrates, though perhaps to an extreme degree, much that is going on in many parts of the country, to alienate the affections of the poor from their social superiors. In Southleigh and its neighbourhood I could trace but too clearly the extent to which this alienation was going on. Mr. Gordon is not the only proprietor in

the parish, though he is the principal one, and the village belongs to him. Of none of the parish squires—nor, indeed, of any of the surrounding proprietors—did the villagers speak either with respect or affection. On inquiring into the origin of this hostile feeling, I invariably found that it was traceable to a belief that the proprietors cared not what became of the labourers. Even apart from those considerations of duty and benevolence which should prompt a landlord to bind himself with his people in the strong bonds of a mutual sympathy, the calculations of prudence should suggest the adoption of a humane and considerate fine of conduct. I have been astonished at the extent to which I have found Socialist doctrines prevailing amongst the rural poor. They know nothing of Socialism as a distinct political theory; but its principles had made their way amongst them to a considerable extent—their progress being promoted, if it was not originated, by the daily contemplation of their own wretched lot. They contend that they have "a right to live, and to live comfortably, as well as the best of them"—and they begin to reason with themselves that they cannot do this until land is treated, not as a property, but as a trust. They have at present no organization or mutual understanding by which they might attempt to carry such doctrine' into practice; but they are becoming more and more imbued with these sentiments, and many of them will tell you so.

But bad as are the tenements usually occupied by the poor, they are not, except in rare cases, quite so revolting in their character, and in the scenes to which they give rise, as are some tenements which have a claim to be regarded in the light of public buildings. These are the parish houses, which are Mattered in considerable numbers over the southern and western districts. They are the houses in which the poor were accommodated previously to the erection of the union workhouses. In many cases, since the workhouses came into use, these parish houses have been sold, and the proceeds applied to defraying pro taute the expense of building the workhouses. But in others, the overseers will not part with them, keeping them for the purpose of letting, and thus deriving a profit from them. They are generally let at a lower rent than ordinary cottages, and thus become the resort of those in the most wretched circumstances, who crowd into them by dozens, and fill up almost every crevice of them with lodgers. One of these I saw on the borders of Devonshire and Cornwall, and not far from Launceston. It consisted of two houses, containing between them four rooms. In each room was a family, who used it both night and day; the lower rooms were about twelve feet square; in one of them were a man and his wife and five children; in the other were a man and his wife and eight children; in this latter there were but two beds—the father and mother and two children occupying one, and the other six being huddled together into the remaining bed. They lay "head and foot," as they termed it—that is to say, three with their heads at the top, and three with them at the foot of the bed. The eldest girl was between fifteen and sixteen, and the eldest boy between fourteen and fifteen. The closeness of this room was overpowering. The beds were necessarily large, and occupied most of the floor; indeed, when the whole family was assembled, several of the children were placed upon the beds to keep them out of the way. In this way the beds may be said to have never been cold. How can health be retained or morals preserved under such circumstances as these ?...

Is it not horrible to think of men and women being brought up in this foul and brutish manner in civilized and Christian England! The lowest of savages are not worse cared for than these children of a luxurious and refined country.""

This *long letter* was reported in other publications where the people, so described, were titled as "the white slaves of England" while their landlord, Mr. Gordon, lived as the equivalent of a millionaire today.

A labourer earned only seven shillings per week at this time, so had little choice where to home himself and his family. In 1852, one family were noted that from the earned seven shillings, one shilling would go to the farmer for rent of the family cottage and they were obliged to pay 6 shillings per bushel of wheat, of which the family bought 3 pecks a week (4 pecks per bushel). In the family there were seven in total and after rent and wheat allowance, all that was left of the man's wage was 1s.6d. Appropriately the writer thus stated "how did they live?"

The winters in such hovels and poor conditions proved even more dangerous for these rural residents than the rains or winds of other seasons. In Wellington, Somerset, one boy of 12 lost both his legs from the severe winter of 1849. A worse case, some 60 years earlier, was reported of two women who were found dead on St. Cyres Hill in the December of 1791. They had been travelling back from the Saturday market in the evening and had lost their way in the snow. Both ladies were subsequently found on the Sunday; both of them left large families, one having eleven dependant children. One of the women was found still holding the bridle of her horse, which had devoutly remained by her side.

As part of their wages, labourers were expected to be provided with ale or, more commonly in Devon, cider to drink during the working day. Water was often dangerous to drink: in 1832 Honiton lost 300 people to a cholera epidemic. A labourer would be allowed between "a quart" and 3 pints a day of their preferred beverage. This was such a staple part of the

labourers life and pay that when Anthony Bacon, a political candidate openly supported a tax of '4 shillings per hogshead' on cider in 1763, the streets were said to have run red, and even the Gissage was tinted pink with the blood spilt in the ensuing riots! The winning candidate, Sir George Younge, promptly saw the proposals abolished.
Everyone in the family was expected to work at as early an age as possible. Lace-making was the most common form of female employment around Honiton and one would be able to see women and children around their lace pillows morning and night. These women were paid very small amounts of money and sometimes not even money at all. In 1852 a writer asked a child lace-maker what she earned and was told it was 1s.6d; however, the girl was usually paid in butter and sugar, for if she was paid in money the buyer expected to be supplied with 7d worth of lace for only 6d payment and, in turn, fourteen pence payment for a shilling's worth of lace.
In the long evenings of winter, the poor would struggle to work at this low paid craft by rushlights. The rushlight was a very common form of household lighting for very poor families. The common rush plant would be collected, dried, and then the stalk would be dipped in tallow fat and allowed to set. The light from these primitive candles was poor and a twelve inch stalk would only provide the user with a maximum of about 15 minutes of light. The majority of people lit their home with the more common tallow candles - the same concept as the rushlight but instead of a stalk, it was made from a central wick covered with many layers of animal fat that gave longer periods of better light. These were generally bought from a dealer.

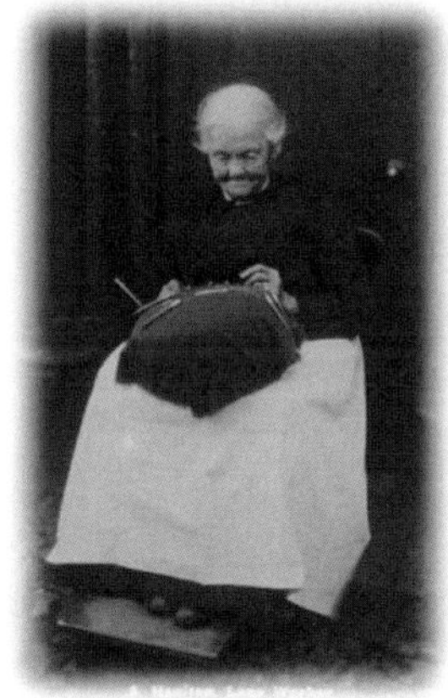

Mrs. Adelaide Salter (nee Billing) a Honiton lace-maker who, at the time of her death in 1939, had been making lace for over 60 years

One step down from the poor labourer were the residents in the dreaded and infamous workhouses where, in 1851, nearly 20% of the residents were failed or infirm agricultural labourers.

Chapter 3
The Honiton Poor Law Union & Workhouse

"The able-bodied men's dining-room on Sundays gave one as near an approach to hell as anything on this earth... The men boasted that prison had no worse terrors than that place."
Enquiry of Workhouse Conditions: Will Crooks, 1906

With the dissolution of the monasteries, under the reign of Henry VIII, a great amount of relief for the poor of the land had been destroyed and by the end of the 16th century it had become clear that government intervention was needed. The Elizabethan Poor Law Act of 1601 gave the responsibility of the poor to their individual parishes. This was often given in a form of 'out-relief' that would include food, clothing and other bare necessities. By the 1720s, it was becoming more common for parishes to have a local workhouse in order to deter any other than the very desperate from claiming relief. The Oxford English Dictionary's earliest reference to a workhouse is that of Exeter in 1652. In 1732 there were an estimated 700 workhouses in operation and in 1738 Honiton had its own one built. The old Honiton Workhouse was located on the site where 'Summerland Place' now stands. The land and building were owned by Allhallows Charity and some three houses were demolished to complete its construction. The workhouse had a garden, space for some 60 people and in 1793 it was described as "large, neat and healthy." This building was the parish workhouse for nearly a century until the entire poor relief system was reassessed under The Poor Law Amendment Act of 1834.
The following was a description of a typical workhouse just before the Act of 1834, as printed in the *'Report from the Commissioners inquiring into the Administration and Practical Operation of the Poor Laws, 1834.'*

"In parishes overburthened with poor we usually find the building called a workhouse occupied by 60 or 80 children (under the care, perhaps, of a pauper), about 20 or 30 able-bodied paupers of both sexes, and probably an equal number of aged and impotent persons, the proper objects of relief. Amidst these, the mothers of bastard children and prostitutes live without shame and associate freely with the youth, who have also the examples and conversation of the frequent inmates of the county gaol, the poacher, the vagrant, the decayed beggar, and other characters of the worst description. To these may often be added a solitary blind person, one or two idiots and not unfrequently are heard among the rest, the incessant

raving of some neglected lunatic. In such receptacles the sick poor are often immured."

It was clear from this report that by the early 1800s the Act of 1601, and all its subsequent amendments, were excessively out of date and that the need for an entirely new way of dealing with the poor was required.
The Act of 1834 was set about to completely reform and change the way in which the poor were provided for. Its main aim was to do away with 'outdoor relief' and form the basis of care from the confines of a solitary building for each Union, an idea that had already been implemented in many of the country's parishes, including Honiton. The dreaded 'workhouse', possibly the most infamous creation of the Victorian era, was immortalised by one of the age's most famous protagonists, Charles Dickens. The doing away with 'outdoor relief' was not, however, completely successful as many unions, including Honiton, actually requested a "relaxation" of this rule during the winter months when it was more cost effective.

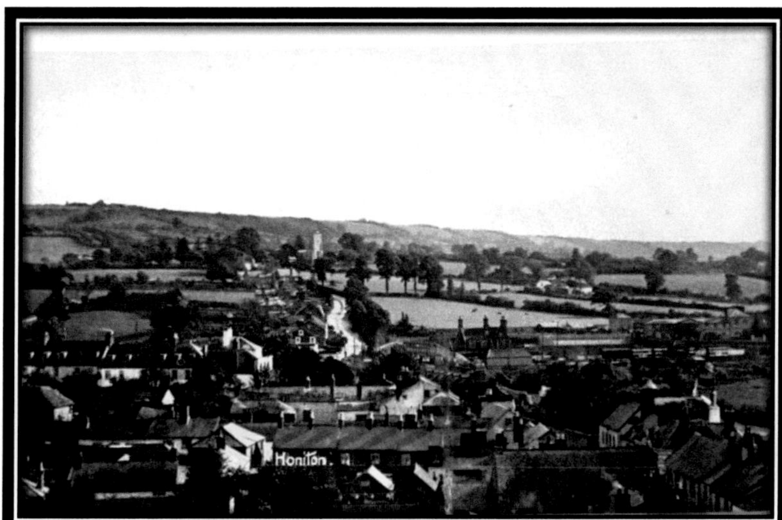

Honiton workhouse can be seen centre-right of the image and of note the undeveloped fields in the centre were once a part of Livermore Farm.

One of the Act's first tasks was to set about dividing the 15,000 or so parishes of England and Wales into new administrative units called 'Poor Law Unions' each run by a locally elected Board of Guardians. It was, at this time, when the old workhouse of Honiton was pulled down and a new Union Workhouse erected where the hospital now stands. The new 'Honiton Union' Workhouse was built in 1836 and opened in 1838, at a cost of £5,022, with room for 230 'inmates'. The newly formed 'Honiton Union' was comprised of 28 parishes including: Awliscombe, Branscombe, Broadhembury, Buckerell, Combe Raleigh, Cotleigh, Dunkeswell, Farway, Feniton, Gittisham, Harpford, Honiton, Luppit, Monkton, Northleigh, Offwell, Ottery St. Mary, Payhembury, Plymtree, Salcombe, Sheldon, Sidbury, Sidmouth, Southleigh, Talaton, Upottery, Ven-Ottery and Widworthy. The Workhouse of Honiton, as stated, only had places for 230 individuals with a catchment area covering 23,793 people in 1851, meaning there were over 100 people for each space the workhouse allocated!

The workhouse was the last resort for those who had nowhere else to go and was a purposely unpleasant place so that only the truly desperate would enter. Local people hated the Honiton establishment so much that many even refused to walk past it! Mothers would be separated from children, wives from husbands and possibly punished if an attempt was made to speak to each other.

Each individual was segregated into specific groups...

1. Aged or infirm men.
2. Able bodied men, and youths above 13.
3. Youths and boys above seven years old and under 13.
4. Aged or infirm women
5. Able-bodied women and girls above 16.
6. Girls above seven years old and under 16.
7. Children under 7 seven years of age.

No contact between these groups was permitted; the residents would be split into four sections, or wings, of the workhouse. Men, women, boys and girls would exercise, work, sleep, eat and be educated in entirely separate quarters: no intermingling was allowed. One story spoke of a labourer who gave his notice to leave the workhouse with his wife and children when he was told **"You cannot take your wife out. We buried her three weeks ago"!**

The most frowned upon groups were the 'able bodied men', as the authorities saw their mere presence as pure idleness.
The entrance to one union workhouse had an unofficial, local name of the 'Archway of Tears.' Whilst inmates were free to leave when they wanted, the question was 'where would you go?!' and even when leaving, one was expected to give 'reasonable notice': one man, who fled a workhouse, over the wall, was sentenced to be whipped. During their residency, no-one was permitted outside the workhouse without permission.
The Honiton Workhouse inmates were forced to wear badges so that, when in the town, locals would know they were resident and this social stigma was just as much as a deterrent from entering. In exchange for bed and board, the people forced to live in these institutions were expected to 'work' and adhere to the vigorous rules. Everyone was expected to be up at 6am, work until 6pm with intervals for meals, and retire for the night at eight; the punishment for not adhering to the rules was severe. A woman, in 1842, who was caught being noisy and swearing, was locked up for 24 hours with only bread and water; another, in the same year, was sent to prison for two months for breaking a window and one child caught fighting in school had his cheese ration withheld for an entire week!
Women were often made to perform menial tasks such as domestic work, cleaning and sewing; the men, however, were subjected to much more laborious work such as rock crushing, wood chopping and even bone crushing. Crushed bones were sold for agricultural fertiliser and the crushing process was a sickening procedure in which the inmates were expected to crush "green bones" - bones which gave off "putrid emanations" as the fat and gelatine contained within them had started to rot. Some inmates, overcome by hunger, were reduced to picking the scraps of meat from the bones they crushed; even the sucking of the bone marrow was not unknown. The process of bone crushing was banned in Honiton and other workhouses in 1845.
People in the workhouse were also not allowed to vote and although the majority of the inmates' financial situation would forbid them such a luxury, the authorities made it clear that anyone entering must forfeit such rights for the sole reason of being poor.

Whilst resident at the workhouse the 'inmates' could expect 3 square meals a day; however, the quality of the food was poor, both in taste and nutrition...
For breakfast...

- Women were permitted one pint of tea, with bread and butter

- Men, girls and boys could expect bread and gruel (flour and oatmeal) with the exception of some older men, who were allowed a pint of tea, with bread and butter.

Dinner consisted of a different dish, depending on the day...

- Monday: Pease soup, herbs, with bread; men and women a pint of table-beer; boys about half a pint.
- Tuesday: Beef and mutton puddings, with vegetables; beer allowance was the same as Monday for the remainder of the week.
- Wednesday: Boiled beef and mutton (sometimes pork with it), hard puddings, bread, vegetables.
- Thursday: Mutton and beef-suet puddings.
- Friday: Beef and mutton puddings, with vegetables.
- Saturday: Irish stew-meat, potatoes, herbs.
- Sunday: Boiled beef and mutton (sometimes pork with it), hard puddings, bread and vegetables.

And lastly for supper...

- Women were permitted a single pint of tea, with bread and butter or cheese.
- Men and boys could expect bread and butter or cheese; men, one pint of beer or tea each; boys, about half a pint.
- Girls and smaller children would be given bread and butter and milk or water to drink.

Beer drunk by children was routine in Victorian Britain as water supplies were more than often hazardous and, interestingly, in 1892, a gallon of "less [than] 10%" volume ale, cost one shilling (about 3p a pint).
The Honiton Workhouse baked its own bread and it is worth noting that vegetables, with the exception of potatoes, were only served four times out of the twenty one meals a week. This was because vegetables were an expensive commodity in the 19th century whereas food such as meat and grain were cheap: only the best for the poor and destitute!

The medical care of the Honiton Workhouse was not much better than the working or living conditions. In the 1840s, the treatment and monitoring of these 'paupers' could be viewed as incredibly poor. Over a documented seven year period, from 1842 to 1849, there were several cases that illustrated complete disregard for the residents' health and/or safety:

- One individual was noted to have died from inflammation of the lungs which had been "neglected".

- A 93 year old sustained a broken neck and thigh bone, whilst in residence, later dying from her injuries.
- One person was recorded to have "burnt to death" with another perishing from a milder case of "severe" burns!
- And one patient was "discharged" from the Exeter Hospital with 'paralysis' and, subsequently, died at the workhouse in 1843.

A report published in 1866, surprisingly, stated that the conditions of the Honiton Workhouse were overall of a good standard. The sick wards were, however, described as "dark and low, and insufficient" with a need for "better accommodation". The appointed doctor was not resident but visited daily, leaving the majority of care to one "paid" and two unpaid nurses. Tuberculosis, or the 'white death' as it was known, was also recorded to have been a big killer of the workhouse paupers.
A later report from 1894 reiterated the opinions of 1866; however, some details contained in the report may not be so favourably looked upon through our modern, more civilised eyes...

"The bedsteads are low and narrow, of a very old-fashioned type, not suitable for old or bedridden folk, especially when of large stature. The bedding is straw... We do not quarrel with the straw bed; when fully filled it is quite comfortable... Among the men two patients were in bed. One was a chattering imbecile, who was also blind; he was too long for his bed, and looked thoroughly uncomfortable; he must have disturbed the ward with his unceasing talk... there are no baths or bathrooms... The nurse, for there is only one, has been in the service of the Board for thirty years... the nurse above mentioned is not trained, nor is she a certified midwife... There is no night nurse"

The report also stated that the workhouse had no running hot water or a gas connection, even though gas had been in Honiton since 1835, and that the fireplaces were all of a "small" size.

In 1892, it was found by the medical officer of the time that the condition of the drains was "not only defective" but "obsolete" and a full inspection was carried out. The account that the inspector found gives an insight into the sanitary conditions of the Honiton Workhouse as well as a rough, general description of the layout of the Workhouse itself. From the report it was stated that the workhouse had separate day rooms and wash/bath houses with toilets for men, women, boys and girls. There was also a scullery, board room, infirm ward, detached hospital building, new sick wards and a nursery on the first floor. The men and women had their own exercise yards whilst the children's was split in two and were covered in loose stones. The establishment's water supply came from a large water tank situated in the centre of the building. Most of the piping was poorly ventilated, honeycombed with holes and made of lead and most of the drains and toilets were described as "defective". All of the waste water was discharged from the building through an open outlet onto the roadway where there was said to be nothing to prevent the escape of "sewer gas", making the experience just as pleasant for any passersby! The following are the most disturbing problems listed in the report:

"The drain from the wash house commences from the bell trap near door and runs underneath the building to men's yard, and is very defective, being honeycombed by rats"

"Upon emptying the soft water tank in the woman's yard, it was found that a large amount of deposit had found its way onto the tank and from the smell arising there from was evidently contaminated by sewage matter to a large degree."

"The iron soil pipe from master W. C. was tested + found defective the position of this pipe is such that sewer gas <u>must</u> find it's way into the building from the defect."

It was, therefore, the opinion of the inspector that...

"The present system of drainage , and the sanitary appliances + water supply are wrong in principle, defective in arrangement + workmanship and I have no hesitation in giving my opinion that it is very unavoidable to stop short of a complete re-construction."

Repair work was enacted but the question as to how long the workhouse had been operating with such poor sanitary conditions is unknown.

There was, however, a kind sense of 'Christian spirit' from the people of Honiton toward the unfortunates in the workhouse: throughout the minute books there are references to kind gestures and gifts to the inmates. A Miss Susan Venn entertained the inmates of the workhouse for "tea" in April 1892 as she was unable to provide a Christmas tree: due to an influenza outbreak, Mr. Edmunds and others distributed gifts to the paupers at Christmas and New Year 1891 and other people of the town were also noted to have donated items such as 'cuffs for the children' and 'rabbits' for eating.

The Victorian era provided little care for those with mental disorders and care was generally that provided by the sufferers' families. Honiton Workhouse, like many others, offered no separate support for the mentally challenged: they were given no concessionary treatment, being dealt with as all other inmates. The descriptions of such individuals in Honiton were listed in documents as 'idiots', 'lunatics' and 'imbeciles'- although medical terminology of the time, shocking by modern standards.

Many people suffering from such afflictions had either developed dementia in later life, simply suffered the equivalent of a nervous breakdown or depression, or were born with conditions such as cerebral palsy or down's syndrome and after home care became no longer possible, for whatever reason, had nowhere else to go but the workhouse...

Edgar Ling was an unfortunate soul in this situation: listed as an "imbecile" he was believed to have been born in Somerset in 1863 and spent most of his childhood in the Honiton Workhouse with his birthplace listed as 'not known'. When he came of age he was ejected to a lodging house in the High Street where he worked for a short time as a 'general labourer' but this obviously proved too much for his fragile mind as by the 1890s he was back in the union house. He remained there until he died aged 50, in 1913, having spent virtually all his life in this establishment. Another example of such a poor individual was that of John Leatt who was born in Ottery St. Mary. He spent some of his earlier life with his brother William, who was a farmer in Ottery St. Mary, and in 1851 his occupation was listed as "idiot". After a spell in the Honiton Workhouse he was sent to work as a labourer on a small farm in his hometown but, like Edgar Ling, he did not manage to hold the position for long and was later re-homed in the workhouse. John spent the remaining 20 odd years of his life in this institution until he died there in 1898, aged 80.

Frederick Rapsey, who was born in Honiton 1865, was an "idiot from birth"; his father William was a butcher in New Street and after the death of his mother in 1874 the family fell apart. William lost his business and was forced to become a labourer: living as a lodger with a poor shoemaker, his son Frederick had no alternative but to enter the workhouse around the age of 10 and William's two other surviving children were forced to take up similar poor lodgings elsewhere in the town. William struggled to support himself alone as old age got the better of him and by 1891 he was also condemned to the workhouse, with his son. William Rapsey died there in 1898, whilst his son Fred died in Exeter in 1936 after spending the majority of his life in the workhouse.

Care of such people was equally sad: in February 1892 a porter, at the workhouse, attempted to attack Frederick Raspey and the assault was reported to the Honiton Poor Law Union. The following was the Union's decision... "alleged assault was of a very trivial character" and that there was "hope that they (the master, porter and inmates) would endeavour in the future to work more amicably together for their own comfort and that of the inmates."

It was at this time, towards the end of the 19th century, that workhouses were focusing more on medical care, like hospitals of today, and such recommendations were reflected in the report of 1894.

The predominant residents of the Honiton Workhouse were the elderly, the orphaned and the unmarried women with child/ren. In Talaton lived the Hellings family. William Hellings was a labourer who, in later life, was forced to live on a meagre Chelsea Pension which supported his younger wife, Elizabeth, and their young children. When William died his pension died with him and his widow attempted to raise her "idiot" daughter Elizabeth and youngest child William alone whilst her other daughter, Jane, was sent to work as a servant on one of the larger Talaton farms. Elizabeth senior, sadly, died in 1868 leaving her family in turmoil. Elizabeth's daughter, Elizabeth, worked for a time, in her weak state of mind, as a servant and Jane fell pregnant, out of wedlock, subsequently giving birth to her daughter in the Honiton Workhouse. Elizabeth also fell pregnant and joined her sister in the workhouse in around 1875. Jane spent 16 years in the workhouse until her only daughter, Mary, died there at the age of 16. There are many documented cases of children who were born in the workhouse, never seeing the outside world. After the death of her dependant child, Jane was released and later found poor lodgings in her home town where she worked as a charwoman. She died there in 1898, aged 55. Elizabeth herself died in the workhouse in 1886 whilst her daughter, Ann, was sent to Monkton, at an early age, to work as a nursemaid. William and Elizabeth's other child, William, never married and worked as a live-in farm servant for the remainder of his days.

Elderly members of the parish often resided with their children after the death of their partner or when it became impossible for them to live alone. In 1851, more than one in four of all households in England had a member of their extended family residing with them. This was not, however, always possible and with nowhere else to go, the elderly and infirm were forced to enter the dreaded workhouses.

Charles Dunning was a tailor, born in Combe Raleigh. He and his wife, Susan, spent much of their lives in Northleigh where they had at least 5 children. It appears that the couple outlived 4 of their offspring and Susan herself died in 1882. With old age advancing, and having nowhere else to go, Charles ended up in the Honiton Workhouse where he died in 1892 aged 93.

Sarah Ridgeway was born in Sheldon in 1815 and later married Daniel Rowland, an agricultural labourer. The family lived in Luppit for a time before moving to Honiton where, for a while, they lived a poor existence in 'Manor Place'. Daniel died, still working as a labourer, aged 75 and his wife of some 50 years, struggled on as a lace-maker, living in a small property in New Street. After a long and arduous life in which she had had 16 children, she sadly spent that last decade of her life in the workhouse where she died, aged 93.

Martha Salter was born in Buckerell where her father ran a farm. She remained on the farm her entire life until her father died and her unmarried brother, William, took over. Martha left the farm when William died in 1873 and went to live with a relative on Great Hale Farm, then aged in her late 70s. Her nephew, Hayman Collins later evicted his aunt and having nowhere else to go she entered the workhouse. Miss Salter had spent the majority of her life on the family farm in Buckerell, so much so that in the last reference to her occupation she was referred to as a "farmer's daughter" then aged in her 90s! It must have been devastating for her to not only be evicted from her lifelong home, but then to be disowned by her own relative and sent to the 'poor house' where she died in 1891, aged 94, unwanted and alone. Of note, at the time of her death, Martha Salter was the oldest resident of the town and one of only 4 other people aged over 90, three of whom were also in the workhouse.

In Victorian England the average life expectancy was 40 years but this was due mainly to the high infant mortality of the time and many people who survived childhood did manage to survive beyond early middle age. Reaching one's 70th was admirable; 80 was quite rare, so much so that one gentleman who died in 1858, aged 86, was described as being of "extreme old age"! 90 was exceptionally rare and, as already stated, only two people in the entire town reached this point in their lives in 1851. A centenarian was almost unheard of and in 1861 there were only 82 people in the whole of England who had reached an age of over 100 years. The age was so uncommon that one census enumerator, of the same year, felt the need to write that one gentleman of Gloucestershire, who was 102 still "[had] all his faculties"! These extraordinary individuals seem to have been much hardier than one may think for only a few of these people were reduced to the workhouse and over one quarter of them were still supporting themselves and their relatives. Several of them were amazingly still working and, incredibly, one Cornish man was still working as an agricultural labourer at 101! Many of these people in 1861 were residing with family members and, of interest, one lady of 102 from Devon was being cared for by her whippersnapper nephew who was 80! When Mrs. Mary Sprague died in Honiton in 1940, aged 102, she is believed to have been the first such person to reach the age of 100 in the town in at least a century.

Children who were orphaned also often resided with family; however, this was often not possible. In 1861 22% of all children in England had lost one parent by the age of 10 and 1% had lost both, leading to so many of these poor unfortunates ending up in the local workhouse where, sadly, most of them died. At one British workhouse, in 1859, the question arose as to how the children of the said establishment should be taught religious values: one man present said *"I think it a thousand pities to lose so much time about a matter of no consequence, because every man knows that, from the system of the house, not one of these children will be alive this day twelve months."*

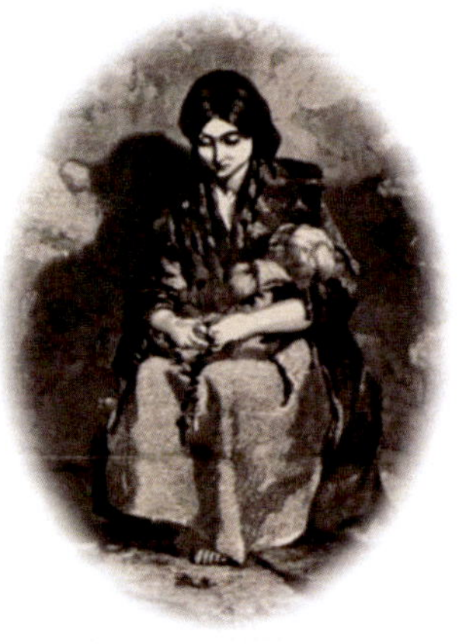

Unmarried, expectant women were also a thorn in the authority's side: some parishes were known to have transported women in labour to a neighbouring parish so that they would not be responsible for them. Up until 1831 a single pregnant woman would be forced to identify the father, who was then given one of two options: marriage or imprisonment! However, before the days of DNA, the identification and proof of liability of a father was hard and in an age not exactly favourable to women, justice was not always achieved. In 1854 a James Snell, of Little Torrington, was ordered by the local authorities, to pay an Eliza Shepherd 1s.6d per week for the maintenance of his 'bastard' child until the age of 13. Snell appealed the decision and the former ruling was quashed with the result being that Miss Shepherd was ordered to pay Mr. Snell £9.12s "towards his cost in this half sustained."

In a country with so little support for unmarried mothers, they had little choice but to enter the workhouse, especially as in many cases their family would disown them. Any father of such illegitimate children was not by any means off the hook, so to speak. William Pike, a married farmer of Hole Farm, Branscombe had had two children by Sarah Rendell, a poor labourer's daughter, and she had subsequently ended up in the Honiton Union Workhouse in 1891. The Poor Law Union demanded that he pay 2 shillings per week per child towards their upkeep, as well as 36s.12d costs. Another man was imprisoned for one month for failing to provide monies to the Union for support of his illegitimate child. This 'penny pinching' from relatives did not stop at neglectful fathers: there are many examples where the Honiton Poor Union wrote to sons and daughters demanding weekly sums, usually 1s.6d., for mothers and fathers who had ended up in the parish workhouse.
The following is an extract of correspondence between Somerset House and Honiton concerning the clothing of illegitimate children:

""Sirs. Honiton, Devon, 27 January 1841.
I AM instructed by the Board of Guardians of the Honiton Union to call your attention to the case of illegitimate children born in the workhouse, who, of course, have no clothes except those which belong to the Union ; by the prohibitory order, no out-relief can be granted to the mothers of these children, and the Board are desirous of being informed whether they can grant clothes to the children to enable the mothers to take them out of the house, as without this power it is quite clear that the mothers and children must remain in the house many years. Your early reply will oblige."

Somerset House responded with the minutes from a meeting of a few years prior...

COPY of Minute of Poor Law Commissioners, 29 October 1839.
THE Poor Law Commissioners have lately had their attention particularly called to the subject of allowances of clothing to paupers.
1. The practice of allowing clothing to adult paupers out of the workhouse appears to be so rare, as not to call for any remarks on the part of the Commissioners.
2. The practice of making allowances of clothing to the children of able-bodied labourers going into service appears to prevail in many Unions, and several applications have lately been made to the Commissioners to sanction allowances of this description. It is manifest that the practice of making allowances of clothing to the children of labourers going into

service cannot increase the total amount of employment; that every person who obtains employment on account of the allowance of clothes from the parish must prevent another person, who has not that advantage, from obtaining employment ; employment; and, consequently, that such allowances are detrimental to the independent labourer. Such allowances are in the nature of premiums upon pauper apprenticeships, the evils of which have been already pointed out by the Commissioners on various occasions...

3. With respect to allowances of clothing to paupers in the workhouse, it is desirable that persons residing a short time in the workhouse should not on leaving it be furnished, except under very particular circumstances, with a fresh suit of clothes. In some places where such an allowance had been made, the result has been, that able-bodied men previously to entering the workhouse have disposed of their clothes, and clothed themselves in rags, not sufficiently decent to work in, knowing that they would receive a complete suit on leaving the workhouse ; and no way has been found of preventing this evil, except by keeping to the strict rule of giving to a pauper who leaves the house no other clothes than those he had on when he entered it. Persons permanently domiciled in the workhouse, and especially children who have remained in it from an early age, must on quitting it be furnished with a decent outfit of clothing. Young persons who have been brought up in the workhouse, and who leave it for service or apprenticeship, ought, in the opinion of the Commissioners, to be furnished with such an outfit of clothing as is usually possessed by young persons not being paupers in a similar condition.

EXTRACT from a Letter of the Board of Guardians of the Longtown Union, to the Poor Law Commissioners ; dated 7 November 1843.

"WHETHER they can legally give clothing to a bastard child when taken from "the workhouse by its mother, no other being left by her in the house? "

EXTRACT from a Letter of the Poor Law Commissioners to the Board of Guardians of the Longtown Union; dated 11 November 1843.

" THE Commissioners desire to state, that the Guardians can furnish necessary clothing to paupers in the workhouse ; and if, on a pauper quitting the workhouse, he have no other sufficient clothing, the Guardians may properly allow the pauper to take with him the clothing supplied to him whilst in the workhouse."'"

As can be seen, every single shilling spent on residents of the workhouse was scrutinised and any feelings of sympathy or empathy for the paupers was simply not considered. Another report, published in 1846, commented on the fact that the authorities actually thought that the poor

wished to become paupers in order to obtain better living conditions and that "every penny bestowed to render the condition of the pauper more eligible than that of the independent labourer [as] a bounty on indolence and vice." Considering the typical labourer's hovels, as described in the last chapter, this may be truer than one may think!
Many workhouses' officials were even known to give the paupers "fictitious errand" such as carrying rocks and delivering blank papers "directed as letters" for no other reason than "to torment them."

There is some evidence that the Poor Law Union of Honiton was not totally unscrupulous towards its dependants. Many poor people were granted 'outdoor relief' so that individuals could go and live with relatives in other parishes rather than be tied to the Honiton Workhouse. The original plans of the 1834 Act had not succeeded in doing away with this 'outdoor' relief and, as an example, the total outdoor relief of the Honiton Union, for one week in January 1892, totalled £122.15s.12d.
There was also much communication between Poor Law Unions concerning people who were resident in a union's workhouse but not indigenous to their said parish. If a man/woman from Honiton was residing in Bristol, for example, and had ended up in the local workhouse, the Poor Law Union of Bristol would write to the Honiton authorities asking for a weekly sum to help support the pauper, and the Honiton Poor Board were often known to have written to such other unions for paupers not from the Honiton Area. In earlier days if an individual fell on hard times they would have been sent back to their parish of birth to receive relief but with the age of the railway people were moving around much more so this method became more common practise.

In 1851, there was a total of 93 people in the Honiton Workhouse compared with 96 in 1861.
The following are some details of those who were unfortunate enough to be in the Honiton Workhouse in 1851...
The Honiton Workhouse was run by the master and matron, John and Mary Coren, and in total there were six members of staff, including a 35 year old school mistress called Ann Chown, a 68 year old nurse Caroline Pile, a 36 year old porter James Orchard and his 33 year old wife Sarah, who was the cook. The wages of the staff were deliberately low so as to save money for the Poor Law Commission that governed them. Many references were made to the workhouse being similar to prison and whereas the Governor of a Victorian prison would be paid around £600 a year, the Master and Matron of a workhouse would be paid, collectively,

about £80. All other staff wages reflected this and only led to more friction between the inmates and those who governed them.
The earliest known Master of the Honiton Workhouse was Philip Passmore and his wife Elizabeth, whose son and daughter, in 1841, were a porter and schoolmistress of the same establishment. In about 1845, John and Mary Coren became the Master and Matron. John Coren had previously been a schoolmaster at the Union Workhouse of St. Thomas. The Corens remained at the workhouse for over 25 years when, in about 1861, the couple moved to the workhouse of Warham in Dorset and the Honiton Workhouse was taken over by Edwin Murrant.
Mary Ann Lewis was a 27 year old servant from Buckerell; she had ended up in the workhouse for having a child out of wedlock. In fact, she had two children, both of whom were born in the workhouse, the eldest being 6. By 1853 Mary had married and moved to Payhembury. Both her children, William and Albert, died but she went on to have a further 5 by her husband, Caleb Webber.
John and Thomas Moore were born the sons of a tailor who resided in Queen Street. Both their parents died and the two brothers ended up in the 'poor house' aged 12 and 6. John did not survive the 1850s but Thomas got out of the workhouse and became a gardener and went back to live in Queen Street, where he married.
Another three children who were unfortunate enough to be living here were the Richards sisters, Georgina, Julia and Harriet. Georgina was sent to Hampshire to work, which was quite common when children came of age. There she married a Robert Goodman in 1866 but by 1881 she was in Oxford Road Union Workhouse where she was listed as a laundress. Her sister, Julia, was sent to work in Devon where she married a gentleman 20 years her senior; by 1881 she was a tailoress with 3 children. Sister Harriet is not thought to have survived to adulthood and it was unlikely the family would have ever seen each other after the workhouse years.
Thomas Dommett was an elderly labourer who ended up in the Union workhouse with his 15 year old son when his wife, Sophia, died in 1850. After leaving the workhouse son, Thomas, went to live in Somerset where he married; however, he left his young family in the same poor circumstances as his young life had been: he died in his early 40s leaving his wife with 6 children to feed.
There is one happier story though: George Berry was a ten year old boy who was in the workhouse in 1851. He later married a woman called Charlotte in 1862 and obtained a respectable trade as a tailor in Ottery St. Mary where he lived at Butt's Hill. The couple had 8 children and were married for 47 years; he died in Ottery St. Mary in 1913, aged 73.

Although treatment and conditions improved in the early twentieth century, many workhouses were still in operation until the establishment of the Welfare State in 1948. Honiton workhouse became a hospital in 1930 yet many older members of the town still always saw the building as nothing other than a place of poverty and dispair. A local man clearly remembers, from the early twentieth century, men of the workhouse wearing cream coloured trousers, making them easily recognisable, reminiscent of Victorian conditions. Such 'uniforms' were made one time by a local woman called Miss. Trace. During the war years the old maternity ward was used as a home for evacuee mothers. 'Marlpits Hospital', as the workhouse later became known, came under the control of Devon County Council from 1930 and by the mid 1950s the establishment was "one of the few hospitals in Devon" that catered for the "very old and very young". At around the same time, a proposal was put forward to rename the premises in order to speed up the transition from workhouse to hospital but this never came to pass. Marlpits Hospital "had become a place to get better, not to die in". By 1985 it had become obvious that the old workhouse and added extensions had finally outlived their usefulness. With overcrowding, lack of privacy, poor staffing, little room for expansion of newer equipment and serious fire risks in the original building, it was demolished and in 1996 the new Honiton Hospital was opened on its old site. Today only one wall of the old morgue survives with the remainder of the building having been, as stated, demolished and redeveloped.

For a lucky few there were several charities in Honiton that aided the poor and in many cases stopped them from having to face the misery of the Union Workhouse.

Chapter 4
Town Charities

"Charity suffereth long, and is kind"
The Bible, I Corinthians

By 1851 there were a number of established charities founded by generous benefactors or rich former members of the community. These charities included either money obtained from land rentals or dividends, as well as specific homes for the elderly or infirm.

Allhallows Charity

In 1524 a knight by the name of Sir John Kirkham, and Elizens Harding, conveyed to Sir William Carew, another knight, and Henry Faireman, the then rector of Honiton, as well as 15 others, all of their combined lands, predominantly in Honiton and Yarcombe, as well as other parishes in Devon. John Kirkham was born and buried in Paignton and was High Sherriff of Devon in 1523 - the same time that he founded the Allhallows Charity. Mr. Faireman and Sir Carew, with their heirs succeeding them, were entrusted to use these lands "for the reparation of the Chapel of Allhallows... and other charitable uses and purposes".

The lands held in trust for this property included some 18 properties which, in 1820, had an annual rental value of £26.7s.11½d and were collectively valued at £174.8s.0d. Many of the properties included in the charity were destroyed by the terrible fire of 1765 and later building leases were granted for their continuation. Amongst the lands and properties included the old headmaster's residence of Allhallows School and the old parish workhouse: the headmaster's residence was granted rent free and the annual rent for the workhouse was just over £3. The headmaster's residence was the large building that presently stands next to Allhallows Museum and included land behind the house, the other side of Silver Street, from the entrance to what is now Newlands to the corner of the Working Man's Club. This land was once all part of the Grammar School.

Beaumont's Gifts

Henry Beaumont, in 1589, donated a farm called Raphayes in Buckerell, to the poor of the town. The farm consisted of ten fields and two orchards that totalled over 26 acres of land and the annual rent of £66, in 1814, was given to the poor of the town.

Henry Beaumont also left £800 to the trustees of the Trust he had established to purchase further lands which he gave to the poor of Honiton "for ever."
Mr. Beaumont's wife, Elizabeth, left a further 40 acres of land that was located in the parish of 'Abbot's Isle', Somerset to the poor of the town in 1595. The property was known as 'The Steevely Lands' "Upon trust to distribute the rents, fines, and profits of the premises yearly, quarterly, monthly or weekly, as need should require, amongst the most aged impotent and poor people inhabiting the said parish of Honiton, as the feoffees should think fit." (feoffees being an old name for trustees).

Thomas Marwood's Gift

The once physician of Elizabeth I also remembered the poor of Honiton parish in his Will dated 1617. He donated some land once known as 'Grubblehayes' as well as 5 cottages and gardens. Grubblehayes was about ¼ acre plot of land and two of the houses were once called 'Lambert's Lilly' and 'Akerman's'. The location of these houses made renting them to potential tenants difficult, so in 1764 they were simply rented to poor people, free of charge.

Hayes Trust

A plot of land, called 'Hayes', was bought in Buckerell in about 1655 with monies left by a number of benefactors, including £100 from James Rodge (the lace dealer), £70 from a John Saunders, £20 from a John Frey and £10 from a Mr. John Chase. By 1799 the plot of land consisted of nearly 13 acres; however, some land had to be sold to the tenant farmer of the time for tax reasons. The rents and profits were yearly distributed to the poor of the parish.

Cole's House and Gray's Houses

In 1661 the Honiton Charities purchased a house, and in 1665 a further two, with surplus monies obtained from rents of their existing properties. The tenants, at the time of purchase, were Humphrey Cole and William Gray; hence their respective names. However, by the early 19th century the properties had been lost: records showed that rents were paid on Cole's House up to 1699 and that Gray's Houses were being used as alms houses in the same year. The last entry concerning these houses was written in 1700 stating that they had been "burnt down, and the ground waste" with the location of them then, and still, unknown.

Warwick Lane Trust

In 1658 an Alexander Cornelius, and others, sold seven houses in Warwick Lane (now Queen Street) to a Tristum Stoning for which he paid £111 for the freehold. The houses were bought on the condition that Mr. Stoning use the rents for the good of the poor of the parish. In 1659 Mr. Stoning gave the properties to the people of Honiton for the same usage.

Bridewell Houses

Orlando Seale sold to his brother, Samuel Seale, in 1675, a property occupied by the site of the old Globe Inn for the good of the poor of the town. The Honiton Charities later bought the freehold and in about 1820 the land was leased for development.

Stocker's Land (Henry Marwood's Gift)

In 1675 Henry Marwood left £100 to his brother, John, to purchase lands where, once again, the rent could be used for the good of the poor of Honiton. Stocker's Land was a house with 18 acres of land in the parish of Luppit. This charity was aimed primarily for relief of "poor aged labourers".

St. Margaret's Alms Houses

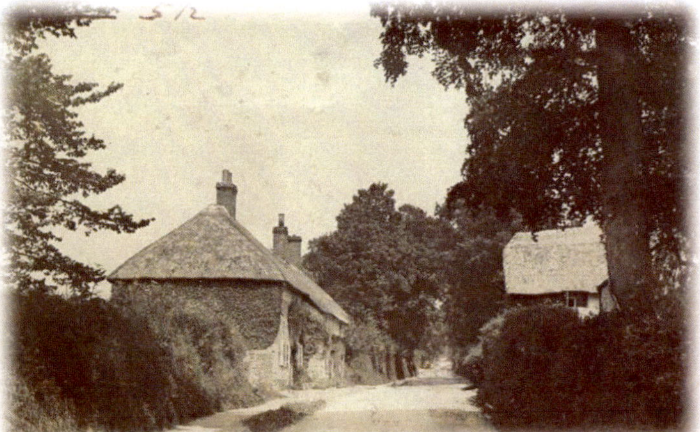

St. Margaret's Alms Houses

St. Margaret's Charity consisted of a chapel and houses for the use of leprous individuals and included several plots of land that were rented yearly so that the inhabitants of the houses could have an annual allowance.As already stated, St Margaret's was thought to have been established by William de Tracy in the 12th century. The hospital was "re-founded" and enlarged by Thomas Chard, last Abbot of Forde, a descendant of William de Tracy who, in 1530, completed restoration work on the previously dilapidated buildings. It was John Chard, a descendant of the Tracys, who was charged with misgoverning the Trust in 1642 along with his father Richard. The rector and churchwardens stepped in and decided that the Charity should be employed for the relief and habitation of one governor and four leprous persons "for ever", as wished by the original founder. As leprosy was becoming less common by the 17th century, it was decided that poor people may also use the charity. John Chard was ordered to pay over £37 for the "prosecution of that commission" and in the same year all the lands belonging to St. Margaret's were valued at £25 per annum. The hospital consisted of the chapel, a house and garden for the elected governor, as well as eight other houses for the poor residents. Originally there were only 4 houses, not including the governor's residence, and in 1807 it was decided to construct four more the other side of the Exeter Road. The new houses cost £293.13s.4d to build, the majority of which was taken from monies generated from the sale of timber from the lands of the Charity. In 1844 the Charity consisted of 8 fields that were rented for the benefit of their inhabitants. The fields were rented annually by auction.

The elected governor was appointed to read prayers to the poor of the alms houses on Wednesdays and Fridays in the chapel.
The money raised from the rented lands was distributed thus. In 1672, each of the four residents was given £4 per year; in 1694 this was raised to 1s.5d per week and the governor was given £5.16s.8d. per annum. By 1807 each poor person was given 2s.6d. a week and the governor 3s. The alms receivers were also given about 12 shillings each at Christmas and were given extra monies in case of sickness. They were also permitted to cut wood from the hedgerows of the estate for firewood.
The cottages of St. Margaret's were a blessing for many but these properties were small, many of which only had 2 rooms and were known to have housed up to 5 people. The residents were predominantly old members of the parish, often widow/ers who had an average age of 71 (in 1851).
By the 1960s the alms houses were still home to six dependant elderly residents but the dwellings were in serious need of repair and updating and the Charity's meagre annual income of about £100 could provide no such improvements or meet repair bills, amounting to an estimated five

figures. In 1971 most of the Charity's money had been spent on the continual repair work and the reluctant choice was made to sell the almshouses, after the last of the residents had been relocated. About £1,600 was raised from the property sales and this was later merged with 'Honiton United Charities'. St. Margaret's Chapel, however, survived as a place of worship a little longer and only became a private dwelling within the last fifteen years. Today, both St. Margaret's Chapel and the old almshouses are private dwellings.

Other Gifts and Bequests

There were also many money donations made by a variety of different people that were included in the Honiton charities, including a gift left by Sir John Ackland enabling bread to be distributed every Sunday and a bequest left by Richard Minifie, which was distributed on 21st June and at Christmas. Elizabeth Harris left a sum of £50 in 1782 so that bread could be given to the poor on Christmas Day and a Rev. John How left £300 for the aid of a Sunday school, resulting in the establishment of a day school in 1813 "free of expense" to poor children. Elizabeth Harris' bequests were still annually in use well into the twentieth century. During the recession of the 1930s, hundreds of unemployed queued for their bread rations; in 1957 over 30 old people were given a loaf but by 1962 the interest on the original £50 could only provide 24 loaves. However, in the same year other benefactors made it possible for each caller to be given a loaf, a shilling and an orange for the Christmas festivities.

The charities of Honiton were managed and run by a steward, a position once held by two generations of the Gidley family. Robert Gidley introduced a new management system of the trusts, on his obtaining the position in 1760; he was succeeded by his son, Courtenay Gidley of Elmfield, in 1800. The steward was responsible for the overseeing of the charities on behalf of the trustees.
The distributions of these bequeathed gifts were not, however, as black and white as their beneficiaries may have hoped for. The Honiton Charities were described as being "much neglected" for much of the eighteenth century and the loss of two of the purchased houses (Cole's & Gray's) is evident of this. St. Margaret's Hospital had also, in 1642, been "misgoverned" by two of the trustees who had used the profits of the land for their "own private use." In this period, before dispensation being granted by the Government to such charities, very little of the overall monies actually made its way to the poor individuals. From September

1817 to September 1818, a total of £400 was paid out from the Honiton Charities but only £75.6s.0d. was actually distributed to the poor. The problem was that much of the money was spent on property maintenance, insurance and staff wages, leaving just under 20% to go to the actual people who needed it the most!

The money raised from all the separate charities was consolidated and was generally handed out three times annually: St Luke's Day, Good Friday and Christmas Day. This is how it was distributed in 1820...

- On Good Friday the rents raised from Grubblehayes, which amounted to £4, were distributed at 1 shilling per person.
- On St Luke's Day (18th October) money raised from 'Stocker's Land' was given out: the total money raised was between £2 and £3, each person applying for it getting sixpence.
- At Christmas the poor were given anything between two to seven shillings.
- On November 5th money raised from the 'Bridewell Houses' was given to the poor in stockings, shoes and books for poor children as wished by the beneficiaries.
- In addition to these set dates of relief, the overseers of the charities also paid, on average, 5 shillings to those who were the poorest of the poor throughout the year.

All these charities still exist today as 'The Honiton United Charities'. Six of the aforementioned charities joined forces with the 'Thomas Marwood' Charity in 1929 with a further 8 joining in 1969.

There were a small handful of other types of relief for people who had fallen on hard times. Nathaniel Sydenham, of the High Street, was a Chelsea Pensioner who had served in the 41st Foot Division from 1811 to 1838. Chelsea Pensions, one of the first 'pension' schemes, were granted to people who had either sustained injury or had served a duration of over twenty years service in the army. The income was given from the Royal Chelsea Hospital, (founded in 1692 by Charles II), but this was only about 6 shillings a week. Henry Braid, a gardener of New Street, was a Greenwich pensioner (for services to the Navy) - the equivalent of a Chelsea Pensioner. There were, in fact, fewer than 5 people in the whole Honiton Parish on such pensions and the allowance was generally so low that all recipients were forced to continue working. Interestingly, a Peter Macleod and his wife survived on the sole income derived from his Greenwich

Pension throughout the 1840s and 1850s. They lived at an old telegraph cottage, used during the Napoleonic wars, situated on the top of St Cyre's Hill which, even today, is an isolated location*1. Impersonating a Chelsea Pensioner was not generally considered a good idea as for much of the Victorian era it was deemed a capital crime. 'Old age pensions' did not come into effect until 1909 and even then only people aged over 70 were eligible.

If a poor person did not wish to enter the workhouse and was not granted enough (or any) relief from local charities, the only other alternative to put food on the table was to turn to crime, punishments of which could be severe.

Chapter 5
Crime & Punishment

"Crime takes but a moment but justice an eternity"
Ellen O'Grady

Whether forced to turn to a life of crime to simply feed your starving family, or from choice, those on the wrong side of the law in bygone days were not in the best of places. Individual's opinions on religion and the voicing of them today, are generally accepted but two centuries ago they were crimes that carried severe penalties. Blasphemy, denying the Holy Scripture or the Almighty, was punishable by fines or imprisonment. Breaking the rules of the Sabbath by drunkenness, for example, was another crime of this class. It was not officially until 1994 that anyone could accept entrance fees for any form of entertainment on a Sunday, effectively banning all sporting events. Public performance in theatres and such were also illegal until 1972. Virtually all recreational ventures on Sunday were at the very least frowned upon and when the playing of games was permitted on Sundays on Allhallows playing field in 1939, it caused great friction with a local religious committee.

Piracy, which many could be forgiven for thinking was extinct by this time, was still practised and anyone caught was executed for treason. Burglary and robbery were, under "common law", capital offences but punishment was usually transportation.

Transportation was the fate of many an unlucky criminal and at the end of their term the convicted were given the choice of whether to return home or remain. If they chose the latter they were given a portion of land and a supply of tools to start afresh. Less than some 10% of those sent abroad returned home after they had paid their debt to society. Transportation was abolished in 1857.

As an example of the types of crime and punishment of the time, I give you the following. In Devon, in 1835, there were 518 people convicted of various crimes - of these: 191 were acquitted, 326 were sent to prison, fined or whipped and 95 were transported for life, 14 years or 7 years. In the same year, nationally, a total of 34 people were executed. It may not be surprising that the majority of those executed were those guilty of murder, or intent to commit murder, but interestingly, 3 of them were convicted of sodomy, one for housebreaking and 7 for arson! Execution for sodomy may seem harsh by today's standards but anyone so convicted would have been grateful they were not caught in such an act during the

reign of Richard III when the punishment could be hanging, burning at the stake, stoned to death, buried alive, or drowned!
As harsh as these punishments may seem through twenty first century eyes, they did seem to reduce crime levels. Over a 30 year period from 1784 to 1814 there were only 60 people convicted of murder. This does not, of course, take into account the significantly smaller size of the London population of the time but it gives one an example of how levels of crime were much lower than today!

One of the most common forms of crime in the eighteenth and nineteenth century was that of the infamous highwayman and the serene picturesque roads surrounding Honiton were by no means a safe haven.
One of the first recorded thefts from a local stage coach happened at 2pm on Monday 10th February 1752 when the Exeter Stage coach was robbed only 1 ½ miles from Honiton, on the Cullompton Road. The robbery was committed by a single highwayman who stole 20 guineas in money and "then rode off with his booty." The report gave a good description of the man who was said to have been dressed in a "brown Great Coat with a plain Cape, and a green plush close bodied coat, with yellow Buttons and Button holes in each flap: His waistcoat was of a dark Colour and trimmed with narrow Gold lace." The man was known to have been waiting some three hours in Exeter for the coach to leave and was well acquainted with the amount of money carried by each passenger. One gentleman on the coach had a gun pointed at him and was told "give me your money", the gentleman offered him silver but the highwayman knew he had more about his person, at which point the gentleman revealed a purse which contained 16 guineas. The highwayman was identified as a William Jennings and he was later captured and executed at Heavitree gallows on April 11th 1752.
Another highwayman robbed two women on the Exeter road in 1754 and foolishly went to Exeter with his stolen money to buy a "brace of pistols" at which point he was apprehended and sent to prison.
Only 3 years later another man, John Gard of Honiton, was convicted of robbing the Northern Mail Coach, a robbery which he was said to have got away with upwards of £4,000!

Begging was the fate of many a poor man/woman but in Honiton in the 18th century a new law was enforced to prevent them. Any vagrant who had been publicly begging was ordered by a magistrate to be shaved and his hair dressed by a barber. It was said that a beggar was seldom seen in the town after the rule was inaugurated.

"A great vagabond" called Charles Ford was also the last man to be put in the town stocks in 1812. 'Stocks' were first mentioned in literature in 1227 and later the 'Stock Acts' of 1350, 1376 and 1405 instructed every parish that ran its own affairs to have stocks present. Towns and villages were actually downgraded to hamlets if public stocks were not installed!
A common form of punishment for crimes in the town was to be whipped whilst being pulled along by a cart through the streets. The last two men to be so treated in Honiton were John Rice and Robert Pile who had been caught stealing apples. This form of punishment for men was outlawed in 1827; too late for Mr. Pile and Mr. Rice though!
The previously mentioned ducking stool was latterly used, particularly for women who were guilty of misconduct. The last person to be 'ducked' in the town was a woman who was found drunk on a Sunday morning in the cellar of a local maltster. There was once a town ducking stool, pillary and stocks present, which were thought to have been introduced to the town during Isabella de Fortibus' ownership of the Manor. A 'pillary' was similar to the stocks; it consisted of a hinged wooden frame in which the villain was restrained by the wrists and neck. Onlookers and passersby were then obliged to pelt the said individual with whatever they wished. The pillary was abolished in 1817.

Stealing was one of the most common forms of crime but punishment, if caught, could be severe. One Robert Potter, a boy apprentice of Cotleigh, was indicted for stealing some money from a servant in the same household. It was a case of mere suspicion as no money was found on the boy, nor were there any witnesses to the crime. However, the parish constable thought otherwise. In a bid to get a confession from the boy the constable tied cords around the boy's thumbs by which he suspended him from a peg on the wall so that his toes were just touching the ground. He then proceeded to pour cold water down the boy's arms. This all took place on Christmas Eve 1823. The constable obtained his confession and the boy was sent to prison. Fortunately for the boy he was later acquitted of any wrong doings.

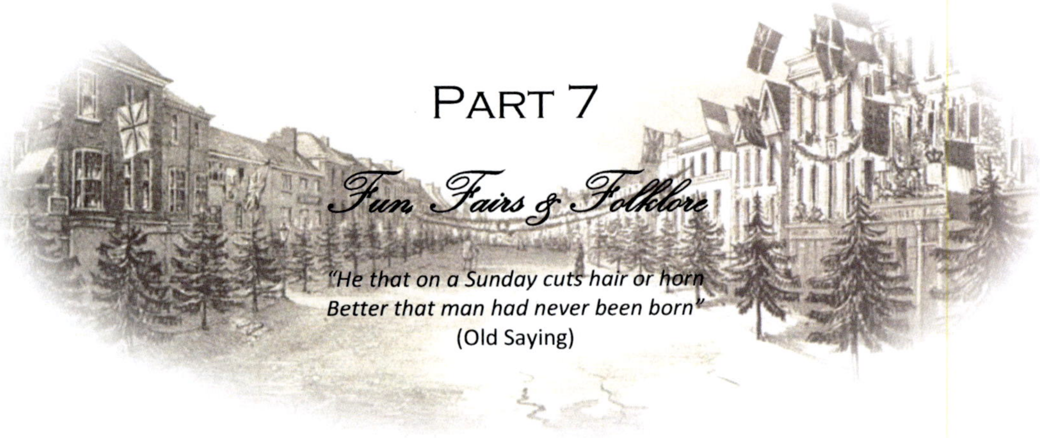

PART 7

Fun, Fairs & Folklore

"He that on a Sunday cuts hair or horn
Better that man had never been born"
(Old Saying)

Chapter 1
Fun & Amusements

"Live and work but do not forget to play, to have ***fun*** *in life and really enjoy it."*
Eileen Caddy

For the majority of the 19th century, people of Honiton did very little other than work and sleep; however, the small amount of time they had in between these two main parts of their day is so discussed in this chapter.

Up until the early twentieth century, work occupied some 12 hours of 6 days of the week and Sunday was strictly for religion. However, by 1913, Thursdays had become half a working day in Honiton, with shops closing at 1pm leaving a whole afternoon for people to pursue their own personal interests. This weekly early closing day was still in practise in the town up until the 1980s.

Before the advent of the half day, Honitonians enjoyed their free time in many ways, as they do today; however, leisure time was spent according to how much money one could afford to throw at such non essential avenues of pleasure.

Richer members of the rural scene could afford to have parts of their homes converted for recreation. In the early Victorian period the then Rector of Offwell had a small boating pond constructed in the grounds of the old rectory, still existing today as a wildlife reserve, and by the end of the 19th century the residents of Springfield House (now Manor House School) had had a tennis court built just beyond the house. Many other affluent members of Honiton society spent lots of money on their gardens. Mr. Flood, of Rookwood, had 'pleasure grounds', 'shrubberies', extensive lawns and carefully cultivated gardens. C. S. Flood was also a keen

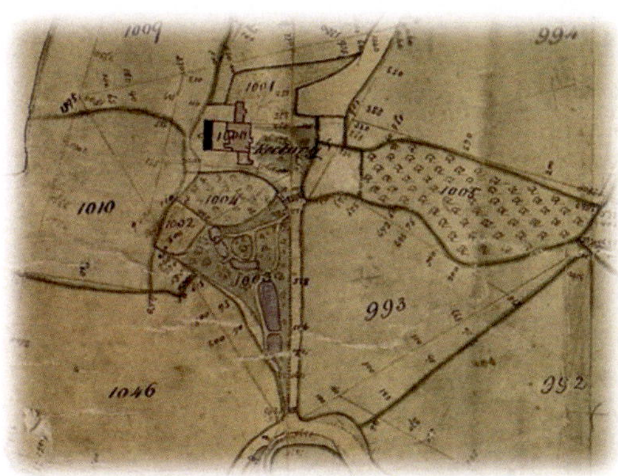

Aerial view of the old rectory from 1844 complete with its carefully laid out water features (blue).

breeder and racer of horses. The old rectory (now Old rectory farm) had "tastefully laid out" grounds amongst fish ponds which were later, sadly, filled in.

The richer town's people would have also attended events at the Dolphin Assembly Rooms. The Assembly Rooms were, as already mentioned, opened in 1824 with a public dinner for 80 people rejoicing with numerous toasts and a "brilliant" firework display that was held in the High Street. In 1851 a concert was held there where classical music was played by local man William Haydon Flood. Among his piano pieces, he played a piece composed by another local musician, Edwin Flood. Nearly all such events took place at the Assembly Rooms and there are many references to dinners being held there for either private parties or, for example, as in 1850, a dinner for some 120 people of the town where young, old, poor and rich were said to have attended. Numerous lectures were also well attended at the Assembly Room among which was a talk on "A Day in a Coal Mine" and a "Lecture on Phrenology"!

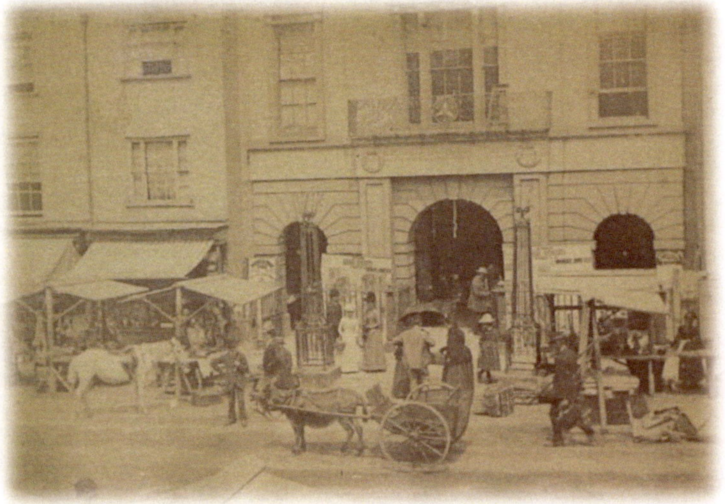

Market day outside the old Assembly Rooms.

Once the Assembly Rooms were known as 'Manor Assembly Rooms' with the aforementioned words boldly situated just below the roof line; the name later changed to 'Dolphin Assembly Rooms'. In the twentieth century they were simply known as the 'Assembly Rooms' and later named 'The Old Pannier Market', the wording of which was once situated over the arched entrance. Today this old listed building is a bed shop.

The average guy or gal in Honiton made do with much more down to earth, and more importantly, affordable ways of relaxing and socialising. Card playing was one of the most popular pastimes or evenings of "tea and supper, with cards between and spirits and water after." Some of the most popular card games played were 'Pope Joan', 'Three Card Loo', 'Whist & Swabbers', 'Long Whist' and 'Cribbage': Honiton people were said to have been "great" at them. The game 'Whist & Swabbers' was played like normal whist, but four of the cards from the deck were used as 'the swabbers' or 'swabs'- the ace of trumps, ace of hearts, jack of clubs and two of clubs. The dealer would supply a pool or a fixed sum for the 'swab' cards, of, say, one shilling and as each player who held one of these cards, played it, he/she drew 3d from the pool. Sometimes the ace of hearts would be the ace of trumps in which case it would be worth double. This game was said to be a popular choice of "some old ladies" of the town who kept the pool at a *safe* 2d or halfpenny per swab! 'Three Card Loo' was another popular Victorian card game. The basic idea was that a pool was formed and each player dealt three cards. Having seen their hand, they could either fold, free of charge, or elect to play, thereby undertaking to win at least one trick for one third of the pool. Any player failing to do so was 'looed' and added an amount to the pool, which was then carried forward and thus increased.
There were also a number of clubs and societies that once met weekly or monthly and among them included 'The Honiton Bible Society', who met from 1814, and 'The Honiton and District Gardening Association'.

Fishing was a popular pastime of many a local resident, just as it still is today. In the 19th century, trout and even salmon were caught from the River Otter. One of the largest trout known to have been caught in this period was ¾lb which was caught near Tipton Bridge, a popular fishing spot. The trout were said to have been "small but very strong" averaging about 6 ounces each, with examples weighing a pound being "rare". A local author noted that the

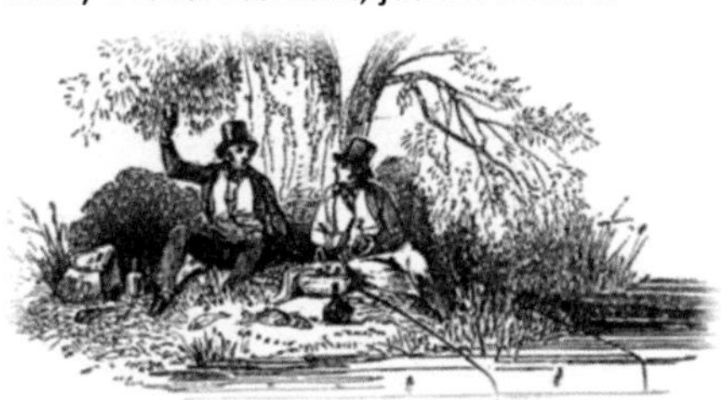

most he had ever known caught in one day was "eight dozen" whilst he himself could average between three and four dozen in the same amount of time. In the eighteenth century the Otter was deemed "famous" for its supply of trout. Samuel Taylor, a gentleman writing an angling publication, who was travelling through the town in the late eighteenth century, was told by the landlord of a local inn that this once "famous" supply of fish was no more, due to the fact that the freeman of the town had, in recent years, been given certain privileges towards catching the trout and that there were none to be caught within some miles of the town. Undeterred by this, the gentleman set off for the river and after only an hour and a half had "caught a fine dish of Trout". On his return to town he showed his catch to "several gentlemen reputed to be the best anglers in the town" who showed great "astonishment" at his feat considering they had been out fly-casting that, and the previous, day without success. Mr. Taylor had unwittingly proved not only that the trout of the Otter were still numerous but also that the reputations of Honiton's "best anglers" may need to be re-assessed!

The Otter was also a place where people enjoyed swimming, at a spot down School Lane once known as 'Head Weir'. Even in the early twentieth century, the town's people were still using this spot in the absence of a town swimming pool. In the nineteenth century it was reached by going down School Lane and crossing through a field known as 'Road Close'. This bathing spot was where a weir had been constructed, further downstream, for the benefit of the mills, allowing the water to reach a depth of up to 10 feet and thus being perfectly suitable for swimming. There was even, at one time, a spring and diving board present. This spot is now situated on the other side of the Honiton Bypass *1 and 'Road Close' has ironically been built on by the aforementioned section of road!

There were also some other general amusements that took place in the town over the years.

In 1766 a large cock fight was held in the town - a competition between owners from East and West Devon. Sixty two birds were entered in this event and the winnings were £4 for each winning bird and £42 for the overall winner: a substantial prize for the time.

Horse races were also often held on St. Cyres Hill and were known as 'The Honiton Races'. One such race that took place on 28th August 1828 had a "purse" of 30 sovereigns to be won. There was one race of note that took place in the town in 1806. A horse dealer from Chard made a "considerable bet" claiming that a distance of 100 miles could be completed by one horse over a period of "sixteen successive hours". The feat was attempted by travelling from Honiton to Exeter and back again six times, with an additional 4 miles added at the end so that the distance of one hundred miles could be completed. The gentleman set off at quarter past four in the morning, arrived at the city at quarter to six and made his first return to Honiton by ten the same morning. The race was completed in thirteen hours and fifty minutes. At the time this was a considerable achievement and gives us an idea of how limited people of yesterday were in their modes of transportation! Such wagers were well documented but unfortunately, once again, the area's indifference to the treatment of the beasts carrying the riders was often overlooked. A wager held between two gentlemen in 1830, which involved a race from Illminster to Exeter and back again for a stake of £50, resulted in the death of one of the horses at Honiton "from excess of punishment and fatigue." In the same report it was stated that "the inhabitants of the neighbourhood...are justly indignant at the atrocious cruelty" of such animals.

Public events and royal occasions were also greatly celebrated in the town. During the Napoleonic Wars the numerous victories on land and sea were commemorated by coloured candles, stuck in potatoes, being displayed in every window. The Coronation of Queen Victoria in 1838 saw the town witness to many celebrations. Business was suspended for the day and

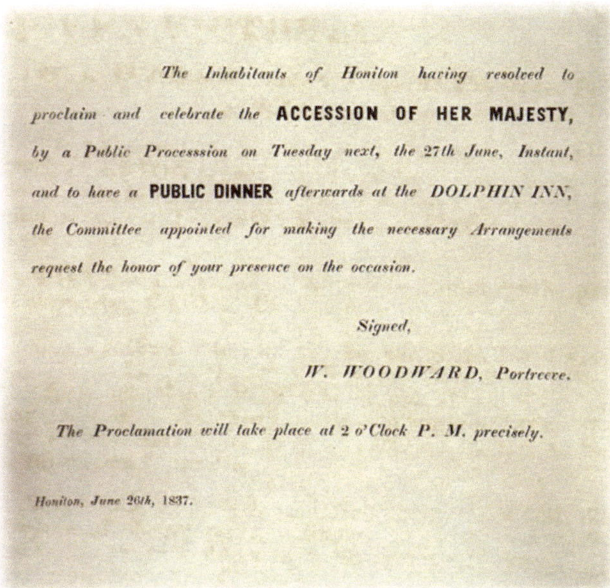

The Inhabitants of Honiton having resolved to proclaim and celebrate the **ACCESSION OF HER MAJESTY,** *by a Public Procession on Tuesday next, the 27th June, Instant, and to have a* **PUBLIC DINNER** *afterwards at the DOLPHIN INN, the Committee appointed for making the necessary Arrangements request the honor of your presence on the occasion.*

Signed,

W. WOODWARD, Portreeve.

The Proclamation will take place at 2 o'Clock P. M. precisely.

Honiton, June 26th, 1837.

amongst the children feasting on the cakes and buns at the free teas were great processions with bands.

""There were the schoolchildren; the ladies, two-and-two; lacemakers with garlands; Female Club also with garlands. Then another band, followed by the clergy "in full canonicals"; constables with staves; the bailiff with his mace; the Portreeve; the Aletasters; members of the Friendly Societies in their regalias; followed in the rear by the traders, sporting bright colours, and "the gentlemen and inhabitants of the town three and tree.""

Friendly societies were organisations that attempted to get the poorer classes to contribute some of their meagre wages towards collection funds that may bring them assistance in their dotage such as boot and sickness clubs. Several such groups existed in Hontion in 1850 including a 'Trademen's Friendly Society' (formed in 1848) as well as 'Friends United' and the 'New United Brethren'.

The jubilees of King George III and Queen Victoria were also greatly celebrated occasions in 1809, 1887 and 1897.

The golden jubilee of Victoria was so immense that the town even had the archway over 'Old School Lane' erected. Great celebrations were also held when George IV, William IV and Victoria were crowned; there was even a party when the Prince of Wales, the future Edward VII, recovered from typhoid in 1872.

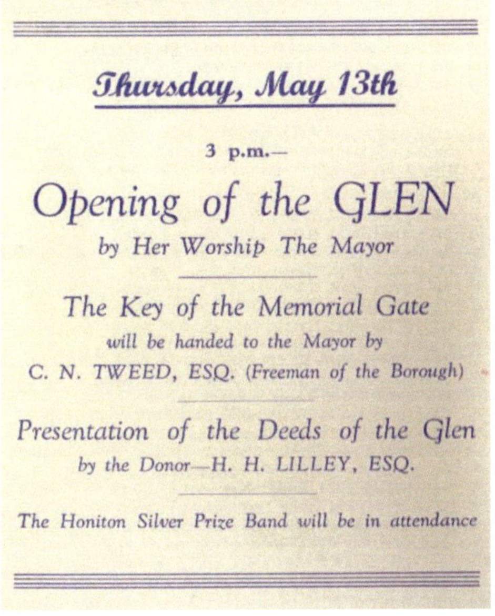

Thursday, May 13th

3 p.m.—

Opening of the GLEN

by Her Worship The Mayor

The Key of the Memorial Gate

will be handed to the Mayor by

C. N. TWEED, ESQ. (Freeman of the Borough)

Presentation of the Deeds of the Glen

by the Donor—H. H. LILLEY, ESQ.

The Honiton Silver Prize Band will be in attendance

Such celebrations were an old custom in Honiton; there is even knowledge of a celebration of a royal birthday in 1695, when great drinking parties were held and bonfires lit. Possibly the grandest of all such celebrations was that of the Coronation of George VI on 27th May 1937. For the entire festivity week, women dressed in red, white and blue dresses, the bells of St. Michael's were rung, over 700 hundred local children were given commemorative mugs and medals, a public tea for 2,500 burgesses was put on, there were 30 sporting events organised, the inmates of the workhouse were given cigarettes, tea and a shilling each, there was a maypole and ballet dancing, 300 people attended a dinner & dance at the Dolphin, a 20 foot bonfire was lit at Kirton's Scrap Yard, parades swept the High Street, St Michael's Church was lit up by red flares and the cream on the cake was when the Glen was presented to the town the following day by Major Lilley. The celebrations of the Silver Jubilee of George V, some two years earlier, saw similar extravagance. From 6.30am on the morning of May 6th 1935 events took place to commemorate the grand occasion, which included church services, whist drives, sporting events, a public dinner and dancing and community singing. The day finished at 10pm with bonfires and firework displays held on Gittisham Hill, Hembury Fort Hill and Roundball.

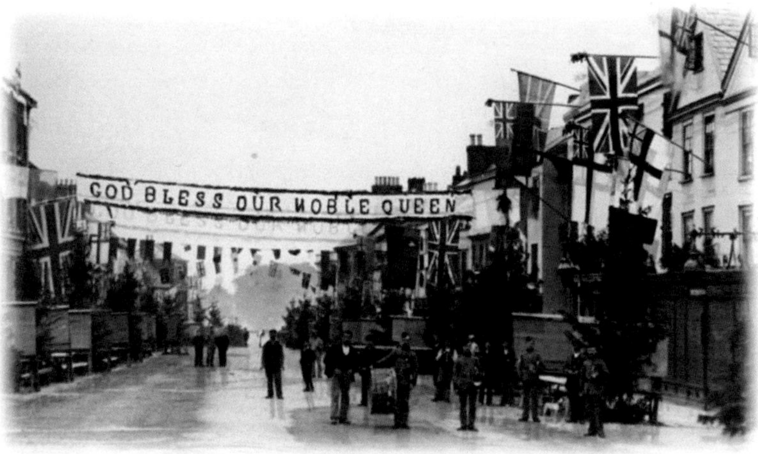

Celebrations for Queen Victoria's Diamond Jubilee in 1897

In 1856, when the Crimean War ended, the whole street was lined with fir trees, tea was provided for all the ladies and children and dinner for all the poor, with all the town tradesmen marching in a procession. In the evening there was a public dinner and the next night a great ball was held. Election time in Victorian Honiton also had a lighter, more comical, side to it. The previously mentioned butcher, Jasper Salter, who was the "town wag", always held "mock elections" at the east end of town, known as

"Scotland", for reasons unknown. He used to ""issue and address signed "Cleaver.""

The arrival of the railway in the town was another occasion that saw great celebrations. On July 18th 1860 all shops were closed and a "general holiday" was declared. A "public tea" for "thousands" was put on along with other refreshments served in the open air whilst dancing and bands celebrated the railway arrival. The new station was decorated for the occasion and the event was concluded with a public dinner at the Dolphin on the following evening, July 19th.

The previously mentioned James Townsend, local attorney, had a pack of harriers whose kennels were situated in Clapper Lane; the Rev. Marker of Gittisham also kept harriers which were used in hunting parties. The Honiton Borough 'Reform Club' sold their "curs and puppies" in the 1830s after being "driven out of a field" by the "loyal and constitutional pack". The following is an extract from the advertisement in which the pack of hounds were to be disposed of by "public competition" that gives an interesting insight into the breeds and names of such dogs that once hunted with such clubs...

""Lot I – JANUS, a wiry-hair'd SCOTCH TERRIER, with a smooth face and slippery tongue,-is remarkably snappish at present, but is nevertheless quite harmless, being

"Willing to wound, but yet afraid to bite."

Justice to the Public compels to the Proprietors to state, that he possesses "no game" whatever having on numberless occasions shewn the white feather!

Lot II. A "SLENDER" Pup, called "SOCINIAN,"-breed unknown-must therefore be classed among the Mongrels.-Hunted in the Whig Pack for many years....Has lately been the CERBERUS at the WHIG BASTILE , where he barks and snaps at the unfortunate inmates with wonderful sagacity.

Lot III. A COCK-EYED PUPPY, called ISSAC, much addicted to running on the false scent.-Hunted with the STEWART Pack, over the CONSERVATIVE PRESERVES, in 1837, when after having secured the Game, the smooth-faced terrier, JANUS, (lot I,) with cunning peculiar to that matchless animal, snatched it from his mouth, and falsely had the credit of being the first dog in the Pack. During the late hunt this Pup refused to join the cry, but slunk away with his tail between his legs-the Club are therefore determined to get rid of him at any price.

Lot VI. SURLY DICK, a most singular animal, being and out-and-out BULL-DOG, with a cloven foot. Not having been seen near cold-water since Saturday, is supposed to be labouring under hydrophobia, and is therefore confined at home, securely muzzled.

Lot V. GRUB, an old hound, with a Government Collar round his neck—has lately been detected trespassing on CORN Fields, and must therefore be sold, to prevent mischief to the Farmer.

Lot VI. A lop-ear'd SHEEP-DOG, called CHINO,-has done the dirty work of the Pack for some time.

Lot VII. A little TURN-Spit, called DUKEY, who will do anything but work, and drink anything but water.

The remainder of the Pack being dogs of inferior note will be disposed of in one Lot.""

The sale, for those who attended, was to be refreshed with "a cold collation of baked duck and cheap bread"!

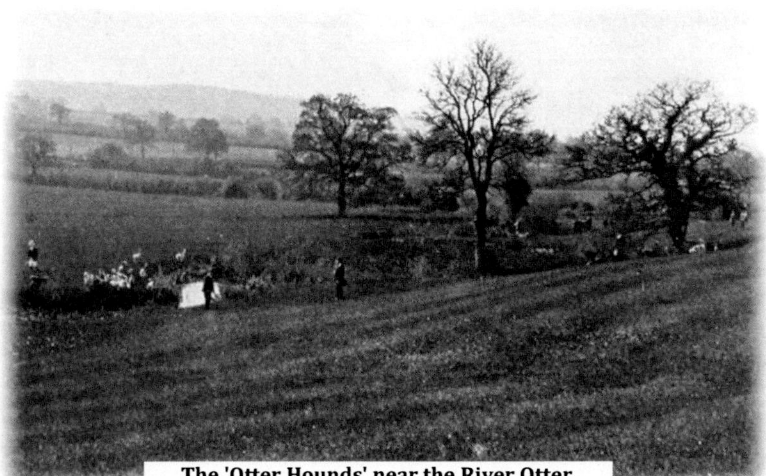

The 'Otter Hounds' near the River Otter.

The town was also occasionally visited by travelling exhibitions and circuses with amusements such as a "wild beast show". The town was also once visited by a troupe of mountebanks who were said to have last performed in the town in 1847 in a field behind the old King's Arms Inn.

The attraction was a small scale circus that played in the open air and there was also a raffle for a leg of mutton at which tickets were sold at one shilling each.

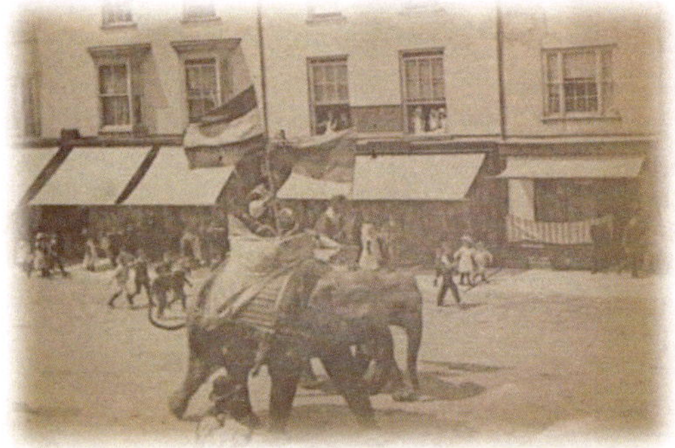

Above & Below: Two shots of when the circus was in town!

Another visiting attraction to the town was that of the shollers, a group of travelling actors.

Their visits were highly anticipated by the locals and they would usually remain in the town for a number of weeks. The sholling company would usually set up base in a barn or skittle alley and Cowley Farm barn was one of the most popular locations. Cowley's barn was known locally as "The Theatre Royal" when the shollers were in town and the elite of the town would watch the performances in full evening dress. One of the most well known shollers was a man known as 'one eyed Palmer', having formerly lost an eye. His last visit was in 1852 when he located himself at the Kings Arms skittle alley. The last ever sholling company to visit the town was said to have been in 1857 when a gentleman called Mr. Rogers visited Honiton with his wife, two daughters,

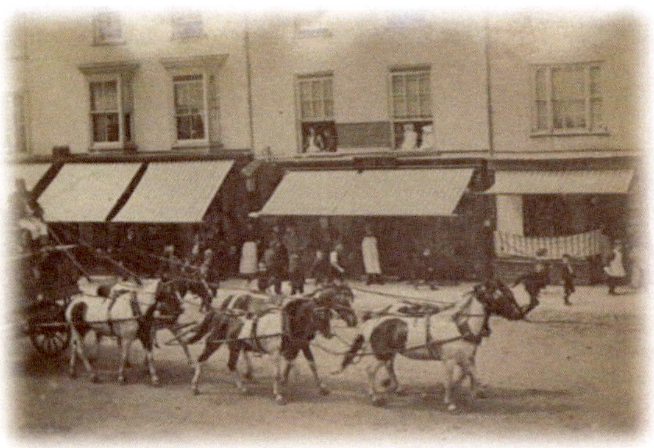

two brothers and their wives. This last performance was held at the skittle alley belonging to The Fountain Inn.

The lace-makers of the town also had their own annual festivities. On July 1st they would have a service at the church followed by a procession through the town which ended with tea at the Golden Lion and dancing into the evening. This was a rather old tradition known to have existed as early as 1778.

Sports

Honiton Cricket Club: this was one of the earliest organised sport societies established in the town, being founded in 1881. The earliest known cricket ground was on Allhallows playing field. The Pavilion still exists today, having been built in 1889. The club was later said to have moved to a field near the Copper Castle and in 1920 it moved to Camp Field, near the present day Heathfield Industrial Estate, the first game being played there on 22nd May 1920. The club moved back to Allhallows after the school vacated the site in 1938 and it is now situated at Mountbatten Park.

Honiton Rugby Club: established in 1883, the first match was played at Budleigh Salterton in the same year. Some notable members were, amongst others, Harry Banfield of the Dolphin Hotel, Derek Steele-Perkins, Dr Finlay, W. E. Sprake, H. H. Lilley of Miller and Lilley and Mr. A. Dimond of Dimond Stationers. The club's present day clubhouse, on Allhallows playing field, was established in 1978.

Honiton Golf Club: the idea for the golf club was put forward by Arthur F. Bernard, a local Justice of the Peace who resided at Combe Raleigh, on the 14th April 1896. The club's first Captain was Rev. A Marwood-Elton and the first President was The Honourable Viscount Sidmouth. The club, which was originally a nine hole course, only later becoming 18 holes, initially charged an annual subscription of 1 guinea. The first club house, a small iron shed, was replaced by a new wooden building in 1931 and the present day building was built in 1976 with the old clubhouse now used as greens-keepers sheds. During WWII the club lost 9 of its 18 holes for the growth of potatoes, only becoming a 14 hole course in 1966 and a full 18 again in 1986. The original concept of the club was abandoned in 1904 but was re-founded in 1922.

Other sporting clubs were established in the early twentieth century, including the Honiton Football Club in 1920 and the Honiton Bowling Club in 1921.

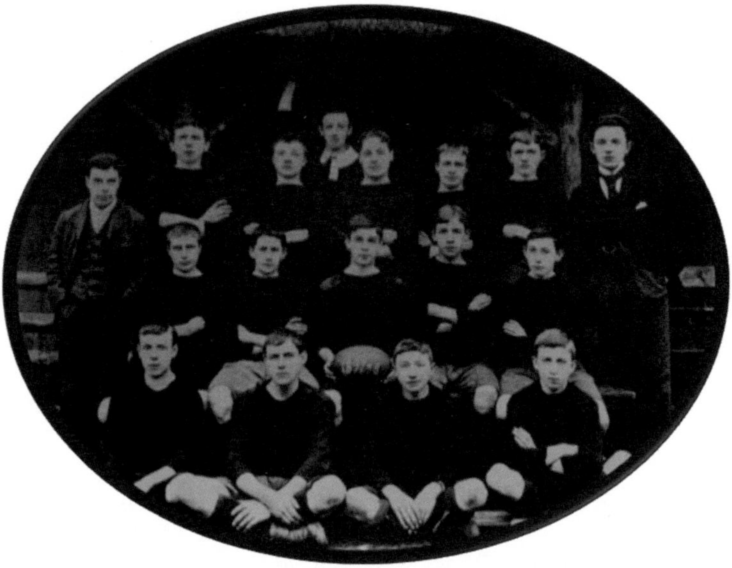

Honiton Rugby Club Team 1897-1898

Chapter 2
Honiton Fair, Show & Markets

"Oh what a day we're having I'm sure,
For the Honiton people both rich and poor"
Ode to the Honiton Show, William Skinner

Throughout the working year the good old people of Honiton could look forward to many other annual events that brought money, merriment and business to the town. In all, there was an annual fair, two great markets, a weekly market and, later, an annual show.

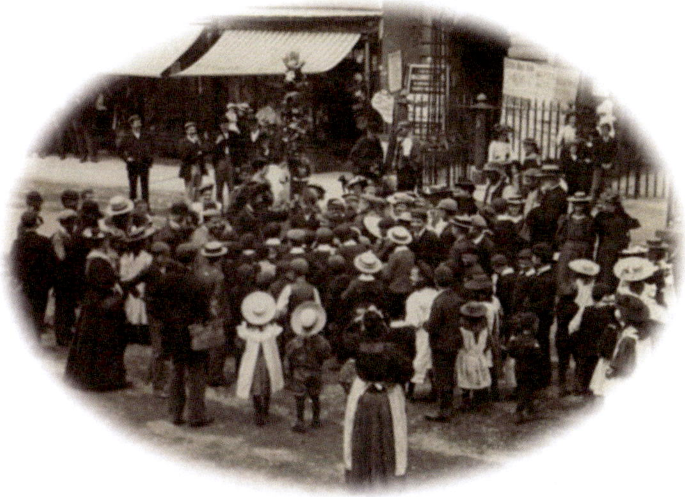

The Opening of Honiton Fair about 1895.

The right for a fair was first granted in 1221 when, as previously mentioned, it was held on Allhallows Day. On 22nd June 1247 the date of the fair was changed by King Henry III to St. Margaret's Day, July 20th a position it has held to this day. Today the fair is held on the first Tuesday on or after July 19th but in Victorian times was held on the first Wednesday after July 19th being originally held on the Tuesday. Once it was a three day event of amusements, feasting and drinking but today is a one day event. On the Tuesday, the Town Crier would carry a glove on a pole decorated with flowers and shout the following:

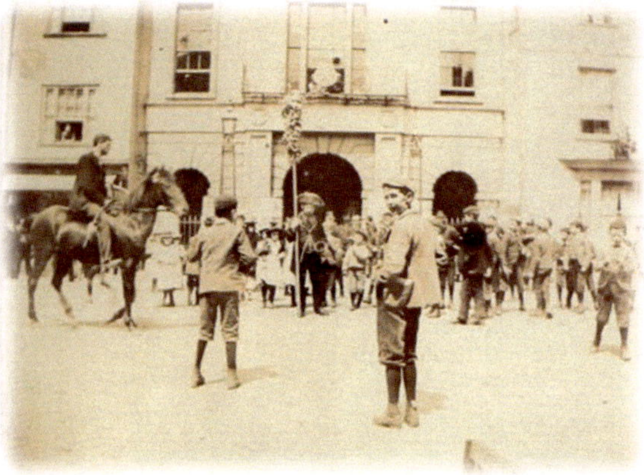

"Oyez! Oyez!
Oyez!,
The Glove is up,
the fair is begun,
No man can be
arrested until it is
taken down
again."

The glove was then carried to, and placed outside, the old Kings Arms Inn where it would remain until the following night. The Kings Arms was once the centre of the great cattle fair that was held on the following day (Wednesday). The Crier would then enter the Kings Arms where outside the crowd would "wait impatiently" as hot pennies were thrown from the upper storey windows. 'Hot Pennies,' as this is known, is still practised annually. Today these pennies are only warm compared to earlier times when they were "well-heated" so much so that many children suffered "burnt fingers" which they "cooled in the stream running beside the pavement". The throwing of these "hot" pennies was thought to have originated when

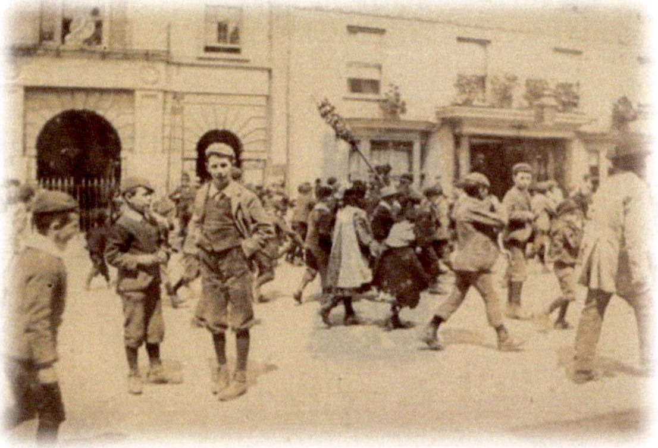

rich threw them to the poor to amuse themselves as the peasants burnt their hands in their desperate attempts to grab the money. The actual origins of this ancient custom are unknown but one suggestion was that it started in the reign of King Stephen, some 900 years ago. Another old custom, practised well into the twentieth century, was to 'dunk' a schoolboy into one of the leats or "dipping places" that used to flow down the High Street.

On Wednesday night the glove would be paraded down to the White Lion and displayed there, for this was the sight of the horse fair that took place on the Thursday. On the Friday evening the Town Crier would go around ringing his bell signalling the end of the fair. Although the fair still remains an annual Honiton event, it is a shame that The Kings Arms, The White Horse and the vitally important finger cooling stream are all now gone.

The word *"Oyez!"* used three times in succession is a mediaeval term used to proclaim the opening of a court of law. It is still used in the 'Supreme Court of The United States' and originates from the Anglo-French meaning "hear ye".

The reference to "no man can be arrested" was thought to be an ancient tradition, giving those who owed money the right to be given a pardon for the three days of the fair. A gentleman travelling through Honiton during fair time in the 1860s commented that "those three days' grace... served as an invitation to evil-doers to visit the town."

Farquaharson wrote the following about his memories of fair time:

- *"On the Monday in the fair week the county folks used to bring in vegetables which were exposed at New Street corner for sale.*
- *On the Tuesday at noon the glove was hoisted and the fair legally commenced. During the afternoon booths and shows would arrive and having taken up their ground would erect their standings. The favourite position for a show was outside the Kings Arm's Inn facing down the street. The shows, surrounds and swings always stood east of the King's Arms some years however any very large exhibition would stand facing up the street opposite the Baptist Chapel.*
- *On Wednesday morning the fair would begin in earnest, from opposite St Paul's to Marwood House the horned cattle stood so thickly as to occupy the roadway. From opposite the Baptist Chapel to the bridge would be pens for pigs and sheep, the centre of the town would be occupied by stalls covered with gingerbread and toys. If there were any Cheap Jacks they stood opposite the church, and in its immediate neighbourhood were stall of fancy articles. At noon all the cattle pigs and sheep would leave the town but at every road leading were place men with long stoves to demand a ticket from the drover as an assurance he or his*

master had paid the fair dues. The after part of Wednesday was devoted to enjoyment every tradesman kept open house where his county customers eat and drank ad lib. In the evening the street would be throughed with pleasure seekers.

- *On Thursday the first part of the day would be quiet but in the afternoon the horse fair would be held at the west end, no horse being allowed higher than the Golden Lion. The stock usually for sale were fit for farm purposes.*
- *On Friday the fair being over all the shops were closed, and till late years, pony racing, climbing the pole and even badger baiting were carried on in the street.*
- *On Saturday there was a kind of wind up, some of the shows and booths still remaining and the tradesmen still having their customers to see them. During the fair the servants were decked in their best and wore especially smart caps. Of late years tradesmen have taken their assistants for an excursion on the Friday. Honiton fair falling as it does between the hay and corn harvest affords the farmer leisure time to attend it."*

Although, officially, this was only supposed to be a three day event, it is evident it was more a week of selling, buying and festivities!
In 1863 there were said to have been 340 bullocks and 1,340 sheep driven into the town on fair day. Oxen were bought for between £15 and £18, cows with calves for £12-£16, sheep sold for about 36 shilling each, lambs went for between 20 and 25 shillings and rams were much more expensive, reaching prices of anything up to £7. These numbers were also said to have been "not nearly so large as before." The sale of animals was such a big part of the annual event that in one national publication of 1851 the fair was actually referred to as the "cattle fair" of "July 20th."
Cleaning of the town, after the event, was an arduous task lasting several days after the fair: even on the "Saturday the odour of carbolic" could still be detected! However "before many days [had] passed quaint old Honiton [settled] down into its usual sleepy quietude" once again!
There was another known annual fair held on Easter Monday at the western end of town which was known as the 'Turk's Head Fair'. This must have once been a well frequented event but had virtually fallen into extinction by the mid 19th century, by which time there was only one stall present that was held by a local confectioner called John 'Jacky' Saunders. Jacky was an old man by the 1850s and it is believed that the fair finally

died with him in the 1870s, if not before. By the 1950s the fair was held in a field along King Street which is now a housing estate called 'Fairfield Gardens'. The fairs once held in that long gone field included stereotypical English pastimes such as the helter-skelter, gingerbread stalls, 'Gondolas with their fair organs', boxing rings and fortune tellers. The field was also host to circuses that once visited several times a year. The field was once owned by a local haulier called Henry Proll who used to transport coal from the train station to the old Honiton Gas Works.

In 1852 the first annual 'Honiton and East Devon Poultry Exhibition', or its full name of 'Honiton and East Devon Association for the Improvement of Domestic Poultry', was held in the town. In 1853 it was held on Wednesday and Thursday of December 28th and 29th in the market house. The "Poultry House" that was once said to have adjoined the Market House was specially glazed for the event so that all the birds could be comfortably displayed to visitors. In total, 416 birds were entered and despite heavy snowfall and frost the attendance was said to have been "good". Chickens, pigeons, turkeys, geese and ducks were entered into the competition, of which the finest specimens were awarded prizes for their respective owners. A number of local people won first, second and third places alongside entrants who had travelled from places as far as Glastonbury, Bridport, Plymouth, Bristol and even London. It is not known how long this annual event lasted but it is hard to imagine today an exhibition of ducks and chickens in Honiton High Street just before the New Year celebrations!

There were also two "great markets" held annually, directly after Lady's Day and Michaelmas, 25th March and September 29th respectively and more specifically "the second Saturday in April, and the Saturday before October 18th." These markets dealt with large scale sales of livestock which included horses, cattle and sheep, etc. In 1837 it consisted of some 2,000 sheep alone, but this was quoted to be "not so numeracy supplied" as in previous years!

The original right for a weekly market was thought to have been granted by King John with evidence of a market as early as 1199 and was originally held on Sunday; later changed to Saturday. The actual market Charter was granted by King Henry III on December 28th 1257. The town of Honiton recently celebrated the 750th anniversary of this event, in 2007, where many members of the town and market adorned themselves in mediaeval dress. In addition to Saturday, there were once two other weekly markets held on Tuesday and Thursday and today only the Tuesday and Saturday markets survive. Saturday was, and still is, the most "well attended" and the visitor of two hundred years ago could expect to meet a number "of market people with panniers, crookes and gambades." Whilst much was sold in the streets from stalls, the sale of poultry, cheese and corn were bartered for in the market house (next to the Dolphin Inn). The weekly Saturday market would have once been the highlight of the town's working week. One would see farmers chatting to their friends about the highs and lows of their week whilst they haggled and bid for the best and latest additions to their animal

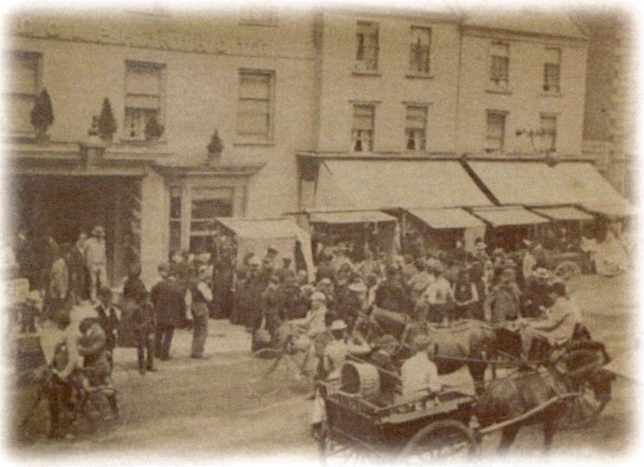

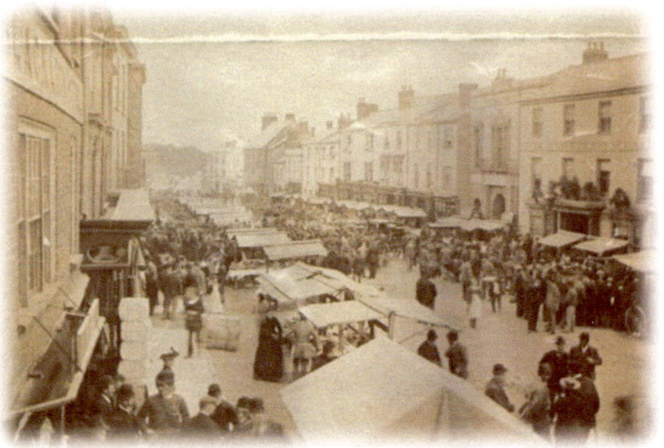

stocks. Wives, coming into town with their husbands, would frequent the drapers for clothing to be made and repaired whilst catching up on the latest gossip and news with their friends. Sons and daughters would be present to assist their fathers and mothers and it would be the one time of the week when prospective couples could catch each other's eyes through the crowds and possibly partake of a kiss behind one of the stalls!

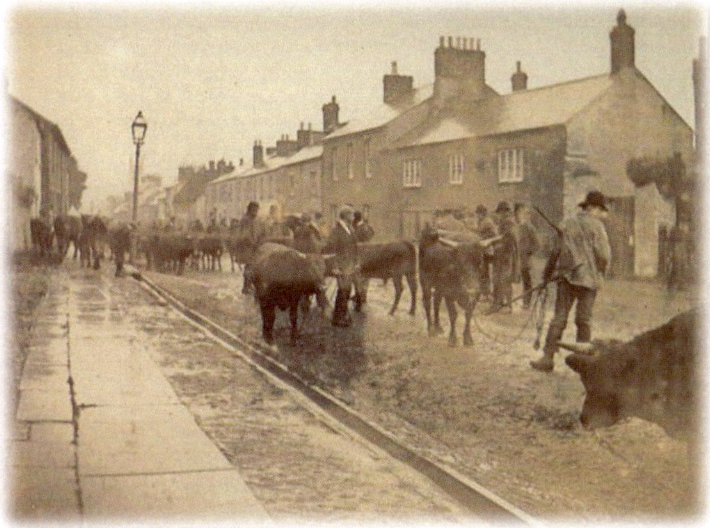

Cattle on market day.

In its earlier days the town market "was locally looked upon as one of the most successful west of Salisbury." In Vancouver's General View of Devonshire he wrote:

> *"The district here mentioned, is justly famous for its rich butter, which is highly admired in the London market, under the denomination of Dorsetshire butter; as well as for its sweet, veined skimmed-milk cheese (scarcely an oleagenous particle in it) with which Honiton market, and from thence Exeter, and the greatest part of Devonshire is supplied."*

The Honiton Market was also mentioned in the story of 'Reuben Apsley' by Horace Smith where one character named Lady Crockatt was so refined that she would "buy no fish except out of Honiton market"!

The following was written of Honiton Market in 1907:

"Butchers in their neat blue or snow-white coats leave their shops to the care of the subordinates and themselves take their stand in the open street and dispense the finest viands from the hooded stalls. Green grocers make artistic displays of the season's delicacies. Seed merchants label their neat packages with showily depicted illustrations and attract many customers, whilst interspersed amongst the stalls are goods which especially tempt the youngsters, and emporiums at which articles can be secured at apparently ruinous prices. A Fish Market, stocked with the latest catches from dear old Beer, nestling between Devon's cliffs a few miles off is actually established each week in the main street. Vendors of cast off army horse clothing, saddler and suck-like do a thriving trade, and every now and then a vendor of medicines, which are guaranteed to cure all the ills to which flesh is heir, may be found at Honiton Market."

By the early 20th century it was becoming obvious that the large numbers of cattle and livestock in the High Street on market days was not only unhygienic but was also starting to cause problems for the motor car which had just started to appear on the roads. It was, therefore, decided to relocate the sale of these beasts to a new site located in Silver Street. Honiton Cattle Market was paid for, and opened, by the Lord of the Manor, Mr. Marker, on October 8th 1910. The principal auctioneers were the old Honiton family of 'T. D. Hussey & Son.'

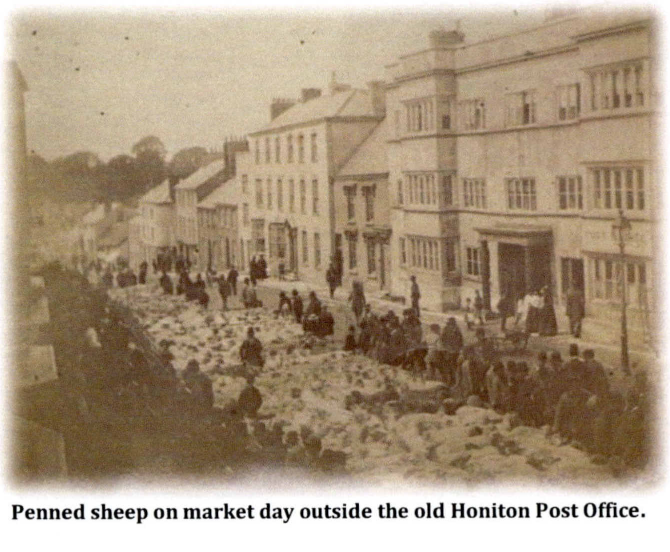

Penned sheep on market day outside the old Honiton Post Office.

Edgar Pulman wrote the following about his early memories of the new cattle market:

"In the early days there were no cattle lorries and the animals were driven for miles from the farm to the market. I have seen cows with full udders and milk dripping from their teats being driven along the roads. As soon as they have been through the auction they were taken to the old Cowley Dairy which adjoined the market, this was compulsory and there was always a representative of the R. S. P. C. A. in attendance to see this was carried out."

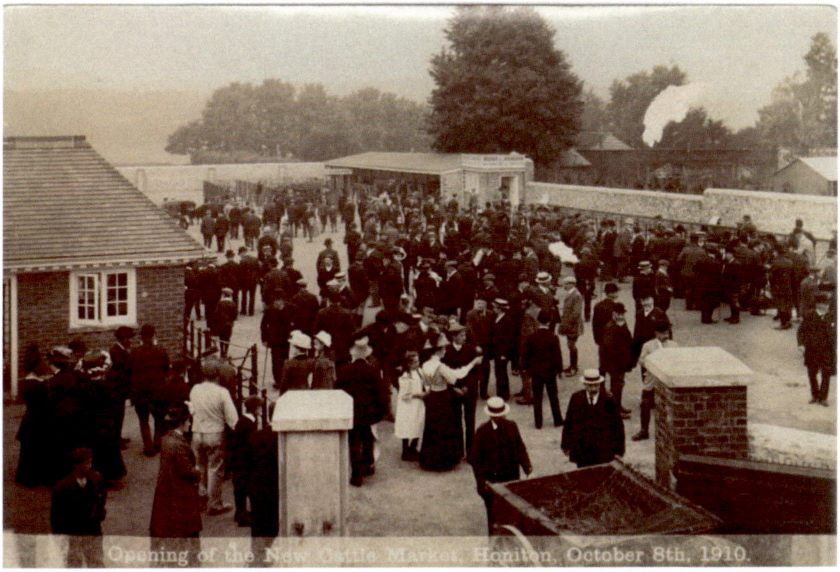

The Honiton cattle market never recovered the devastating effects of the 2007 foot & mouth outbreak and after centuries of bovine being driven into town the market ceased. The nearest cow sales today are held in Exeter and Taunton.

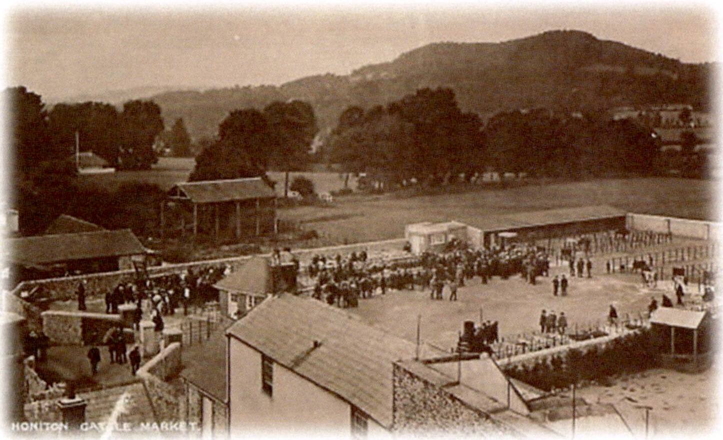

Honiton Cattle Market in 1915

Today over 40% of all first time marriages end within the first fifteen years but in Victorian times the vows you made on your wedding day really were "until death you do part". However, if a husband did become tiresome of his wife for making lumpy porridge or not having supper ready on time, there were ways other than divorce or murder in which he could rid himself of her. In the 1830s a man by the name of Henry Broom got the Town Crier to march the streets and announce that his wife was to be put up for auction at the Honiton Fair. The "woman, fine grown, and of handsome person, about twenty-five years of age" was paraded to the market place where the auctioneer, who was her husband of three years, started the auction. The sale aroused a lot of interest and whilst potential buyers agreed the young maiden was both "youthful" and "pretty" some feared that a droop at the corners of her mouth gave warnings that "admiration should be tempered by caution"! Amongst the crowds of people, a local painter put in the first bid of half a crown. Several other locals made subsequent bids but the winning gentleman, by the name of Thomas Tremlett of Awliscombe, won the woman for a final bid of one pound. The terms appeared satisfactory to all as "all went their way smiling, as if they meant to be happy ever after"! A similar documented case involved that of a railway labourer who also offered his wife for sale at one of Honiton's markets in 1857. The legality of these two transactions may be uncertain but in the 1857 case it was said that a "deal was

effected"! This 'poor man's divorce', as it was once known, was a serious transaction to all the relevant parties as a wife was once deemed the property of her husband, which could be sold like any other possession. There are hundreds of documented examples of such sales occurring throughout the country.
In 1869 the annual profits of the market tolls and fair was £300 and the rights for this annual revenue were purchased first by Lord Marker in 1872 for the sum of £2,000. In the twentieth century the rights for the market tolls were owned by Honiton Borough Council until 1974 when East Devon District Council was formed. In 2009 East Devon District Council handed the rights of the tolls back to the town council.

Honiton Show was first held in 1890 when the Buckerell, Awliscombe, Feniton and Gittisham Agricultural Association decided that the need for a local annual show of the area's finest beasts should be displayed and judged. The first was held on Bramble Hill on September 30th of the same year with admission of one shilling and the show's first president was Lord Sidmouth. In 1921 the ground, having outgrown its Bramble Hill location, moved to Heathfield and by the end of World War II it had relocated once again to the bottom of Ottery Moor Lane, where the sports ground is presently located. It was later held at a field off Monkton Road and in 2003, land that was bought from Roebuck Farm became the Show's present permanent fixture. No show was held during the Great War and the Second World War but ever since then there has been a Honiton Show annually in the first week of August.

Chapter 3
Local Customs & Beliefs

"Foul superstition howsoe'er disguised"
Lord Byron

Old Honiton had many strange local customs and superstitions that would today be viewed as almost mediaeval. Virtually all of these have long been forgotten and no longer practised which is in some ways a shame as many of them are old pieces of local culture and tradition that have been lost forever.

Celebrations and Customs

Many of the religious days of the year were marked by feasting or parties in a time when the church had much more influence over people's lives. Shrove Tuesday, as today, was the day when pancakes were made and at Easter a special cake was also prepared. During Lent the women of the town were expected to attend church in black. On Easter Monday children mounted Church Hill to 'clip' the parish church of St Michael's. This was done by everyone holding hands until an unbroken circle was formed around the church.

"The ceremony was performed amid crowds of people and shouts of joy, by the children of the different charity schools who, at a certain hour flocked together for the purpose, the first comers placed themselves hand in hand with their backs against the church and were joined by their companions who gradually increased in number till at last the chain was of significant length to completely surround the edifice as soon as the hand of the first had touched that of the first the party broke up and walked in procession to the next church where the ceremony was repeated."

The term 'clipping' comes from the Anglo-Saxon 'clippen' meaning 'embrace fondly'. If this ceremony was not performed it was believed the whole parish would have 12 months of bad luck.
Work by candle light was also suspended at Easter time as an old rhyme stated "be the Easter high or low, out the candle we must blow." Easter Monday would also have seen the popular attraction of a bull being baited in the High Street.

On May 29th boughs of oak trees were placed outside every door; this was to commemorate 'Oak Apple Day', a celebration of the restoration of the monarchy after the Civil War. This festivity was officially abolished in 1859. Whitsun Monday, another old religious holiday, was devoted to the annual dinners of the majority of local clubs who met at their respective headquarters and marched, fronted by a band and their own banners, to the church and then paraded through the town. After the procession the day was spent feasting with "gooseberry pies" and "summer cabbages". The night before St John's day, June 23rd, parties were held "when the good people held their revels". This day was to commemorate St. John the Baptist.
Michaelmas, September 29th, was celebrated by most households preparing roast goose; a tradition started by Elizabeth I who chose the said bird for the celebration of the defeat of the Spanish Armada in 1588. She specified it should be served every year at the royal table and many people subsequently followed the custom. Michaelmas was a celebration of the end of the harvest season and has always been a well recognised festival. November 5th would have once seen a large bonfire lit on Church Hill with the town Portreeve leading a procession to the spot. This custom had gone from Honiton by about 1808 after a prankster apparently set fire to the Portreeve's wagon and the ceremony was thus abandoned. Until relatively recently, one of the town's main firework displays was still performed on Church Hill by the Lions Club but it carried none of the former traditions. It was, in fact, law that all citizens of England celebrate "with unfeigned thankfulness" this day until 1859 when the law was repealed. Celebrations of November 5th were known to have become raucous, rowdy occasions: in the festivities of 1882 a valuable window was smashed and an old coach was seized and thrown on the town bonfire, reminiscent of the events on Church Hill of some 70 years before!
At Christmas 'mummers' would visit the town's houses. The performing of mummers was an ancient custom of masquerades playing out stories of King George and the Dragon and other mythological stories. Despite Christmas being a Christian festival, these very popular mummers' plays dated back to pagan times. Mummers were also known to have performed in Sidmouth around the same time and some maintain the custom to present times. On the same night a man travelled around the town playing tunes with his violin under bedroom windows to wish the inhabitants a Merry Christmas and Happy New Year. On Christmas day he would call back for some form of reward for his previous night's work! People would also splash out on more expensive coloured tallow candles, specially made for the season by local tallow chandlers. Many makers of

these candles gave them away free to their customers; some were said to have been as long as 2 feet and "thick in proportion"! These candles were often not burnt but preserved as their fat was said to be a perfect remedy against cuts and sores!

The Romans had given each calendar year as an average of 365¼ days but this system left an accumulative error of 8 days every millennium. By the 16th century there were 10 of these days. The Gregorian calendar was introduced in 1582 with the advent of leap years in order to do away with the accumulation of erroneous days from the old Roman system. Britain, however, did not adopt it until 1752 and even up until Victorian times, many local people still celebrated Christmas on its former date of January 6th (11 days after Dec 25th) some whole century after the new time-keeping method was introduced into the country. This is also why Christmas time is associated with snow, for originally Christmas was at a time when snowfall was much more common (January rather than December)!

Another common Christmas ritual, which was performed until around the 1950s, was that of the 'Ashen Faggot'. It was a particularly important tradition at the 'White Hart Inn' at Offwell where an ashen faggot was once burnt every Christmas Eve for generations. At one festive celebration at the White Hart it took two men to carry the faggot in. The 'Ashen Faggot' was a bundle of sticks that was bound together with either wire or hemp and was carried into the pub on Christmas Eve and later burnt.

Even Christmas left little leisure time for local people. In 1859, when Christmas Day fell on a Sunday, there was a meeting held by local tradesmen to decide whether or not to "suspend business" on Monday 26th December "in order to give [their] assistants" the day off! Luckily for the downtrodden employees, the shopkeepers gave them their "general holiday".

Lastly is a long forgotten New Years Eve celebration that was once a common sight in the High Street on December 31st. On New Year's Eve a large group of people would gather in the High Street and on the strike of midnight of the clock of St. Paul's a local man would sing "The Miner's Dream of Home". This song dates from 1890 but it is not known how many New Years were celebrated in the town with this tune. The last two people to perform this piece were William Rattenbury and William Long. The custom ceased at some point in the 1930s.

Beliefs and Folklore

People of Victorian Honiton had a very superstitious nature about them and believed in a variety of strange rhymes and myths. Many of these beliefs probably date back centuries, being handed down from one generation to the next and today one would be lucky to find anyone who can remember any such saying or legend let alone the practise of them.

To give one an idea of just how superstitious people of the time were, I refer to an event which took place not far from the town in 1855. On a winter's morning of that year a collection of strange footprints was

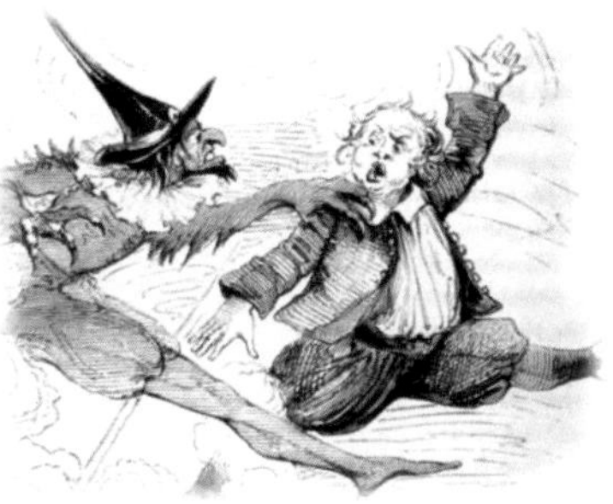

discovered in the snow that stretched for many miles across the south of Devon. These peculiar tracks to many resembled that of a bipedal, cloven- hoofed entity and many people were terrified to venture out of their homes after dark for a considerable time after this event as they truly believed these tracks were those of the Devil.
It was thought that a newly born child should not be passed through an open window as this would stunt its growth. It was also commonly practised to take a baby *upstairs* before being taken *downstairs* as this would prevent any falls later in life. Children's nails were never supposed to be cut for the first twelve months of its life, as the child would grow up to be a thief: the nails were bitten off by the mother or a nurse. The bitten off nails, as well as things such as locks of cut hair and milk teeth, had to be carefully disposed of for if a witch got hold of them she could endanger the child's wellbeing.
People of the area were keen to get their new born children baptized as soon as possible for if the child died without being christened it would be doomed to hunt with the black hounds of Squire Cabell for eternity. Cabell reputedly sold his soul to the Devil and since his death in 1677 he and his black hounds have been seen roaming Dartmoor. It was the story of Squire Cabell that inspired Arthur Conan Doyle to write his famous book 'The Hound of the Baskervilles'.
One should also never cut his/her hair or nails on Sunday for fear of bad luck befalling them...

*"He that on a Sunday cuts hair or horn
Better that man had never been born"*

To cut one's nails on a Monday morning, without thinking of a fox's tail, would guarantee the cutter a "present" in the coming week! So basically if you had never heard the saying, everyone who trimmed their nails on a Monday morning would receive a gift!

Funerals were occasions that displayed customs centuries old. Mourners of the deceased would always start the funeral procession at the foot of Church Hill with a hymn or psalm and would continue with their song until reaching the old church. When a person of significant standing in the town died, the chief mourners, along with the family doctor and lawyer, were given a scarf, gloves and a silk hat band that stretched nearly to the waist to wear for the procession. The Sunday after the funeral, the mourners would all congregate in the parish church for the ceremony of the departed and no one would stand until the service was complete, as a sign of respect.

There was one woman in Victorian Honiton, believed by many to be a witch, who was thought to make nightly trips on her broomstick. This woman was feared amongst the town's people and when passing her in the street people would deliberately be overly friendly to her in an attempt to prevent her putting a spell on them; out of sight, however, "no abuse was too great"!

In 1874 there was one woman in Honiton who had breast cancer and after failing to fight the illness through conventional medicine she went to see a local woman called Emily Fish, who was a herbalist. She visited Mrs. Fish for eight months and with her remedies failing, the herbalist made up a potion of "neats-foot oil", "litharge" and "acetic acid" which she applied to the tumour. Several weeks later the cancer sufferer died and Mrs. Fish was brought before a coroner's jury where she was found guilty of manslaughter!

The two types of witches were "the white witch" and "the black witch"; the latter was the evil one you would want to avoid but the white witch was "corrective of the spells of the other". White witches were both men and women and were occasionally consulted about stolen goods or ailments thought to have arisen from the activities of a black witch. One magistrate stated that in his twenty years in office he had seen "numberless" cases in which witches were consulted for such causes. There were some well known white witches around the local area and among them was a very well known individual in Exeter called Tuckett and another in Chard.

The Honiton area has quite a long history of witches; a large stone, outside 'The Hare and Hounds' public house on the Sidmouth Road, is known as the 'Witches Stone'. This large boulder has a variety of myths attached to it, including that it was a powerful rock that witches used to destroy their enemies with and that it was also the slaughter stone of a coven of witches. The stone is said to roll down the hill when the bells of Sidbury Church chime at midnight to drink from the River Sid and to wash away the stains of blood that have been spilt on it over the years. Originally it was thought to have been a boundary stone between Gittisham and Sidbury but no such boundary stone in the area was of similar size to this one. It was once reported to have been 5 feet 10 inches in length and 5 feet 2 inches in breadth and weighing in at an estimated ton. In 1951 the stone was placed in an upright position by an archaeological group and as it has sunk into the soil over the decades, only a small portion of it is visible today.

A traveller through Honiton in 1760 noted the presence of a ducking stool, used for obtaining confessions from any suspected witches. The device was said to have been located near the Gissage and described as an armed wooden chair fixed on a pole some 13 feet long which was hinged so that the operator could lower and raise the accused into the water. If the persecuted sank (or drowned) they were innocent and if they swam they were clearly a witch and were thus hanged: no way out really if suspicion fell on you! To render a black witch's spell harmless one had to draw blood from her body. One man in Stockland, in the mid 19th century, believed that a local woman had charmed his cattle and by scratching her arm with a thorn branch he thought it would dissolve the curse. His attempt, however, ended in him appearing before a magistrate - perhaps the witch cursed him too when he tried to attack her! Another Devonshire magistrate stated in 1852 that "three or four months past he had had four similar cases" such as that of the Stockland witch. A similar example to that of the man in Stockland is one that was known to have occurred in Clyst St. Lawrence. A local farmer grabbed a woman, whom he suspected of cursing his pig, and stuck a pin in her arm in order to draw blood and hence break her spell. The strange thing about this was that it happened in 1924: quite a few years after one would expect such superstitious practises to occur!

If you were a member of a local Victorian village and a witch was causing you problems, there was one very common and ancient practice you could rely on to relieve yourself of the horrid hag. Sticking pins in the heart of a sheep or cow, and then carefully stowing it somewhere in your abode, was thought to cure any evil and protect your home from wickedness. One such example of this was found behind a beam in the kitchen of the farmhouse of what is now 'Devenish Pitt Riding School', Farway. It was believed to have been put there in the 1870s as protection against a local witch. A similar, more sinister, item was found in a house in the village of Farway itself. In 1990 the new occupant of an old village cottage found, in the corner of the bread oven, a small clay item resembling the shape of a man and, like the heart, it had pins thrust into it. This could have possibly been the home of the aforementioned witch causing problems for the old farmer of Devenish Pitt!

The myths of witches in the town itself go back many centuries before the Victorian era. In 1665 a woman called Elizabeth Brooker, who worked in a draper's shop, had a visit from an elderly woman on market day who asked for a pin. Elizabeth took one from her sleeve but the woman demanded to be given a larger one which could not be supplied. The old woman left the shop angrily saying "she should hear farther from her, and that she would wish e'er long she had given the pin as desired." The next day Miss. Brooker found a pin had been inserted in her thigh so far that she could barely see the head. Elizabeth visited a reputable local surgeon but suffered a "fortnight's illness" before the pin could finally be found and removed. The surgeon even stated that the pin was "bewitched" and that "perhaps the devil was let off easy this time" for the elderly woman suspected of cursing her was never found.

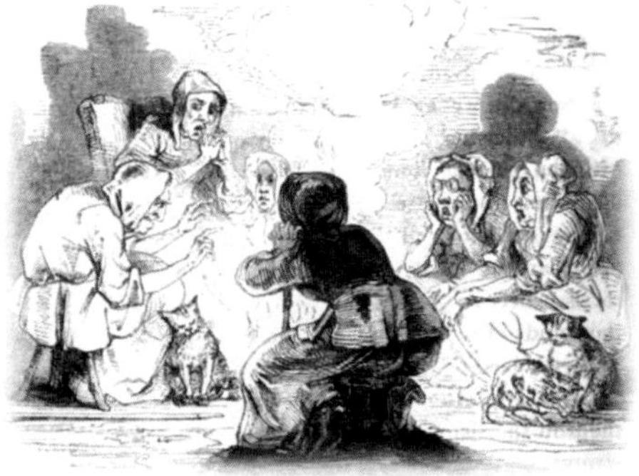

There was another well known witch who resided in Membury in the early part of the 19th century. This old woman was responsible for many evil doings, particularly directed at her neighbour who was a farmer. Her name was Hannah Henley and over the years she cast spells that killed his horses and sheep, turned his cattle mad and blind, caused his brother to die in agony and killed the family's youngest child. She also put a curse on the farm when she was refused items that she demanded, such as food and money. The farm's butter could not be made, bread failed to bake in the oven and 'milk would not set'. The family were on their way to ruin until, fortunately for them, she died. Her bruised and mutilated body was found wrapped in a bed sheet on a high branch of a tree near her cottage on the morning of Good Friday, 1841. It appeared to those who discovered her that she had been dragged through her bedroom window by some supernatural force and pulled vigorously through a thorn bush. Many locals believed that the devil had been angry with her and had thus taken her life. "In her time Hannah Henley was the most famous witch in East Devon" and local people would have most definitely told stories about her in front of an open fire on cold winter's nights for many years after her death.

There was also a Rector of Combe Raleigh in the 17th century known as Dr. Knott who was once believed to be a wizard. The stories of him lasted right through to at least the mid nineteenth century.

Although such suspicion and persecution of witches slowly ebbed away, the practising of witchcraft was not actually made legal until 1951 when the 'Witchcraft Act' of 1735 was finally repealed.

Other strange local customs included that anyone bitten by a mad dog had to be smothered to death between two feathered pillows; serious cases of small pox were also resolved by this method. This was apparently once orchestrated in Gittisham for a man who had been bitten by a rabid dog, proving these 'old wives tales' were strongly believed and commonly practised. All other small pox sufferers would be kept in a room with all windows and doors shut and a continual fire burning in the room to keep the sufferer as warm as possible. The belief was that by keeping the patient hot the disease would be "sweated out".

There was another strange remedy for scalding, which was recounted in a tale of a child who was burnt at the Honiton Fair of 1868. The child of a Sarah Sheppard, who had previously had an eye scalded from an ember from a fire burning at Honiton Fair of the same year, was later severely burnt from spilling a saucepan of boiling water. The following was quoted by a witness:

"I met Sarah Sheppard about nine o'clock on Thursday coming on the road with the child in her arms, wrapt in the tail of her frock. She said her child was scalded: then I charmed it as I charmed it before, when a stone hopped out of the fire last Honiton fair and scalded its eye. I charmed it in the road. I charmed it by saying to myself, "There was (sic) two angels

come from the north, one of them being fire and the other frost; in frost, out fire," & I repeat this three times; this is good for a scald. I can't say it is good for anything else. Old John Sparway told me this charm many years ago. A man may tell a woman the charm, or a woman may tell a man: but if a woman tells a woman or a man a man, I consider it won't do any good at all."

The child, unfortunately, died from its injuries but, obviously rather than contacting a physician, the mother believed this 'charm' would save her infant!

Whilst many would be partying on the previously mentioned eve of St. John's, others may have slipped away to the old parish church of St Michael's where, at midnight, s/he would be able to see the spirits of those who were to die in the coming year, pass through the porch door. However, if you wished to be involved, you had better take some coffee with you, for if you were to fall asleep whilst watching the procession, it was said that you, too, would die. Whilst at the church you may also be fortunate enough to see the spirits of the departed rise from their graves and dance around the graveyard after hanging their shrouds on their tombstones!

Bachelors and spinsters may also decide to spend the night away from the festivities of St. John's Eve. It was thought that if any such unmarried person set up a table with a clean cloth laid with uncut cheese, a jug of cider, a loaf of bread and a plate and knife and sat in total silence with all the windows and doors open in the night's darkness, a premonition of the person they would marry would enter the house and partake of the food at midnight. If a word was spoken, however, the event would end. A young maiden could also go out at night and knock on the door of the henhouse to find out about her fate with the young men of the parish. If the hens cackled at this disturbance it was said that she would never marry; however, if the cockerel crowed she would be married within a year.

St. Swithin was an eighth century Bishop of Winchester who cast his anger over those who moved his body from Winchester Churchyard on July 15th by bringing down 40 days of rain. It has, therefore, always been believed that if it rained on July 15th (St. Swithin's Day) it would rain for 40 more, and in Honiton the day was also noted as having particular powers in forecasting the weather. A Mr. Berry of the town wrote in 1918 that:

- "In 1912 it rained on the 15th, and we had rain on 36 days after.

- In 1913 it did not rain on that day, and there were only 14 wet days after.
- In 1914 rain on St. Swithin's day was followed by 31 wet days.
- In 1915 a wet St. Swithin's was again followed by 31 wet days.
- In 1916 there was no rain on the 15th and only for 11 days after.
- Last year it rained and we had 33 wet days after."

Not a bad argument for the purpose of proving the old legend correct, at least in Honiton anyway!

If the belief of witches, superstitions and spells is not enough for you, how about pixies?! A person having been "pixie-led" was a common term some 150 year ago in Honiton. A farmer in the 1860s had set out for home from a friend's house after dark and despite being familiar with the road, he got lost and wandered around for the remainder of the night. When dawn arrived he found himself back where he had started and fully believed that he had been misled or 'pixie-led' by some mischievous pixies! Beliefs in such supernatural beings were rife throughout the Victorian countryside.

Many people who had bought, or moved to, a new house would often use a poker to draw a cross in the hearth before lighting the house's first fire as was practised to ward off evil of a witch. A cross drawn by a poker was also said to be the perfect remedy for a fire that was stubborn in igniting. Fires in the sitting room of one's home could only be lit between November 1st and May 5th.

People who committed suicide were buried at one of the town's crossroads with a stake through their heart. Some were buried at midnight in the parish church, so no one would see, but no religious service would be performed. Suicide was one of the worst sins for a Christian and was still a capital offence up until 1961!

On New Year's Day anyone leaving their house for the first time that year was encouraged to bring back some article or money that he had not taken out with him/her. In doing so the householder was guaranteeing prosperity for the coming year. To see the new moon through glass or trees for the first time was said to signify bad luck for the next month but when viewed in the open, or over the right shoulder and then saluted with a bow, would bring the individual good luck for the next 4 weeks.

Among the town's numerous myths and superstitions lingered some supernatural entities, for "every dark lane had its ghost".
The Dolphin Hotel (now Montomery's) was used as a hospital during the Civil War and the ghost of one who died there is still believed to roam the floors. He is thought to look out on to the town from one of the windows on the first floor.
During the Monmouth Rebellion, many people of the West Country, and subsequently Honiton, lost their lives in these battles for power. One such man, on the side of Monmouth, who fought at the Battle of Sedgemoor, is said to haunt Lower Marlpits Hill; it was said, on returning home to his cottage that once stood a little further up from St. Michaels's, he was caught by Royalists and was hacked to death in front of his wife and children. This gaunt figure has been seen wearing a "broad-brimmed hat" and a "flowing coat" on several occasions. The fullest account of a sighting was from pupils from 'Summerland College' who were walking up the hill, near the old cottage in 1904. The figure apparently appeared in his torn and tattered, mud covered brown coat and approached them; the children were the only ones to witness the gentleman whilst the mistress did not see anything. On hearing the experience of her students the headmistress of the school unearthed the story of the murdered man. The cottage was pulled down in the 1930s and the sightings seem to have stopped with its demolition. This author remembers hearing the story of the ghost as a child but has not heard anyone talk of it in more recent times.
Another spectre was once said to haunt a spot not far from the railway station. In 1902 it became routine for the boys of the parish to go "ghost hunting" at a piece of waste ground once occupied by some burnt cottages near the railway line. Such groups of children were said to often flee in "panic" when the apparition of a "man in blue" appeared before them. However, this ghostly gentleman is thought to have been nothing more than a joke started by such a group of adolescents and after several *sightings* the myth became a temporary urban legend!
Manor House, once the Golden Lion Inn, is another of the town's buildings that was once said to be haunted. Many people who worked for the local firm 'Gribble, Booth & Taylor', who once occupied part of the property, were said to have known about the ghost in the 1980s. The Railway Inn is also a property in the town once reputed to be haunted by an "elderly couple." Another sinister spectre is said to wander the A373 between Honiton and Awliscombe. Several sightings dating back to the 1960s involve a strange entity appearing before road users, causing many of them to swerve in order to avoid an accident but when looking back, found nothing there. These occurrences have been reported at a section of the

road where an old stone wall runs parallel to the highway. There was once an archway in the wall that has since been bricked up and since then the sightings appear to have stopped.

The last known supernatural being in the town was only known to have appeared once to a group of ladies some two hundred years ago. One summer's afternoon two young ladies from Gittisham had come to visit two sisters living in the town. After tea the four embarked on the walk back to Gittisham and as they passed the Turk's Head Inn, until recently 'Slades Countrywise', they saw a girl kneeling beside a pond that once stood opposite the inn. The girl appeared to be washing her hands in the water and one of the party recognised her as a local girl called Grace Seale and bid her a good afternoon. The girl turned and stared at the group but did not speak and then turned back to the water. The four friends, shocked at Grace's rudeness being usually a "well mannered" individual, shortly afterwards parted company. The sisters had left the other two members of their group at the lane leading to Gittisham and then they themselves had turned and started home. On their return to the inn they noticed a group of people outside and were shocked to find out that the body of the aforementioned Grace Seale had just been found in the River Otter, some two fields away from the inn, where it had lain for several hours. The women had witnessed the girl by the pond long after she had died and the story was known to have been told many times since the eventful day.

Epilogue

I now conclude my book about the Devonian market town of Honiton. I hope you have found it as interesting to read as I have to write. I finish with the ending quote from Richard Archibald Farquharson's text 'The History of Honiton' from 1891 which has been an invaluable resource to this work...

""Gentle Reader I have concluded my task, be not too critical but pardon my shortcomings and believe I have honestly done my best to describe the place where my early and happiest days were spent and in my conclusion let me say of Honiton as Goldsmith did of Livsoy:

"In my wanderings round this world of care
In all my griefs and God has given my share
I still had hopes my latest hours to crown
Amidst these lowly bowers to lay me down
To husband out lifes' taper at the close
And keep the flame from wasting by repose
I still had hopes, for pride attends me still,
Amongst the swains to show my book-learned skill,
Around the fire an evening group to draw,
And tell of all I knew and all I saw
And as a hare, whom horse and hound pursue,
Pants to the place from which at first he flew
I still had hopes, my long vexations past
Here to return and die at home at last.""

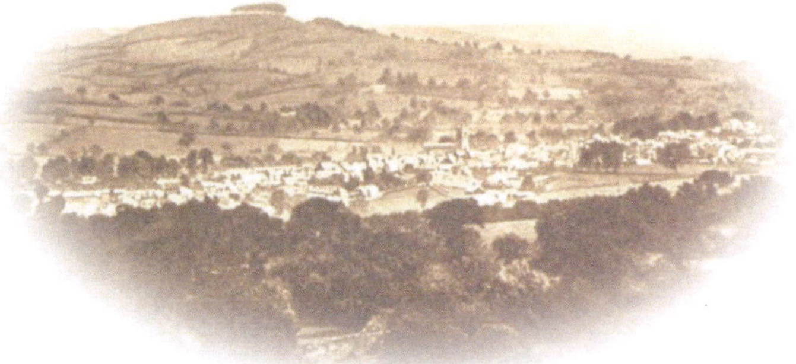

The End

Acknowledgements

Many people have kindly contributed to this work and this author would like to thank those who made this publication possible.

I am hugely indebted to the following: *Ancestry.co.uk* for allowing me full access to their archives; the *staff of Honiton Library,* in particular librarian *Jenny Wood MBE* who kindly gave me permission to use documents and photographs; *Colin Wright* of *belsey & copp* for his kind advice, assistance and guidance; Francis Martin of the Battishorne Trust for his kind donation towards publication costs and last, but by no means least, *Arthur Dimond* whose kind generosity provided the majority of images for this work, as well as allowing me to borrow and view his Honiton archives.

I would also like to thank and mention the following individuals and organisations who kindly assited me and/or gave me access to their personal stories, archives, documents, images and research:
Alec Farquharson ; 1911census.com; Martin Street Photography's Sepia Collection ; Grace Upton; Mary Ed Hartnell; Icam Archive Systems Ltd; Manna House BnB; Mr. & Mrs. Gammon of Tracey Mill Trout Farm; Graham York Rare Books; Mr. & Mrs. Hodgetts of Cheneys Farm; Mrs. Nichols; Mr. & Mrs. Tonks of Broadacres; Gerard O' Brien; Owen Tratt; Betty Davey; Oaklands Guest House; Ken Martin; Dr. R. Essame; Charlotte Wizgel; Elaine Currie; Mike Roy Read; David Johnson; Peter Hussey; Ruth Tucker; David Appleyard for his kind permission to use the painting of The Dolphin by Joseph Appleyard(http://www.josephappleyard.co.uk); Chris, Alan & Lyn Darrant; Mark Walker; Adrian Pearson & Manor House School; Shirley Nielson; Alan Rosevear; Stephanie & Noel (recently departed) Walmsley-Kastner; Kath & Norman Broom; The Vine Inn; Staff of Westcountry Studies Library; Devon Records Office for kind permission to reproduce their images that can be found on pages 166, 172, 226, 232, 234 &235 (reference numbers 1733Z/1/70/4, 1733Z/I/74/4, 1733Z/I/74/5, 1733Z/VII/41/3, 1733Z/VII/41/4, 1733Z/VII/39/9 & 1733Z/VII/41/5 respectively); Gerald & Pamela Sweetland; Michael Slade; Elsie Stanbury; Andrew Billing of Honiton Photographics; Staff at St Paul's Church & Honiton Parish Office; Mr. & Mrs. Wheatley-Brown of Monkton Court Hotel; Peter Eyles; Mr. & Mrs. Underwood; Terry Farebrother; George Roulson and everyone else who kindly contriubuted.

I would also like to thank my family for their continued help and support.

Key Source Material

- The History of Honiton; (manuscript); Richard Farquharson; 1891.
- Honiton: An Old Devon Market Town; M. Edmunds; Westcountry Books; 1993.
- Honiton Lace; P. M. Inder; Exeter Museum Publications; 1977
- Around Honiton; Les Berry & Gerald Gosling; Chalford; 1995.
- Old Farming Days: Life on the Land in Devon & Cornwall; Robin Stanes; Halsgrove; 2005.
- The Romance of the Wool, Lace & Pottery Trades in Honiton; J. R. W. Coxhead; 1951
- The History of Allhallows School; J. R. W. Coxhead; 1959.
- Honiton in old Picture Postcards; H. J. Yallop; European Library-Zaltbommel/Netherlands; 1983.
- The Independent Chapel, Honiton, Donald H. Cooke, 1971.
- The History of the Honiton Lace Industry; H. J. Yallop; University of Exeter Press; 1992.
- Honiton Report; Devon County Council & Honiton Borough Council; 1973.
- An Introduction to Inn Signs; Eric R. Delderfield; 1967.
- Mate's Illustrated Honiton; Mates & Sons; 1903
- Tithe Map of Honiton; Devon Record Office.
- Pigot's Directory of Devonshire; 1844
- Kelly's Directories of Devonshire; 1883; 1889; 1893; 1902; 1906; 1910; 1914; 1919; 1923; 1926; 1930; 1935; 1939.
- White' Directories of Devonshire; 1850; 1878.
- Billings Directory of Devonshire; 1857.
- Honiton Memories; Shirely Nielson; Honiton History Society; 2003.
- Memoirs of Edgar Pulman; unpublished; 1989.
- General View of Agriculture of the County of Devon; Charles Vancouver; 1808.
- Western Morning News Archives
- Folklore, Myths & Legends of Britain; Readers Digest; 1973.
- Honiton: Past and Present; Chips Barber; 2000
- Travels in Victorian Devon: Illustrated Journals & Sketchbooks 1846-1870; Compiled by Jeremy Butler; 2000
- Daily Life in Victorian England; Sally Mitchell; 1996.
- Devon and It's People; W. G. Hoskins; 1968.
- Victorian Britain; Brenda Williams; 2005.
- Honiton Inns; Trevor Hitchcock; 2009.
- A Statistical Account of the British Empire; J R McCulloch; 1837.
- Black's Guide to Devonshire; Adam & Charles Black; 1864.
- The Beauties of the Shore; Or, A Guide to the Watering-places on the South East Coast of Devon; D. M. Stirling; 1838.
- Lost Crafts: Rediscovering Traditional Skills; Una McGovern; Chambers; 2008
- The Time Traveller's Guide to Medieval England; Ian Mortimer; Vintage; 2008

Appendix

I - VI

Year of Fire	Day & Date	Duration	Place	Details (if any)
1672				
1679	May		High Street	"a great part of Honiton was burnt... on both sides of the street"
1699				Houses belonging to the poor of town destroyed
1747	Sunday; 19th July	afternoon July 19th to 4am July 20th	High Street	3/4 town burnt; started opposite Allhallows Chapel; started from overheated baker's oven; part of shambles burnt
1752	January			Premises of Mr Maynard; serge-maker; destroyed. £1400 of damage
1754	Tuesday; July 2nd			
1765	Tuesday; 30th July			Locals burnt down flour mills
1765	Wednesday; 21st August	1pm to 8pm	High Street (east)	3/4 town (140 houses) destroyed; Allhallows Chapel & Meeting house destroyed, one recorded death
1777	Saturday; 1st February			
1778	Monday; 9th March			
1779	Sunday; March 14th			Fire started intentionally; 14 houses destroyed
1790	Friday; 3rd Sept	3 hours		Soap house of Mr Kerslake; several buildings engulfed
1790	Saturday; 15 May		High Street	39 houses destroyed; started in stables of Golden Lion Inn
1797	Thursday; 24th August		High Street	47 houses destroyed; Honiton Bank burnt; £10,000 worth of damage
1820			High Street (north)	White Lion & several houses destroyed
1828				Paper Mills destroyed by fire
1830			High Street	White Lion destroyed again
Bet 1830-1840			Mill Street	Malthouse & other businesses destroyed
1840			High Street	Swan Inn & several other properties burnt (now site of present Baptist Chapel)
1846			High Street (south side of east end)	Several cottages engulfed
1847			High Street	Two Fires: Lamb Inn stables and later a mill in Mill Street burnt
1850			Outskirts	Hale Farm & premises destroyed
1852				Carpenter's Arms & adjoining houses burnt
1853	December (2nd fire)		Silver Street/New Street	Two Fires: houses in Silver Street burnt & later Mr Woodgates house in New Street virtually destroyed
1862			High Street (east)	Cottages consumed
Bet 1862- 1871			High Street	Chopping Knife Inn & adjoining houses burnt
1871				London Inn obliterated
1886	Thursday; 11th March		New Street	Little damage occurred
1887			New Street	Tudor cottages destroyed
1911	Sunday; 26th March		Church Hill	St Michaels destroyed

Chronological list of Honiton Fires.

I

Minister	Start	End	Notes
Walter	1224	1244	
Sir Henry de Monfort ?	1272	1276?	unconfirmed
Sir Adam Paen	16th Feb 1276	1285?	
Master Guyde Tillbrok	Rector in 1285		
Henry de Pykeney		1314	Resigned
Richard de Wydeslake/Wideslade	13 Jan 1314		
Philip de Puntyngdon/Puntingdon	13 Jan 1325		in post in 1349
Sir John de Southdone/Bysouthdown	Rector in 1358	after 1377	
Richard Gardiner	?	1391	Cessioned
Richard Madeford/Mudeford	3 Feb 1391		Exchanged Parish with Rector of Widecombe
Edward Fsysch/Fishacre	25 Jan 1399	1408	Exchanged Parish with Rector of Shirwell
Robert Fynor	27 Nov 1408	1412	Died in Post
John Sueynton/Sileynton	15 Jan 1412	1433	Exchanged Parish with Rector of St Mildred's, London
Thomas Smith (Smyth)	12 July 1433	1442	Exchanged Parish with Rector of Compton, Hampshire?
Richard Lawe	22 May 1442	1450	Died in Post
John Rigge/Rugge	23 Mar 1450	1459	Died in Post
Thomas Frome	15 Feb 1459		
Geoffrey Newchurch		1487	Died in Post
John Melbury	6 July 1487	1500	Died in Post
John Yeate/Yeale	10 Oct 1500	1505	Died in Post
Henry Ferman/Feyrman/Faireman/Firman	17 May 1505	1527	Died in Post
Richard Denys	16 April 1527	1529	Cessioned
Nicholas Carew	28 Mar 1529	1539	Resigned
Philip Bale	3 Jan 1539	1559	Last Catholic Rector
Robert Slade	1554/1559	1587	Thought to have died in post
Hugh Dowrish	10 May 1587		
Robert Slader		1596?	
John Robins	1598	1605	Died in Post
Philip Nichols	18 Feb 1605	1614	Died in Post
John Eedes	16 May 1614	1637	Ejected due to being a Royalist
Dennis Prideaux	20 Nov 1637	1648?	Ejected
Francis Sourton	1648	1662	Resigned for non-conformity
Ozias Upcott	8 Jan 1662	1699	1st Rector who resided in old rectory
Ezra Cleaveland	28 July 1699	1740	Died in Post
Hon Charles Bertie	15 Nov 1740	1746	Cessioned
Charles Bertie	15 Jun 1761	1788	Died in Post
Edward Honeywood/Honywood	6 Dec 1788	1812	Died in Post
Henry Allewright Hughes	26 May 1813	1827	Cessioned
Villiers Henry Plantagenet Somerset	16 July 1827	1855	Died in Post
John Fielder Mackarness	1855	1869	Left position to become Bishop of Oxford
Michael Ferrebee Saddler	1869	1895	
Hugh John Fortescue	1895	1908	
Frederick Leslie Courtenay	1908	1935	Died in Post
Andrew Augustine Fane de Salis	1935	1962	
Richard Andrew Babington	1963	1972	
Robin Mark George Morrell	1972	1978	
James William Irvine Trevelyan	1978	2000	
Jane Barbara Hedges	2001	2005	First female Rector of Honiton
Susan Emma Roberts	2006	Present	

Honiton's Rectors

II

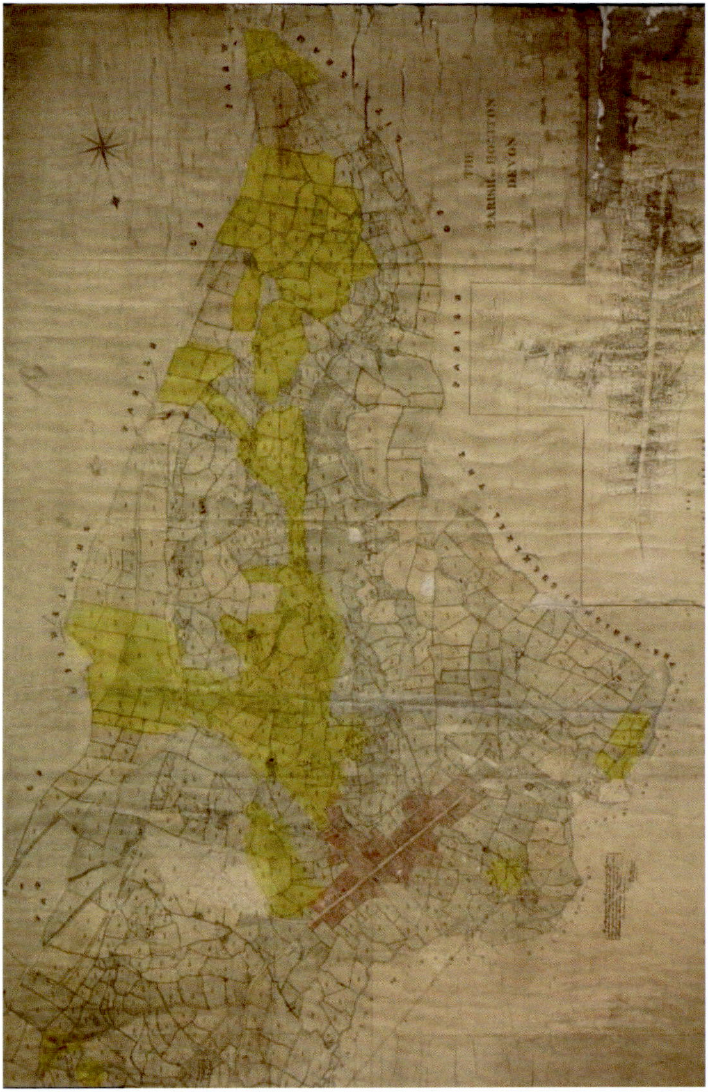

Honiton Manor Lands (shaded in yellow) 1844

III

Co-ordinate References

Boundary Markers (pg. 12)

1. 50°47'1.23"N 3°10'11.29"W (Wadmore Lane)
2. 50°46'25.44"N 3°10'51.87"W (Boundary Oak)

Milestone (pg. 252)

1. 50°47'48.36"N 3°10'10.64"W (Located on A35)

Telegraph (pg. 332)

1. 50°48'44.81"N 3°12'33.45"W

Farms ('Farms & Fields' Chapter from pg. 161)

1. 50°47'15.44"N 3°11'25.87"W (Brand)
2. 50°48'2.48"N 3°11'25.26"W (Cowley)
3. 50°47'11.15"N 3°11'3.40"W (Gardeners)
4. 50°47'2.16"N 3°11'43.65"W (Roundball)
5. 50°46'57.57"N 3°11'46.28"W (Roundball Fields)
6. 50°46'36.86"N 3°11'17.06"W (Stout)

Mills (pg. 192)

1. 50°48'28.02"N 3°10'52.63"W (Northcott Mill)

Roads (from pgs. 253-256)

1. 50°47'33.60"N 3°11'9.25"W
2. 50°47'27.67"N 3°11'12.96"W
3. 50°47'16.71"N 3°11'2.50"W
4. 50°47'35.76"N 3°11'39.14"W
5. 50°47'12.39"N 3°11'42.52"W
6. 50°46'36.99"N 3°10'11.90"W

IV

Toll House Locations (pgs.264-266)

1. 50°47'51.61"N 3°10'38.47"W (Copper Castle)
2. 50°48'24.99"N 3° 9'17.33"W (Cheeseway Ash)
3. 50°48'3.61"N 3°11'7.37"W (Clapper Lane)
4. 50°47'28.75"N 3°10'49.14"W (Lower Marlpits)
5. 50°47'9.01"N 3°10'26.16"W (Higher Marlpits)
6. 50°47'3.32"N 3°12'1.82"W (Gobsore)
7. 50°47'45.79"N 3°13'7.91"W (Traflagar Bridge)
8. 50°46'29.53"N 3°10'45.68"W (Appledoor)
9. 50°48'7.52"N 3°10'53.10"W (Holyshute)
10. 50°48'13.63"N 3°12'20.47"W (Stoneyford)
11. 50°47'39.47"N 3°12'30.28"W (Turk's Head)
12. 50°47'59.98"N 3° 9'32.85"W (Hutgate)

Fun, Fairs Folklore (pg. 340)

1. 50°48'13.64"N 3°11'36.07"W (Bathing Spot: nearest known location)

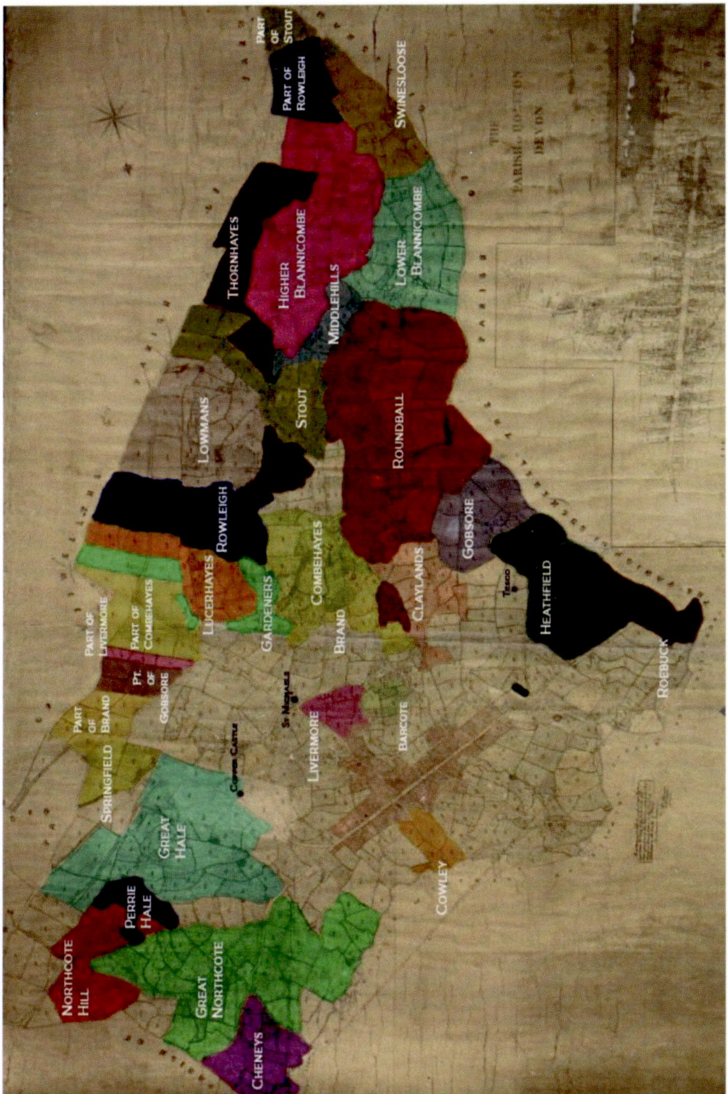

Farm Lands 1844. (The unmarked pink area, nr. Cowley, is the old town boundary)

V

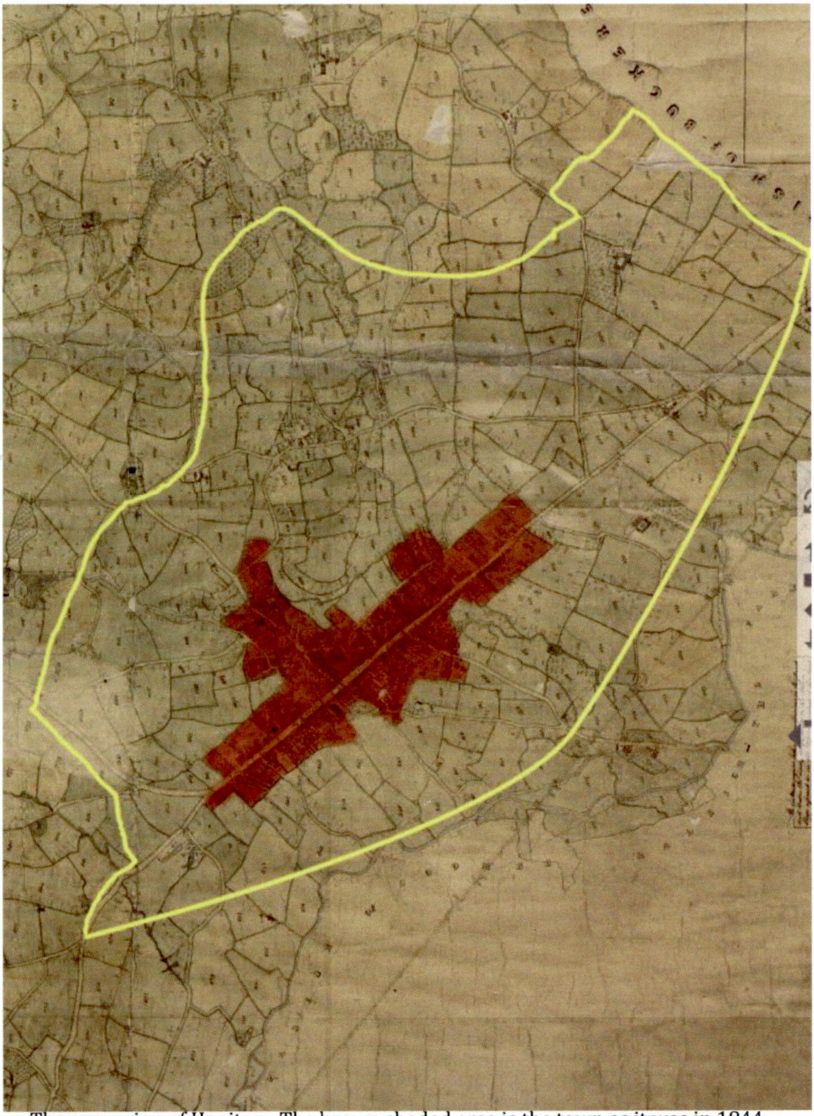

The expansion of Honiton. The brown shaded area is the town as it was in 1844 and the yellow border is the approximate extent of the town boundaries today.

VI